Grounding Urban Natures

Urban and Industrial Environments

Series editor: Robert Gottlieb, Henry R. Luce Professor
of Urban and Environmental Policy, Occidental College

For a complete list of books published in this series, please see the back of the book.

Grounding Urban Natures

Histories and Futures of Urban Ecologies

Edited by Henrik Ernstson and Sverker Sörlin

The MIT Press
Cambridge, Massachusetts
London, England

This book was set in Stone by Westchester Publishing Services, Danbury, CT. Printed and bound in the United States of America.

Library of Congress Cataloging-in-Publication Data is available.

Names: Ernstson, Henrik, 1972– editor. | Sörlin, Sverker, editor.
Title: Grounding urban natures : histories and futures of urban ecologies / edited by Henrik Ernstson and Sverker Sörlin.
Description: Cambridge, MA : MIT Press, [2019] | Series: Urban and industrial environments | Includes bibliographical references and index.
Identifiers: LCCN 2018042912 | ISBN 9780262039918 (hardcover : alk. paper) | ISBN 9780262537148 (pbk. : alk. paper)
Subjects: LCSH: Urban ecology (Sociology)--Case studies. | Urbanization--Environmental aspects--Case studies.
Classification: LCC HT361 .G76 2019 | DDC 304.2/091732--dc23
LC record available at https://lccn.loc.gov/2018042912

10 9 8 7 6 5 4 3 2 1

Contents

Preface: A Diverse Urban World

Henrik Ernstson and Sverker Sörlin

Grounding Urban Natures: Histories and Futures of Urban Ecologies grew out of an interest in getting serious about the diversity of urban experience and urban natures. In the last ten to twenty years there has been an increasing push to develop a global understanding of urbanization and how to solve a host of environmental problems. We thought it was time to dig down into the multiple histories through which urban natures, in their varied forms and connections to social and political processes, have been shaped across the world. Given our own empirical studies, especially in Stockholm and Cape Town, we wondered what we could learn by gathering together authors who had extensive knowledge of other cities around the world and who could write in textured ways, with historical depth, about urban nature and its politics.[1] How could this mode of writing *from* a particular location help us come to grips with the highly uneven mega-phenomenon of contemporary urbanization? Could such a grounded approach help to uncover a more comprehensive view of urban natures and their political ecologies, past and future?

Incidentally, we articulated these initial thoughts about this book project in a parking lot on the University of Cape Town campus, and this geographical position has continued to inform our work. Above us was the Rhodes Memorial, a symbol of the city's colonial past, representing the colonial benefactor who provided the land for the university on the slopes of Table Mountain. We found it disturbing to be subsumed, as it were, under his gesture—one that came from deep within the British imperial project and afforded us the chance to look out over—and to risk overlooking—the Cape Flats, a large expanse of windy and flood-prone land that since forced removals under apartheid in the 1960s has been the home to the majority of people, while considered, as John Western phrased it, the city's "outcast."

In taking in this view, *grasping* the city from a distance and detachment founded on a problematic legacy, we sensed an uncomfortable resonance with some of the frameworks being developed by scholars and colleageus in the environmental sciences—frameworks related to their (and our) concern for urban sustainability and yet, we thought, quite insensitive to the texture of the everyday comings and goings of urban life and the multiple histories of urban nature. Instead of promoting situated case studies across the world, we have witnessed the increasing circulation of simplifying models that gestures to be valid everywhere. This risks missing the very situated character of *how* urban nature is related to multiple meanings, various historical experiences, and different forms of politics based on race, gender, ability, and class. Simply put, the political stakes that are inherently attached to urban environments will be misunderstood or silenced as a result of simplification. There, between Rhodes and Cape Flats, we intuitively felt a need for a book that could problematize this environmental scientific gaze and break with ingrained bias and tradition on how cities and environments are thought and studied.

Metaphorically speaking, we wanted a collection of chapters that pushed us to think "the city" and "urban nature" more through the textured realities of Cape Flats than through the city's historical "centre," and that could demonstrate a range of methods by which our real concern for urban and ecological crises can be grounded. Thus, we asked authors from various disciplines to use their rich understanding about particular cities across the global South and North to speak of urban nature from those locations, bringing the texture of place and time to bear on how they theorize and understand urban nature.

Thematically the book is organized into three major parts: "Unexpected Natures," "Popular Natures," and "Technological Natures," placed in between the introduction (part I) and the conclusion (part V). The thematic parts bring together studies and conversations on how to expand what can be considered as urban nature in part II, followed in parts III and IV with a focus on values, knowledge, and imaginations of urban nature through the perspectives of both ordinary people and experts. Emphasizing, as each author does, the grounded approach of their chapters, each chapter also demonstrates how different combinations of theory and method can be used to unpack urban nature. This has in its own right, apart from theoretical insights and grounded narratives, produced a collection of methodologies that will be of inspiration to critical urban environmentalists.

Apart from the chapters, the introduction and the conclusion to this volume bring together thus far quite disconnected conversations. There we combine urban environmental studies on one hand, including the whole gamut of thought from "cyborgs" and "more-than-human" formations to "social-ecological systems," and on the other other the more recent developments in urban studies of postcolonial or "Southern" urbanism, which strives to retain the texture of places when theorizing the urban. Within this broader terrain of thought, we try to grasp the diversity of natures and urban worlds that we are now all firmly part of—how they are shaped and formed through time and place, and who can claim to have legitimate knowledge about them. Taken together, we believe strongly that it is important socially, environmentally, and politically to diversify the understanding of urban natures at this historical moment of worldwide urbanization—and *Grounding Urban Natures* is a contribution in this direction.

Note

1. For an extensive review of urban environmental studies, see the introduction to this book. For our own studies, see, for instance, Ernstson and Sörlin (2009, 2013) and Ernstson (2013), and the research-based documentary film *One Table Two Elephants* (von Heland and Ernstson 2018), which was filmed in Cape Town and situates questions about race, nature, history, and knowledge in a postcolonial city.

References

Ernstson, Henrik. 2013. "Re-Translating Nature in Post-Apartheid Cape Town: The Material Semiotics of People and Plants at Bottom Road." Actor-Network Theory for Development Working Paper Series, edited by Richard Heeks, no. 4. Manchester: Institute for Development Policy and Management, School of Environment, Education and Development, University of Manchester. http://hummedia.manchester.ac.uk/institutes/cdi/resources/cdi_ant4d/ANT4DWorkingPaper4Ernstson.pdf.

Ernstson, Henrik, and Sverker Sörlin. 2009. "Weaving Protective Stories: Connective Practices to Articulate Holistic Values in the Stockholm National Urban Park." *Environment and Planning A* 41(6): 1460–1479.

Ernstson, Henrik, and Sverker Sörlin. 2013. "Ecosystem Services as Technology of Globalization: On Articulating Values in Urban Nature." *Ecological Economics* 86: 274–284.

von Heland, Jacob, and Henrik Ernstson. 2018. *One Table Two Elephants*. Documentary film, 84 minutes. World premiere at CPH:DOX 2018, Copenhagen International Film Festival, March 20. http://bit.ly/1T2E-film.

Western, John. 1981. *Outcast Cape Town*. Berkeley: University of California Press.

Acknowledgments

This book has its origin in the project "Ways of Knowing Urban Ecologies," funded by Formas, the Swedish research council for sustainable development. Gathering together excellent interdisciplinary scholars from urban ecology, human geography, and environmental history, the project developed case studies on contested urban natures and the inclusive and exclusionary logics of natural resource management around wetlands, sand dunes, forests, coastal ecosystems, and agricultural fields in Cape Town, New Orleans, and Stockholm.

As part of this research group, we were intrigued by the wider story of urban nature that was flashing by in the local stories of our case studies; while highly textured and particular, maybe even peculiar, the stories extended to inform our thinking about urban nature and environmental politics elsewhere. It was these initial thoughts that gave rise to this book's effort to tie together and make sense of local experiences on a wider scale but through grounded, textured studies and stories. This prompted us to form a wider group, which first included Amita Baviskar, Lance van Sittert, and Richard A. Walker, all of whom contributed chapters, and later to invite Martín Ávila, Jia-Ching Chen, James Evans, Lisa Hoffman, Jens Lachmund, Joshua Lewis, Lindsay Sawyer, and Anne Whiston Spirn to contribute to this volume as well.

We wish first of all to acknowledge all of the chapter contributors. We have been blessed with their skills in writing beautiful prose, their curiosity and dedication to the project, and their rich understanding of the places they write from. Through our shared and constructive dialogues, we sought collectively to understand more nuances of the "social lives of urban nature," once suggested as a possible title of the book by Amita Baviskar. As you will see throughout the volume, the contributors offer extended lessons and piercing insights, honed through long-term fieldwork and archival work and based on their commitment to their disciplines and interdisciplinary dialogues. Their chapters are in their own right crucial contributions to the growing "wild libraries" of urban nature.

We also acknowledge early important discussions and research presentations from human geographer Jane Battersby and anthropologist Lesley Greene, both from the University of Cape Town; environmental historian Paul Warde from Cambridge University; Andrew Karvonen, human geographer at KTH Royal Institute of Technology, Stockholm; and Lise Sedrez, environmental historian from Universidade Federal do Rio de Janeiro.

We also thank the group of PhD students who took our course on urban ecology "as science, culture, and politics," co-organized with Joshua Lewis. The students offered rewarding discussions of the book's chapters and the wider interdisciplinary topics at the heart of our project. Amita Baviskar and Lisa Hoffman very kindly gave lectures to students and the general public. Ideas and some draft chapters were also discussed at a PhD workshop at Portland State University, and we thank the main organizers, Anthony Levenda, Erin Goodling, and Marissa Matsler, as well as Amy K. Coplen, Zbigniew Grabowski, and Thaddeus Miller for support and Nathan McClintock for hosting. Two conferences shaped parts of the material and its framing: a special session at the annual conference of the Association of Environmental History (ASEH) in San Francisco and the Stanford University conference "Urban Beyond Measure: Registering Urban Environments of the South," organized and chaired by the first editor and Jia-Ching Chen, with crucial assistance from Jacob Doherty and support from Stanford anthropologists James Ferguson, Thomas Blom Hansen, and Sylvia Yanagisako. We thank Martin Emanuel for delivering a commissioned bibliography and literature search for the project, and Jessica Rattle in Cape Town and Susanna Lidström in Stockholm for additional support. For institutional support, we thank Gordon Pierie, Edgar Pieterse, and Maryam Waglay at the African Centre for Cities at the University of Cape Town, and Nina Wormbs and Marco Armiero at KTH Royal Institute of Technology in Stockholm. We are deeply indebted to the wonderful group of younger and senior scholars who were part of the original "Ways of Knowing Urban Ecologies" project: Jane Battersby, Thomas Elmqvist, Marnie Graham, Mary Lawhon, Joshua Lewis, Susan Parnell, and Jessica Rattle. We thank our dear colleague Jacob von Heland for his intellectual support and feedback.

Throughout the course of working with the book, our respective home institutions and colleagues have been supportive in providing space for discussions and sharing ideas. They include the Division of History of Science Technology and Environment at KTH Royal Institute of Technology in Stockholm and its KTH Environmental Humanities Laboratory, the African Centre for Cities at the University of Cape Town, and the Department of Geography at The University of Manchester. We also thank the History Department at Stanford University, especially Richard Roberts and Monika Wheeler, as well as Laura Hubbard at Stanford's Center for African Studies, and the Institute for Advanced Study at Princeton University and its School of Social Science.

We thank MIT Press for their help throughout the production process of the book, in particular Beth Clevenger's steadfast support, including Robert Gottlieb and Anthony Zannino, and we send a heartfelt thank you to John Donohue for deft copy-editing and guidance in the final stages.

Finally, we acknowledge Formas for supporting this project as part of two interdisciplinary research grants ("Ways of Knowing Urban Ecologies," 250-2010-1372, and "Socioecological Movements in Urbanized Ecosystems," 211-2011-1519), and we also thank the Marcus and Amalia Wallenberg Foundation for additional generous support.

On a more personal note, we extend our gratitude to family and friends for company and comfort, not least during long working sessions in the southern Cape and in California. Sverker especially to my daughter Lydia, now nineteen, for grounding urban natures with me on foot in streets, parks, forests, and along shores. Henrik to *mi compañera* Andrea Eckstein, and to my son Dante, now fourteen, and my daughter Lea-Mo, now sixteen, for their solid and warm support throughout.

I Introduction

1 Toward Comparative Urban Environmentalism: Situating Urban Natures in an Emerging "World of Cities"

Henrik Ernstson and Sverker Sörlin

The city and the urban are a network of interwoven processes that are both human and natural, real and fictional, mechanical and organic. ... [T]his hybrid socio-natural "thing" called "the city" is full of contradictions, tensions and conflicts.
—Erik Swyngedouw, "The City as a Hybrid"

We need to ... invite the animals back in [and] re-enchant the city.
—Jennifer Wolch, "Zoöpolis"

The Greek term *theorein*: a practice of travel and observation, a man sent by the polis to another city to witness a religious ceremony. "Theory" is a product of displacement, comparison, a certain distance. To theorize, one leaves home. But like any act of travel, theory begins and ends somewhere.
—James Clifford, "Notes on Travel and Theory"

There is a global discourse forming around urban ecology that risks simplifying how cities and nature are understood together. Its models range from tech-driven "smart cities" to ecology-driven "biophilic," "resilient," or "eco-cities"; to attempts at formulating "a science of cities." While we recognize that a global response to urban sustainability is important, we question discourses that seem intent on creating unifying frameworks through which to think about and act on urban ecology in all cities. If there is anything that the rich traditions of urban studies, critical environmental studies, and environmental history have shown, it is that place and time matter for how things play out. This book draws upon a wide tradition of thought and research from the humanities and the social sciences concerning ways that cities and nature have been conceptualized together and seeks to offer multiple perspectives for the study of urban natures.

Its publication comes at a time when two great trends are coming together: unprecedented ecological crisis and a new scale and reach of worldwide urbanization. For us, these developments do not call for unifying and universalizing frameworks; rather, they require in-depth, textured, and detailed case studies that can situate the study of urban ecology and its politics within cultural, social, and environmental contexts, while remaining connected to critical projects of justice, emancipation, and sustainability.

Our aim, on the one hand, is to demonstrate how accounts from particular cities and places help to bring out a crucial politics of urban nature that is often misrepresented or silenced in global models of urban ecology. We call this approach *grounding urban natures*. On the other hand, the chapters of this book also demonstrate that cities are interconnected in countless ways: with other cities, with their hinterlands, and with yet other hinter-hinterlands in an ever-complex web of flows of people, materials, capital, and ideas. This means that no city is an island, and cannot be studied as such—a central premise of urban studies since its inception. In this profound sense, cities are shaped by things and events far away, caught up in what have been called "worlding practices," that capture how cities and their ecologies are shaped by human and sociocultural practices that translate technologies, institutions, laws, ideas, knowledge forms, and modes of resistance from one context to another. We live in cities and urban natures shaped by past events and wider geographies that have been folded into the particular places we study and dwell in. Taken together, *grounding*, or digging down where we stand to develop textured case studies, and *worlding*, a way of understanding how urban natures carry many other places within them, constitute our approach to studying urban environments.[1]

Our introduction lays the groundwork for this approach by first reviewing the history of ideas about urban nature and urban ecology. What we are after is to seek out the wider intellectual adventure that has unpacked urban nature in increasingly new, sometimes unexpected ways—in short, the history of the discovery of urban natures, emphasizing the plural of nature. This history can of course only be partial and truncated, given our constraints of space, but it does demonstrate that the scholarly study of urban nature, or what we intermittently will call urban ecology or the urban environment, has several intellectual and ideological beginnings. However, the review also indicates that most of these beginnings lie firmly in the West and global North, either in the cities of Europe and North America or in

Western academic institutions. This, we suggest, has created a problematic bias in how cities and urban ecology have been conceived and theorized in schools of thought as different as cybernetic social-ecological systems theory, industrial ecology, and neo-Marxist political ecology. While we recognize that these heterogeneous approaches to urban ecology have been immensely productive and important in unearthing and making visible the variety and multidimensionality of urban natures, we also mean that they need to be "provincialized," leaning here on a postcolonial tactic from Dipesh Chakrabarty, in order to sensitize, critique and problematize how these approaches and understandings, sometimes gestured as universal, come from somewhere, thus carrying their own provincial flavor, shaped by their geographical and intellectual origins.[2]

In the second section of this chapter, we will draw upon the concerted effort in urban studies of rethinking cities based on the experience of the global South. Since the 1990s, this effort, at times called "Southern urbanism" or "postcolonial urbanism," has drawn upon postcolonial critique to question how cities and urbanization have been studied through North American and European models, arguing for expanding the locations and cities from where theory can be constructed outside the Western canon. At this time of global history, a time when urbanization is expanding and becoming enfolded within so many different cultural, social, and environmental contexts, we need to be more cautious in how study and theorization of urban environments are done. This means to revisit how Paris, London, New York, Los Angeles, and Tokyo, for instance, have influenced or biased urban thought while expanding our discussions with studies and theorizations from, say, Delhi, Lagos, Johannesburg, Guatemala City, and Katmandu—but also smaller cities that historically have fallen off the map of urban studies.[3] One of the overall goals of this book is indeed to integrate this productive impulse from Southern urbanism into critical urban environmental studies so as to reflectively decenter European and North American bias while expanding the locations from where we can think urban nature and urban ecology.

What is important to remember from Southern urbanism, however, is that urbanization should *not* be conceived as essentially different "there" from what it is "here"—a regionalist misreading of Southern urbanism that has sometimes plagued its reception. Rather, the argument has to do with *how* we theorize cities and urbanization more generally, such that we start thinking urban environments from multiple locations and recognize that theory-making is an act of translation from one context to another wherein no *one* location (or geographical point) can be more valid than any other in constructing knowledge. At the heart of Southern urbanism consequently lies a highly reflective and comparative agenda for urban environmental studies. Indeed, when the rich legacies of urban environmental studies, which we review in the first section of this chapter, are brought together with Southern urbanism, which we review in the second section, it opens toward what we call *comparative urban environmentalism,* a crucial field of study in this historical moment of worldwide urbanization.

This chapter works to define this field of comparative study. We argue that our book, which brings together multiple disciplines and authors that in textured ways speak about urban nature from multiple locations, represents a first step in developing this field. We also recognize that much more is left to do, not least to develop thoroughly comparative projects. In the following we review the history of thought about urban nature and then demonstrate the decentering effect of Southern urbanism. We conclude by summarizing the chapters of the book.

The Wild Growth of Urban Environmental Studies

Nature features prominently in the long historiography of cities and urban forms.[4] Within Western thought, urban nature has featured as beauty and recreation, as in the history of gardens and urban design. Nature occupies a certain place in histories of urban infrastructures, such as water works and sewage systems, and in histories of public health, as in the sanitary movement of the late nineteenth century. Nature also has a central and defining role in the history of major city planning ideas, such as Ebenezer Howard's "garden cities" from 1903, Frank Lloyd Wright's "Broadacre City" from 1932, and Le Corbusier's modernist visions of "towers in a park" from 1933, as well as in the functionalist planning of Stockholm's expansion along subway lines and motorways in the 1950s. Across these engagements, urban nature as a signifier features in radically different shapes, sizes, smells, and textures, and it has never received a clear meaning. When clear meanings have arisen, it has been in ideological discourse, often in planning, as the counterpoint to the built or planned city so that very idea of the city in mainstream and popular discourse was developed as a counter-phenomenon to nature—the city was what nature was not. Despite insightful interventions—such as that of Raymond Williams in 1973, who demonstrated just how extremely intertwined and complex the relation between "city" and "country" has been over time, or that of William Cronon in 1991, who used the rise of Chicago in the nineteenth century to tease out how "first" and "second" nature, the natural and human-constructed, are melded together through the capitalist market—the dichotomies of nature/society, urban/rural, and country/city have been a major trope in planning and thinking about cities and urban environments.[5] Our intention here is not to define urban nature, but rather to use this rich, multifaceted, and oftentimes ambiguous word to gather a whole range of literatures that seemingly have not been brought together before, but which strongly have something to do with each other. Indeed, despite the pervasiveness of nature and the "green," it is striking that until very recently there has been little interest in bringing various uses of "urban nature" into some kind of history of urban nature.

As the chapters in this volume demonstrate, though, sophisticated work on urban natures has grown rapidly across the scienes and humanities, especially since the late 1980s and 1990s. This has ranged from, for instance, landscape ecologists showing that urban landscapes can function as safe havens for pollinators through the mosaic of private gardens and public parks.[6] Rather than as a source of pollution and a destroyer of habitat, the city is here read as something that counteracts regional decline of pollinators because of the increasing industrial monoculture imposed on rural areas. The recognition of urban nature has furthermore allowed ecologists and economists to measure the value of street trees, parks, bushes, and meadows as part of "urban ecosystem services" or "green infrastructure," showing in numerous studies how these elements of urban nature are beneficial to public and individual human physical and mental health.[7] Within the humanities, historians have worked to correct the view of environmental history as essentially rural. In contrast to Donald Worster's "agroecological perspective" from 1990, which narrowly centered untouched "wilderness" and excluded the built environment, scholars from North America and Europe in the late 1990s, and then from Brazil, India, and South Africa in the 2000s, have uncovered how nature, while not featuring centrally in more popular stories of modern cities, has extensively shaped and been shaped by cities.[8] Taken together, urban nature, variously referred to as urban ecology or the urban environment, has been enriched across disciplines and linked to various phenomena, ranging from large-scale infrastructure systems to fundamental social conflicts to intimate ideas about cleanliness, sexuality, and the self.

Indeed, the enormous growth of cities and their disproportionate contribution to the contemporary human experience and the total human ecological footprint, including climate change, has generated an upsurge in literature and overturned old ideas that placed nature and culture in separate containers. It is thus timely to revisit the many beginnings of thinking urban nature and try to bring sometimes disparate threads together into a wider modern history of its study. The thought that "the city" needs to be viewed as both social and natural at the same time, as cyborgian, socionatural, or socioecological, has become firmly established within several disciplines in the last two decades, and increasingly in policy and practice. This is an exciting development that ties together a longer, albeit far from mainstream Western intellectual tradition of urban thought that has questioned the dichotomy of cities as separate from nature, with Lewis Mumford claiming already in 1938 that cities are "a product of the earth...a fact in nature, like a cave, a run of mackerel or an ant-heap," and David Harvey famously remarking in 1996 that "there is nothing unnatural about New York city."[9] In the next section we trace some of the modern beginnings of this revolutionary idea.

From Parisian Botany and Baltimore Complexity to the "Urban Planet"

A science-based journey of the discovery of urban nature can be drawn from botany and ecology to cybernetic and complex systems theory. While much earlier examples of urban botany can be found, for its modern scientific beginning, botanist Paul Jovet could be taken as a candidate for a "first" dating of the discovery of urban ecology.[10] Paired with rich illustrations, he studied urban wastelands of Paris in the 1930s and 1940s, recognizing "that urban vegetation was a distinctive kind of ecological *mélange* (mixture) comprising a bewildering array of plants from all over the world...[that] was itself in a state of constant flux through the impact of human activities such as construction or *piétinement* (trampling)."[11] This interest carried over to the more systematic and influential vegetation studies of Herbert Sukopp and his research group in 1950s postwar West Berlin, then an enclosed city within the Soviet bloc. Sukopp's group radically expanded the spaces of interest for biologists and ecologists. Following Jovet, they showed how biological and ecological sciences, mainly used at the time to study "untouched wilderness" outside cities, could be used to study the novel vegetation assemblages in "wastelands" and deserted "bomb lots" left in Berlin after World War II.[12] This wider vision, diagrammed in biodiversity maps that spatially located "valuable" plant communities within the wider city, made urban nature visible *alongside* more conventional components of cities—for example, railway lines, industrial zones, houses, and parks— suggesting its equivalence. While such biodiversity maps have since the 1990s become an integral part of many city planning offices across the world, for quite some time this field-based work was nonetheless a marginal activity with little impact on architectural theory or urban planning.

If Jovet and Sukopp represent a botany and landscape ecology origin of urban nature studies, one grounded in the field sciences, a shift came in the late 1960s and 1970s with the growth of linear systems theory and cybernetics. This was paired with the strengthening of the environmental movement and growing concerns over pollution, congestion, waste flows, and other "side effects" of a consumerist society, which demanded environmental models of the whole city. Abel Wolman, followed by Howard T. Odum and others, began in the 1960s to model entire cities as mass/energy flow systems. Borrowing from electrical engineering and cybernectics, they developed linear input-output metabolic models of cities, what some has referred to as an early "conceptual model of cities as urban ecosystems."[13] This inspired a series of empirical studies that developed course-scale linear input-output models that quantified energy and mass flows in Brussels, Tokyo, and Hong Kong between 1974 and 1981, among others by Paul Duvigneaud.[14] Rather than the Cartesian mapping technique of Sukopp, which focused on land use and the ecology *in* the city with a focus on plant communities, these conceptual models tried to grasp the ecology *of* the city with a focus on inscribing the city's ecology within wider human-made and industrial systems, often drawing arrows of different thicknesses to represent quantities of energy and mass flows. Noteworthy is that efforts to grasp the ecology of the city had surfaced earlier, albeit in more organisist terms, with Sukopp noting studies of Munich and Stuttgart as early as 1920, where "cities...were compared to organisms, with parks and gardens as the 'green lungs.'"[15]

Despite this scientific knowledge production that treated cities as intimately linking social and natural processes, the idea of the city as socionatural or hybrid was only partially accepted within the subfield of urban ecology in the 1980s, and also there contested. The real paradigmatic breakthrough came with the wider discursive shift in ecology itself. The modern discipline of ecology had been dominated by a view of "balance in nature" since its inception in the late nineteenth century in works by Frederic Clements and Arthur Tansley. In the early 1970s, "nonequilibrium theory," which radically broke with this idea of balance, emerged. The theory described ecosystems not on progress toward a stable optimal or "natural state" in a series of successions (e.g., a coral reef) but as more dynamic and chaotic. Depending on a combination of changes in the abundance of organisms (e.g., algae-eating fish diminishing due to fishing), chance disturbances (e.g., storms) or climatic factors, there was a possibility of ecosystems shifting to another state with radically different properties (following our example, an algae-dominated reef).[16] Richard C. Lewontin was first in proposing the idea of "alternative stable states" in 1969, with C. S. Holling developing the idea further in his seminal 1973 article on how the distinction between "stability" and "resilience" of complex systems changes natural resource management.[17] Whereas Lewontin, with Richard Levins, went on to develop a Marxist dialectical approach to biology,[18] later picked up by urban political ecology (UPE) in the 1990s and that included explicit recognition of power and capitalism in the shaping of socioenvironmental dynamics, Holling in contrast went on to found an overtly more apolitical and managerial approach, today known as social-ecological systems (SES) theory, which integrated "resilience" as a notion of purportedly accepting change and uncertainty to "keep options open" in retaining key system functions.[19] In relation to wider social changes, Lewontin and Levins's model was certainly more in tune with the 1970s' radical critique of consumerist societies, whereas recent historical research has explained the mainstreaming and success of resilience and SES theory in terms of how it fit with the rise of neoliberal capitalism in the 1980s.[20]

When imported into urban ecology, the managerialist nonequilibrium idea mobilized bigger and more comprehensive funding toward an urban-based formulation of SES. This funding enabled in particular the launch in 1997 of the first urban-based long-term ecological research program in Baltimore, Maryland, and Phoenix, Arizona, which systematically applied a complex adaptive systems framework, with an associated study in Seattle.[21] Here we we find a similar ambition as in the 1970s in setting out to measure just about everything. From measuring flows of nutrients, energy, and materials, to air quality, biodiversity, and soil composition, including ambitious efforts to measure human interaction with urban terrestrial and aquatic ecosystems, human health, and "cultural resources"—but with the difference this time around to combine such measurements with a spatial awareness and a desire to capture complexity at ever-finer-grained resolutions.[22] Groups in Europe followed, especially in Stockholm and Helsinki, where a more pronounced integration of the role of the public in managing green spaces was achieved. These latter groups also integrated more fully the use of landscape ecological principles, for instance how pollinators and birds "link" otherwise disconnected urban ecosystems. While each group used its home city as a laboratory,[23] there was increased comparative work, which represented a major interdisciplinary expansion from the linear input/output models of the 1970s. However, in spite of this growing integration between social and ecological disciplines, the mainstream SES approach developed with little explicit attention to how fundamental societal conflicts and power shaped urban ecologies (albeit with some notable exceptions).[24]

The emergent SES model of the city, today referenced in studies around the globe, was a quite basic unit of social and ecological subsystems with feedback loops. Socionatural dynamics that operated on a city were "boxed in" to analyze pathways toward adaptive governance and to "nurture" social and ecological sustainability. SES and resilience perspectives, however, were critiqued from the beginning for internalizing crisis and unsustainability caused by a capitalist and consumerist society. Recipes for (co-)management of natural resources and ecosystem services were foregrounded, addressing symptoms instead of root causes to ecological crisis.[25] Some claimed that SES scholars risked depoliticizing environmental research: "the scientific assumptions of resilience ecology run the risk of political foreclosure because they frame the governance choices that are available, often in feedback mechanisms that are seemingly neutral."[26]

Nonetheless, the SES discourse has spread beyond North American and European academies and has come to articulate with a much wider scale than what earlier ecologists had achieved. Fusing (circa 2010) with Earth System and Geosphere/Biosphere research—ramped up by the twin policy focus on urbanization and climate change (and increasingly "the Anthropocene")—urban SES theory has become part of what can only be described as something akin to a "global urban ecology," a universalist claim to knowledge that carries within its highly sophisticated yet arcane and jargon-heavy discourse a technomanagerial response for an "urban planet." The recent ambitious edited volume *Urban Planet*,[27] significant for this development, carries a global outlook impregnated with a complex systems view that effortlessly moves between local, city to planetary scale but without engaging profoundly with critical social scientific theory of power, capitalism, or resource exploitation, nor how knowledge is structured by a business- and tech-dominated political economy.[28]

Research within the urban SES tradition has more generally aimed to structure knowledge, be that qualitative, quantitative, social, or ecological, within a basic feedback model. In relation to our focus on ethnographic, historical, and textured research, most such work, if at all mentioned, typically features as "examples" of system dynamics, as curiosa perhaps, or as a way to "fill in data" in already established conceptual models of cities. While highly productive, and surely offering possibilities toward much more situated work, the urban SES school has come to underrepresent finer-grained understandings of how politics, power, and capital is part of "the system" under study, and thus profoundly influencing socioecological processes. Indeed, conspicuously absent in the development of urban SES are the newer and more radical approaches to study life in the city that came to dominate urban studies from the 1970s.

Capital, Power, and Cyborgian Urbanization

The wider shift in the social sciences, partly as a product of the radical social movements that swept the West in 1968 and in the early 1970s, resulted in the growth of a more critical and reflexive study of cities, which came to influence also how urban nature was approached. These critical roots can be traced to when urban geography decisively broke off from "a sort of orthodoxy" that had dominated urban analysis since the rise of the Chicago School of Urban Sociology in the late 1920s.[29] Rather than studying the city as a mosaic, often using biological or ecological metaphors to build wider theoretical constructs, the city was placed in the wider force field of a capitalist society. Drawing on Marxist and feminist analyses, urban dynamics were explained not from an idea of some kind of "natural" succession but as the results of power, conflicts, subcultures, and the militarization of urban space, where the "the city" was viewed "as a theater of class struggle." One important consolidation of these energies from the mid-1990s, took the form of urban political ecology (UPE).

Drawing its theoretical language from primarily Marxist geography, UPE emphasized the double-sidedness of the city as both social and material.[30] The city has a physical reality of buildings, cars, streets, and parks, but it is also highly stratified in terms of social hierarchies and status. UPE means that these two manifestations of reality are interlinked in how social relations of power and wider flows of capital have produced them both. To unpack this double-sidedness, scholars developed a methodology that differed radically from, for instance, the SES school. Rather than boxing in the city as "a system," scholars focused on what was flowing through the city and traced how water, waste, sewage, electricity, and even fat—but also forests, plants, and wetlands—were shaped by their own biophysical properties, as well as geographically extensive social relations of power. As Erik Swyngedouw explained:

> If I were to capture some urban water in a glass, retrace the networks that brought it there and follow Ariadne's thread through the water, "I would pass with continuity from the local to the global, from the human to the non-human" (Latour 1993, p 121). These flows would narrate many interrelated tales: of social and political actors and the powerful [and unequal] socio-ecological processes that produce urban and regional spaces.[31]

Through long monograph case studies (early studies included Guayaquil, Athens, Durban, and New York, among others) such "sociomaterial" or metabolic flows were traced (using archives, interviews and observations) as shaped by social actors, practices, and infrastructures. Explanatory narratives treated this "urbanization of nature" as simultaneously material, discursive, and symbolic and fundamental to the circulation of capital, the generation of profits, and the creation of inequality and structures of oppression.

This had the effect to politicize the urban environment. Urban nature was moved *out of* the realm of engineering, planning, environmental, and ecological expertise *into* discussions of justice, politics, and public contestation.[32] This was a clear break with the "scientistic" approaches to urban ecology that we have reviewed so far. Instead of objective measurements and amassment of data, urban metabolic flows—alongside parks, wetlands, trees, and so on—were wrought from the hands of engineers and experts and used as entry points to understand asymmetrical power relations that make up our urban worlds. Rather than diagrams, models, or maps, UPE scholars developed rich explanatory narratives that traced the actors, practices, infrastructures, and spaces that extended far beyond the city's nominal borders and involved the circulation of money, materials, and ideas that produce unequal urban environments. This historical and geographical method of radical contextualization followed a Marxist tradition to unpack the commodity form, here viewed ultimately as "the city," constructed as a reflection of capitalist power. Indeed, the objective in UPE was not so much to understand, say, water, wetlands, or the environment per se, but the social power configurations that mediate them. To secure housing and healthy water or sanitation for all, or to lower environmental pollution, did not lie with technical or managerial procedures but in changing underlying social relations of power.

UPE has more recently been challenged and extended by drawing on a range of critical theories. This has included "embodied urban political ecology" using feminist, antiracist, and postcolonial approaches,[33] including feminist analyses of water inequality in Delhi[34] or "situated urban political ecology" that draws on postcolonial theory[35] to "abolitionist ecology" that foregrounds how the legacies of slavery and racialized uneven development has shaped urban environments in US cities.[36] Important work has also drawn upon queer theories, studies of ontological politics, and decolonial perspectives,[37] and in bringing radical political theory in closer communication with environmental studies, all with the aim to interrupt and repoliticize technomanagerial governing of urban environments.[38] UPE also prefigured current interests in "planetary urbanization," where "the city" as the territorial home of urban studies has been wrought inside out to uncover the extensive "operational landscapes" that fuse material and labor together in shaping urban, suburban, and rural landscapes across the world.[39]

However, while UPE's view of the city as a "socio-natural thing" has proved important in foregrounding socioenvironmental activism and unsettling technomanagerial discourses on urban sustainability, a last crucial perspective on urban nature decenters a lingering anthropocentrism that we find in both UPE and SES theory.

Invitations to the Multispecies City

Since the 1990s, a critique of UPE's neo-Marxist ways of dealing with power and the hybrid nature of the city has grown into a "more-than-human" approach that strives to deal with and critique an anthropocentric bias in thinking environments and "the urban." This has focused on so-called nonhuman agency, the idea that it is not only humans and their relations to each other that make up and change the social world.[40] Rather than what in Western thought has been considered as inert objects, "non-humans" have entered the sphere of analysis—including mammals, micro-organisms, genes, machines, algorithms, winds, vegetation, and chemical compounds—for how they meddle and constitute relations that shape the social world, changing our lives beyond our capacity of control.

This interest in the "vibrancy" or "vitality" of matter (that has only par-tially been drawn upon in UPE and that goes beyond Marxist analysis of the commodity) has ushered in a curious and subversive way of viewing the city as a more-than-human geography.[41] This has questioned anthropo-centric ideas of Western thought and, alongside it, for whom the city is for. Already in 1996, Jennifer Wolch drew upon "animal geographies" in her article "Zoöpolis" to critique Western anthropocentric notions of urbaniza-tion, so hard-wired to "progress rooted in the conquest and exploitation of nature by culture." She called, in line with Donna Haraway and several others, for "re-enchanting the city…to bring the animals back in."[42] Ten years later, Stephen Hinchliffe and colleagues emphasized that "urban liv-ing spaces involve much more than human worlds and are often prime sites for human *and* nonhuman ecologies."[43]

These studies have aimed at heightening the sensibilities through which different modes of living can be registered. This has included "experi-ments in engaging with urban water voles" in Birmingham, where citizens and scholars, using sight, smell, and touch, shifted from creating "faith-ful representations" of other species to instead building practices of "cre-ative address" to engage them.[44] Rather than a politics of *representing* other species through human-made artifacts, as for instance in endangered spe-cies lists, what is sought is a more direct form of embodying a more-than-human politics, a heightening of bodily senses into what could be called an "affective" urban ecology. This has included experimental ways of design and speculation around cohabitation with spiders, cockroaches, and scor-pions,[45] and also the writing of multispecies ethnographies to learn how penguins and flying foxes in Sydney understand their urban life within a symbolic animal universe of "successive and meaningful events."[46]

The bulk of this work has been been done in collaboration with artists, designers, and community groups and focused on developing practices of *learning with nonhumans* how to dwell and live together. This has raised fundamental questions of how to organize a common life between species when there is no mutual language or simple way of establishing common rules.[47] In the human social realm this has challenged urban policy that relies on market-based mechanisms, which is deemed overly anthropocentric and economistic, but on the same grounds equally challenged nature conservation approaches, "adaptive governance" as framed by SES, and human-centric framings of politics as in UPE's focus on oppressive social structures. Instead more "local and immediate interventions" have been developed that seek rereading the city as a multispecies place, which in turn can destabilize human-centric authority and knowledge of the city.[48] This provokes changes in public discourse of who can be seen as part of the city, and thus for whom the city should be designed for. The foundation for a new city, what Thom van Dooren and Deborah Bird Rose call a "more equitable multispecies city," lies in experimenting with affective practices that render humans and nonhumans sensible to each other.[49]

Wild Libraries of Urban Natures

Bringing this first part of the chapter to a close, we can now retrace the journey we have covered. From the Promethean view of a human-centric city, a city where, as expressed by an excited news reporter in New Orleans in 1920, "Man has measured strength with Nature and conquered,"[50] we have arrived at a quite different notion of the city, a "Zoöpolis," a vibrant multispecies city of entangled human and nonhuman life struck through with all sorts of politics, human and more-than-human.[51]

This traverse illustrates that the increasing commitment to study and problematize urban nature has surely created a wild library of literatures that deal with urban nature in very different ways. Indeed, although our survey of an expansive field is far from exhaustive, lacking contributions from planning, architecture, art, industrial ecology, and so on,[52] it shows that even though the field contains radically different viewpoints and ideological commitments, the sheer energy of it has established, through a slow buildup in the late twentieth century but in earnest only after 2000, a seismic shift in how the city is viewed. That social and natural processes, the city and the country, are deeply intertwined, which in the early twentieth century was only marginally articulated in Western academia, has become mainstream and common. A challenge therefore is to bring urban research communities into closer and longer-term debate and collaboration in addressing major social and environmental problems, including how cities produce oppressive social structures and undermine the living conditions of various species, together with how to organize a more just life in common. However, in such integrative efforts lie the risk of falling back on trusted frameworks that are too rigid for making sense of our new urban world. Mainstream policy, from the local to the international scale, tries too often to *pin down* urban nature as a stable object of knowledge, thereby risking cutting out the richness and multiple qualities attached to urban natures. Indeed, while models and diagrams can be powerful precisely because they turn complex questions of land use and planning into something "digestible in a single sweep of the eye," they also run the risk of oversimplifying the problems of cities, which at times need to stay complex.[53]

To this richness of urban nature, there is however another important layer of critique and literature that must be integrated, especially given the new phase of worldwide urbanization that we find ourselves in. Given the review above, with some exceptions, most research and theory development on urban ecology and urban nature has so far been carried out within Western academia and in cities of Europe and North America. With ongoing integrative efforts to face global challenges, we must ask how this intellectual origin influences how "urban nature," "urban ecology," and "urban environments" are thought and codified as theory, politics, and policy. What is needed is a rereading of the richness of the literature on urban nature from an expanding urban horizon, including non-Western locations.

Southern Urbanism: Taking in a "World of Cities"

Our turn to Southern urbanism lies in its interest to understand cities based on place-specific accounts, and its push to theorize and develop comparative studies from locations outside the given Western legacy, that is, to allow for the wider "world of cities" to participate as we think urban ecology, politics, and sustainability in the twenty-first century.[54]

Formulated from within a broader frame of "thinking from the South," Southern urbanism emerged in the mid-1990s through a postcolonial critique of knowledge production around cities and urbanization.[55] Why rely on theories formulated during the "first wave" of urbanization, from say the 1820s to the 1950s in Europe and North America? Why continue to center on these particular cities today when conditions of urbanization have changed so radically and are played out so differently? Consider for instance

how life in most Euro-American cities during the initial phase of urban
studies in the early twentieth century was structured around the rhythm
of the five-day work week.[56] This rhythm was such an everday background
pulse for scholars and policymakers and must have profoundly influenced
how they framed questions and solutions to urban problems, which in turn
entered into theories and historiographies of urban and modern life.[57] Yet,
this rhythm is becoming increasingly obsolete and is already being replaced
by a different one for a large proportion of urban dwellers in growing and
emerging cities in Africa, Asia, the Middle East, and continuously in Latin
America—but also in Europe and North America. Indeed, while the twentieth century, the golden age of Euro-American industry-led urbanization, saw
about 2.5 billion new urbanites, the same growth will take only four decades
in the present century, when developing regions will account for 93 percent,
with over 80 percent of this growth occurring in Africa and Asia.[58]

The need to reconsider our thinking about cities and urban ecology
must be set in this wider context of material change on the ground.[59] How
urban environments are formed and contested will play out quite differently. Some simple statistics on cities of Africa help to drive this point
home. For instance, while a small urban African middle class is growing,
the United Nations has estimated that more than 60 percent of the population of cities in Africa is expected to continue to live in so-called slums
or informal settlements in the foreseeable future. This means that a very
different urban infrastructural landscape has been growing that relies not
only on government-built pipes and cables to access water, electricity, and
the disposal of solid recyclables and human waste, but on heterogenous
configurations of practices, markets, and technologies that undermine
simplistic dichotomies that have organized urban theory for a long time,
including private/public, formal/informal, rural/urban, and human/nonhu-
man.[60] Kampala, Uganda, for instance, five decades after independence, has
around 1.7 million inhabitants, with one million estimated to live in self-
constructed neighborhoods (sometimes termed "slums") with slim chance
of steady work due to slow industrialization and a shrinking public sector.[61]
Even in comparatively wealthy Cape Town, South Africa, formal unemployment rates reach over 60 percent in major parts of the city.[62] Changes in the
rhythm of the city and the varied and emergent uses of urban space have
prompted new and grounded empirical analysis, radically changing how
we can view "the city," its physical and cultural production, and who can

claim to have knowledge about it.[63] Following from this, there has been a sharp change in the economic dynamics that underpin the production of the built environment. Only 3 percent of Africa's urban households, it has been estimated, can obtain private mortgages to build houses, and since the tax base for public investment is also low, there is a radically different terrain for financing the production of the built environment. This stands in stark contrast to the frenzy of building in many Asian cities, for example in China and Singapore, where the speed of infrastructure investments often outpaces those of industrializing Euro-America in previous centuries. Wherever you turn, basic pillars of city building, along with urban life and ecology, have changed fundamentally and in ways that established frameworks formulated in the global North cannot fully comprehend.

Given these material and cultural changes, we stress that Southern urbanism does not deny the validity of earlier theory but asks of all theorization to "keep open the possibility," as Jennifer Robinson states, "of being disrupted by understandings of urbanization from elsewhere."[64] There is an invitation here to build on what was before, but in reflective and critical ways, retaining the texture of places when theorizing the urban. This foregrounding of texture and thinking with "multiple elsewheres" as a mode of producing theory contains an important view of knowledge production and speaks directly to our concern with how universalistic, often quantitative, but also conceptual models presume to speak for all cities and urban environments, without recognizing how these models have been shaped by their "home" cities. Comparative urbanists have critiqued Western academia, constituted as it was in the time of the great explorers and to serve colonial and imperial projects,[65] in that it tends to gesture toward building universal theory and models while skillfully hiding its provincial and circumscribed origins. In other words, to act as if theory comes from nowhere, thus rejecting (or having been trained to overlook) that, as James Clifford insisted, "like any act of travel, theory begins and ends *somewhere*."[66]

This abstraction of theory from its *particular* places and traditions of construction, while gesturing to be universal and applicable everywhere—a nonsituated analysis—can be exemplified by contemporary trends in urban ecology. One is the tendency to create ever bigger datasets and ever more general models to understand cities and urban ecologies. At the Santa Fe Institute, for example, physicists are developing a "science of cities" based on the assumption that cities are made up of overlapping networks that structurally resemble elephants and mice. The claim is made that similar "scaling laws" that govern the ratio between the length of blood vessels and body mass across very different-sized animals could also hold for certain urban variables across differently sized cities, regardless of sociocultural or biophysical context. This implies a disturbingly simplistic understanding of cities, at least in terms of how they are to live in, how they operate, and how they can be changed. The authors don't hide this assumption but take it as their goal to prove that "they are manifestations of the same average idealized city."[67] By amassing quantitative data from a large number of cities across quite disparate variables, from kilometers of water pipes, number of supermarkets, and incidents of HIV/AIDS to the amount of innovations and patents registered from city firms, stable patterns emerge that can be used to deduce general properties of this "idealized city." This produces outputs expressed as tables of cities ranked in performance, innovation, or total resource effectiveness. Another example of abstraction comes from the social-ecological systems-based approach that emerged in Baltimore, Phoenix, Stockholm, and Helsinki, which we reviewed in the previous section. As this SES approach has traveled the world from its Euro-American "home laboratories" in the early 2000s, there has been very little reflection on how it might fit other cities and "systems," what it might not "capture," or its bias.[68] Rather, it carries the trademark of Western academia to hide away its origins. While certainly making room for more social and ecological contextualization and on-the-ground observations than the fully quantitative "science of cities" approach from above, the SES conceptual framework—structured around "feedback loops," "slow" and "fast" variables to account for change at the systems level—gestures to be applicable to all cities without changing its main framework. The problem with such an approach in the present moment of novel and worldwide urbanization is that each city tends to be codified through already established variables so that every place and city appears to look and function in fundamentally the same way, only exhibiting *variances* in the intensity of system variables.

This work of abstraction, which "science of cities" and SES approaches exhibit, comes with at least three problematic effects that apply more generally to similar frameworks. They rely on a strict bounding of the city, what has been referred to as "methodological cityism,"[69] disregarding to a large extent *how* particular cities have become interconnected with nearby and distant rural and urban geographies. This goes against much economic, geographical, urban, and indeed ecological research. These frameworks also risk producing an ahistorical city without spatial form and socioenvironmental context. "Science of cities" translate cities into "scores" that are difficult to contextualize in any real city, not least fast-growing cities in the global South. The SES approach makes the city appear as a functional system that cuts out differences and specificities. What is also problematic is how these models travel. By "packaging" all possible cities as *variances* of an "idealized city," these models privilige certain expertise and knowledge that favors overview and abstraction while often gesturing that in-depth and place-based analysis from history, sociology, geography, or vernacular ways of knowing are simply "examples" of dynamics or as curiosa when discussing strategic planning. This risks silencing to different degrees how cities are place-specific constructions with particular history and spatiality, exhibiting path-dependent trajectories when it comes to infrastructure, the built environment, and how political and decision-making systems have been configured.[70]

Taken together, what Southern urbanism helps to drive home, and what the chapters of the book help us to see, is that global and universalistic models can suffer from a *simplification syndrome*. While scholars and theorists invest in their models and stick with them, the empirical world of cities keeps producing an ever-increasing variety. In tuning their models to reflect such novel dimensions, but without giving up on their model of an ever-expanding range of cities—that is, attempting to do comparative urbanist work without serious critical reflection—scholars construct stylized urbanities while moving farther away from the realities of the particular cities about which their models are supposed to say something.[71] Indeed, for all of the ever-increasing computer power, urban statistics, and case studies from different world regions, the desire to grasp "the city" or urbanization as a whole ends in a nonplace, a utopia where statistics and numbers perform "*the* city," *qua* modeled city.[72] Moreover, it is this stylized model city that often and too easily becomes slotted into policy debates, urban planning, and scenario planning.

Toward Comparative Urban Environmentalism

Our project of comparative urban environmentalism is not about discarding what has been thought before, but in accounting for a wider urban experience and in acknowledging from where ideas about cities, nature, and urbanization have come and how they have traveled.[73] A key term for this rethinking is *location*, especially in the way that it has been developed in postcolonial and feminist theory: what is the *location* from where we stand when we talk, theorize, and make statements about the world.[74] *Location* means not simply a physical point or place, but a historical-geographical epistemological location, a place that has been shaped by wider social, cultural, and economic processes that have shaped certain ways to make sense of the world. In practice and politics, this means at least to become more self-ware of what informs one's thought—what is the history of the thoughts and ideas we carry and use—and to use this insight to elaborate what other (geographical-historical) *locations* could contribute in thinking the city anew.

Southern urbanism offers a way to deal with a radically new urban terrain within a generative comparative frame. Three main strategies for comparative work can be highlighted. First, the in-depth case study, which features in the chapters of this book, follows Southern urbanism's emphasis to take each city seriously for what it can offer to theory. Sensitive to the notion of *location*, Robinson emphasizes that in-depth case studies should include attention to when analytical constructs do not make sense. These "untranslatabilities and analytical disjunctures" are signs of when theory has hit its margin or, rather, when the particular provincial origin of a theory becomes apparent.[75] These are important productive moments for the comparative urbanist. This is nothing new to case study analysis of course, but here it is set within a radically changing urban world, which should reinvigorate in-depth studies.

Second, another of Southern urbanism's powerful impulses is to explore new ways of comparing cities through how they are connected, what Robinson named "productive geographies."[76] This could mean, for instance, drawing on AbdouMaliq Simone's comparative geography of "black urbanism," which theorizes the city and the environment based on the experiences of those who were never officially welcomed to the city but who were still there *making* the city.[77] This starting point could lead to comparative studies of how environments and urban infrastructures were used, shaped, and reworked by slaves and their descendants in southern US cities, the black majority in South Africa, Jews in seventeenth- to twentieth-century Europe, Palestinians in Israeli cities, slum dwellers in Kampala, or South East Asian contract workers in present-day Dakar or Qatar. Rather than taking the city center or the "whole" of the city as its object, such studies require a multisited research design that is both careful in composing a comparative geography and attuned to how differences play out when launching new readings of urban environments.[78] Another comparative method of interest, which has been in development for some years, lies in "mobile urbanism," a relational framework developed by Eugene McCann and Kevin Ward that follows urban policies.[79] The comparative work lies in decentering the whole idea of "the city" as the confined territorial space in which problems arise and are solved. Instead, a wider geography is brought into focus that views the urban landscape—its firms, people, ecosystems, and associated policy frameworks (within which "problems" are conceived and their "solutions" hatched)—as produced across vast international policy circuits that link together conference rooms, academic departments, geopolitics, local politics, and wider political economic conditions in order to study how policies are constructed, travel, and influence local settings, expertise, and land use. "Green indicators"—including building norms, public health standards, and biodiversity measures—are examples of policies that could be followed, but so could more comprehensive ideas such as "green infrastructure" and ecological engineering, but also practices and activism around environmental justice, which impact urban environments, placing certain stakeholders in the know and sidelining others.[80] Thus, rather than comparing cities either by holding one variable constant (laboratory style, according to the simplification syndrome), or by grouping cities based on simplistic and externally imposed attributes, productive geographies are crucial for a comparative urban environmentalism agenda, opening fresh and radical space to generate new concepts informed by many elsewheres.[81]

Third, retaining a postcolonial sensibility within a comparative urban environmentalist project means, among other things, attending to differences without essentializing them.[82] Rather than denouncing "regional studies," Ananya Roy (in debate with Jennifer Robinson) has argued that an artful attention to regional academic traditions—what she refers to as "conceptual vectors" that are historically produced depending on relations to the world from this location—could be crucial in bringing about a more diversified way of theorizing the urban.[83] The power of her approach lies in a postcolonial sensibility that appreciates that the "local" is never just that, but is always shaped and formed in a current of historically produced influences and practices that stretch out from, and connect to, other places, in a process that has been referred to as "worlding."[84] Roy quotes Edward

Said, who insisted that "theory is a response to a specific social and historical situation," that is, *that theory is of this world* and can only ever be effective as critique and action when treated as such. This is an argument against universalism as the legacy of Northern theory.[85] Clifford likewise wrote that the insight of Said "challenges the propensity of theory to seek a stable place, to float above historical conjunctures,"[86] which is precisely the propensity we encountered in the more universalistic approaches reviewed above.[87] Conseqently, the notions of "conceptual vectors" and "worlding" allow for studies of what might be called the "genius of the local" (borrowing here from the expression "genius of paganism" from Andrew Apter and Harry Garuba), which means a logic to confront *and* appropriate the wider world—connect with it for better and worse—while developing able and contextualized responses to pressing problems and possibilities.[88] In-depth case studies that carve out and articulate the logics and practices of this "genius of the local" could highly enrich urban and environmental studies, bringing to bear the rich legacies of "local"/"regional" ways of making sense of worldly matters, unearthing *how* things matter as responses to pressing needs and wider flows. To theorize in the context of such work could mean to articulate conceptual vectors that are rooted in particularities, and yet may hold relevance for other contexts, and thus to encourage conversations across places and disciplines.

Through these three comparative methods (the in-depth case study, productive geographies, and conceptual vectors), a main thrust of our book is to merge the two conceptual revolutions we have reviewed—the rapid and diverse growth of urban environmental studies that undermines long-standing dichotomies of culture and society as separate, and the development of postcolonial sensibilities through Southern urbanism. Turning now to our book's chapters, it is mainly through its textured case studies that possibilities emerge to rethink urban environments *across widely different contexts*.

Building from Comparative Accounts and the Book's Contribution

The intersection of urban environmental studies and comparative or Southern urbanism has gained attention and already forms a good base on which to build our comparative urban environmentalist agenda. A good example of this is the volume *Ecologies of Urbanism in India*, which provides a rethinking of established thought through categories and experiences from urban India, including studies of fire, water, air pollution, planning, and waste.[89] Departing from African urbanist thought, there has been efforts to "provincialize" urban political ecology, drawing on studies of contested biodiversity, the "incremental infrastructure" of electricity, and the politics of alcohol flows.[90] Others have pushed to challenge the "modern infrastructure ideal" of centralized networks with studies from Latin America, Africa, and India;[91] developed ways to situate environmental politics between "vital infrastructures" of informal waste workers in Dakar and a global recycling industry;[92] and formulated "alternative visions" of urban theory based on long-term studies in African cities.[93] Following "green aesthetics" rather than exact maps and numbers, attempts have been made to understand how Delhi officials have governed and demolished slums.[94] Yet others have developed "cinematic ethnography" and used camera and film to richly situate a multitude of experiences of urban nature among contested plants, wetlands, and silenced histories in the postcolony.[95]

Like these studies, and many not mentioned, the chapters of this book bring forward *locations* from which to rethink urban natures. Across its chapters, the book takes us on a journey among cities that grew from the "first wave" of urbanization in Europe and North America, to cities of the "second wave" of urbanization in Latin America and parts of Asia, to the "cities at the speed of light" in Asia and the "rogue urbanism" of Africa to understand how urban nature is shaped, deployed, and contested as discourse and material reality.[96] The book is thus seeking not a new theoretical framework, but an approach or platform for comparative urban environmentalism.

Part II, "Unexpected Natures," includes chapters that demonstrate the variety of urban natures. The argument is obvious but important as a starting point: urban nature is broader than the fixed *things* of "green space," such as parks or cemeteries. Urban nature is *process*—part cultural, part biophysical—and includes built natures, such as infrastructures of pipes and sewage; private and public gardens; parks and ornamental spaces; and also weeds and all kinds of animals, including domesticated species, wild species, and unwanted synanthropic species such as lice and rats. This is developed by Joshua Lewis (chapter 2), who focuses on the extensive reworking of the coastal delta of New Orleans, USA, by port and real estate elite interests in the early twentieth century. In particular, he shows the strengths of a historical approach to urban ecology, which reveals not only how elites tried to domesticate a coastal urban landscape through a technological fix in the form of a submerged water siphon, but also the simultaneous and dialectical production of "phantom landscapes," emergent and dynamic ecologies that distribute benefits and vulnerabilities in highly uneven patterns. In chapter 3, Lindsay Sawyer takes us to Lagos, Nigeria, where she starts her ethnography-based narrative with a simple scene from when the Lagos State Beautification Task Force was rolling out a "a carpet of neat grass" under a Chinese-constructed light-rail system close to the informal settlement of Badia. This nexus of rising nation-states in Africa and Asia serves as a starting point for her exploration of how urban nature has always served ideological projects, here tied to Afro-positive desires for a "world city." Against this, though, she also looks at the filling of marshes with everyday waste as a skillful means for the urban poor to gain a foothold in the city. To speak *from* a particular location, but in a way that it can influence thought and action elsewhere, Anne Whiston Spirn (chapter 4) draws on her long-term collaboration with schoolchildren, teachers, and residents of Mill Creek, Pennsylvania, in developing her notion of "landscape literacy" as a tool of empowerment. This community of color, shaped by segregationist redlining, resides in a town that had been on top of a submerged floodplain and is beset as a result by cave-ins that have swallowed cars and even caused human causalities. Whiston Sprin describes how children, teachers, and she and her university students collaboratively develop capacities to read and construct a collective history of the landscape that in turn empowers their ability to stake out claims and show that they have relevant knowledge to shape future planning of the landscape. Concluding this section, Martín Ávila and Henrik Ernstson (chapter 5) take us to a quite nightmarish situation in the city of Córdoba, Argentina, where scorpions who have found a huge habitat under the city in its aging sewage infrastructure creep up through the shower grates to cause fear and danger in private homes. Drawing on animal geographies and more-than-human approaches, they use design and speculation to consider how it could be possible to cohabitate with nonhuman animals that are stubbornly part of the city and that we instinctively do not like.

Part III, "Popular Natures," demonstrates how popular movements—and "in-place" ways of acting and knowing—have reworked and resignified the values and meanings of urban nature, always in relation to state and other powers, and thereby affected who can claim to know urban nature. Thus, Richard A. Walker (chapter 6) examines how and why the San Francisco

Bay Area, a focal point of Western capitalism for a long time, has come to include a patchwork of over 200 protected areas covering 1.75 million acres. Developing the notion of a "metro-natural landscape," he unpacks the formation of a century-old popular movement, as well as the role of legislation, science, and the regulatory powers of the state in creating this extensive urban landscape. In a somewhat different vein, Lisa Hoffman (chapter 7) inquires into the production of urban subjects and government rationalities through an ethnography of environmental volunteers who pull out invasive plants in the coastal city of Dalian, China—an ethnography that also demonstrates the intimate making of new socialities through chopping, cutting, and sharing. Moving to larger complexes of urban nature, Amita Baviskar (chapter 8) explores how green spaces and urban publics actively constitute each other in Delhi, India. Through her delicate account of the hidden—but threatened—peri-urban forest of Mangarbani and her strolls among loving couples at central Delhi Ridge park, she explores how nature is caught up and has become meaningful for different social groups, but also how India's rising middle class has tried to enroll urban nature in particular and exclusionary ways. As a transition to part IV, Jens Lachmund (chapter 9) focuses on Berlin and examines the shifting but interlinked models of urban nature that developed during the twentieth century. These span from viewing nature as part of an "organic whole" to the development of biotope protection with urban ecologists after the second world war, to more recent notions of urban nature that have emerged from civic gardening in a popular movement.

Part IV, "Technological Natures," explores how abstract models of urban nature used in urban planning actually work. The construction, circulation, and use of these models is part of a wider history of how technomanagerial "solutions" flow between cities and across countries and regions to influence urban planning and state action. Here we focus on the mobility of such models, the rationalities they construct, and the politics they have engendered. Thus, based on a close reading of letters and diaries, Lance van Sittert (chapter 10) shows how a bird sanctuary in Cape Town during apartheid functioned as a "laboratory site," first for the development of "fortress conservation" and then, as the urban origin of an expansive model of community-based conservation, which is, however, still shaped by class and racial dynamics. Reiterating the close connection between the extended laboratory and ecological governance, James Evans (chapter 11) develops a critique of "the rise of the savior ecologist" for urban governance on a planet marked by climate change. Focusing on Baltimore, he examines how a highly mobile policy discourse that is based on SES theory (and coded through the use of concepts such as "ecosystem services," "green infrastructure," and "resilience") problematically attempts to "abstract universal principles for urban ecology and its governance from specific places." If Evans focused on the scholars that have abstracted urban ecology, in the next chapter (chapter 12), Jia-Ching Chen traces a more concrete form of abstraction through how the urban master-plan has been revived in the construction of the idealized Chinese "eco-city." The city in focus, Yixing, shows how administrative tools reclassify what was before rural farmland into spaces for urban "greentech" (especially for solar photovoltaics factories). This leads to massive land dispossession and calls attention to the wider rural-urban dynamics in the making of ostensive environmental values through statecraft. Indeed, the technological natures that are analyzed in part IV only *appear* to follow the vision that architects, ecologists, and planners had laid out, where the real consequences for people and the environment are emergent from failing to recognize how land and biophysical processes are part of social and political processes.

In our conclusion as editors (chapter 13), we engage with the tension between textured, situated studies and a concern with the global scale by digging deeper into the word pair of "grounding" and "worlding." Building upon lessons from critical environmental studies, environmental history, and Southern urbanism, the chapter aims to construct a cross-cultural standpoint or scaffolding for studying urban nature and environments in a world of cities. Seeking as well to bring together the rich comparative material from the chapters into a broader conceptual framing, it calls attention to how the textures of these particular studies of different cities across the global North and South not only contribute to how we can understand urban natures, but also help to question and critique overly abstract frameworks for studying urban nature, ecology and environments.

Conclusion

This chapter started with the assertion that global models and discourse on urban environments and urban ecology risk simplifying how cities and nature are understood together. This would misrepresent or silence urban environmental politics, distort how policy is made, and fail to respond to the grave urban and environmental crises of which we are part. While a global response to urban sustainability is important, we have sought a radically different way of accomplishing this by thinking urban environmental theory and policy through situated, textured, historical, and comparative studies. We did this by thinking in terms of *grounding* as a mode of digging where we stand to develop textured case studies, and *worlding* as a way of understanding how particular urban natures carry many other places and natures within them. These notions constitute our comparative urban environmentalist approach that combines two fields, urban environmental studies and Southern/postcolonial urbanism, which until now have been viewed as quite unrelated fields. Drawing on these fields, we suggested three comparative methods—in-depth case studies, productive geographies, and conceptual vectors—that can make possible a study that views urban nature as multifaceted, sociomaterial, and always contested, and which incorporates into the study of urban nature a critical reflection from where and by whom theory is produced. We believe that this mode of constructing theory and policy is more in tune and more responsive to the multiple ecological crises and radically shifting modalities of urbanization that we are witnessing today.

Notes

1. As we develop here in chapter 1 and further in chapter 14, our approach emphasizes "situated knowledges" in contrast to universal knowledge (Said 1983; Clifford 1989; Rose 1997; Haraway 1998, quote on p. 575; Chakrabarty 2000; Howitt and Suchet-Pearson 2003; Rich 2003 [1984]). This recognizes that all social theories are dependent upon a process of abstraction, which in turn is dependent on one owns positionality or location in the world. Our previous developments along this line for urban environmental studies together with colleagues is found in Ernstson 2013a, 2014; Lawhon 2013a, 2013b; Ernstson, Lawhon, and Duminy 2014; Lawhon, Ernstson, and Silver 2014; Silver 2014, 2015; and Lawhon et al. 2016. We recognize "grounded theory" (Glaser and Strauss 1967) but we do not build upon it here; rather we side with how it has been critiqued (Thomas and James 2006).

2. Chakrabarty 2000.

3. Robinson 2002.

4. A more extensive review of this wide literature would be necessary. Here it suffices to mention that the following articles and reviews have been helpful in preparing

our presentation: Alberti 1999; Sukopp 2002; Keil 2003, 2005; Braun 2005; Heynen, Kaika, and Swyngedouw 2006; Melosi 2010; Kennedy, Pincetl, and Bunje 2011; McDonnell 2011; Pickett et al. 2011; Gandy 2013; Heynen 2014; Pataki 2015; and Rademacher 2015. See also key references to urban ecology and urban environmental history in subsequent notes.

5. Williams 1973; Cronon 1991. See also Cronon (1995).

6. See, for instance, Colding, Lundberg, and Folke (2006).

7. The earliest article that explicitly uses the term "urban ecosystem services" is Bolund and Hunhammar (1999). Since then, there has been a frenzy of publications, first from North America and Northern Europe, and for the last ten to fifteen years expansively from China. Gómez-Baggethun et al. (2013) have written a succinct review with over two hundred references to "urban ecosystem services," which includes "disservices," in line with the subfield's taxonomic inclination. Their review draws together findings from landscape ecology (e.g., on pollination), environmental education, public health, and environmental psychology, including early work on how forest groves, parks, and birdsong can provide "restorative experiences" for humans (Kaplan 1984, p. 189). See also a similar review by Haase et al. (2014). For a critique of ecosystem services, see McAfee (1999) and Kull, de Sartre, and Castro-Larrañaga (2015); and in the urban context: Ernstson (2013b); Ernstson and Sörlin (2013); and Depietri et al. (2016).

8. Urban environmental history has expanded since the late 1980s and early 1990s. See Melosi (2010) for a brilliant review of the field and a critique of Worster's (1990) "agroecological perspective in history." For early arguments and examples of key studies, see, for North America: Melosi (1993, 2010), Rosen and Tarr (1994), Keyes (2000), Steinberg (2007), and Walker (2007); and, for Europe: Winiwarter (2004), Schott, Luckin, and Massard-Guilbaud (2005), Clark (2006), Isenberg (2006), and Massard-Guilbaud and Thorsheim (2007), with the latter noting an early focus in Europe on "urban technical networks" (p. 692). The field has expanded to other geographical and cultural contexts: see, e.g., van Sittert (2003 and chapter 10, this volume) on South Africa; Sedrez (2005) on Brazil; and Sharan (2014) on India. In archeology, a further excavation of the role of urban nature has been done for ancient and pre-Colombian societies: see Redman and Kinzig (2003), Isendahl (2010), and Sinclair et al. (2010).

9. Mumford 1938, p. 1961 (as quoted in Braun 2005, p. 636); Harvey 1996, p. 186.

10. We are here following Gandy (2013).

11. Gandy 2013, p. 1303.

12. Lachmund (2013) has written the key account on the Berlin School of early urban ecology led by Herbert Sukopp. This account is also closely followed and

expanded in Matthew Gandy's film *Natura Urbana*, released in 2018 (https://www.naturaurbana.org/).

13. Alberti 1999, p. 606. In their review, Kennedy, Pincetl, and Bunje (2011, p. 1965) note "two schools of urban metabolism," one using energy equivalents following Odu, and a second tracing "a city's flow of water, materials and nutrients in terms of mass fluxes," so-called material flow analysis (MFA). Since 1960 there has been over fifteen full-city studies, mainly European and Asian cities, and after a quiet spell in the 1980s the interest in MFA has grown. For another good review, see Cadenasso, Pickett, and Grove (2006).

14. The studies of the cities were Brussels by Duvigneaud (1974), Tokyo by Miyawaki, Okuda, and Suzuki (1975), and Hong Kong by Boyden et al. (1981). The Hong Kong study *The Ecology of a City and Its People* was an early proponent of human ecology and the first project in UNESCO's urban settlements section of the Man and the Biosphere Program. On the latter and on the role of UNESCO in the wider context of international environmental politics in the post war decades, see Warde, Robin, and Sörlin, *The Environment: A History of the Idea* (2018), especially ch. 6, "The Earth Is One But the World Is Not."

15. Sukopp (2002, p. 378) mentions studies of Munich in 1920 and Stuttgart in 1954.

16. For this paradigmatic shift in ecology, see Daniel B. Botkin's *Discordant Harmonies: A New Ecology for the Twenty-First Century* (1990). Nonequilibrium ecology was also known under more colorful names such as "dynamic ecology," the "ecology of chaos," "discordant nature," and "ineluctably contingent nature," as noted by Karl S. Zimmerer (1994, with references therein) in his argument to integrate "new ecology" within human geography. See also McDonnell (2012).

17. See Lewontin (1969) and Holling (1973, p. 21). The latter meant that whereas stability emphasized the goal to maintain "a predictable world," resilience accepted change and uncertainty.

18. Lewontin and Levins 1985; Lewontin and Levins 2007, pp. 101–108.

19. Quotes from Holling (1973, p. 21). For an uncritical insider's account of the growth of the resilience perspective in environmental studies, see Folke (2006).

20. See Nelson (2014, 2015). Her argument is developed further in Braun (2015) and in Swyngedouw and Ernstson (2018). Together these scholars imply that resilience theory offered a view of nature, which capital in a neoliberal worldview required—a more reflective, yet malleable notion of nature that could be exploited within a liberal market-based society. This interest of a "collaborative" and "co-constituted" nature has been heightened within market-based societies due to the fear of global warming and climate change (Swyngedouw and Ernstson 2018). We also note how

Nelson (2015) argues for a yet radical potential within the now highly mainstreamed resilience theory discourse. This seems counterintuitive given Nelson's and others' arguments about neoliberal capitalism's cultural power to subsume critique. One might instead suggest to approach Lewontin and Levins's (1985) more radical take on nonequilibrium ecology.

21. The earliest book-length articulation of this perspective is Alberti (2008). Other key early publications include Alberti (1999), Pickett et al. (2001), Redman and Kinzig (2003) from North America, and Elmqvist et al. (2004) and Yli-Pelkonen and Kohl (2005) from Europe. There has been increasing collaboration across the Atlantic: see, for instance, Ernstson et al. (2010b) and the synthesis by Niemelä et al. (2011). Interestingly, in the literature commenting on this scientific development, we have noted a North American bias in describing the origins of urban SES theory, with generally less recognition of the early work from groups in Stockholm and Helsinki. These Nordic groups were earlier and more pronounced in making use of landscape ecology (e.g., "mobile link species," pollinators and seed-dispersing birds), but also in more explicitly integrating social theories. This included the use of social/ ecological network analysis, "urban commons" frameworks, and discussions on the role of "local ecological knowledge," which developed into sophisticated theories of multiscale governance of social-ecological systems (see, e.g., Yli-Pelkonen and Kohl 2005; Borgström et al. 2006; Andersson, Barthel, and Ahrné 2007; Ernstson et al. 2010a; Colding and Barthel 2013).

22. A glimpse of this ambition and desire can be gleaned from figure 2 in Pickett et al. (2001) and figure 1 in Pickett and Cadenasso (2006). See also Cadenasso, Pickett, and Grove (2006).

23. See Evans's (2011 and chapter 11 in this volume) treatment of the relation between scientific practice, truth, and "the experimental city."

24. See Ernstson's (2013b) effort to integrate social-ecological systems theory (and its emphasis on complexity) with urban political ecology (with its insistence on social power and environmental justice). For empirical SES studies with an environmental justice dimension, see, e.g., Boone et al. (2009) for Baltimore and Kinzig et al. (2005) for Phoenix.

25. For early critique of the resilience discourse, see Nadasdy (2007) and Hornborg (2009), and, as mentioned, Nelson (2014, 2015). For critique of urban resilience and SES, see Evans (2011), Ernstson (2013b), and Swyngedouw and Ernstson (2018), but also Mugerauer's (2010) critique on the absence of "the richness of the everyday lifeworld" in SES analysis.

26. Evans 2011, p. 232. See also Evans, chapter 11 in this volume.

27. Elmqvist et al. 2018.

28. Haraway 1991; Harvey 1996; Moore 2015.

29. All quotes in this paragraph of the main text are from from Scott and Storper (2015, p. 2). We here follow their effective summary of how the Chicago School of Urban Sociology (Park, Burgess, and McKenzie 1925) was replaced by Marxist analyses developed by Henri Lefebvre 2003 [1970], David Harvey (1973), and Manuel Castells (1977 [1972]), and feminists-Marxist analyses of Linda McDowell (1983) and Doreen Massey (1991). Interestingly for our review is that the Chicago School, which is also known as "urban ecology," is often mentioned in urban resilience and SES literature as an inspiration (see, e.g., McDonell 2011). Conspicuously absent are the newer and more radical approaches to study life in the city, which in many ways replaced the Chicago School. For our project of a critically grounded analysis of urban nature and urban ecology, inspiration can actually be found in both, given the Chicago School's emphasis on ethnographic detail and the feminist-Marxist school's emphasis that power shapes urban environments (as in urban political ecology [UPE]).

30. Urban political ecology (UPE) draws on Marxist thought from Henri Lefebvre, David Harvey, and Neil Smith, with inspiration from William Cronon's *Nature's Metropolis* (1991) and Raymond Williams's *The Country in the City* (1973). It also made crucial imports from actor-network theory (ANT) and science and technology studies (STS), using notions like "quasi-objects" (Latour 2005) and "cyborgs" (Haraway 1991). A seminal text is Erik Swyngedouw's "The City as a Hybrid: On Nature, Society and Cyborg Urbanization" (1996), although urban case studies is also developed in early feminist political ecology (Rocheleau, Thomas-Slayter, and Wangari 1996). Important early studies, which focused on water, include Swyngedouw's *Social Power and the Urbanization of Water* (2004) on Guayaquil, Ecuador; Gandy's *Concrete and Clay* (2002) on New York; Kaika's *City of Flows* (2005) on Athens, Greece; and Loftus's "The Metabolic Processes of Capital Accumulation in Durban's Waterscape" (2006) on water privatization in Durban/eThekwini, South Africa. The field was consolidated through reviews by Keil (2003, 2005) and the edited volume by Heynen, Kaika, and Swyngedouw (2006), where an expanded range of sociomaterial flows and quasi-objects were used as entry points for critical analysis, including water, fat, food/hunger, and parks and suburban lawns. Further studies emerged on urban forests (Heynen 2006), rivers (Rademacher 2011), green corridors (Evans 2007), and waste (Njeru 2006), among others. For reviews of UPE, see Keil (2003, 2005), Zimmer (2010), Kaika and Swyngedouw (2011), Heynen (2014, 2015, 2017), Lawhon, Ernstson, and Silver (2014), Rademacher (2015), and Loftus (2017). For a recent edited volume, see Ernstson and Swyngedouw (2019).

31. Swyngedouw 2004, location 461.

32. As Cook and Swyngedouw (2012) point out, there are affinities but also differences between urban political ecology and environmental justice literatures.

33. Doshi 2017, p. 125.

34. Truelove 2011.

35. Lawhon, Ernstson, and Silver 2014; Ranganathan 2014.

36. Heynen 2015.

37. See also studies on "queer ecologies" (Gandy 2012) and ontological politics (Holifield 2009; Ernstson 2013a, 2014).

38. See Swyngedouw (2009) on the "postpolitical city." See Ernstson and Swyngedouw (2019) and Swyngedouw and Ernstson (2018) on postfoundational political thought.

39. See Brenner and Schmid (2011, 2014), who have developed Henri Lefebvre's (2003 [1970]) idea of the "complete urbanization of society." On "operational landscapes," see Arboleda's (2016) case study of a Chilean mining town.

40. See Pellizzoni (2016) for a review.

41. Such approaches rely heavily on actor-network theory, assemblage thinking, or vitalist approaches. For urban work, see, for instance, Braun (2005), Bakker and Bridge (2006), and Hinchliffe and Whatmore (2006). More generally, see Bennet (2010) and a thorough review in Pellizzoni (2016).

42. Wolch 1996, p. 21. See also Emel and Wolch (1998) and Haraway (2003).

43. Hinchliffe et al. 2005, p. 643; emphasis added.

44. Hinchliffe et al. 2005, pp. 646, 648.

45. Ávila 2012. See also Martín Ávila's project "doomestics" as referenced in Ávila and Ernstson, chapter 5 in this volume.

46. van Dooren and Rose 2012, p. 4. This line of work draws upon the early work from the 1930s by Estonian biologist Jacob von Üexkull, who precisely explored the social and meaning-making worlds, or *Umwelt*, of other species (von Üexkull 2010 [1934]; for a review, see Kull 2001).

47. Stengers 1996, 2005. There is a strong resonance in this literature with von Üexkull's "semiotic approach in biology" (von Üexkull 2010 [1934]). Inspiration is also drawn from actor-network theory's preoccupation with the construction of knowledge from the 1980s, Donna Haraway's cyborg-feminist situated approach to science, and an approach to power and resistance drawn from Gilles Deleuze (see Hinchliffe et al. [2005] on this last point).

48. Hinchliffe 2008; Holifield 2009; Ernstson 2013a.

49. Quotation from van Dooren and Rose (2012, p. 1). See also Ávila and Ernstson, chapter 5 in this volume.

50. We acknowledge the archival work by Joshua Lewis for this quotation, which is from newswriter Thomas E. Dabney, *The New Orleans Item*, May 2, 1920. The news article can be seen in figure 2.1 in Lewis's contribution to this volume (chapter 2).

51. Wolch 1996.

52. Among several equally vibrant literatures that we have not included, we can mention practice-related fields of architecture, planning, design, and the arts; animal studies; and more technical fields, such as industrial ecology, material flow analysis, and sanitation and health. For industrial ecology and material flow analysis, see reviews by Fischer-Kowalski (1998), Fischer-Kowalski and Hüttler (1999), and Kennedy, Pinctl, and Bunje (2011). For architecture, landscape architecture, design, and planning, see Laurie (1979), Birch and Wachter (2008), Müller, Werner, and Keleey (2010), and (here integrating SES theory) Pickett, Cadenasso, and McGrath (2013). For animal studies in the city, of which we have highlighted some, see Wolch (2002), Brantz (2010), and Biehler (2011), as well as van Dooren and Rose (2012). Further from cultural studies and ecocritical thought, see Bennet and Teague (1999).

53. From an article referencing the 2012 exhibition *Grand Reductions: Ten Diagrams that Changed Urban Planning*, curated by Benjamin Grant and the San Francisco Planning and Urban Research Association (Badger 2012).

54. See Robinson (2005, p. 757). See also Edensor and Jayne (2012).

55. We use "Southern urbanism" and "comparative urbanism" (Nijman 2007; Robinson 2011) as umbrella terms, including and relating to "postcolonial urbanism" (Roy 2014, 2016) and "global South urbanism." There is no space to further capture the subtle but important differences bedtween these terms. Southern, comparative, and postcolonial urbanism nonetheless grew from empirical studies done in Africa, Asia, and Latin America in the 1990s. A recent summary of debates and developments can be found in the extensive *Routledge Handbook on Cities of the Global South*, edited by Sue Parnell and Sophie Oldfield (2014); see also *For the City Yet to Come* by AbdouMaliq Simone (2004a), *Learning the City* by Colin McFarlane (2011), *Rogue Urbanism* by Edgar Pieterse and Simone (2013), and special issues organized by McFarlane and Jennifer Robinson (2012) and Robinson and Ananya Roy (2016). Inspirational, even foundational works outside urban studies include Indian historian Dipesh Chakrabarty's *Provincializing Europe* (2000), Australian sociologist Raewyn Connell's *Southern Theory* (2007), and the provocative book by South African anthropologists Jane Comaroff and Jean L. Comaroff, *Theory from the South: Or, How Euro-America Is Evolving toward Africa* (2011). For a critique of this perspective from within urban studies, see the debate started by Scott and Storper (2015) with response from Mould (2015).

56. Of course, there were variances in how this "rhythm" of the city played out along class, race, and gender lines.

57. We thank Jim Ferguson, Stanford University, for the metaphor of rhythm.

58. Parnell and Pieterse 2014, p. 7 (quoting United Nations Population Fund 2007, pp. 7–8).

59. For statistics in this paragraph, if nothing else is stated, see Parnell and Pieterse (2014, pp. 15–18).

60. See the research tradition on urban infrastructure beyond the "modernist ideal," which has developed from studies in cities of the global South: Kooy and Bakker (2008); Jaglin (2014); Coutard and Rutherford (2016); Monstadt and Schramm (2017); and Lawhon et al. (2018). Two broader theoretical schools can be highlighted, those like Furlong (2014), who builds on science and technology studies, and others like Silver (2014, 2015), who builds from Simone's provocation to view "people as infrastructure." For an effective review, see Lawhon et al. (2018).

61. Schoebitz, Niwagaba, and Strande 2016, p. 2.

62. Petersen et al. 2015, p. 4. For more details, see Charman et al. (2015).

63. Pieterse 2008; Pieterse and Simone 2013; Bhan 2016.

64. Robinson 2014, p. 62. For further development, see Robinson (2016).

65. See in particular Connell's treatment in *Southern Theory* (2007).

66. Clifford 1989, p. 1.

67. Bettencourt et al. 2007, p. 7302.

68. See early critique of the universalizing tendency of resilience theory in Nadasdy (2007) and Mugerauer (2010).

69. Angelo and Wachsmuth 2015.

70. While similar pitfalls of rehearsing the theory, rather than pursuing the case, is evident within all schools of urban theory, including UPE in its use of shorthands such as "metabolic rift," or "neoliberal natures" (Parnell and Robinson 2012; Lawhon, Ernstson, and Silver 2014), their emphasis on ethnography, historical-geographical methods and the long-monograph format of analysis allows for place-specific contextualization and reflections over theoretical bias.

71. Ernstson and Sörlin 2013.

72. A longer treatment would be necessary, but we do not think our argument concerning a "nonplace" stands against James Evans's (2011) sharp observation that place actually becomes more important for urban SES theory in making truth claims: "With the death of the detached observer [when studying adaptivity and resilience] and the incorporation of research, planning and administration into the system under study, so the possibility of abstract 'placeless' knowledge also dies" (p. 233). We agree, but when such knowledge travels, postcolonial critique is still valid, as it is not the city itself that travels, nor the place-bounded "truth spot" that urban resilience scholars pursue (Evans 2011). But what travels are precisely the narratives, artifacts, and ideas of researchers, which was what postcolonial theory,

starting with Said (1983), critiqued in the first place. It is through this traveling of narratives, journal articles, diagrams, photos, PowerPoint presentations, researchers, and PhD students that new "truth spots" can be created in new places to strengthen the theory further. We affirm with Evans that "as objectivity recedes from view, truth becomes synonymous with success.... Resilience [and its SES scholars] privileges places that have the capacity to become truth spots" (p. 232). Note that Evans (2011) draws upon and extends Gieryn's (2006) concept of "truth spot," which the latter developed to critically analyze how the Chicago School of Sociology (also known as "urban ecology"; see note 30) in the 1920s used the city as a laboratory for developing social scientific theory.

73. For this argument in relation to critical environmental studies and urban political ecology in particular, see Ernstson, Lawhon, and Duminy (2014), Lawhon, Ernstson, and Silver (2014), and Lawhon et al. (2016).

74. See discussions in Said (1983), Clifford (1989), and Rich (2003 [1984]); for an application, see Garuba (2003).

75. Robinson (2016, p. 20). She here references Tariq Jazeel (2014) and his "Spivakian sensibilities," and she includes a reference to Colin McFarlane (2010).

76. Robinson 2014; see also Robinson 2002, 2016.

77. Simone 2011.

78. Robinson 2014.

79. McCann and Ward 2011. While not urban, see much earlier geographical and relational work in the same vein by John Law (1986) in his development of actor-network theory (ANT).

80. McFarlane, Desai, and Graham 2014.

81. We here rely with appreciation on Robinson's article in *Progress in Human Geography* from 2016, but we can add that her notion of a "virtual field of conceptualization," and her sometimes quite abstract language in discussing comparative studies—that is, she tends not to develop her comparative agenda from concrete and situated studies—have invited critique that in her formulation of "global urban studies," she risks reasserting universalism as a legacy of Northern theory (Lawhon et al. 2016; Roy 2016).

82. Roy 2014, 2016.

83. Connell 2007, pp. 65–68; Roy 2009.

84. Roy 2016. See also Roy and Ong (2011).

85. The quote is from Said (1983, p. 168), which is requoted by Roy (2014, p. 16).

86. Clifford 1989, p. 4.

87. See also Ahluwalia (2005, p. 141), and in environmental studies, Howitt and Suchet-Pearson (2003). Here again we can point out the risk that Roy (2016) has noted in Robinson's "global urban studies" formulation of comparative urbanism (Robinson 2014, 2016). See also note 81.

88. The expression "genius of paganism" comes from Andrew Apter's (1992, p. 166) anthropologial study of the Yoruba people of Nigeria, who goes on to define its logic as that which "confronts and appropriates the outside world to control it from within its kingdoms and cults" (ibid.). South African literature scholar Harry Garuba (2003, p. 264) develops the expression further in his animist interpretation of cultural practices through a close-reading of African postcolonial literature.

89. Rademacher and Sivaramakrishnan 2013. For an early interdisciplinary contribution, but without an explicit urban focus, see the edited volume *Nature in the Global South* (Greenough and Lowenhaupt Tsing 2003).

90. Ernstson 2013a; Lawhon 2013a; Lawhon, Ernstson, and Silver 2014; Silver 2014. See further from Graham (2015) on biodiversity and "postcolonial nature conservation."

91. Furlong 2014. Further references in note 60.

92. Fredericks 2014.

93. Myers 2011. See also Myers (2003, 2005).

94. Ghertner 2015.

95. von Heland and Ernstson 2018.

96. Quotes are from titles by Roy (2011) and Pieterse and Simone (2013), respectively.

References

Ahluwalia, Pal. 2005. "Out of Africa: Post-structuralism's Colonial Roots." *Postcolonial Studies* 8(2): 137–154.

Alberti, Marina. 1999. "Modeling the Urban Ecosystem: A Conceptual Framework." *Environment and Planning B* 26: 605–630.

Alberti, Marina. 2008. *Advances in Urban Ecology*. New York: Springer.

Andersson, Erik, Stephan Barthel, and Karin Ahrné. 2007. "Measuring Social-Ecological Dynamics behind the Generation of Ecosystem Services." *Ecological Applications: A Publication of the Ecological Society of America* 17(5): 1267–1278.

Angelo, Hillary, and David Wachsmuth. 2015. "Urbanizing Urban Political Ecology: A Critique of Methodological Cityism." *International Journal of Urban and Regional Research* 39(1): 16–27.

Apter, Andrew. 1992. *Black Critics and Kings: The Hermeneutics of Power in Yoruba Society.* Chicago: University of Chicago Press.

Arboleda, Martín. 2016. "In the Nature of the Non-city: Expanded Infrastructural Networks and the Political Ecology of Planetary Urbanisation." *Antipode* 48: 233–251.

Ávila, Martín. 2012. "Devices: On Hospitality Hostility and Design." Högskolan för design och konsthantverk (HDK; School of Design and Crafts). Doctoral thesis. Gothenburg: University of Gothenburg.

Badger, Emily. 2012. "The Evolution of Urban Planning In 10 Diagrams." *CityLab,* November 9. https://www.citi.io/2015/03/25/the-evolution-of-urban-planning-in-10-diagrams/.

Bakker, Karen, and Gavin Bridge. 2006. "Material Worlds? Resource Geographies and the 'Matter of Nature.'" *Progress in Human Geography* 30(1): 5–27.

Bennet, Jane. 2010. *Vibrant Matter: A Political Ecology of Things.* Durham, NC: Duke University Press.

Bennet, Michael, and David W. Teague, eds. 1999. *The Nature of Cities: Ecocriticism and Urban Environment.* Tucson: University of Arizona Press.

Bettencourt, Luís M. A., José Lobo, Dirk Helbing, Christian Kühnert, and Geoffrey B. West. 2007. "Growth, Innovation, Scaling, and the Pace of Life in Cities." *Proceedings of the National Academy of Sciences of the United States of America* 104(17): 7301–7306.

Bhan, Gautam. 2016. *In the Public's Interest: Evictions, Citizenship and Inequality in Contemporary Delhi.* Athens: University of Georgia Press.

Biehler, Dawn. 2011. "Embodied Wildlife Histories and the Urban Landscape." *Environmental History* 16(3): 445–450.

Birch, Eugenie L., and Susan M. Wachter, eds. 2008. *Growing Greener Cities: Urban Sustainability in the Twenty-First Century.* Philadelphia: University of Pennsylvania Press.

Bolund, Per, and Sven Hunhammar. 1999. "Ecosystem Services in Urban Areas." *Ecological Economics* 29(2): 293–301.

Boone, Christopher, Geoffrey Buckley, J. Morgan Grove, and Chona Sister. 2009. "Parks and People: An Environmental Justice Inquiry in Baltimore, Maryland." *Annals of the Association of American Geographers* 99(4): 767–787.

Borgström, Sara T., Thomas Elmqvist, Per Angelstam, and Christine Alfsen-Norodom. 2006. "Scale Mismatches in Management of Urban Landscapes." *Ecology and Society* 11(2): article 16.

Botkin, Daniel B. 1990. *Discordant Harmonies: A New Ecology for the Twenty-First Century.* New York: Oxford University Press.

Boyden, Stephen, Sheelagh Millar, Ken Newcombe, and Beverley O'Neill. 1981. *The Ecology of a City and Its People: The Case of Hong Kong*. Canberra: Australian National University Press.

Brantz, Dorothee, ed. 2010. *Beastly Natures: Animals, Humans and the Study of History*. Charlottesville: University of Virginia Press.

Braun, Bruce. 2005. "Environmental Issues: Writing a More-than-Human Urban Geography." *Progress in Human Geography* 29(5): 635–650.

Braun, Bruce. 2015. "New Materialisms and Neoliberal Natures." *Antipode* 47(1): 1–14.

Brenner, Neil, and Christian Schmid. 2011. "Planetary Urbanization." In *Urban Constellations*, edited by Matthew Gandy, 10–13. Berlin: Jovis.

Brenner, Neil, and Christian Schmid. 2014. "Planetary Urbanization." In *Implosions/Explosions: Toward a Study of Planetary Urbanization*, edited by Neil Brenner, 160–163. Berlin: Jovis.

Cadenasso, Mary L., Steward T. A. Pickett, and J. Morgan Grove. 2006. "Dimensions of Ecosystem Complexity: Heterogeneity, Connectivity, and History." *Ecological Complexity* 3(1): 1–12.

Castells, Manuel. 1977 [1972]. *The Urban Question: A Marxist Approach*. London: E. Arnold. Translated by Alan Sheridan from the French original, *La question urbaine*. Paris: Maspero.

Chakrabarty, Dipesh. 2000. *Provincializing Europe: Postcolonial Thought and Historical Difference*. 2nd ed. Princeton, NJ: Princeton University Press.

Charman, Andrew J. E., Leif M. Petersen, Laurence E. Piper, Rory Liedeman, and Teresa Legg. 2015. "Small Area Census Approach to Measure the Township Informal Economy in South Africa." *Journal of Mixed Methods Research* 9(2): 1–23.

Clark, Peter, ed. 2006. *The European City and Green Space: London, Stockholm, Helsinki and St Petersburg, 1850–2000*. Aldershot, UK: Ashgate.

Clifford, James. 1989. "Notes on Travel and Theory." *Inscriptions* 5: 1–7. http://ccs .ihr.ucsc.edu/inscriptions/volume-5/james-clifford/.

Colding, Johan, and Stephan Barthel. 2013. "The Potential of 'Urban Green Commons' in the Resilience Building of Cities." *Ecological Economics* 86: 156–166.

Colding, Johan, Jakob Lundberg, and Carl Folke. 2006. "Incorporating Green-Area User Groups in Urban Ecosystem Management." *Ambio* 35(5): 237–244.

Comaroff, John, and Jean Comaroff. 2011. *Theory from the South: Or, How Euro-America Is Evolving toward Africa*. Boulder, CO: Paradigm Publishers.

Connell, Raewyn. 2007. *Southern Theory: The Global Dynamics of Knowledge in Social Science*. Cambridge: Polity Press.

Cook, Ian R., and Erik Swyngedouw. 2012. "Cities, Social Cohesion and the Environment: Towards a Future Research Agenda." *Urban Studies* 49(9): 1959–1979.

Coutard, Olivier, and Jonathan Rutherford, eds. 2016. *Beyond the Networked City: Infrastructure Reconfigurations and Urban Change in the North and South*. London: Routledge.

Cronon, William. 1991. *Nature's Metropolis: Chicago and the Great West*. New York: Norton.

Cronon, William, ed. 1995. *Uncommon Ground: Rethinking the Human Place in Nature*. New York: Norton.

Depietri, Yaella, Giorgos Kallis, Francesc Baró, and Claudio Cattaneo. 2016. "The Urban Political Ecology of Ecosystem Services: The Case of Barcelona." *Ecological Economics* 125: 83–100.

Doshi, Sapana. 2017. "Embodied Urban Political Ecology: Five Propositions." *Area* 49(1): 125–128.

Duvigneaud, Paul. 1974. "L'ecosysteme URBS: L'écosystème Urbain Bruxellois." *Mem. Société Royale de Botanique de Belgique* 6: 5–35.

Edensor, Tim, and Mark Jayne, eds. 2012. *Urban Theory beyond the West: A World of Cities*. London: Routledge.

Elmqvist, Thomas, Xuemei Bai, Niki Frantzeskaki, Corrie Griffith, et al., eds. 2018. *Urban Planet: Knowledge towards Sustainable Cities*. Cambridge: Cambridge University Press.

Elmqvist, Thomas, Johan Colding, Stephan Barthel, Sara Borgström, Andreas Duit, Jakob Lundberg, Erik Andersson, et al. 2004. "The Dynamics of Social-Ecological Systems in Urban Landscapes." *Annual New York Academy of Science* 1023: 308–322.

Emel, Jody, and Jennifer Wolch, eds. 1998. *Animal Geographies: Place, Politics, and Identity in the Nature-Culture Borderlands*. London: Verso.

Ernston, Henrik. 2013a. "Re-Translating Nature in Post-Apartheid Cape Town: The Material Semiotics of People and Plants at Bottom Road." Actor-Network Theory for Development Working Paper Series, edited by Richard Heeks, no. 4. Manchester: Institute for Development Policy and Management, School of Environment, Education and Development, University of Manchester. http://hummedia.manchester.ac.uk/institutes/cdi/resources/cdi_ant4d/ANT4DWorkingPaper4Ernstson.pdf.

Ernston, Henrik. 2013b. "The Social Production of Ecosystem Services: A Framework for Studying Environmental Justice and Ecological Complexity in Urbanized Landscapes." *Landscape and Urban Planning* 109(1): 7–17.

Ernston, Henrik. 2014. "Situating Ecologies and Re-distributing Expertise: The Material Semiotics of People and Plants at Bottom Road, Cape Town." In *Symposium on the Interdisciplinary PhD Program in Urban Design & Planning at the University of Washington, 6 May*, 1–20. Seattle: University of Washington. http://depts.washington .edu/urbdpphd/symposium/Ernstson4.pdf.

Ernstson, Henrik, Stephan Barthel, Erik Andersson, and Sara T. Borgström. 2010a. "Scale-Crossing Brokers and Network Governance of Urban Ecosystem Services: The Case of Stockholm." *Ecology and Society* 15(4): article 28.

Ernstson, Henrik, Mary Lawhon, and James Duminy. 2014. "Conceptual Vectors of African Urbanism: 'Engaged Theory-Making' and 'Platforms of Engagement.'" *Regional Studies* 48(9): 1563–1577.

Ernstson, Henrik, and Sverker Sörlin. 2013. "Ecosystem Services as Technology of Globalization: On Articulating Values in Urban Nature." *Ecological Economics* 86: 274–284.

Ernstson, Henrik, and Erik Swyngedouw. 2019. *Urban Political Ecology in the Anthropo-Obscene: Interruptions and Possibilities*. Abingdon, UK: Routledge.

Ernstson, Henrik, Sander Van Der Leeuw, Charles L. Redman, Douglas J. Meffert, George Davis, Christine Alfsen, and Thomas Elmqvist. 2010b. "Urban Transitions: On Urban Resilience and Human-Dominated Ecosystems." *Ambio* 39(8): 531–545.

Evans, James P. 2007. "Wildlife Corridors: An Urban Political Ecology." *Local Environment* 12(2): 129–152.

Evans, James P. 2011. "Resilience, Ecology and Adaptation in the Experimental City." *Transactions of the Institute of British Geographers* 36: 223–237.

Fischer-Kowalski, Marina. 1998. "Society's Metabolism: The Intellectual History of Materials Flow Analysis, Part I, 1860–1970." *Journal of Industrial Ecology* 2(1): 61–78.

Fischer-Kowalski, Marina, and Walter Hüttler. 1999. "Society's Metabolism: The Intellectual History of Material Flow Analysis, Part II, 1970–1998." *Journal of Industrial Ecology* 2(4): 107–136.

Folke, Carl. 2006. "Resilience: The Emergence of a Perspective for Social-Ecological Systems Analyses." *Global Environmental Change* 16(3): 253–267.

Fredericks, Rosalind. 2014. "Vital Infrastructures of Trash in Dakar." *Comparative Studies of South Asia, Africa and the Middle East* 34(3): 532–548.

Furlong, Kathryn. 2014. "STS beyond the 'Modern Infrastructure Ideal': Extending Theory by Engaging with Infrastructure Challenges in the South." *Technology in Society* 38: 139–147.

Gandy, Matthew. 2002. *Concrete and Clay: Reworking Nature in New York City*. Cambridge, MA: MIT Press.

Gandy, Matthew. 2012. "Queer Ecology: Nature, Sexuality, and Heterotopic Alliances." *Environment and Planning D: Society and Space* 30(4): 727–747.

Gandy, Matthew. 2013. "Marginalia: Aesthetics, Ecology, and Urban Wastelands." *Annals of the Association of American Geographers* 103(6): 1301–1316.

Garuba, Harry. 2003. "Explorations in Animist Materialism: Notes on Reading/Writing African Literature, Culture, and Society." *Public Culture* 15(2): 261–286.

Ghertner, D. Asher. 2015. *Rule by Aesthetics: World-Class City Making in Delhi.* New York: Oxford University Press.

Gieryn, Thomas F. 2006. "City as Truth Spot: Laboratories and Field-Sites in Urban Studies." *Social Studies of Science* 36(1): 5–38.

Glaser, Barney G., and Anselm L. Strauss. 1967. *The Discovery of Grounded Theory.* Chicago: Aldine.

Gómez-Baggethun, Erik, Åsa Gren, David N. Barton, Johannes Langemeyer, Timon McPhearson, Patrick O'Farrell, Erik Andersson, Zoé Hamstead, and Peleg Kremer. 2013. "Urban Ecosystem Services." In *Urbanization, Biodiversity and Ecosystem Services: Challenges and Opportunities,* edited by Thomas Elmqvist, Michail Fragkias, Julie Goodness, Burak Güneralp, Peter J. Marcotullio, Robert I. McDonald, Susan Parnell, et al., 175–251. Dordrecht: Springer.

Graham, Marnie. 2015. "Postcolonial Nature Conservation in Practice: The Everyday Challenges of On-Ground Urban Nature Conservation, Cape Town, South Africa." *GeoJournal* 82: 43–62.

Greenough, Paul, and Anna Lowenhaupt Tsing. 2003. *Nature in the Global South: Environmental Projects in South and Southeast Asia.* Durham NC: Duke University Press.

Haase, Dagmar, Neele Larondelle, Erik Andersson, Martina Artmann, Sara Borgström, Jürgen Breuste, Erik Gomez-Baggethun, et al. 2014. "A Quantitative Review of Urban Ecosystem Service Assessments: Concepts, Models, and Implementation." *Ambio* 43(4): 413–433.

Haraway, Donna J. 1991. *Simians, Cyborgs, and Women: The Reinvention of Nature.* New York: Routledge.

Haraway, Donna J. 1998. "Situated Knowledges: The Science Question in Feminism and the Privilege of Partial Perspective." *Feminist Studies* 14(3): 575–599.

Haraway, Donna J. 2003. *The Companion Species Manifesto: Dogs, People, and Significant Otherness.* Chicago: Prickly Paradigm Press.

Harvey, David. 1973. *Social Justice and the City.* London: Edward Arnold.

Harvey, David. 1996. *Justice, Nature and the Geography of Difference.* Oxford: Blackwell.

Heynen, Nik. 2006. "Green Urban Political Ecologies: Toward a Better Understanding of Inner-City Environmental Change." *Environment and Planning A* 38(3): 499–516.

Heynen, Nik. 2014. "Urban Political Ecology I: The Urban Century." *Progress in Human Geography* 38(4): 598–604.

Heynen, Nik. 2015. "Urban Political Ecology II: The Abolitionist Century." *Progress in Human Geography* 40(6): 839–845.

Heynen, Nik. 2017. "Urban Political Ecology III: The Feminist and Queer Century." *Progress in Human Geography* 42(3): 446–452.

Heynen, Nik, Maria Kaika, and Erik Swyngedouw, eds. 2006. *In the Nature of Cities: Urban Political Ecology and the Politics of Urban Metabolism.* London: Routledge.

Hinchliffe, Steve. 2008. "Reconstituting Nature Conservation: Towards a Careful Political Ecology." *Geoforum* 39(1): 88–97.

Hinchliffe, Steve, Matthew B. Kearnes, Monica Degen, and Sarah Whatmore. 2005. "Urban Wild Things: A Cosmopolitical Experiment." *Environment and Planning D: Society and Space* 23(5): 643–658.

Hinchliffe, Steve, and Sarah Whatmore. 2006. "Living Cities: Towards a Politics of Conviviality." *Science as Culture* 15(2): 123–138.

Holifield, Ryan. 2009. "Actor-Network Theory as a Critical Approach to Environmental Justice: A Case against Synthesis with Urban Political Ecology." *Antipode* 41(4): 637–658.

Holling, Crawford S. 1973. "Resilience and Stability of Ecological Systems." *Annual Review of Ecology and Systematics* 4(1): 1–23.

Hornborg, Alf. 2009. "Zero-Sum World: Challenges in Conceptualizing Environmental Load Displacement and Ecologically Unequal Exchange in the World-System." *International Journal of Comparative Sociology* 50(3–4): 237–262.

Howitt, Richard, and Sandie Suchet-Pearson. 2003. "Ontological Pluralism in Contested Cultural Landscapes." In *Handbook of Cultural Geography*, edited by Kay Anderson, Mona Domosh, Steve Pile, and Nigel Thrift, 557–569. London: Sage.

Isenberg, Andrew C., ed. 2006. *The Nature of Cities: Culture, Landscape and Urban Space.* Rochester, NY: University of Rochester Press.

Isendahl, Christian. 2010. "Greening the Ancient City: The Agro-Urban Landscapes of the Pre-Hispanic Maya." In *The Urban Mind: Cultural and Environmental Dynamics*, edited by Paul Sinclair, Gullög Nordquist, Frands Herschend, and Christian Isendahl, 527–552. Uppsala: Uppsala University Press.

Jaglin, Sylvy. 2014. "Regulating Service Delivery in Southern Cities: Rethinking Urban Heterogeneity." In *The Routledge Handbook on Cities of the Global South*, edited by Susan Parnell and Sophie Oldfield, 434–447. London: Routledge.

Jazeel, Tariq. 2014. "Subaltern Geographies: Geographical Knowledge and Postcolonial Strategy." *Singapore Journal of Tropical Geography* 35(1): 88–103.

Kaika, Maria. 2005. *City of Flows: Modernity, Nature and the City*. New York: Routledge.

Kaika, Maria. 2017. "'Don't Call Me Resilient Again!' The New Urban Agenda as Immunology ... Or ... What Happens When Communities Refuse to Be Vaccinated with 'Smart Cities' and Indicators." *Environment & Urbanization* 29(1): 89–102.

Kaika, Maria, and Erik Swyngedouw. 2011. "The Urbanization of Nature: Great Promises, Impasse, and New Beginnings." In *The New Blackwell Companion to the City*, edited by Gary Bridge and Sophie Watson, 96–107. Oxford: Wiley-Blackwell.

Kaplan, Rachel. 1984. "Impact of Urban Nature: A Theoretical Analysis." *Urban Ecology* 8(3): 189–197.

Keil, Roger. 2003. "Progress Report: Urban Political Ecology." *Urban Geography* 24(8): 723–738.

Keil, Roger. 2005. "Progress Report: Urban Political Ecology." *Urban Geography* 26(7): 640–651.

Kennedy, Christopher, Stephanie Pincetl, and Paul Bunje. 2011. "The Study of Urban Metabolism and Its Applications to Urban Planning and Design." *Environmental Pollution* 159(8–9): 1965–1973.

Keyes, Jonathan J. 2000. "A Place of Its Own: Urban Environmental History." *Journal of Urban History* 26(3): 380–390.

Kinzig, Ann P., Paige Warren, Chris Martin, Diane Hope, and Madhusudan Katti. 2005. "The Effects of Human Socioeconomic Status and Cultural Characteristics on Urban Patterns of Biodiversity." *Ecology and Society* 10(1): article 23.

Kooy, Michelle, and Karen Bakker. 2008. "Splintered Networks: The Colonial and Contemporary Waters of Jakarta." *Geoforum* 39(6): 1843–1858.

Kull, Christian A., Xavier Arnauld de Sartre, and Monica Castro-Larrañaga. 2015. "The Political Ecology of Ecosystem Services." *Geoforum* 61: 122–134.

Kull, Kalevi. 2001. "Jakob von Uexküll: An Introduction." *Semiotica* 4: 1–59.

Lachmund, Jens. 2013. *Greening Berlin: The Co-production of Science, Politics and Urban Nature*. Cambridge, MA: MIT Press.

Latour, Bruno. 1993. *We Have Never Been Modern*. Cambridge, MA: Harvard University Press.

Latour, Bruno. 2005. *Reassembling the Social*. Oxford: Oxford University Press.

Laurie, Ian C., ed. 1979. *Nature in Cities: The Natural Environment in the Design and Development of Urban Green Space*. Chichester, UK: John Wiley & Sons.

Law, John. 1986. *Power, Action, and Belief: A New Sociology of Knowledge*. London: Routledge and Kegan Paul.

Lawhon, Mary. 2013a. "Flows, Friction and the Sociomaterial Metabolization of Alcohol." *Antipode* 45(3): 681–701.

Lawhon, Mary. 2013b. "Situated, Networked Environmentalisms: A Case for Environmental Theory from the South." *Geography Compass* 7(2): 128–138.

Lawhon, Mary, Henrik Ernstson, and Jonathan D. Silver. 2014. "Provincializing Urban Political Ecology: Towards a Situated UPE through African Urbanism." *Antipode* 46(2): 497–516.

Lawhon, Mary, Jonathan D. Silver, Henrik Ernstson, and Joe Pierce. 2016. "Unlearning [Un]Located Ideas in the Provincialization of Urban Theory." *Regional Studies* 50(9): 1611–1622.

Lawhon, Mary, David Nilsson, Jonathan Silver, Henrik Ernstson, and Shuaib Lwasa. 2018. "Thinking through Heterogeneous Infrastructure Configurations." *Urban Studies* 50(4): 720–732.

Lefebvre, Henri. 2003 [1970]. *The Urban Revolution*. Translated by R. Bonnono. Minneapolis: University of Minnesota Press.

Lewontin, Richard C., and Richard Levins. 1985. *The Dialectical Biologist*. Cambridge, MA: Harvard University Press.

Lewontin, Richard, and Richard Levins. 2007. *Biology under the Influence: Dialectical Essays on Ecology, Agriculture, and Health*. New York: Monthly Review Press.

Lewontin, Richard C. 1969. "The Meaning of Stability." *Brookhaven Symposia in Biology* 22: 13–24.

Loftus, Alex. 2006. "The Metabolic Processes of Capital Accumulation in Durban's Waterscape." In *In the Nature of Cities: Urban Political Ecology and the Politics of Urban Metabolism*, edited by Nikolas C. Heynen, Maria Kaika, and Erik Swyngedouw, 173–190. London: Routledge.

Loftus, Alex. 2017. "Political Ecology I." *Progress in Human Geography*, first online October 18 https://doi.org/10.1177/0309132517734338.

Massard-Guilbaud, G., and P. Thorsheim. 2007. "Cities, Environments, and European History." *Journal of Urban History* 33(5): 691–701.

Massey, Doreen. 1991. "Flexible Sexism." *Environment and Planning D: Society and Space* 9(1): 31–57.

McAfee, Kathleen. 1999. "Selling Nature to Save It? Biodiversity and Green Developmentalism." *Environment and Planning D: Society and Space* 17: 133–154.

McCann, Eugene, and Kevin Ward, eds. 2011. *Mobile Urbanism: Cities and Policymaking in the Global Age*. Minneapolis: University of Minnesota Press.

McDonnell, Mark J. 2011. "The History of Urban Ecology: An Ecologist's Perspective." In *Urban Ecology: Patterns, Processes, and Applications*, edited by Jari Niemelä,

Jürgen H. Breuste, Thomas Elmqvist, Glenn Guntenspergen, Philip James, and Nancy McIntyre, 5–12. Oxford: Oxford University Press.

McDowell, Linda. 1983. "Towards an Understanding of the Gender Division of Urban Space." *Environment and Planning D: Society and Space* 1(2): 59–72.

McFarlane Colin. 2010. "The Comparative City: Knowledge, Learning, Urbanism." *International Journal of Urban and Regional Research* 34(4): 725–742.

McFarlane, Colin. 2011. *Learning the City: Knowledge and Translocal Assemblage.* Oxford: Wiley-Blackwell.

McFarlane, Colin, Renu Desai, and Steve Graham. 2014. "Informal Urban Sanitation: Everyday Life, Poverty, and Comparison." *Annals of the Association of American Geographers* 104(5): 989–1011.

McFarlane, Colin, and Jennifer Robinson. 2012. "Introduction—Experiments in Comparative Urbanism." *Urban Geography* 33(6): 765–773.

Melosi, Martin V. 1993. "The Place of the City in Environmental History." *Environmental History Review* 17: 1–23.

Melosi, Martin V. 2010. "Humans, Cities, and Nature: How Do Cities Fit in the Material World?" *Journal of Urban History* 36(1): 3–21.

Miyawaki, A., S. Okuda, and K. Suzuki. 1975. *Vegetation in the Surrounding of Tokyo Bay.* Yokohama: n.p.

Monstadt, Jochen, and Sophie Schramm. 2017. "Toward The Networked City? Translating Technological Ideals and Planning Models in Water and Sanitation Systems in Dar Es Salaam." *International Journal of Urban and Regional Research* 41: 104–125.

Moore, Jason W. 2015. *Capitalism in the Web of Life: Ecology and the Accumulation of Capital.* London: Verso.

Mould, Oli. 2015. "A Limitless Urban Theory? A Response to Scott and Storper's 'The Nature of Cities: The Scope and Limits of Urban Theory.'" *International Journal of Urban and Regional Research* 40: 157–163.

Mugerauer, Robert. 2010. "Toward a Theory of Integrated Urban Ecology: Complementing Pickett." *Ecology and Society* 15(4): article 31.

Müller, Norbert, Peter Werner, and John G. Keleey, eds. 2010. *Urban Biodiversity and Design.* Chichester, UK: Wiley-Blackwell.

Mumford, Lewis. 1938. *The Culture of Cities.* New York: Harcourt, Brace and Co.

Myers, Garth. 2003. *Verandahs of Power: Colonialism and Space in Urban Africa.* Syracuse, NY: Syracuse University Press.

Myers, Garth. 2005. *Disposable Cities: Garbage, Governance and Sustainable Development in Urban Africa.* Hampshire, UK: Ashgate.

Myers, Garth. 2011. *African Cities: Alternative Visions of Urban Theory and Practice.* London: Zed Books.

Nadasdy, Paul. 2007. "Adaptive Co-management and the Gospel of Resilience." In *Adaptive Co-management: Collaboration, Learning and Multi-level Governance*, edited by Derek Armitage, Fikret Berkes, and Nancy Doubleday, 208–227. Vancouver: UBC Press.

Nelson, Sara Holiday. 2014. "Resilience and the Neoliberal Counter-revolution: From Ecologies of Control to Production of the Common." *Resilience* 2(1): 1–17.

Nelson, Sara Holiday. 2015. "Beyond the Limits to Growth: Ecology and the Neoliberal Counterrevolution." *Antipode* 47(2): 461–480.

Niemelä, Jari, Jürgen H. Breuste, Thomas Elmqvist, Glenn Guntenspergen, Philip James, and Nancy McIntyre, eds. 2011. *Urban Ecology: Patterns, Processes, and Applications.* Oxford: Oxford University Press.

Nijman, Jan. 2007. "Introduction—Comparative Urbanism." *Urban Geography* 28(1): 1–6.

Njeru, Jeremia. 2006. "The Urban Political Ecology of Plastic Bag Waste Problem in Nairobi, Kenya." *Geoforum* 37(6): 1046–1058.

Park, Robert E., Ernest W. Burgess, and Roderick D. McKenzie. 1925. *The City.* Chicago: University of Chicago Press.

Parnell, Susan, and Sophie Oldfield, eds. 2014. *The Routledge Handbook on Cities of the Global South.* London: Routledge.

Parnell, Susan, and Edgar Pieterse, eds. 2014. *Africa's Urban Revolution.* London: Zed Books.

Parnell, Susan, and Jennifer Robinson. 2012. "(Re)theorizing Cities from the Global South: Looking beyond Neoliberalism." *Urban Geography* 33(4): 593–617.

Pataki, Diane E. 2015. "Grand Challenges in Urban Ecology." *Frontiers in Ecology and Evolution* 3(57): 1–6.

Pellizzoni, Luigi. 2016. "Catching Up With Things? Environmental Sociology and the Material Turn in Social Theory." *Environmental Sociology* 2(4): 312–321.

Petersen, Leif M., E. J. Moll, M. T. Hockings, and R. J. Collins. 2015. "Implementing Value Chain Analysis to Investigate Drivers and Sustainability of Cape Town's Informal Economy of Wild-Harvested Traditional Medicine." *Local Environment* 20(9): 1040–1061.

Pickett, Steward T. A., Geoffrey L. Buckley, Sujay S. Kaushal, and Yvette Williams. 2011. "Social-Ecological Science in the Humane Metropolis." *Urban Ecosystems* 14(3): 319–339.

Pickett, Steward T. A., and Mary L. Cadenasso. 2006. "Advancing Urban Ecological Studies: Frameworks, Concepts, and Results from the Baltimore Ecosystem Study." *Austral Ecology* 31(2): 114–125.

Pickett, Steward T. A., Mary L. Cadenasso, J. Morgan Grove, C. H. Nilon, R. V. Pouyat, Wayne C. Zipperer, and R. Costanza. 2001. "Urban Ecological Systems: Linking Terrestrial Ecological, Physical, and Socioeconomic Components of Metropolitan Areas." *Annual Review of Ecology and Systematics* 32(1): 127–157.

Pickett, Steward T. A., Mary L. Cadenasso, and Brian McGrath, eds. 2013. *Resilience in Ecology and Urban Design: Linking Theory and Practice for Sustainable Cities*. Dordrecht: Springer.

Pieterse, Edgar. 2008. *City Futures: Confronting the Crisis of Urban Development*. London: Zed Books.

Pieterse, Edgar, and AbdouMaliq Simone, eds. 2013. *Rogue Urbanism: Emergent African Cities*. Johannesburg: Jacana Media.

Rademacher, Anne. 2011. *Reigning the River: Urban Ecologies and Political Transformation in Kathmandu*. Durham, NC: Duke University Press.

Rademacher, Anne. 2015. "Urban Political Ecology." *Annual Review of Anthropology* 44(1): 137–152.

Rademacher, Anne, and K. Sivaramakrishnan. 2013. *Ecologies of Urbanism in India: Metropolitan Civility and Sustainability*. Hong Kong: Hong Kong University Press.

Ranganathan, Malini. 2014. "Paying for Pipes, Claiming Citizenship: Political Agency and Water Reforms at the Urban Periphery." *International Journal of Urban and Regional Research* 38(2): 590–608.

Redman, Charles L., and Ann P. Kinzig. 2003. "Resilience of Past Landscapes: Resilience Theory, Society, and the *Longue Durée*." *Conservation Ecology* 7(1): article 14.

Rich, Anne. 2003 [1984]. "Notes toward a Politics of Location." In *Feminist Postcolonial Theory*, 29–42. New York: Routledge.

Robinson, Jennifer. 2002. "Global and World Cities: A View from off the Map." *International Journal of Urban and Regional Research* 26(3): 531–554.

Robinson, Jennifer. 2005. "Urban Geography: World Cities, or a World of Cities." *Progress in Human Geography* 29(6): 757–765.

Robinson, Jennifer. 2011. "Cities in a World of Cities: The Comparative Gesture." *International Journal of Urban and Regional Research* 35(1): 1–23.

Robinson, Jennifer. 2014. "New Geographies of Theorizing the Urban: Putting Comparison to Work for Global Urban Studies." In *The Routledge Handbook on Cities of the Global South*, edited by Susan Parnell and Sophie Oldfield, 57–69. London: Routledge.

Robinson, Jennifer. 2016. "Thinking Cities through Elsewhere: Comparative Tactics for a More Global Urban Studies." *Progress in Human Geography* 40(1): 3–29.

Robinson, Jennifer, and Ananya Roy. 2016. "Debate on Global Urbanisms and the Nature of Urban Theory." *International Journal of Urban and Regional Research* 40(1): 181–186.

Rocheleau, Dianne E., Barbara Thomas-Slayter, and Esther Wangari, eds. 1996. *Feminist Political Ecology: Global Issues and Local Experience*. London: Routledge.

Rose, Gillian. 1997. "Situating Knowledges: Positionality, Reflexivities and Other Tactics." *Progress in Human Geography* 21(3): 305–320.

Rosen, Christine M., and Joel A. Tarr. 1994. "The Importance of an Urban Perspective in Environmental History." *Journal of Urban History* 20: 299–310.

Roy, Ananya. 2009. "The 21st-Century Metropolis: New Geographies of Theory." *Regional Studies* 43(6): 819–830.

Roy, Ananya. 2011. "Cities at the Speed of Light: Asian Experiments of the Urban Century." Public Lecture, May 12. London: London School of Economics and Political Science. http://www.lse.ac.uk/website-archive/publicEvents/events/2011/201105 12t1830vNT.aspx.

Roy, Ananya. 2014. "Worlding the South: Toward a Postcolonial Urban Theory." In *The Routledge Handbook on Cities of the Global South*, edited by Susan Parnell and Sophie Oldfield, 9–20. London: Routledge.

Roy, Ananya. 2016. "Who's Afraid of Postcolonial Theory?" *International Journal of Urban and Regional Research* 40(1): 200–209.

Roy, Ananya, and Aihwa Ong, eds. 2011. *Worlding Cities: Asian Experiments and the Art of Being Global*. Oxford: Wiley-Blackwell.

Said, Edward. 1983. *The World, the Text and the Critic*. Cambridge, MA: Harvard University Press.

Schoebitz, Lars, Charles B. Niwagaba, and Linda Strande. 2016. *SFD [Shit Flow Diagram] Report Kampala*. Report for SANDEC (Swiss Department of Sanitation for Development) and EAWAG (Swiss Federal Institute of Aquatic Science and Technology), Dübendorf.

Schott, Dieter, Bill Luckin, and Geneviève Massard-Guilbaud, eds. 2005. *Resources of the City: Contributions to an Environmental History of Modern Europe*. Aldershot, UK: Ashgate.

Scott, Allen J., and Michael Storper. 2015. "The Nature of Cities: The Scope and Limits of Urban Theory." *International Journal of Urban and Regional Research* 39: 1–15.

Sedrez, Lise. 2005. *The "Bay of All Beauties": State and Environment in Guanabara Bay, Rio de Janeiro, Brazil, 1875–1975*. Ann Arbor, MI: University Microfilms.

Sharan, Awadhendra. 2014. *In the City, Out of Place: Nuisance, Pollution and Urban Dwelling in Modern Delhi, c.1850–2000*. Oxford: Oxford University Press.

Silver, Jonathan. 2014. "Incremental Infrastructures: Material Improvisation and Social Collaboration across Post-colonial Accra." *Urban Geography* 35(6): 788–804.

Silver, Jonathan. 2015. "Disrupted Infrastructures: An Urban Political Ecology of Interrupted Electricity in Accra." *International Journal of Urban and Regional Research* 39(5): 984–1003.

Simone, AbdouMaliq. 2004a. *For the City Yet to Come: Changing African Life in Four Cities*. Durham, NC: Duke University Press.

Simone, AbdouMaliq. 2004b. "People as Infrastructure: Intersecting Fragments in Johannesburg." *Public Culture* 16(3): 407–429.

Simone, AbdouMaliq. 2011. *City Life from Jakarta to Dakar: Movements at the Crossroads*. New York: Routledge.

Sinclair, Paul J. J., Gullög Nordquist, Frands Herschend, and Christian Isendahl. 2010. *The Urban Mind: Cultural and Environmental Dynamics*. Uppsala: Uppsala University: Department of Archaeology and Ancient History.

Steinberg, Theodore. 2007. *American Green: The Obsessive Quest for the Perfect Lawn*. New York: W. W. Norton.

Stengers, Isabelle. 1996. *Cosmopolitiques*, vol. 1: *La guerre des sciences*. Paris: La Découverte.

Stengers, Isabelle. 2005. "The Cosmopolitical Proposal." In *Making Things Public: Atmospheres of Democracy*, edited by Bruno Latour and P. Wedel, 994–1003. Cambridge, MA: MIT Press.

Sukopp, Herbert. 2002. "On the Early History of Urban Ecology in Europe." *Preslia, Praha* 74: 373–393.

Swyngedouw, Erik. 1996. "The City as a Hybrid: On Nature, Society and Cyborg Urbanization." *Capitalism Nature Socialism* 7(2): 65–80.

Swyngedouw, Erik. 2004. *Social Power and the Urbanization of Water: Flows of Power*. Oxford: Oxford University Press. Kindle.

Swyngedouw, Erik. 2009. "The Antinomies of the Postpolitical City: In Search of a Democratic Politics of Environmental Production." *International Journal of Urban and Regional Research* 33(3): 601–620.

Swyngedouw, Erik, and Henrik Ernstson. 2018. "Interrupting the Anthropo-obScene: Immuno-Biopolitics and Depoliticizing Ontologies in the Anthropocene." *Theory, Culture & Society* 35(6): 3–30.

Thomas, Gary, and David James. 2006. "Reinventing Grounded Theory: Some Questions about Theory, Ground and Discovery." *British Educational Research Journal* 32(6): 767–795.

Truelove, Yaffa. 2011. "(Re-)Conceptualizing Water Inequality in Delhi, India through a Feminist Political Ecology Framework." *Geoforum* 42(2): 143–152.

United Nations Population Fund (UNFPA). 2007. *State of the World Population 2007: Unleashing the Potenial of Urban Growth.* New York: United Nations Population Fund.

van Dooren, Thom, and Deborah Bird Rose. 2012. "Storied-Places in a Multispecies City." *Humanimalia* 3: 1–27.

van Sittert, Lance. 2003. "The Bourgeois Eye Aloft: Table Mountain in the Anglo Urban Middle Class Imagination, c. 1891–1952." *Kronos* 2(2): 161–190.

von Heland, Jacob, and Henrik Ernstson. 2018. *One Table Two Elephants.* Documentary film, 84 minutes. World Premiere at CPH:DOX Copenhagen International Film Festival, March 20 http://bit.ly/1T2E-film.

von Üexkull, Jakob. 2010 [1934]. *A Foray into the Worlds of Animals and Humans.* Minneapolis: University of Minnesota Press.

Walker, Richard. 2007. *The Country in the City: The Greening of the San Francisco Bay Area.* Seattle: University of Washington Press.

Warde, Paul, Libby Robin, and Sverker Sörlin. 2018. *The Environment: A History of the Idea.* Baltimore, MD: Johns Hopkins University Press.

Williams, Raymond. 1973. *The Country and the City.* New York: Oxford University Press.

Winiwarter, Verena. 2004. "Environmental History in Europe from 1994 to 2004: Enthusiasm and Consolidation." *Environment and History* 10: 501–530.

Wolch, Jennifer. 1996. "Zoöpolis." *Capitalism Nature Socialism* 7(2): 21–47.

Wolch, Jennifer. 2002. "Anima Urbis." *Progress in Human Geography* 26(6): 721–742.

Worster, Donald. 1990. "Transformations of the Earth: Toward an Agroecological Perspective in History." *Journal of American History* 76: 1087–1106.

Yli-Pelkonen, Vesa, and Johanna Kohl. 2005. "The Role of Local Ecological Knowledge in Sustainable Urban Planning: Perspectives from Finland." *Sustainability: Science, Practice, & Policy* 1(1): 3–14.

Zimmer, Anna. 2010. "Urban Political Ecology. Theoretical Concepts, Challenges, and Suggested Future Directions." *Erdkunde* 64(4): 343–354.

Zimmerer, Karl S. 1994. "Human Geography and the 'New Ecology': The Prospect and Promise of Integration." *Annals of the Association of American Geographers* 84(1): 108–125.

II Unexpected Natures

2 The Disappearing River: Infrastructural Desire in New Orleans

Joshua Lewis

When readers of the *New Orleans Item* picked up the newspaper on May 2, 1920, they saw a peculiar front page headline: "NEW ORLEANS BUILDS OWN UNDERGROUND RIVER: Great Siphon Under Industrial Canal Solves Drainage Problem" (see figure 2.1). Officials at the Port of New Orleans were eager to highlight the completion of their much-touted but already problem-plagued drainage siphon. After years of engineering setbacks, neighborhoods being flooded by raw sewage, and financial scandals surrounding the Industrial Canal and Inner Harbor project, the maritime elite mobilized the local press to trumpet the huge concrete tube that was supposedly poised to resolve a major infrastructural contradiction: the right of way for the port's new shipping canal happened to cross precisely at the point where the city's immense drainage volume reached its site of "final disposal" in a small tidal creek called Bayou Bienvenue. In the mercurial waterways and swampy soils of the continent's largest river delta, port engineers poured concrete in the deepest open excavation in the history of human settlement in the Mississippi Delta—over eighteen meters below sea level. This would be a difficult endeavor even for contemporary engineers, as the soil at those depths is a mucky mix of quicksand, water, and highly rot-resistant bald cypress forests buried by ancient floods. During the winter of 1919, dredging machines were shattered and costs soared as layer upon layer of ancient forests were dug, sucked, chopped, and dynamited out of the way by the labor gangs. Deeper still, engineers found layers of fine riverine sediments, hardened sand, and seashells where an ancient shoreline extended. One port official kept a pile of the primeval shells on his desk to illustrate the geologically epic scale of the project. A local journalist who often doubled as the port's foremost advocate and mouthpiece explained to the public what was implied in the simultaneous completion of the

Figure 2.1
Front page of the *New Orleans Item*, May 2, 1920, hailing the construction of the drainage siphon. The top diagram shows the four chambers of the siphon; the bottom diagram shows the siphon design, with drainage water being sucked underneath the Industrial Canal and into Bayou Bienvenue.

Inner Harbor, the municipal drainage system, and the concrete siphon that held it all together:

> Man every day is surpassing Nature. ... He turns rivers from their course and mingles oceans. ... If a mountain is in his way, he obliterates it. He plays hide-and-seek with hurricanes. ... He creates machinery like cosmic forces. The highest study of mankind is not Man, but the works of Man. In New Orleans, Man has measured strength with Nature and conquered. ... He has joined the river and lake, building gargantuan foundations for his work on the quicksands themselves. And as an incident in the general plan, he created a disappearing river. ... This is the famous drainage siphon—the great quadruple passage of steel and concrete. ... The Florida canal approaches to within a hundred or so feet of the Industrial Canal, then dives 40 feet underground, passes beneath the shipway, and comes to the surface on the other side, not far from the pumping station where it is lifted into Bayou Bienvenue.[1]

The siphon was engineered and celebrated as anti-nature. To engineers its capacities emerged from its design and its durable materials: concrete, steel, and iron. But it was perhaps more like the four-chambered human heart than an ultimate engineering triumph over the vacillations of nature. It became a troublesome and invisible anxiety to its managers, prone to leaks, clogs, and total breakdowns. The siphon's concrete chambers conveyed fetid sludge, sewage, storm water, natural gas, electricity, hurricane storm surges, chicken coops, auto parts, fish, seeds; an ultimately unknowable miscellany of things was pushed and pulsed through its chambers by people and by the forces of the deltaic environment.

Through the history of the siphon, this chapter addresses how infrastructure participates in the production of urban natures. Attending to the agency of infrastructural artifacts and networks in the sociomaterial production of urban space is now a well-established approach for research into the dynamics of the urban environment.[2] Urban infrastructure represents a useful research object for questions around how the uneven form of the built environment and the dynamics of urban ecological systems are entangled in the contested politics of a heterogeneous and globally interconnected urban polity. The history of capitalist urbanization in the biophysically dynamic Mississippi River Delta provides an instructive context to explore these themes. In a terrain built by and subject to regular flooding, engineers have struggled to create infrastructural networks that can achieve fixity and efficiency in a place defined by flow and flux. Infrastructures that rework and interconnect waterscapes have been mobilized to drive urban spatial expansion, improve public health conditions, and facilitate waterborne commerce. Each of these impulses suggests an idealized form of the deltaic environment: urbanized, sanitary, and navigable.

In early twentieth-century New Orleans, it happened that these desires and the water infrastructures they spawned overlapped in the same low-lying drainage basin. Engineers heralded the drainage siphon as a way to simultaneous enroll one territory into different spatial agendas that prioritized fundamentally different social goals and material flows. This amalgam of canals, locks, pipes, pumps, and streams comprise an *urban infrastructural ensemble*. "Ensemble" alludes more to the intent of engineers than an actually smooth coordination of the various technological, human, and ecological actors involved. This network of water infrastructure was always a precarious work in progress, susceptible to being destabilized by social and material forces. Nonetheless, the creation of this ensemble in New Orleans established the stubborn physical structures that have configured patterns of urban inequality, flooding, and ecological change to the present day. The siphon is a useful empirical artifact to ground an inquiry into these processes, as it served as a critical nexus undergirding the overall modes of urbanization evident in the region. Embedded and stubborn, the siphon was encountered by generations of managers who worked to conserve its functions and divine its idiosyncrasies. Though the siphon's chambers disappeared under the ship channels, freighters, and wharves of the port's Inner Harbor in 1921, it reemerged as an agent in strange places—in the flooded bedrooms of a public housing facility, in the frustrated mind of the engineer, in the bodies of delta wildlife, and on the dinner plates of the urban elite.

Promoters of sustainability and resilience as modes of urban governance often fail to recognize how crucial material infrastructure networks can be to achieving more socially just and ecologically benign urbanization outcomes. This chapter is thus a contribution to an emerging critical and historical literature concerning urban infrastructure.[3] The siphon's transition from a marvel of technological modernism, to an invisible transformer of regional waterscapes, to a participant in the devastation of neighborhoods highlights how aging clusters of urban infrastructure are sources of economic and ecological sustainability challenges in cities. As the urban polity's most physically enduring collective venture, the meaningful adaptation of urban infrastructure is often technically and politically difficult.[4] For example, city governments are typically able to overhaul their drainage and sewer systems only once in a century, if that often. The long time scales involved in these adaptations give way to spatially persistent patterns of uneven development and hazard exposure, and in some cases, particularly in the case of water infrastructure, these aging networks help structure the biophysical parameters around which ecological systems adapt and organize. Over many decades, it becomes difficult to separate "urban nature" from the infrastructures that configure the flows of water, influence soil conditions, and transport materials over a certain territory. As coastal cities worldwide begin to confront rising seas, the careful adaptation and repurposing of these infrastructures is a critical, if formidable, task. These trends call for detailed historical accounts of how those infrastructures came into being, what interests they served, how they became ecologically and socially embedded, and who has stood to gain and/or suffer from their adaptation.

The ensemble in which the siphon performed is implicated in patterns of social and geographic relations that anthropologists have called "infrastructural violence," wherein societal cleavages and oppressive public policies are legible in the engineering of the urban environment, where they raise questions of environmental justice and social equity.[5] The historically rooted and enduring entanglements of infrastructure, neighborhoods, and urban nature are of crucial concern here. An important task for scholars, planners, and policymakers lies in acknowledging and grappling with what Kaika and Swyngedouw call "the urban dowry"—the aging and problematic material inheritance of urban infrastructural systems.[6] The story of the "disappearing river" offers a textured account of how infrastructure is more than concrete and steel. The siphon produced urban nature in unexpected forms, while capitalists, municipal authorities, engineers, and ordinary citizens contested the benefits, constraints, and hazards presented by their troublesome infrastructural inheritance.

Pathogens, Swamps, and Choke Points

The siphon was not so much "an incident" in any single plan as our opening quotation implies, as it was a technological intervention intended to mitigate three ecological conditions endemic to the Mississippi River Delta: deadly pathogens and their vectors, unstable swampy soils, and navigational choke points in waterways. First, sanitary engineers were in pursuit of the politically ideal circulation of urban wastes; second, real estate developers were planning to produce suburban enclaves on former swamps and elevated reclaimed land; and third, port planners were working to provide an alternative port approach free of the sandbars and shoals of the Lower Mississippi River.

The growing political and economic pressures to fight disease in the city and expand the port's capabilities in the late nineteenth century brought the interest of planners, engineers, and capitalists to the city's eastern margins. The lowest terrain in the swampy depression where the siphon was constructed was one of the lowest points in the Mississippi Delta; even before it sank further in the twentieth century, it was barely a meter above sea level. Most settlement in the region tended to cluster along the high ground of the Mississippi River's banks and ancient distributaries, which form ridge lines rising from the swamps. The eastern margin of the city has always been its most flood prone, due to its position in the basin of Bayou Bienvenue, a sinking expanse of swamps and marshes that drain directly into the estuaries of the Gulf of Mexico. The inland reach of the basin was at the turn of the century a freshwater swamp forest with a canopy dominated by bald cypress trees and an understory of freshwater marsh

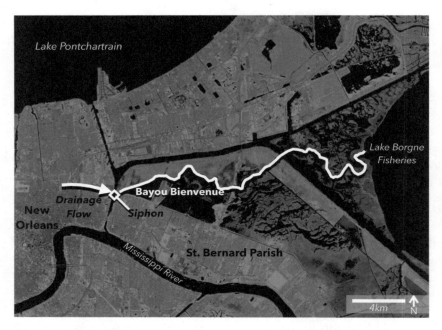

Figure 2.2
The siphon and the neighborhoods, infrastructures, and ecosystems it tied together.
NASA Landsat 7 imagery. Processing by Joshua Lewis.

plants and dwarf palmetto shrubs. The seaward reach of the basin is tidally influenced, and freshwater swamp forests gave way to brackish and salt marshes as Bayou Bienvenue emptied into Lake Borgne, an estuary of the Gulf of Mexico (see figures 2.2 and 2.3). The flat terrain means that without major river floods, storm surges, or technological intervention, water was relatively stagnant and the tidal range low.

Viruses, bacteria, and insects played an important role in how the siphon ended up being situated where it was. Outbreaks of yellow fever during the summer months could claim thousands of lives in New Orleans, especially those of recent immigrants who had no acquired immunity to the disease. In one particularly virulent outbreak in 1853, 10,000 of the city's 150,000 died of the infection.[7] A local journal noted in 1850 that it had "become fashionable to regard New Orleans as 'The Wet Graveyard' ... little more than a vast necropolis."[8] The swamp-loving *Aedes aegypti* mosquito, brought to Louisiana from Africa along with thousands of enslaved African people, was yellow fever's vector. Malaria, typhoid, and cholera were also

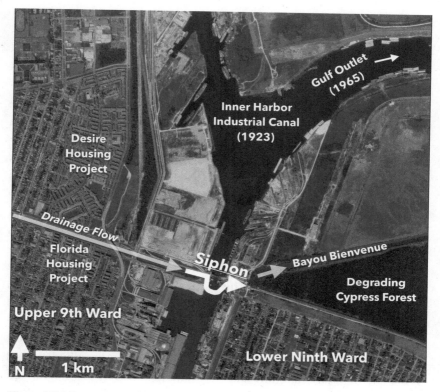

Figure 2.3
Aerial photograph showing the neighborhoods and hydrological features in the siphon's environs. Imagery courtesy of US Geological Survey. Processing by Joshua Lewis.

persistent problems for the poorer residents who lived in the saturated areas away from the river's natural ridges.

While pathogens and mosquitos created a real public health crisis in the city, they also jeopardized the city's role as a control point in the flow of commodities and financial capital between the Mississippi Valley and Atlantic trade routes. The constant presence of deadly pathogens in the city represented a significant source of economic risk for the city's elite. Cargoes that had docked in New Orleans during outbreaks were often forced into quarantine when arriving at other ports, thereby slowing the movement of capital and goods. The city's ruling elite stood to gain from more efficient drainage and disease eradication by improving the reputation of the city as a safe space for investment and trade.

The decision to drain many of the swamps in the city limits was a given by the 1890s, when a board of engineers and public health experts was charged with developing a municipal drainage system. Drainage pumps and canals have long been a feature of the city's landscape, but an interconnected comprehensive system required new hydrological planning. The municipal drainage system was informed by a topographical survey of the city carried out in 1893. The translation of flat swamplands into an artifact registering the smallest differences in elevation enabled the drainage advisory board to determine where gravity could assist their efforts most.[9] This influenced the critical decision about *where* the "final disposal" of the city's massive drainage flows would go. Based on the survey, engineers saw three options: the Mississippi River, Lake Pontchartrain to the north, and Bayou Bienvenue / Lake Borgne to the east (see figures 2.2 and 2.3). The river was a nonstarter, because of the huge energy costs of pumping the city's drainage from its neighborhoods (at or around sea level) against gravity into the river (which is above sea level). This left the estuary of Lake Pontchartrain, and Bayou Bienvenue, a tidal creek that emptied into Lake Borgne.[10] While pumping to Lake Pontchartrain was easiest from a technical and topographical perspective, this location was complicated by its status as a resort space for the city's elite, the emerging plans for an extensive suburban land reclamation project along the lakeshore, and its relatively low tidal range. As the advisory board noted, there were "numerous pleasure resorts along the shore," and thus they concluded that it was

> desirable to protect lake [Pontchartrain's] water even from slight pollution. The lake is landlocked, which prevents a rapid tidal flow in and out, or any material circulation of its water. Under these circumstances, as is the case at present, a pollution becomes a serious matter. A discharge into the lake of the ordinary flow and of that from light storms should therefore be avoided.[11]

The third option, on the other hand, had several advantages. A two-kilometer stretch of Bayou Bienvenue's inland reach had already been straightened, dredged, and renamed the "Florida Canal" decades prior, and some pumping infrastructure was already in place. In addition, Bayou Bienvenue was chosen by surveyors as the municipal boundary, meaning wastewater could ride the city limits until it reached the ambiguous jurisdictions of the remote tidal estuaries. Thus Bayou Bienvenue emerged as the preferred site of "final disposal" for the city's drainage. Engineers foresaw only minor modifications to make this line of action feasible. In explaining their preference for the Bayou-Lake Borgne site, the board explained that Bayou Bienvenue's drainage basin was

> mostly uninhabited and a slight pollution of the water has no disadvantages. It is open to the Gulf [of Mexico], and the tides rise and fall more rapidly [than in Lake Pontchartrain]. The greater fluctuations cause a more complete dispersion and a more rapid removal of the drainage water. The mean level is several inches lower than Lake Pontchartrain. The distance from the city to the lake is somewhat greater, but Bayou Bienvenu[e], which by dredging can readily be made of sufficient size to convey the drainage water, runs from the [Gulf] nearly to the levees of the city and can be utilized, without detriment, to receive the drainage flow. It is, also, the natural outfall for the drainage of a large part of the city.[12]

Perhaps the project's boosters were engaging in wishful thinking when they characterized the Ninth Ward of New Orleans and neighboring St. Bernard Parish as "virtually uninhabited." In truth, thousands of working-class families lived in the immediate vicinity of the project. Recent immigrants from Ireland, Germany, and Italy, decedents of free people of color and the enslaved, and long-established fishing villages were spread throughout the basin. Land in the area was poorly served by existing drainage and transportation infrastructure, but was comparably cheap and was drawing in hundreds of new residents annually in the 1910s.

By 1916, drainage engineers successfully connected the city's main stormwater system to Bayou Bienvenue. New electric-powered drainage pumps were sucking a filthy slurry of stormwater, groundwater, soil, garbage, and raw sewage into the Florida Canal and Bayou Bienvenue, where it flowed gradually toward the Gulf, dispersing somewhat into the cypress forests in the bayou's basin along the way. During intense rainstorms, however, relief canals could still carry drainage (hopefully diluted) into Lake Pontchartrain. Through this plan the engineers and municipal authorities hoped to constrain the various effects of infectious disease, maintain the elite recreational uses along Lake Ponchartrain, and maximize the territory that could be effectively drained and reclaimed. The mobilization of the bayou as a waste sink was imperative for these various elite desires to be achieved simultaneously.

These efforts were remarkably effective at stemming outbreaks of malaria and yellow fever, as well as bacterial cholera. The last yellow fever outbreak occurred in 1905. The death rate for malaria and cholera dropped from 177 per 100,000 in the 1880s to 18 per 100,000 in 1919, adding almost twenty years to the average resident's life span between 1900 and 1920. Still, death rates for non-whites were nearly double that of whites in 1919.[13] Municipal drainage was only one component of the progressive sanitarian effort to eradicate pathogens and insects, but according to the drainage authority superintendent in 1919, the "great sanitary works" were "the foundation upon which the improved health conditions have been built."[14] But Bayou Bienvenue's capacity to assimilate and carry the "most objectionable" drainage waters was also a foundational component of the system. The nutrient rich, turbid, and infected waters that had created the "wet graveyard" of the 1800s were in their most concentrated form pushed into the swamplands east of city. Once the system was built out, all it took was the pull of a lever, and suddenly Bayou Bienvenue's drainage basin more than doubled in spatial scale, prime mosquito habitat was destroyed, and new territory was opened up for urban land reclamation and capital investment. Sanitary engineering was delivering tangible and politically popular outcomes in transforming the city's relationship to its swamplands and resident pathogen vectors.

Bayou Bienvenue's utility to the city's leadership was not relegated to its capacity to accommodate waste flows and fight disease. The Bayou's channel and low-slung basin became enrolled in a wide-ranging vision developed by port officials to circumvent long-standing navigational choke points in the Mississippi River. Transportation geographers define choke points as "locations that limit the capacity of circulation and cannot be easily bypassed."[15] Although New Orleans is only eighty kilometers from the Gulf of Mexico by the shortest line of flight, the route from the mouth of the Mississippi River to the port itself is almost two hundred kilometers. The complexity of the approach to the port from the sea has since the city's founding been a source of frustration for the city's maritime commercial elite. The approach upstream to New Orleans was prone to heavy fog, strong river currents, ever-shifting sandbars, and rough weather. The channel depths necessary for the growing fleet of oceanic steamers left port planners wondering if they might miss out on the benefits of growing cargo holds and deeper draft requirements.

The ultimate solution that circulated among engineers was that of a canal that could anchor private capital and maritime industrial development in the tidewater zone and connect those new facilities to the Gulf of Mexico with a new ship canal, giving ships the alternative of bypassing the lower Mississippi River entirely. The use of navigational locks and inner harbors was expanding worldwide during this time, and the city's maritime elite commissioned civil engineers to draw up a plan for an inner harbor and lock in 1911. The 1911 plan consisted of a navigation canal extending northward from the Mississippi River and radiating into sprawling side channels and commodity-specific harbors. Bayou Bienvenue is featured prominently in the map accompanying the plan, its connectivity to the Gulf of Mexico is made clear, and the navigation canal itself is shown connected to the bayou, but not to Lake Pontchartrain, indicating that in 1911 port officials envisioned the bayou as their best prospect for achieving an alternate route to the ocean.[16] By 1915, port managers were publicly touting the possibility of transforming the bayou into a ship channel.[17] The idea that that a small deltaic stream like the bayou could be enrolled both as the primary waste sink for a growing metropolis *and* a primary artery of global commerce was ambitious in the extreme for such a relatively insignificant water feature. But in 1916, drainage officials, city leaders, and port managers seemed to agree that connecting the city's drainage system with the bayou did not preclude its use as an outlet to the sea.

Although it is shallow and crooked, Bayou Bienvenue attracted the attention of the Port of New Orleans for the same reasons as it did the drainage officials. Its basin was (erroneously) considered sparsely populated, what land existed was near sea level (requiring only one navigational lock), and it possessed a water outlet to the Gulf of Mexico. Observers had long noted the potential of utilizing the bayou as a conduit of global connection. As a visiting journalist wrote in 1836: "There is no quarter of the town for which nature has done so much, and man so little as this suburb. By means of a canal in its rear to connect it with the Bayou Bienvenue...it would be placed within six hours sail of the Gulf of Mexico."[18] Although the city's drainage authorities, the Sewerage and Water Board (S&WB) cooperated in selecting the site for the Inner Harbor, the port's increasing ambitions brought the two sprawling projects into physical and political conflict— one that the siphon was intended to resolve. After acquiring the strip of land between the Mississippi River and the shores of Lake Pontchartrain, drainage officials had initially supported a proposal to dredge a shallow canal that did not connect to Lake Pontchartrain and was designed to carry barges and harbor space for bulk commodities like coal, lumber, grain, gravel, and sand. But with United States involvement in the First World

War increasing and industrial production disrupted in Europe, large-scale shipbuilding emerged as a new possibility for the Inner Harbor. For that, the canal would need to be deeper, and it would need an effective route for sending completed ships to sea. In 1918 a port booster explained the agency's rationale for scaling up the project on the fly:

> This is an era of great and bold conceptions. The war, perhaps more than all else [has] called attention to the fact that the day of petty things had passed, and that communities are either to press boldly forward or decay. In nature niceness is followed closely by rottenness and the finished city is a dead city. The men in charge of the commercial affairs of the port...sensed this early in their visualizations of the canal project.[19]

In mid-1918 the Industrial Canal project was redesigned to be nearly twice as deep and wide as originally conceived, catching drainage officials off guard. When excavation began, port engineers intended to utilize the bayou as an outlet to the gulf and its shoreline for industrial development.[20] By 1919, however, port officials again hesitated and decided that connecting the new canal with Lake Pontchartrain would not necessarily preclude the use of the bayou as an outlet. As it was reported in the press, the decision to connect the Industrial Canal to Lake Pontchartrain was triggered by the urban nature emerging in the bayou as it was enrolled as a waste sink. Port officials who visited the bayou only a few days after the drainage engineers had fully networked the bayou into the drainage system found that the influx of nutrient rich and turbid water had "killed all the fishes" and was producing a "very bad odor."[21] The "separated" drainage and sewer system had problems with seepage and contamination of the drainage lines, vexing engineers and infuriating residents. An unruly urban nature was emerging. As new pipes were laid, the land around them rapidly subsided, leading to leaks and cracks in both lines and permitting what they carried in them to intermingle. This was a particularly serious problem in the bayou, because it was receiving the "dry weather" drainage load, which was not diluted by stormwater, and at times was more sludge than runoff. To avoid acute pollution in the Inner Harbor and gain more connectivity, port engineers decided to open a channel into Lake Pontchartrain.

This decision created a serious problem for drainage engineers and land developers. The new design severed the drainage system from Bayou Bienvenue, and pumping drainage into the Inner Harbor would pollute Lake Pontchartrain. The resolution to this contradiction was negotiated hastily, and port officials agreed to design, finance, and construct a concrete siphon underneath the Inner Harbor to maintain the city's drainage into Bayou Bienvenue. The siphon's designers hoped it could move six thousand cubic feet of water per second, enable safe maritime navigation above it, and help maintain the circulation of wastewater down its path of least social and topographical resistance—into Bayou Bienvenue and the swamps and marshes east of the city. Giving drainage officials assurances that the siphon would be completed by 1919, port engineers severed the bayou from the drainage system before the siphon was completed. In 1918, engineers began excavating their massive pit and laying the foundation of the siphon.[22]

The siphon was enormous, nearly 250 meters long and containing four chambers, each slightly over three meters high. The "daily flow" chamber, which was designed to handle the ambient drainage of the city's moist footprint on days with little or no rain, was a little over a meter wide. The New Orleans drainage system is peculiar in the sense that it is constantly pumping groundwater out of the city, even on sunny days. The storm chambers, designed to handle the city's huge drainage volumes during its frequent and intense rainstorms, were four meters wide. A fourth chamber was included, designed to carry telephone cables, gas lines, and so forth, measuring around two meters wide. Large hydraulically controlled iron gates on either end of the siphon were installed to close the chamber off entirely if necessary.

The hydrological scheme in which the siphon was to perform its lauded disappearing act was plagued by technical problems and delays from the start, and the city's municipal drainage authority, and by extension its citizens, were on the losing end of a decade of contention and animosity between the city's port and drainage authorities. During the siphon's three-year construction, the drainage load was again pumped into Lake Pontchartrain, creating foul odors and high turbidity. Plans to place dredged material along the lakefront and create an elevated wealthy enclave were proceeding, and investors were incensed after drainage officials had assured them that pollution could be avoided.[23]

The port's decision to cut a canal through the city's waste sink turned new sewers under urban neighborhoods into stagnant septic tanks. The city's human wastes also required a siphon underneath the new canal to retain their politically ideal circulation. A temporary pipe released the majority of the city's untreated sewage into the Mississippi upstream of the Inner Harbor, but for the area closest to the canal, in the rapidly growing Ninth Ward neighborhood, no such outlet existed. The sewage simply collected in the new sewer pipes with nowhere to go, leaving a stench rising from the overflowing culverts of raw human waste.[24] Rainstorms flooded the streets, spreading sewage-laden water into homes and schools and threatening to undermine the work of sanitary engineers in combating bacterial cholera. Area residents, organized in civic associations, grew furious with the city's drainage authorities. Civic groups lodged formal protests complaining of flooded streets and overflowing sewage.[25] George Earl, the drainage superintendent, lamented the disruptions that the Inner Harbor project brought on: "Until the siphon under the industrial canal…is completed, it will be impossible for us to relieve the drainage situation."[26] Earl complained rather bitterly in his semi-annual reports at how slow the siphon construction process was, and that shifting political dynamics within the port agency made that entity anything but an honest partner.[27]

The siphon was finally completed in 1921, and in November of that year drainage workers again pulled their levers, and the fetid wastewater was sucked through the siphon and back into Bayou Bienvenue. But incredibly, port officials insisted that the Industrial Canal remain open to Bayou Bienvenue, where tidal influence from the sea led to the bayou flowing "backward" into the Industrial Canal. This was a strange state of hydrological affairs. Keeping the bayou connected to Industrial Canal meant that the city's main drainage volume was being siphoned 250 meters underneath a canal at great cost, so as not to pollute it, only to flow into it from the *opposite* side. Tidal flows then pushed the sludge to the Pontchartrain shoreline. The drainage authorities were outraged by the port's refusal to at least install a movable gate between the bayou and Industrial Canal. The drainage superintendent accused the port of "nullifying the benefits which the design and vast expenditure for a satisfactory…outlet for drainage were intended to produce, just because the authorities operating the Industrial Canal do not see fit to close an opening which they made, for their own convenience, when they started work on said canal."[28] And while the local press proclaimed the glorious completion of the Inner Harbor and the siphon, local engineers were less certain about the legacy of the projects. In 1921 the *Louisiana Engineer*, which noted the cost overruns and drainage disruption brought on by the Industrial Canal project, judged that had those problems been foreseen, the canal never would have been constructed. "The canal is here and here to stay," the engineering editorial observed, adding that "some of us may live to see the day when the Industrial Canal lies idle and choked with water hyacinth [an invasive aquatic plant], a burden to tax payers and a dangerous liability."[29]

The conflicts around the operation of the drainage-navigation network held together by the siphon demonstrate how struggles around the operation of infrastructure can be explicitly—or by proxy—conflicts about competing visions of the form and function of urbanized ecosystems. In the early 1920s unexpected ecological dynamics began emerging in the Bienvenue Basin, diverging from engineering projections and opening a debate about what version of Bayou Bienvenue and its cypress forests was the proper one. Special negotiations arranged between various public authorities made little progress toward resolution, though the port nearly always held the upper hand politically, insisting upon the potential use the bayou as a gulf outlet, at least until an alternative presented itself. With the shadow of epidemic fading, the primary concerns of the hydro-politics of the siphon pitted the port and its maritime capitalists against the drainage authorities and land developers along the lakefront. Local fishing groups and residents of the assumedly "uninhabited" swamps also got involved.

Drainage officials argued in public meetings that the bayou was the "natural outlet" for the city's stormwater. A staff editorial in 1923 framed the bayou's future form as a choice between "a drainage ditch or a navigation canal." On the one hand, the authors noted, huge public outlays had been made under the assumption that the bayou would carry drainage. On the other, port officials were claiming that if used as a gulf outlet, the bayou's shores could soon "bloom with plants industrial where now only marsh grasses rear their heads."[30] By 1926 the port began stepping back from its agenda for Bayou Bienvenue, explaining that its banks were too unstable to hold the "plants industrial" they envisioned a few years prior and that it was too crooked to be used as a deep-water ship channel. In 1927, after close to a decade of bitter wrangling between port and drainage officials, a dam was installed between the bayou and the Industrial Canal, finally restoring the hydrology favored by the drainage officials and land developers. In 1931 the US Army Corps of Engineers definitively concluded that the bayou could not be utilized for deepwater navigation.[31] The bayou was to remain the city's sink for its nastiest waste stream, with the siphon's iron gates acting as a sort of industrial sphincter.

Accounts indicate that the construction of the dam in 1927 and the sudden pulse of wastewater that ensued disrupted bayou ecosystem, much as it had been in 1918, when the area became the sole processor of the city's most rancid outflows. In 1927 local civic associations and fishing groups complained that the bayou was "stagnated and polluted, and following high tide, the waters flow over the lands [in its basin] destroying all vegetation and timber…and have destroyed the fisheries…as far as Lake Borgne, and shrimp waters in Lake Borgne."[32] The construction of the dam diminished the flow of contaminated water into Lake Pontchartrain, and by the early 1930s an immense dredge-and-fill operation was creating new land along the lakefront for suburban subdivisions, amusement parks, and military bases. The dredge-and-fill operation produced hundreds of acres of territory that was higher than surrounding areas and relatively safe from hurricane flooding. The lakeshore development, initially an all-white and upper-class area, has never experienced major flooding since it was built in the 1930s. The siphon helped make the production of this elite high ground possible by materially negotiating the drainage and navigation systems to avoid pollution in Lake Pontchartrain at the crucial time when such a development seemed risky.

The successful development of the lakeshore signified that the siphon and Bayou Bienvenue were at least provisionally enrolled into the overall urbanization scheme and performing their prescribed roles. But before long, the siphon's malfunctions foregrounded questions over who was responsible for repairing and maintaining it. In 1928 the siphon started leaking. Water began seeping through the ceiling of the siphon and into the Industrial Canal, creating lower water pressure and limiting the siphon's performance. The Dock Board, as the architects of the siphon and the entity responsible for its necessity to begin with, took the initiative in repairing the leaks. But after a port barge sank during the operation, the Dock Board sent the drainage authority the bill for the repairs. In 1934 the Louisiana Supreme Court ruled that the drainage authority, which had little role in the design or construction of the siphon, was in fact in charge of its maintenance and was thus liable for the costs of the port's repairs, including the sunken barge. Around the same time, the port was successfully able to negotiate a federal take over of the Industrial Canal locks and secure federal support for dredging a canal just north of Bayou Bienvenue to network the Industrial Canal with the Gulf Intracoastal Waterway system, a federal inland waterway that extended from Florida to Texas. This canal was also the first phase of a linear gulf outlet. For all the port's boasting of the Inner

Harbor's genius, within a dozen years of its completion, its officials skill-fully freed themselves of any responsibility for the operation and mainte-nance of its main technological features, the lock and the siphon.

The Siphon's Backward Behavior

Port expansion during the Second World War created a labor and housing shortage in the city, and port and city planners turned to massive public housing initiatives in the siphon's vicinity. Local officials, confident of the ability of the Inner Harbor project to generate manufacturing jobs, worked to secure huge federal investments in public housing facilities close to the Inner Harbor's wharves. The viable habitation of this marginal and low-lying land relied solely on the siphon's proper functioning. The Desire and Florida public housing facilities were just one part of a decade-long effort by local power brokers to secure public investment in a wholesale trans-formation of the eastern swamps and marshes of New Orleans into a vast maritime industrial complex with a new deepwater ship channel to sea. The farthest inland reach of Bayou Bienvenue's historical basin, along the Florida Canal, was selected for new public housing facilities. That terrain had been used previously as a vast open landfill, and after 1920 it began to sink below sea level as the siphon sucked the groundwater out of the area. By 1965, nearly 30,000 people were packed into poorly constructed apartments built on half a square kilometer of recently reclaimed and still subsiding swampland.[33] In only a few years, the "virtually inhabited" area claimed the highest population density in the entire state of Louisiana.

In 1947 the siphon encountered its first storm surge. As a major hurricane moved through the area, storm surge from Lake Borgne moved through new ship canals and remnant tidal streams, piling up along the Industrial Canal's eastern banks. With hydrological pressure from the bayou pushing against the siphon's eastern outflow and the pumps designed to pull rather than push water toward the gulf, the siphon failed. Quite astonishingly, it actually began flowing backward, spewing seawater into the city. This resulted in a meter or more of flooding in the new public housing facili-ties. The siphon's treachery was kept quiet. It is unclear whether drainage workers simply neglected to close the iron sluice gates, or if the reversal of hydraulic pressure made this impossible. No plans to address the risk of the siphon flowing backward were discussed in the press at the time, and indeed the port was quick to trumpet the resilience of its operations to the hurricane in the local press. The city continued to expand, the port continued excavating deeper canals, the siphon continued to be the city's primary drainage outlet, and prospects of cheap housing and industrial jobs drew more people into the swampy neighborhoods under the siphon's influence. In 1956 the Desire public housing facility, the largest in New Orleans, was opened on a swampy tract just north of the Florida Canal. Within a year or so after residents began moving in, the soil was rapidly subsiding, water and gas lines were breaking, and stairs no longer reached doorways.[34]

The city's powerful maritime elite and public officials were becoming dependent upon the siphon and the Bienvenue drainage basin to assimilate wastes, reorganize maritime transport and industrial production, and absorb new influxes of poor and working-class residents. But the ecological effects of these actions were ricocheting into the world of the elite in unexpected ways. After decades of waste flows through the siphon, ecosystems within its hydrological domain began to reorganize around the new parameters, giving rise to unexpected effects unknown to most people at the time. In May of 1959, an early season tropical storm dumped twenty-eight centimenters of rainfall on New Orleans in a twenty-four-hour period. With no storm surge accompanying the weak system, the city's drainage system, and the siphon, performed as intended. An unexpected outcome of the intense rainfall emerged when coastal biologists visited the mouth of Bayou Bienvenue a few weeks later and found the water to be "extremely turbid."[35] It also contained unusual amounts of inorganic phosphates, which suggested that along with stormwater, the siphon was still conveying large volumes of human waste into Bayou Bienvenue. The biologists noted that while the eutrophication (low dissolved oxygen levels due to inputs of nutrients and blooms of aquatic plants) in Bayou Bienvenue presented problems for wildlife in the bayou itself, the waters of Lake Borgne near its mouth were generating incredibly productive shrimp fisheries. The relative frequency of the rainfall events like the one in 1959 suggests that turbidity and nutrient loading in the bayou was likely tightly coupled with the drainage system in New Orleans for decades. The drainage system–siphon–bayou network was influencing ecological dynamics in unexpected ways many kilometers away from its concrete chambers. The fisheries of Lake Borgne have been a major contributor of fish, shrimp, and oysters to restaurants in New Orleans for centuries. We can speculate (with some amusement) that a tightly coupled nutrient cycle existed in the region during the mid-twentieth century, wherein the nutrients carried in diluted human wastes flowed through the siphon and into Lake Borgne. Under certain conditions, those nutrients enhanced the productivity of the fishery, influencing the price, availability, and perhaps even the flavor of seafood served in the world-renowned restaurants of New Orleans, where the city's elite ate, drank, and entertained visitors. The operation of the siphon was simultaneously penetrating coastal environments and the posh cultural spaces of the city's well-to-do.

The port's Mississippi River Gulf Outlet canal, nearly completed by 1965, was supposed to be the penultimate solution to the constant shoaling in the Lower Mississippi and offer ships a direct route into the Inner Harbor. One of the many problems with this project was that it was actually more of an "inlet" than an "outlet." Its excavation induced widespread coastal erosion and provided a direct route for storm surges into New Orleans. In 1965, Hurricane Betsy flooded the Lower Ninth Ward and St. Bernard Parish in up to three meters of water. Despite the siphon's faulty performance in 1947, drainage officials again neglected to close the siphon's gates before Betsy arrived. Surge again forced its way backward through the siphon and into the Florida and Desire housing developments, an area where now 60,000 mostly lower income residents lived. As the storm's winds began dying down, drainage officials realized that the siphon had again betrayed them, and frantically sent a team of workers in a small boat to close the siphon's western sluice gate, through which saltwater was spewing into the city. Workers managed to stem the flow, but not before seawater collected in the city's densest residential neighborhood. With the siphon out of commission, the water could not be pumped out normally, and instead had to be pumped against gravity to Lake Pontchartrain, a less efficient route that took days to accomplish. The flooding caused serious damage to the Desire and Florida public housing facilities, and residents reported at the time that the event revealed the shoddy construction of the buildings. Residents also noted that the flooding from Betsy marked a deterioration of overall living conditions in the area. As industrial jobs in the Inner Harbor failed to materialize and even Port officials began to regret abandoning a river-based port system, life in the housing projects became one of grinding poverty and deprivation. As more people moved into the area during the 1960s, huge volumes of garbage and unwanted items were thrown into the Florida Canal. The canal became a common place for the discovery of dead bodies, which risked being sucked into the siphon during a storm if not found beforehand. After the Black Panther Party attempted to organize mutual aid and resistance to discriminatory public policies amongst residents, New Orleans police were involved in two shootouts in the Desire housing projects as they tried to arrest Panther members. During these confrontations, multiple vehicles were driven into the Florida Canal and set on fire. The failure of the Inner Harbor project to generate employment meant that the housing projects in the area were basically warehousing poor and working-class people in a hazard-prone landscape and severely limiting the life chances of people living there. Lives hung in the balance when infrastructures and ecosystems were co-mingled in pursuit of narrow economic gain.

Hurricane Betsy did bring about serious public debate around the operation of the siphon. When drainage officials explained in 1965 that the flooding of the city's largest public housing facility could have been avoided with the pull of a lever, elected officials began threatening to reorganize the drainage board with new rules and greater public accountability and to discontinue the use of the siphon. In 1967, drainage authorities sent a scuba diver through an access tube into the siphon to determine if material was clogging it. Chicken coops, auto parts, mattresses, and other mangled refuse were lodged in the chamber, spurring a lengthy cleanup operation. As environmental monitoring became a mainstay of natural resource management in the 1970s, it became clear that the exceptional productivity of the Lake Borgne fisheries had a dark side. When state officials began testing oyster beds for bacterial contamination, they found that along with abundant nutrients, the drainage system–siphon–bayou network was carrying fecal coliform bacteria, which infected oyster tissue and posed a serious public health risk. Emergency fishery closures began in the late 1970s, leading to calls by coastal politicians to scale back the use of the siphon. As the siphon's treacheries accumulated, they exposed not just the adjacent neighborhoods to flood risk, people to illness, and fishermen to losses, but eventually the public authorities and engineers themselves. As the state's leading engineer noted in 1917, failures in infrastructural systems brought both technologies and their managers "to the surface of the great social sea, like a dead fish after an explosion of dynamite in the waters where he swam."[36]

As technological, political, and ecological contradictions grew, the elite's desire for the siphon was waning. Describing the siphon as "old, old, old" in 1974, drainage officials began advocating for a new facility to chlorinate stormwater and pump it directly into the Industrial Canal; it was finally built in 1992. After 1992, Bayou Bienvenue received only the drainage from the Lower Ninth Ward neighborhood and occasional stormwater flows through the siphon, which, in turn, ameliorated some of the pollution issues in Lake Borgne. With the siphon's critical role in the infrastructural ensemble relocated to chemical treatment facilities, the siphon became an increasingly obscure and little-known piece of the urban landscape. Its material demise came at the hands of its institutional parent, the port, whose officials had washed their hands of its maintenance in the 1930s. In 2004 port officials were preparing a long-stalled project to expand shipping access to the Inner Harbor. This required a number of retrofits to existing canal infrastructure, most importantly, the navigation lock at the river and the bridge that extended over the siphon at Florida Avenue. The bridge's construction necessitated severing the siphon from the drainage system, and further, the ceiling of the siphon was around eleven meters below the surface of the canal, a depth that could create problems for the huge ships the port hoped to attract. Civil engineers who designed the bridge were asked to remove the siphon. In 2004 engineers filled the siphon with explosives and detonated it. The concrete was brought to the surface by enormous clamshell buckets and hauled away to a landfill.

Conclusion: Katrina and the Siphon's Phantom Landscapes

A few months after engineers detonated the siphon, Hurricane Katrina struck the Gulf Coast. The severity of the event led to a number of significant changes and retrofits to the infrastructures the siphon once networked. The scope of tragedy and destruction necessary to trigger these reactive measures should give other coastal cities pause. The siphon was gone, but the urban infrastructural ensemble it stitched together was profoundly implicated in the catastrophe. This demonstrates how infrastructures can have effects on urban nature even after they are decommissioned and ostensibly cease to exist. The siphon allowed engineers to embed the city's two core water systems in the same territory. The siphon's influence can be interpreted through the stands of dead cypress, abandoned public housing complexes, and the enormous new flood protection structures in the area. During Katrina, instead of rocketing backward through the siphon, storm surge entered the city from multiple directions, using the networks of drainage canals and navigation canals indiscriminately as it filled the city's low-lying topography. The port's darling Gulf Outlet canal, now maligned as an economic debacle and a "hurricane highway," funneled storm surge into the Inner Harbor, and flood walls along both sides of the Industrial Canal failed, killing hundreds and stranding thousands in the low terrain of the Bienvenue Basin (and elsewhere). Now over a decade after Katrina, 100,000 residents have not returned to their homes in New Orleans. And though Katrina represented the first hurricane to have dramatic impacts outside of the Bienvenue Basin, the areas flooded in 1947 and 1965 were still disproportionately affected. Of the total number of still-displaced people, around half were formerly residents of the Bienvenue Basin.[37] The Desire and Florida housing projects, which were being overhauled and redeveloped at the time, were devastated by the storm. Residents were not allowed to move back into some buildings, and along with the other traditional public housing facilities in New Orleans, the structures were torn down and are gradually being replaced with single-family homes and small apartments.[38] The Florida and Desire areas, the densest population cluster in the region after the 1970s, are now again one of the sparsest places in the city.

The port's Gulf Outlet was ordered closed by the US Congress in 2009, and the Inner Harbor system accounts for only a small fraction of the port's total cargo and employment capacity. The US Army Corps of Engineers has constructed an imposing three-kilometer-long storm surge barrier across Bayou Bienvenue and the salt marshes near Lake Borgne. The billion-dollar structure, completed on an expedited timetable, was hailed by the local press in 2010 as the "great wall" and the "world's largest storm surge barrier," which would enable the city to maintain port activity on the Inner Harbor despite its history of economic, ecological, and humanitarian catastrophes. In 2013 it was reported that the funds for the great wall's maintenance were not forthcoming and that large sections of the wall were actually sinking below the height standards in the design. A legal dispute is raging over which state and federal agencies are responsible for the repairs. An unexpected effect of the project also emerged recently. The Gulf Outlet closure and surge barrier construction constricts tidal flows into the Bienvenue Basin, and freshwater conditions are emerging in wetlands that have been saline for a generation. Environmental activists, and increasingly, corporate foundations, government actors, and philanthropies have begun planting cypress trees along Bayou Bienvenue, within sight of the concrete culverts where the siphon once emptied. Swamp forests and cypress trees—and entire ecosystems themselves—are now emerging as new objects of desire for the region's elite. As swamp landscapes become economically valued as flood protection infrastructure, new relations, and ultimately, novel contradictions are being forged in the muddy terrain of the Mississippi River Delta.

Acknowledgments

The author would like to thank Ashley Carse, Robin McDowell, and Henrik Ernstson for their input and feedback on this chapter. The Swedish Research Council Formas is acknowledged for providing funding for this research through the research grant "Socioecological Movements and Transformative Collective Action in Urban Ecosystems" (MOVE; Dnr: 211-2011-1519).

Notes

1. "New Orleans Builds Own Underground River," *New Orleans Item*, May 2, 1920.

2. Swyngedouw 1997; Graham and Marvin 2001; Kaika 2005; Karvonen 2011; Melosi 2000.

3. Kaika and Swyngedouw 2000; Graham and Marvin 2001; Hommels 2005; Monstadt 2009; Anand 2012; Rodgers and O'Neill 2012; Carse and Lewis, 2017; Lewis and Ernstson 2019.

4. Hommels 2005.

5. Anand 2012; Ferguson 2012; Rodgers and O'Neill 2012.

6. Kaika and Swyngedouw 2000.

7. Colten 2005.

8. Dowler 1850, p. 277.

9. Bell 1899, p. 299.

10. Bayou Bienvenue is a presettlement water feature that drained parts of what is now the 7th, 8th, and 9th wards. It has been used as an engineered drainage outlet continuously since at least the 1880s.

11. New Orleans Advisory Board on Drainage 1895, p. 23.

12. Ibid., p. 24.

13. The Sewerage and Water Board of New Orleans 1919, p. 19.

14. Ibid.

15. Rodrigue 2004.

16. Bernhard and Scott 1911.

17. "Third District Agreed on as Lake-to-River Canal's Site," *New Orleans Item*, July 21, 1915.

18. "City of New-Orleans: Correspondance of the Courier & Enquirer," *Alexandria Gazette*, December 5, 1836.

19. "Great Industrial Canal Enterprise Typifies New Orleans," *New Orleans Times-Picayune*, June 16, 1918.

20. "Levees Inspected by City Officials," *New Orleans Times-Picayune*, March 10, 1918.

21. "Canal Builders Confronted with New Obstacle," *New Orleans Times-Picayune*, March 19, 1918.

22. "Sewer and Water Plan Disarranged in Lower Section," *New Orleans Times-Picayune*, February 2, 1919.

23. Earl 1920, p. 11.

24. Ibid.

25. "Lafayette Avenue Sewerage Offends," *New Orleans Times-Picayune*, July 9, 1920.

26. Earl 1920, p. 11.

27. Ibid.

28. Earl 1922, p. 13.

29. "The Industrial Canal," 1921, p. 186.

30. "Bayou Bienvenue," *New Orleans Times-Picayune*, March 9, 1923, p. 8.

31. "Bayou Channel to Gulf Opposed by Army Office," *New Orleans Times-Picayune*, June 7, 1931, p. 4.

32. "Fight against Damming of Bayou Bienvenu Under Way in Parish," *New Orleans Times Picayune*, April 4, 1927, p. 22.

33. Germany 2007.

34. For more information on the Desire Housing Project, see the New Orleans Community Data Center, http://www.datacenterresearch.org/pre-katrina/orleans/7/16/snapshot.html.

35. The A&M College of Texas 1959, p. 20.

36. Young 1917, p. 13.

37. The Data Center, Neighborhood Statistical Area Data Profiles, https://www.data
centerresearch.org/data-resources/neighborhood-data/.

38. This process actually began in 2002, when conditions in the Desire projects had
deteriorated to a point that federal authorities funded a project to demolish them
and rebuild new homes on the same land.

References

The A&M College of Texas, Department of Oceanography and Meterology. 1959.
"Hydrological Studies for the Corps of Engineers Proposed Mississippi River-Gulf
Outlet Project, Louisiana." US Fish & Wildlife Contract 14-16-008-572, September.
Report 1.

Anand, Nikhil. 2012. "Municipal Disconnect: On Abject Water and Its Urban Infrastructures." *Ethnography* 13(4): 487–509.

Bell, A. N. 1899. "New Orleans: Uprising of the People for Sanitary Improvement
and Drainage and Sewerage. The Sanitarian (1873–1904)." *American Periodicals*,
October 1, p. 359.

Bernhard and Scott. 1911. "Inner Harbor-Navigation Canal. Proposed Development."
Lithograph. Historic New Orleans Collection.

Carse, Ashley, and Joshua A. Lewis. 2017. "Toward a Political Ecology of Infrastructure Standards: Or, How to Think about Ships, Waterways, Sediment, and Communities Together." *Environment and Planning A* 49(1): 9–28.

Colten, Craig. 2005. *An Unnatural Metropolis: Wrestling New Orleans from Nature.*
Baton Rouge: Louisiana State University Press.

Dowler, Bennet. 1850. "On the Necropolis of New Orleans." *New Orleans Medical and
Surgical Journal* 7 (November): 277.

Earl, George. 1920. *Report of the General Superintendent.* Forty-Second Semi-Annual
Report of the Sewerage and Water Board of New Orleans, December 31.

Earl, George. 1922. *Report of the General Superintendent.* Forty-Sixth Semi-Annual
Report of the Sewerage and Water Board of New Orleans, December 31.

Ferguson, James. 2012. "Structures of Responsibility." *Ethnography* 13(4): 558–562.

Germany, Kent. 2007. *New Orleans after the Promises: Poverty, Citizenship, and the
Search for the Great Society.* Athens: University of Georgia Press.

Graham, Stephen, and Simon Marvin. 2001. *Splintering Urbanism.* Oxford: Blackwell.

Hinchliffe, Steven, and Sarah Whatmore. 2006. "Living Cities: Towards a Politics of
Conviviality." *Science as Culture* 15(2): 123–138.

Hommels, Anique. 2005. "Studying Obduracy in the City: Toward a Productive Fusion between Technology Studies and Urban Studies." *Science, Technology & Human Values* 30(3): 323–351.

"The Industrial Canal." 1921. *Proceedings of the Louisiana Engineering Society* 7(5) (October): 186.

Kaika, Maria. 2005. *City of Flows: Modernity, Nature and the City*. London: Routledge.

Kaika, Maria, and Erik Swyngedouw. 2000. "Fetishizing the Modern City: The Phantasmagoria of Urban Technological Networks." *International Journal of Urban and Regional Research* 24(1): 120–138.

Karvonen, Andrew. 2011. *The Politics of Urban Runoff*. Cambridge, MA: MIT Press.

Kelman, Ari. 2006. *A River and Its City: The Nature of Landscape in New Orleans*. Berkeley: University of California Press.

Latour, Bruno. 2005. *Reassembling the Social: An Introduction to Actor-Network Theory*. Oxford: Oxford University Press.

Lewis, Joshua A., and Henrik Ernstson. 2019. "Contesting the Coast: Ecosystems as Infrastructure in the Mississippi River Delta." *Progress in Planning* 129: 1–30.

Melosi, Martin. 2000. *The Sanitary City: Urban Infrastructure in America from Colonial Times to the Present*. Baltimore, MD: Johns Hopkins University Press.

Monstadt, Jochen. 2009. "Conceptualizing the Political Ecology of Urban Infrastructures: Insights from Technology and Urban Studies." *Environment and Planning A* 41(8): 1924–1942.

New Orleans Advisory Board on Drainage. 1895. *Report on the Drainage of the City of New Orleans*. New Orleans: Fitzwilliam and Co.

Rodgers, Dennis, and Bruce O'Neill. 2012. "Infrastructural Violence: Introduction to the Special Issue." *Ethnography* 13(4): 401–412.

The Sewerage and Water Board of New Orleans. 1919. *Fortieth Semi-Annual Report*. December 31.

Swyngedouw, Erik. 2004. *Social Power and the Urbanization of Water: Flows of Power*. Oxford: Oxford University Press.

Young, Samuel. 1917. "Why the Engineer? Who Is He? What Is He?" *Proceedings of the Louisiana Engineering Society* 3(1): 12–16.

3 Natures Remade and Imagined: "World-City" Beautification and Real Estate Reclamation in Lagos

Lindsay Sawyer

Sometime in 2011, men and women in bright orange jumpsuits bearing the letters LAWMA (Lagos State Waste Management Authority) arrived at a patch of scrub between two lanes of Apapa Road in Lagos, Nigeria. Across the road in the neighborhood and market of Badia, which is divided into Badia West, Badia East, and several community areas, residents watched as the Lagos State Beautification Task Force, a subdivision of LAWMA, began to clear what had been a dumping ground for old shipping containers. Gradually they replaced the soil—blackened by diesel soot from tankers going to and from nearby Apapa port—with a carpet of neat grass. At the same time, the massive columns for a new Chinese-constructed light-rail line were being raised, forming a clear visible edge to Badia. The lawn continued to take shape with a few small circular planting beds. A low fence was put up around the area. With no gaps in the fence and no shade over the grass, the park looked quite uninviting, though pretty (figure 3.1). A small path was cut through at one end, fenced in and covered in concrete so that people could cross the road to Badia without disturbing the neat lawn. Despite this small concession to their community and the visually improved vista, the residents of Badia became nervous about the development. During my fieldwork,[1] residents expressed they felt that it was "not for us" and they began "sleeping with only one eye closed."[2]

These fears turned out to be justified. On February 23, 2013, bulldozers arrived in Badia East early in the morning and razed the homes and businesses of an estimated nine thousand people. Many residents were unaware of the seventy-two hours' notice that was supposedly given by the state government and disseminated through local leaders, and they were forcedly stopped from salvaging their personal possessions during the

Figure 3.1
Top: The cleared and fenced ground of Badia East. The light rail line is visible in the background. Five years after the clearance, the land remains undeveloped. *Bottom*: The beautified park from behind the light rail line. Badia East is just visible to the right. Photos by Lindsay Sawyer, 2013.

clearance. Afterward, the Lagos State government gave various and sometimes contradictory reasons for the clearance, even denying that people lived there at all.[3] Nevertheless, most of their justifications centred on the "insalubriousness" of the area and claims that it was unhygienic, unfit for human habitation, and fostered criminality.[4] The residents were offered no compensation or means for relocation.[5] After the area was cleared and fenced in, a billboard went up advertising an "affordable" public housing development, part of the first serious public housing initiative in Lagos for many decades. As construction started, the residents of Badia were still scattered around Lagos. Some, who had nowhere to go, no means to rebuild what they had lost, and no way to afford a place in the new development, slept outside, on the periphery of the construction site.[6]

In identifying two very different urban natures in Lagos, this chapter emphasizes that even though they seem distinct, they have been historically intertwined in a mutually constitutive dynamic. Approaching the urban natures of Badia this way, I hope to complicate what could be a simple opposition between the neat/formal and the messy/informal. The aestheticized park is not just a benign green space; it can be an ideological tool to implement globally circulating ideas about what makes a city a competitive "world city." In turn, Badia East is not simply a site of environmental degradation and poverty but a highly structured, commercialized, and contested urban space.

Like the opening scene, much of this chapter is set in Badia, a low-income neighborhood where these two very different urban natures came together in a violent confrontation that led to the destruction of its eastern part, as described above. Badia is a centrally located neighborhood that has been reclaimed over decades by the incremental and collaborative infilling of its swamps by invested residents. I will refer to this as "popular urban nature," one that is produced primarily by "the people" (even if this is not a coherent group) and as part of the emergent process of popular urbanization.[7] On the other hand, there is an aestheticized urban nature in the form of the new area of beautification, the exclusive public housing project that Badia East was demolished to make way for, and the light-rail line, all of which are part of the Lagos State government's Lagos Megacity Project (LMP), which is seeking to make Lagos into "a liveable megacity for all," but is excluding certain people and places from its vision. Looking at the processes of this exclusion by means of acts of beautification, this chapter

shows how popular urban nature can be a form of resistance to such exclusionary planning methods, as well as an effective though limited and vulnerable urban strategy for achieving gains such as affordable housing and
the creation of livelihoods.[8]

The first section, which traces the pathway of Badia's aesthetic urban
nature, shows that with the continuing use of greening and slum clearance
as tools of urban development, the LMP has parallels with the ideology and
practice of the colonial garden city and thus perpetuates and deepens the
unequal and uneven urban development of Lagos in this way. The second
section emphasizes the state's antagonistic role in the production of popular urban nature, using the neighborhood of Ajegunle, located fairly close
to Badia and another example of popular urbanization, as an example. This
section understands popular urban nature as an effective urban strategy
produced over time, rather than as a casual or chaotic process. The chapter
then returns to Badia in general to look at the factors that have prevented
the residents from securing any long-term gains through this strategy. It
also asks how popular urban nature can serve as an act of resistance when
residents are vulnerable to the confluence of powerful interests and ambiguous land systems at work in the area. Finally, I look to various postcolonial
scholars for how such an understanding of Badia can build into the imagining of alternative urban futures.

Garden City Pathways: Aesthetic Urban Nature and a "Liveable Megacity for All"—But Not Everyone

The greening of elite spaces of the city to make them distinct from "the
rest" is a widely recognized pattern throughout the world.[9] In Lagos, this
spatial strategy is apparent in the current beautification initiative, as well
as in the lasting imprint of colonial garden city methods. The garden city
was more than just an aesthetic precedent; it was a structural one. In her
study of the garden city in colonial Africa, Liora Bigon writes that garden city
ideas and practices have been consistently used "in the creation of racially
divided colonial urban spatiality," although it is still very much understud-
ied in African contexts.[10] As a colonial planning regime, the garden city
can be seen as a precedent for the production and reinforcement of urban
inequality in Lagos through divergent, yet reciprocal urbanisms.[11] That is,
although the greening of space in Lagos now takes a very different form,

in combination with the spatial planning logic of the state, as embodied in the LMP, it has largely the same effect. Thus, to understand what has happened in Badia, this chapter will trace the pathway of the beautified park back to the garden city policies of colonial Lagos in order to identify ideological continuities with aspects of the contradictory, yet mutually constitutive dynamic between the Lagos Megacity Project and popular urbanisms such as Badia. Even though Badia was not formed by such an explicit rhetoric and process of segregation as employed in colonial Lagos, the LMP nevertheless perpetuates and deepens inequality by focussing on development projects that do not directly improve the living conditions of the poor, and in fact often serve to exacerbate them.

In the 1962 map of Lagos Island (figure 3.2), created just shortly after Nigeria gained independence, the dualistic structure of colonial Lagos is clear, and it remains remarkably legible today. In the map, the formerly European Reserve Area of Ikoyi is clearly and spaciously laid out on the eastern side of the island, whereas Isale Eko, the western part from which all of Lagos grew and which housed the vastly larger African population,[12] is a cluster of densely populated winding streets. The two are separated by a "buffer zone" of (originally European) civic and recreational land uses, including schools, government buildings, a prison, a golf course, and a polo ground. Today, despite much development and significant land reclamation that changed the shape of the island, the stark difference in densities between Ikoyi and Isale Eko remains. The buffer zone is much more diverse now, but is still clearly legible as an interstitial space. Ikoyi was designed for European residents in the 1930s and followed the aesthetic principles of a garden city, but they were not applied as strictly as in Europe and the West. Bigon notes that this was often the case in cities of sub-Saharan Africa[13] where, rather than a full application of Ebenezer Howard's concentric model for entire towns that used green belts to separate housing, industry, and civic functions, the notion of the garden city as employed in African cities tended to appear as a set of features including lush vegetation, tree-lined avenues, and colonial style villas set in generous grounds. These features characterized Ikoyi and other elite spaces in Lagos, and to some extent still do. To produce these distinct green spaces fit for modern living, Ikoyi received a disproportionate concentration of colonial investment in infrastructures.[14] At the same time, Isale Eko was largely neglected,[15] as were the growing suburbs outside of the city proper.[16] Moreover, as Daniel

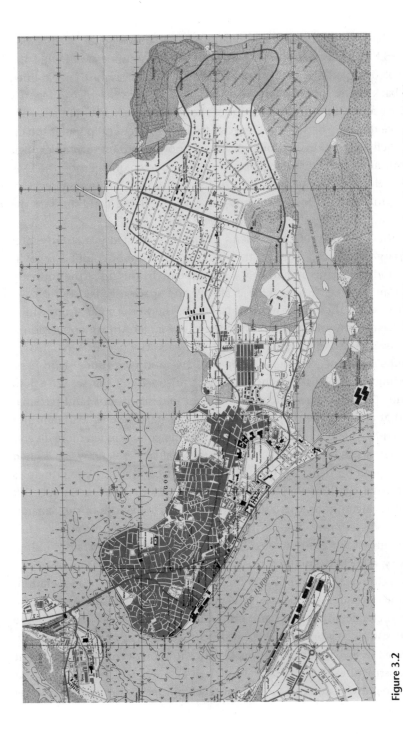

Figure 3.2

Map from 1962 showing spatial division of the extremely dense area of Lagos Island (*left*) and the garden city layout of Ikoyi (*right*).

Source: US Army Corps of Engineers, 1962.

Immerwahr notes, the "colonial government's sole interest in native space was the threat it might pose, from disease or fire, to European space."[17] This lead to "deepening forms of social inequality"[18] marked by sharp differences between the elites' and the ordinary population's living conditions and access to services. Further, and very significantly, those areas of the city that did not resemble the garden city vision were labeled dens of iniquity and disease. Marginalized and even criminalized, these spaces had in fact received little investment, the resulting conditions of which were used as justification for their clearance.[19] This is another familiar story, which extends from Victorian-era Britain to Badia and the present day, of derogatory representations of "slums" and their residents, which serve to criminalize poor people and justify unjust displacement.[20] Further, slum clearances are consistently shown to result in the development of further slum areas,[21] exacerbating existing conditions rather than addressing the uneven dynamics that produce them. Indeed, Badia has been cleared several times over the decades, only to remerge.[22]

The greening of Lagos now takes place under the notion of "beautification," which, rather than segregating a whole island, is diffused throughout the urban fabric. As with the park in Badia, the beautification project targets variously sized spaces mostly next to or between main roads, which are landscaped into fenced green areas. Some are made into parks with benches (but with little to no shading), some into installations of flowerbeds or topiary bearing the slogan of the city, "Eko O Ni Baje O," the curiously pessimistic optimism that is often literally translated as "Lagos will not ruin!" Some include sculptures sponsored by businesses, mostly banks, which brand the spaces and presumably sponsor their upkeep. All are planted with grass and neat, low hedgerows and maintained by LAWMA employees and the beautification task force in their bright orange jump suits and policed by KAI (Kick against Indiscipline) officers in bright green uniforms. The beautified spaces have had a noticeable visual impact on the urban landscape of Lagos.[23] They are (strategically) visible signs of progress by the government, something that has been very rare in Lagos and now lends pride in the city and builds confidence in the state both at home and abroad.

However, it must be remembered that the residents of Badia were made uneasy by the beautified park and clearly felt it was not made for them. And this is really the point, and it fits in with what Asher Ghertner refers to as the "aesthetic governmentality" of world city-making, wherein green spaces are instrumentalized in creating visual distinctions between desirable and undesirable spaces in an aspirational visioning of the future city, in which desirable and undesirable populations are likewise defined.[24] Whereas the green spaces of the colonial city demarcated space along racial lines, greening now demarcates space that is available for an (imagined) disciplined, tax-paying citizen and is attractive by global standards. This is not to say that the green spaces are ever able to entirely exclude certain people; they are in reality blurred spaces. In his work on the "continual reproduction of colonial urban practice" in African cities, William Cunningham Bissel notes that this process has "always remained more aspiration that actuality."[25] Thus, for example, colonial garden cities always had a significant presence of local employees.[26]

The beautification project is a key strategy of the Lagos Megacity Project,[27] which is an umbrella term and does not refer to a coordinated masterplan as such.[28] The separate projects and initiatives are stated as working toward the loosely defined goal of improving the "liveability" of Lagos now that it has reached "megacity status," a quite loose qualification most often based on various statistics indicating that Lagos will have the third largest urban population in the world by 2025. What is important here is that the LMP is appealing to a notion of "megacity" that applies to major global cities like London and New York, not the "megacities" of the global South, which often conjure up chaos and even impending catastrophe.[29] The LMP has very ambitious plans focussing on large-scale infrastructural projects, which are funded through public private partnerships and include the Lagos Light Rail, the Lekki Expressway, the Lekki Free Trade Zone, and Eko Atlantic, the new privately funded luxury island for several hundred thousand inhabitants that has been reclaimed from the Atlantic Ocean. LMP has also made very real improvements to roads and drainage improvements, implemented a rapid transit bus system, and of course pursued beautification. But even as these large- and small-scale projects are transforming the urban fabric of Lagos and rehabilitating the image of Lagos both locally and globally, the megacity aspirations of the LMP can also be seen as embodying an outward-looking vision, modelled on globally circulating referents of a world city.[30] The effect is to deny, or at least ignore, the realities and requirements of a significant portion of the population, as well as to ignore established forms and networks of business and trade.

Moreover, not only do many of the larger initiatives not reach down to benefit the poor, but the LMP has also implemented a host of more disciplinary measures that seek a more orderly city, usually at the expense of the livelihoods and everyday lives of the poor. For instance *okada*, motorbike taxis, which were the cheapest and most popular form of transport, were considered a "nuisance" and banned from all major roads in 2012, while *molue*, the cheapest buses, were banned from the center, causing a serious increase in daily travel costs for many people. The ubiquitous street and market trading and hawking, which sustains a significant proportion of residents, have also been targeted for clearance by the LMP. Traditional markets with their dense rows of wooden stalls are being systematically cleared and replaced by concrete multistorey, mall-like "modern" and "ultra-modern" markets. In what is often a cynical strategy of redevelopment, the original traders are given the first right of refusal to purchase a shop space in these modern malls, but since they have no hope of affording such a space, they are effectively displaced from their livelihoods.

Slum and market clearances have been used as a means for urban development in Lagos from colonial times until the present day.[31] The rhetoric involved has also changed little. As mentioned before, slums have long been represented as dens of criminality and disease, and this has been used as justification for their clearance, especially when unflattering comparisons are made with healthy green spaces. Asher Ghertner writes that this "hygienist discourse" is still in full force in postcolonial cities (and no doubt others),[32] and Matthew Gandy identified it as operating in Lagos.[33] Indeed, before and after the clearance of Badia East, representatives of the Lagos State government described the neighborhood as unhealthy, dirty, full of crime, and unfit for human habitation.[34] Governor Fashola even adopted a heroic stance in justifying the clearance: saying that he had "to take people out of living on a refuse heap," he also promised, in what is incredibly a direct quotation, "We will bulldoze away your difficult conditions."[35] Placing blame for the origins of bad living conditions onto the poor, this perspective absolves the government of responsibility. It denies the realities faced by residents, and obscures the role of the government in exacerbating them. In fact, the effects are even more twisted. As part of the Lagos Metropolitan Development and Governance Project, which is under the LMP umbrella, Badia was meant to benefit from World Bank funding for a new drainage canal, which was built in 2012. However instead of improving the community, the canal likely contributed to the forced eviction of residents as the land became more viable and valuable to the state and the Ojora family, the traditional landowning family of the Badia area who have frequently agitated for the clearance of the land. The next section will examine the role of the government beyond greening initiatives and clearances and the production of popular urban nature in more detail.

The Reciprocal Production of Popular Urban Nature

The development initiatives of the Lagos State government have been active in the production of "slum" urbanisms and popular urban nature in many ways, even as they have condemned and destroyed them. In this section I will give a brief historical overview of this contradictory, mutually constitutive dynamic, as well as the subsequent conditions that led to popular urban nature being used as a strategy of urbanization.

From around the 1930s onward, at the time when the city of Lagos was being carved up into a version of a garden city, not only the "native quarters" of the city, but also the "mushrooming" suburbs outside the municipal boundaries were neglected. Especially after the Second World War and again after the oil boom of the 1970s, a growing migrant population created a demand for low-income housing that the formal housing market and public sector could not fill.[36] Instead a highly effective "informal" market provided housing largely through the plot-by-plot subdivision and sale of indigenous land.[37] This ever-increasing commercialization of land and property, and growing contestation over them, resulted in prices in the suburbs rising sharply over the decades, which, in turn, caused the urbanization of the last available space: the inner peripheries of Lagos—the flood-prone marshes, creeks, and swamps that infiltrate Lagos's central areas due to its low-lying topography—where cheap housing for migrants could be built.[38] This is where the production of popular urban nature eventually emerged as a strategy to reclaim the saturated terrain.

The rapidly urbanizing areas outside of the municipal boundaries of Lagos were not under consistent or effective administration throughout their growth.[39] The areas were thus largely neglected, receiving few services or infrastructure and little planning control in terms of land use or building regulations. As with the development of the land itself, people provided themselves with services in other ways, such as digging unregulated bore-holes for water and, later, using generators for power, developing further independence from, and at times antagonism with, the state. In this way, both the people and the state contributed to the creation of what Bayat refers to as a "void in the domination of the state."[40] The vast majority of these areas developed into the suburbs of Lagos: a very solid but underserviced urban fabric that provides housing for millions of people. As such, the government tolerates it as it has had little capacity to regulate such urban development or offer a formal alternative. Despite developing in a similar way, and offering crucial accommodation for some of the most vulnerable urban residents, the popular reclamation of the inner peripheries has not been tolerated in the same way; instead these precarious areas have frequently been targeted for demolition and clearance.

I will briefly turn to the neighborhood of Ajegunle, which has areas of popular urban nature, to give a very literal example of how the neglect of the government and the administrative confusion contributed to the spread of popular urbanization, and even provides a precedent for neighboring Badia. Ajegunle was consistently neglected by Lagos State government during its crucial periods of growth. Being near the main port of Lagos, Ajegunle grew rapidly with the influx of rural migrants, from a mere 6,000 in the 1950s to 90,000 in the early 1970s,[41] and to at least half a million today.[42] It has large areas of solid ground, which are densely developed, but is run through laterally with swampy creeks (figure 3.3). Up until the 1990s, these creeks were used as a municipal dump[43] for waste taken from the wealthy areas of Lagos (the only areas with any form of waste collection until around ten years ago). The use of the area as a dumpsite contributed to the marginalization and stigmatization of Ajegunle. Yet it also acted as a form of de facto landfill, creating extremely unhealthy land, but land nonetheless on which to build. People are still filling in the creeks with waste and sand this way, producing spaces of popular urban nature.

On a field visit to the creeks of Ajegunle in 2012, as I was walking and talking with a resident, I realized that at some point along the muddy, pothole-ridden road, the street had become entirely covered in litter. As we walked on, the ground became soft, giving way slightly underfoot, and then turning into a bouncing, shifting, stinking mass, with what looked like only old carpet providing a more continuous surface to walk on. This thick ground, extending along the creek at many meters' width, formed

Figure 3.3
Popular urban nature in a creek of Ajegunle. People have collected and used waste
and sand to fill in this wetland to reclaim land to build their houses on. The land is
however not fixed, but constantly slides back into the vegetation. Photo by Lindsay
Sawyer, 2012.

not only a thoroughfare but the foundation for the surrounding homes
and buildings. We were walking on tons of waste and sand that had been
used to incrementally fill in the creek, which is still visible as a substantial
strip of tall green weeds (figure 3.3). During subsequent interviews, residents living in Ajegunle, Badia, and other places with this popular urban
nature described the process of reclamation as a highly organized and commercialized venture. Even in marshy areas in Lagos, "land" is sold in plots.
In one area, an eighty-foot-by-forty-foot plot, on which a tenement house
with many rooms to rent out could be built, the cost would be ₦150,000–
180,000 (US$900–1,000) if it was marshland, ₦450,000 (US$2,700) if it was
solid ground.[44] To give some perspective, around 70 percent of people in
Lagos earn less than ₦40,000 (US$245) per month, and half of those less
than ₦20,000.[45] These plots are usually bought directly from the *Omo Onile*,

the traditional landowning families or their representatives. To reclaim the marshy land, groups of plot-owning residents fill it with waste, especially plastic bottles, wood shavings, and sand until it becomes solid enough to build on. These materials are not "found" or free but are also part of a competitive supply chain. A tipper-load of sand, for instance, sells for ₦34,000 (around US$200) at a market about twenty kilometers away from Badia; around thirty tippers are needed for a shallow fill, and up to seventy for a deep fill. This process requires constant maintenance and the addition of new materials as they settle and disintegrate. Construction materials for wooden or sandcrete houses are in addition to these costs. Considering that rent along the creeks is around ₦1,500 (US$10) per month for a room, the production of popular urban nature constitutes a significant investment that can be made only by long-term, plot-owning residents or speculative investors. As such, the production of popular urban nature forms part of a complex and important local economy that stretches from the tenants who pay rent, to the traders who import building materials. The very poor living conditions created by popular urban nature belies the fact that it not only is a strategy that provides much-needed low-income rental housing, but forms a competitive "real estate" market that is part of the local economy and allows investors and indigenous landowners to capitalize on the last remaining plots of undeveloped land in the central areas of Lagos.

Badia and the "Misrule of Law"

This section returns to Badia to look at how, although popular urban nature can constitute a viable and effective urban strategy, and in the case of Badia formed the foundation of a community for over forty years, it was still vulnerable to the multiple interests that led to its partial destruction in 2013. The multiple land systems at work—traditional, formal, and popular—intersect in such a way as to create what James Holston calls "a misrule of law: a system of stratagem and bureaucratic complication deployed by both state and subject to obfuscate problems, neutralize opponents, and, above all, legalize the illegal."[46] In this system law is brandished by the powerful in such a way that it means "humiliation, vulnerability and bureaucratic nightmare" for the urban poor.[47] Indeed, the ability of powerful interests to manipulate the system left the residents of Badia fundamentally vulnerable.

Although they had occupied Badia over four decades and made the land habitable in the first place, the residents were prevented from consolidating the area into a recognised claim and from gaining such status or power that would have enabled them to resist, or at least have a voice in, the redevelopment of their homes and properties.

After the clearance, the residents were defiant about their ownership and claim to Badia, in which the production of popular urban nature played an important role. One resident told me how his father had helped to reclaim the land and had built the family a house, which they then developed into an eighteen-room rental property that provided them with a good living. [48] Another resident, interviewed by Amnesty International after the clearance of Badia East, whose father was the former *Baale* (local leader) of the area, said, "The government has never helped us, the community raised money, we reclaimed the land here [by filling the swampy area], we constructed the road ourselves and provided electricity ourselves."[49] The social and economics rights lawyer Felix Morka, whose organization had worked with Badia residents for many years, describes how the government has been absent from the development and the practicalities of everyday life of Badia until it moved in to demolish it:

> Like most people in Nigeria, Badia's residents had become highly disillusioned by the unresponsiveness of government, both as a provider and as a regulator. The idea of the state as a social contractor seemed meaningless. Outside of the threatened demolition, the people of Badia did not feel the presence of government, and many did not care about it either. Government was virtually irrelevant to their well-being—their health, education, security, environment, food, housing, water, employment, and their overall well-being. On a day-to-day basis, they had no reason to look to the state for their material needs. With no access to official or alternative sources of information, people were unaware of the social and economic forces propelling the government to destroy the community; the extent of the threat; or the competing interests at play.[50]

Morka's observations make clear not only the independence of the residents of Badia from the state, but also how this became a source of conflict. From the point of view of the state, the residents of Badia were not "productive" members of society, did not pay taxes,[51] and were not even necessarily enumerated residents of the city. Further, the boundaries and even names of all the communities of Badia were understood only locally, and were not formally surveyed. This "invisibility" to officialdom had conflicting effects: on the one hand, it gave the residents strength through inscrutability; on the other, it made them vulnerable by leaving them unrepresented and without a recogniseable voice.[52]

Another source of vulnerability for the residents of Badia came from competing interests over the land. As mentioned, large parts of Lagos developed by means of landowning indigenous families partitioning and selling their land. This has been a highly profitable process for the main families of Lagos, who have often acted speculatively. For instance, as Tade Akin Aina has reported, landowners have sold plots of land in certain areas, but, retaining their inalienable claims to the land in customary law, have prohibited people from building permanent structures so that the larger tract of land could be sold again once the area had appreciated in price.[53] In Badia, the situation was different insofar as the land was in fact given to the first settlers by the federal government as compensation for the loss of their original village in 1973; due to the railway line running alongside Badia, the federal government considered it as under their jurisdiction. However, the Ojora family, one of the main landowning families of Lagos, considers Badia part of their land and asserts that the federal government did not have the right to use the land for relocation. As powerful actors in Lagos, they have mobilized their claim to the land again and again, and their consistent agitation for its clearance arguably led to the many partial clearances the community experienced over the decades.[54] Lagos State government represents another group of powerful actors with interests in Badia. According to the Land Use Act of 1978, the state government has the right to acquire any land "for the public good," and large tracts of land are unaccountably under acquisition, despite a lack of any plan for their use. This was the case with Badia, until it was recently designated as the location for the 1008 Housing Scheme, which is part of Lagos State government's new homeownership scheme, Lagos HOMS. Badia, once a peripheral marshy area, had become a prime location, the nexus between several important transportation junctions including the new Lagos Light Rail line. As such, it had also become a crucial strategic node in the plans of the LMP.

A variety of factors makes it practically impossible for residents in neighborhoods like Badia to obtain formal documentation regarding property ownership and tenure, which, in turn, fundamentally undermines any stability they may have had through owning a plot of land, and further increases their vulnerability. As part of the land acquisition process, the government will pay compensation to residents, but only those with recognized claims and proof of customary or statutory ownership. None of the property-owning residents of Badia had the required documentation that would be recognized by the government—either a certificate of occupancy or any valid proof of conveyance from the *Omo Onile* (the Ojora family). This was due, first, to the nature of Badia's development, where plots are irregular and structures are not compliant with building regulations. Second, the process of official documentation is incredibly time consuming and expensive, costing up to ₦5 million (US$30,000) for a certificate of occupancy, and is likely to involve the repurchase of the plot from the indigenous landowner at the current market price to settle their claims. Furthermore, people often express feeling nervous at having the government know their business. Finally, official documentation is never absolutely secure and is open to contestation in court. In Badia, the state government's claim to the right to acquire land is even contested by the federal government, which claim it is under its jurisdiction, which is in turn again contested by the Ojora family. Consequently, there was little motivation, never mind feasibility, for the residents of Badia to seek forms of documentation that might have provided them with the substance to defend their claims of ownership and demand at least adequate compensation from the government.

So how can the production of Badia's popular urban nature be understood as an act of resistance? Here, it is informative to look to Holston's notion of insurgent citizenship, which is a form of urban struggle wherein "the hardships of illegal residence, house building, and land conflict [become] both the context and substance of a new urban citizenship."[55] Insurgent citizenship is "a process that is an acting counter, a counterpolitics, that destabilizes the present and renders it fragile. ... It bubbles up from the past in places where present circumstances seem propitious for an irruption."[56] In this way, Badia can perhaps be seen to be "an acting counter." First, it constitutes a physical claiming of space that confers a sense of ownership over part of the city to vested residents and provides housing that the government cannot. Second, the production of popular spaces has been a consistent process in the urbanization of Lagos, shaping and being shaped by other formal and informal processes of urban development in mutually constitutive dynamics. In this way, it has troubled the implementation of urban plans and visions such as the LMP, and "irrupts" when these top-down formations perpetuate the uneven dynamics of urbanization again and again. However, in Holston's study of Brazil, this insurgency led to the creation of mobilized citizens who demanded full membership in their city.[57] The urban poor gained political rights, largely through the legalization of their property claims and the provision of services. This has not happened in the popular neighborhoods of Lagos. There, it is difficult in the first place to talk about notions of citizenship where the relationship between the state and the people has, over long decades of political instability and military dictatorship, been one of unresponsiveness paired with brutality on the part of the various states (colonial, military, democratic) and apathy on the part of the people.[58] The people expect little of their government, as the alternative organization of spaces and services shows, but they demand little too. Furthermore, as this chapter has shown, with popular urban spaces inhibited from consolidating physically and their residents limited in their ability to improve their living conditions and to legalize their claims, and with the government making no move to ratify such spaces and instead colluding with landowning families, creating a more stable platform from which to make demands has not been possible. As demand for land in Lagos continues to grow, further pushing out and marginalizing popular spaces, and as the uneven dynamics of Lagos's urbanization seem locked in a status quo that powerful elites are committed to maintaining, what role can the production of popular urban nature play in the future of Lagos? And what can it teach us about how to avoid reproducing these highly unequal dynamics and shift the status quo?

Postcolonial scholars write about the opportunities and perils of the underregulated spaces that make strategies and acts of resistance possible and at the same time vulnerable. AbdouMaliq Simone describes actors in African cities as operating "in the contexts of a 'real power' constituted by imbricating multiple spaces of legality and illegality, formality and informality constantly pieced together and pulled apart."[59] This is the space where what I have been calling mutually constitutive dynamics and Holston refers to as "unbalanced and corrosive entanglements"[60] come together. In Badia, residents could for a time take advantage of such a layered, ambiguous space to create centrally located housing that was demanded by tenants with very low incomes and provided a profitable venture for the landlords. Yet, as this chapter has detailed, these residents were effectively powerless against the deployment of the "misrule of law" by the powerful, who could make it work in their favor and displace and disempower the residents of Badia.

Can these dynamics be made less unfairly weighted against the urban poor, and how can alternative spaces be made less vulnerable?

Working with "Messy Realities"

As a final note, further to showing that popular urban natures are tangled up with state-led rhetoric and policies that have motivated their production and their destruction, and exacerbated their poor conditions at the same time as excluding them from ongoing urban developments, pathways toward more just urban futures can potentially be found in approaches that can make the most of such messy and complex relationships.

It has been an important move by postcolonial urban scholars to recognize the pragmatic, political, and social capacities of alternative modes of urbanization. In what Edgar Pieterse identifies as a "rich vein of postcolonial theorization,"[61] scholars such as AbdouMaliq Simone have reinterpreted the urban in ways that allow for the identification and analysis of alternative systems[62] that are not one thing or the other, but exist on a complex and shifting continuum.[63] Such rethinking has led to a more nuanced understanding of informal processes that are widespread, not marginal, and capable of being organized and effective,[64] as political acts of everyday resistance that come in a variety of forms.[65]

Pieterse recognises that a research practice that "takes care to know what is going on,"[66] that resists generalizations in favor of more "careful elucidations," can contribute to creating more effective implementations of such alternative modes of urbanization.[67] Importantly, Pieterse recognizes that this knowledge must be folded into the efforts of the state, given that the state is necessary to creating better urban futures.[68] Indeed, Badia's popular urban nature is a demonstration of the limits of self-organization: as much as people have provided and claimed for themselves, it is vitally important to recognize that there was only so far that they could go in improving their daily lives without government investment in the provision of infrastructure and appropriate bureaucratic mechanisms. From this perspective, the question becomes how to incorporate the state into alternative futures and how the state can incorporate popular spaces without destroying what makes them viable. Simone warns that this is a difficult project that risks alienating the people it tries to help[69] with overly simplified, linear solutions that risk doing more harm than good.[70] Instead, what postcolonial perspectives point out the need for are partial, tentative solutions that acknowledge the ambiguities and contradictions constantly at work in the production of the urban, or what Pieterse might refer to as the "messy realities."[71] Vanessa Watson calls for new modes of planning that can recognize now-dominant urban conditions[72] and the revalorized notions of informality. She notes that the interface of the "conflicting realities" of underregulated spaces could be a good starting point.[73] Popular urban nature has provided a lens with which to "take care to know" a contested and complex urban space. A careful consideration of the historical, social, and political context of just this small space has exposed a complex web of reciprocal, productive, and destructive relationships between urban processes and all sorts of different groups of actors that must be taken into account for the imagining of alternative urban futures.

Acknowledgments

I would like to thank Megan Chapman and Andrew Maki of Justice Empowerment Initiative for introducing me to the residents of Badia, and to the residents for sharing their experiences with me. I would also like to thank Christian Schmid, Monika Streule, and Ozan Karaman for their collaboration in developing the concept of popular urbanization. Many thanks also to Henrik Ernstson and Sverker Sörlin for their generous guidance and engagement with the chapter, and to Lisa Hoffman for her early encouragement.

Notes

1. The material here is based on several periods of fieldwork in Lagos between 2011 and 2014, which included interviews with residents of a broad cross-section of different neighborhoods. This is part of a wider project from the Future Cities Laboratory of ETH Zurich, "Planetary Urbanization in Comparative Perspective."

2. Displaced residents of Badia in conversation with the author, May 13, 2013 and reiterated in the fact-finding interviews done by Amnesty international.

3. State Commissioner of Physical Planning and Urban Development Olutoyin Ayinde in a television interview, March 2013.

4. Amnesty International 2013.

5. After more than a year in court, with the assistance of a legal NGO and the international attention brought by Amnesty International, the residents achieved nominal compensation from the Lagos State government. The amounts involved are far from adequate, but for their claims to be officially acknowledged by the government constitutes a significant achievement.

6. The construction of the "1008 housing scheme" has since stalled, and the first shaky foundations are weathering badly. Some residents have crept back, but Badia East remains largely empty. The government and the Ojora family colluded in a further partial clearance of neighboring Ijora Badia in 2015.

7. Monika Streule, Ozan Karaman, Christian Schmid, and I are currently developing popular urbanization as a new theoretical category that hopes to describe more adequately people-led processes usually described as "informal," as "self-built," or as "slum" (Streule et al. 2018).

8. The notion of viewing popular urbanisms as an urban strategy was introduced to me by my colleague Monika Streule.

9. See Hoffman (2011).

10. Bigon 2013.

11. See particularly Bissel (2007), who notes that while there is a striking convergence of current urban practice and colonialist discourse, a "remarkably impoverished means of analyzing the historical dynamism of African social spaces" remains (p. 194).

12. Mabogunje 1968.

13. Bigon 2013.

14. Gandy 2006.

15. Immerwahr 2007.

16. Gandy 2006.

17. Immerwahr 2007, p. 7.

18. Gandy 2006, p. 377.

19. Marris 2005.

20. Gilbert 2007; Varley 2013.

21. Agbola and Jinadu 1997.

22. Morka 2011.

23. It is becoming an object of fascination for visitors to Lagos. Dutch photographer Hans Wilschut is currently examining the impact of the beautification through his forthcoming photographic work entitled "The Beautification Project."

24. Ghertner 2010, 2011. See also Watson 2009.

25. Bissel 2007, p. 29.

26. In a different but related vein, Ghertner (2011) looks at residents in Delhi who are displaced by beautification efforts, but who at the same time partly support the need for the city to be "beautified."

27. The LMP was started by Bola Tinubu, the previous governor of Lagos State and first governor of the democratic Fourth Republic of Nigeria. It has been really put into effect by his successor, Babatunde Fashola, who finished his second term in 2015.

28. Governor Fashola has commissioned Model City Plans for wide areas of the city from foreign consultants Dar al Handasah. Most are in the design phase but some are already being implemented; it remains to be seen how effectively.

29. As often referenced, see Davis (2006), but also Rao (2006) and Roy (2011).

30. Roy 2011; Bunnell 2013.

31. Mabogunje 1968; Peil 1991; Agbola and Jinadu 1997; Marris 2005.

32. Ghertner 2011.

33. Gandy 2006.

34. Morka 2011.

35. Governor of Lagos State Babatunde Fashola in a television interview, Channels Television, August 12, 2013.

36. Peil 1991.

37. Barnes 1986; Sawyer 2014.

38. Aina 1989b.

39. Barnes 1986.

40. Bayat 2010, p. 61.

41. Peil 1991, p. 21.

42. Lawanson, Nwokori, and Olajide 2012.

43. Peil 1991; Agbola and Jinadu 1997; Olanrewaju 2001; Agbola and Agunbiade 2009.

44. All prices quoted are for the period between May 2013 and October 2014.

45. Lagos Bureau of Statistics 2012, p. 573.

46. Holston 2008, p. 19.

47. Holston 2008.

48. Displaced resident of Badia in interview with the author, May 13, 2013.

49. Amnesty International 2013.

50. Morka 2011, p. 28.

51. This is despite the fact that the government regularly collected monthly water rates from the residents of Badia for the connection to a water pipe.

52. Again, my colleague Monika Streule must be credited here.

53. Aina 1989a, 1989b.

54. Morka 2011.

55. Holston 2008, p. 4.

56. Ibid., p. 34.

57. Ibid., pp. 8–9.

58. See earlier quotation from Morka 2011.

59. Simone 2001, p. 37.

60. Holsten 2008, p. 13.

61. Pieterse 2014, p. 4.

62. Lawhon, Ernstson, and Silver 2014.

63. Lindell 2010.

64. Simone 2001, 2004; AlSayyad 2004; Huchzermeyer 2011.

65. Bayat 2000; Benjamin 2008; Holston 2008; Kudva 2009; Lindell 2010; Roy 2011; Varley 2013.

66. Pieterse 2014, p. 4.

67. Pieterse 2011, p. 315.

68. Pieterse 2014, p. 23.

69. Simone 2011, p. 362.

70. Simone 2010, p. 8.

71. Edgar Pieterse mentions the idea of messy realities on his webpage, and I find it a particularly useful phrase that deserves further interrogation (African Centre for Cities n.d.).

72. Watson 2009, p. 2260.

73. Ibid., p. 2273.

References

African Centre for Cities. n.d. "People: Edgar Pieterse." https://www.africancentre forcities.net/people/edgar-pieterse/.

Agbola, T., and E. M. Agunbiade. 2009. "Urbanization, Slum Development and Security of Tenure: The Challenges of Meeting Millennium Development Goal 7 in Metropolitan Lagos, Nigeria." In *Urban Population–Development–Environment Dynamics in the Developing World: Case Studies and Lessons Learned*, edited by A. de Sherbiniin, A. Rahman, A. Barbieri, J. C. Fotso, and Y. Zhu, 77–106. Paris: CICRED.

Agbola, T., and A. M. Jinadu. 1997. "Forced Eviction and Forced Relocation in Nigeria: The Experience of Those Evicted from Maroko in 1990." *Environment and Urbanization* 9(2): 271–288.

Aina, T. A. 1989a. "'Many Routes Enter the Market Place': Housing Submarkets for the Urban Poor in Metropolitan Lagos, Nigeria." *Environment and Urbanization* 1(2): 38–49.

Aina, T. A. 1989b. "Popular Settlements in Metropolitan Lagos, Nigeria: A Socio-Economic and Structural Survey of the Habitat of the Urban Poor." *Third World Planning Review* 11(4): 393.

AlSayyad, N. 2004. "Urban Informality as a "New' Way of Life." In *Urban Informality: Transnational Perspectives from the Middle East, Latin America, and South Asia*, edited by A. Roy and N. AlSayyad, 7–30. Lanham, MD: Lexington Books.

Amnesty International. 2013. *If You Love Your Life Move Out! Forced Eviction in Badia East, Lagos State, Nigeria*. London: Amnesty International.

Barnes, S. T. 1986. *Patrons and Power: Creating a Political Community in Metropolitan Lagos*. Bloomington: Indiana University Press in association with the International African Institute, London.

Bayat, A. 2010. *Life as Politics: How Ordinary People Change the Middle East*. Stanford CA: Stanford University Press.

Benjamin, S. 2008. "Occupancy Urbanism: Radicalizing Politics and Economy beyond Policy and Programs." *International Journal of Urban and Regional Research* 32(3): 719–729.

Bigon, L. 2013. "Garden Cities in Colonial Africa: A Note on Historiography." *Planning Perspectives* 28(3): 477–485.

Bissell, William Cunningham. 2007. "Casting a Long Shadow: Colonial Categories, Cultural Identities, and Cosmopolitan Spaces in Globalizing Africa." *African Identities* 5(2): 181–197.

Bunnell, T. 2013. "Antecedent Cities and Inter-referencing Effects: Learning from and Extending beyond Critiques of Neoliberalisation." *Urban Studies* 52(11): 1983–2000.

Davis, M. 2006. *Planet of Slums*. London: Verso.

Gandy, M. 2006. "Planning, Anti-planning and the Infrastructure Crisis Facing Metropolitan Lagos." *Urban Studies* 43(2): 371–396.

Ghertner, D. A. 2010. "Calculating without Numbers: Aesthetic Governmentality in Delhi'sSlums." *Economy and Society* 39: 185–217.

Ghertner, D. A. 2011. "Rule by Aesthetics: World-Class City Making in Delhi." In *Worlding Cities: Asian Experiments and the Art of Being Global*, edited by A. Roy and A. Ong, 279–306. Oxford: Wiley-Blackwell.

Gilbert, A. 2007. "The Return of the Slum: Does Language Matter?" *International Journal of Urban and Regional Research* 31(4): 697–713.

Hoffman, L. 2011. "Urban Modelling and Contemporary Technologies of City-Building in China: The Production of Regimes of Green Urbanisms." In *Worlding Cities: Asian Experiments and the Art of Being Global*, edited by A. Roy and A. Ong, 55–76. Oxford: Wiley-Blackwell.

Holston, J. 2008. *Insurgent Citizenship: Disjunctions of Democracy and Modernity in Brazil*. Princeton, NJ: Princeton University Press.

Huchzermeyer, M. 2011. *Tenement Cities: From 19th Century Berlin to 21st Century Nairobi*. London: Africa World Press.

Immerwahr, D. 2007. "The Politics of Architecture and Urbanism in Postcolonial Lagos, 1960–1986." *Journal of African Cultural Studies* 19(2): 165–186.

Kudva, N. 2009. "The Everyday and the Episodic: The Spatial and Political Impacts of Urban Informality." *Environment and Planning A* 41(7): 1614–1628.

Lagos Bureau of Labor Statistics. 2012. "Basic Statistical Hotline." Lagos: Lagos Bureau of Labor Statistics.

Lawanson, T., I. Nwokori, and O. Olajide. 2012. "Poverty and Environmental Conditions in Informal Settlements of Lagos Megacity: A Time-Line Study of Ajegunle Community (1998–2008)." In *Proceedings of the 4th West Africa Built Environment Research (WABER) Conference*, edited by S. Laryea, S. Agyepong, R. Leiringer and W. Hughes. Abuja, Nigeria.

Lawhon, M., H. Ernstson, and J. Silver. 2014. "Provincializing Urban Political Ecology: Towards a Situated UPE through African Urbanism." *Antipode* 46(2): 497–516.

Lindell, I. 2010. "Between Exit and Voice: Informality and the Spaces of Popular Agency." *African Studies Quarterly* 11(2–3): 1–11.

Mabogunje, A. L. 1968. *Urbanization in Nigeria*. London: University of London Press.

Marris, P. 2005 (1961). *Family and Social Change in an African City: A Study of Rehousing in Lagos*, 2nd ed. London: Routledge.

Morka, Felix C. 2011. "A Place to Live: Resisting Evictions in Ijora-Badia, Nigeria." In *Stones of Hope: How African Activists Reclaim Human Rights to Challenge Global Poverty*, edited by Lucie White and Jeremy Perelman, 17–40. Stanford, CA: Stanford University Press.

Olanrewaju, D. O. 2001. "Urban Infrastructure: A Critique of Urban Renewal Process in Ijora Badia, Lagos." *Habitat International* 25(3): 373–384.

Peil, M. 1991. *Lagos: The City Is the People*. London: Belhaven.

Pieterse, E. 2011. "Recasting Urban Sustainability in the South." *Development* 54(3): 309–316.

Pieterse, E. 2014. "Epistemic Practices of Southern Urbanism." Paper presented at the African Centre for Cities Academic Seminar, February 21. Cape Town: African Centre for Cities.

Rao, V. 2006. "Slum as Theory: The South/Asian City and Globalization." *International Journal of Urban and Regional Research* 30(1): 225–232.

Roy, A. 2011. "Slumdog Cities: Rethinking Subaltern Urbanism." *International Journal of Urban and Regional Research* 35(2): 223–238.

Sawyer, L. 2014. "Piecemeal Urbanisation at the Peripheries of Lagos." *African Studies* 73(2): 271–289.

Simone, A. 2001. "On the Worlding of African Cities." *African Studies Review* 44(2): 15–41.

Simone, A. 2004. "People as Infrastructure: Intersecting Fragments in Johannesburg." *Public Culture* 16(3): 407–429.

Simone, A. 2010. *The Social Infrastructures of City Life in Contemporary Africa*. Uppsala: Nordiska Afrikainstitutet.

Simone, A. 2011. "The Politics of Urban Intersection: Materials, Affect, Bodies." In *The New Blackwell Companion to the City*, edited by Gary Bridge and Sophie Watson, 357–366. London: Wiley-Blackwell.

Streule, M., L. Sawyer, O. Karaman, and C. Schmid. 2018. "Popular Urbanisation—A Comparative Concept of the Analysis of Contemporary Urbanisation Processes." Working Paper, ETH Zürich.

Varley, A. 2013. "Postcolonialising Informality?" *Environment and Planning D: Society and Space* 31(1): 4–22.

Watson, V. 2009. "Seeing from the South: Refocusing Urban Planning on the Globe's Central Urban Issues." *Urban Studies* 46(11): 2259–2275.

4 Landscape Literacy and Design for Ecological Democracy: The Nature of Mill Creek, West Philadelphia

Anne Whiston Spirn

"Nature" is the word Raymond Williams called "perhaps the most complex word in the [English] language."[1] In English, the word "nature" originally described a quality—the essential character of something. Williams identified two additional areas of meaning: "the inherent force which directs either the world or human beings or both" and "the material world itself, taken as including or not including human beings." Nature is an abstraction, writes Williams, a set of ideas for which many cultures have no one name, "a singular name for the real multiplicity of things and living processes." The abstraction of the word itself conceals radical differences in definition from culture to culture, even among individuals within the same culture.[2]

Language structures how one thinks, what kinds of things one is able to express, and how one acts. Language makes it possible to conceive ideas and see new meanings. It can also suppress thought, disguise meaning, and make people blind. Someone's definition of nature influences whether they think cities are part of the natural world, or separate from it, and how they act to shape cities. Someone who believes that the city has degraded "nature" is apt to see only pollution there. Someone who assumes that the city has destroyed or displaced "nature" is not likely to see the effects of the natural processes that still shape its landscape. Ideas of nature have profound effects on how cities are designed, built, and sustained (or not sustained) over time.[3]

Given conflicting definitions and their consequences, I use "nature" sparingly, deliberately, and explicitly. For me, nature is not a place, like a park or a wilderness, and not a particular feature, like a tree or a river. For me, nature consists of the creative and life-sustaining processes that connect everything in the biological world and the physical universe, including humans. These chemical, physical, and biological processes interact with social, economic, political, and cultural processes, over time, to produce landscapes. I use the word "landscape" as freely as I use "nature" sparingly, for I hope to recover the original meanings of the word in Old English and Nordic languages: the mutual shaping of people and place.[4] Landscape, in its original sense, is not mere scenery. It encompasses both the population of a place and its physical features: its topography, water flow, and plant life; its infrastructure of streets and sewers; its buildings and open spaces.

Individuals and societies inscribe their values, beliefs, ideas, and identity in the landscapes they create, leaving a legacy of stories: natural and cultural histories, landscapes of poetry, power, and prayer. Such stories are told and read through a language of landscape with its own elements, pragmatics, and poetics.[5] The language of landscape is a powerful tool. It permits people to perceive pasts they cannot otherwise experience, to anticipate the possible, to envision, choose, and shape the future landscape.

Since 1987, West Philadelphia's Mill Creek watershed and neighborhood has been my laboratory to test and generate ideas about landscape language, landscape literacy, and what Randolph Hester has called "ecological democracy," or how to restore urban ecosystems and build community in synergistic ways.[6] I chose the Mill Creek watershed strategically: it is an urbanized watershed of many neighborhoods, its creek is buried in a sewer, its topography is varied, its population is racially and economically diverse. To further explore issues of landscape literacy, ecological democracy, and the interplay between poverty, race, and environmental quality, I focused on the Mill Creek neighborhood, among the economically poorest in Philadelphia, as an extreme case. It also would prove to be a critical and paradigmatic case.[7]

Landscape literacy enabled residents of the Mill Creek neighborhood to read the environmental, social, economic, and political stories embedded in their local landscape and gave them a way to formulate new stories, to envision how to transform their neighborhood, to both challenge and work with public officials.[8] Just as verbal literacy was a cornerstone of the American civil rights movement of the 1950s and 1960s, landscape literacy empowered Mill Creek residents to recognize and redress injustices embodied in their landscape and to build pride and self-confidence.[9]

Reading the Landscape of Mill Creek

The landscape of West Philadelphia's Mill Creek neighborhood is a catalogue of the failures of twentieth-century urban policy, planning, and design.[10] Some policies and projects were deliberate and insidious in their effects; most were well-intentioned but misguided. The US Federal Housing Administration's guidelines for underwriters, first spelled out in the 1930s, included the race of a neighborhood's population and the age of its buildings; these guidelines contributed to redlining, the banking practice of refusing to grant loans for the purchase of properties on the basis of location.[11] Urban renewal projects of the 1950s, such as the public housing towers inserted into this neighborhood of small-scale row houses, had devastating effects on the place they sought to improve and contributed to the racial segregation of a neighborhood where blacks and whites had lived next door to one another, in identical row houses, for at least a century. New parks, playgrounds, and streetscapes built in the 1960s cracked and subsided within a few decades of construction, and a public housing project built in the 1950s was demolished recently.

The critics of modernist urban planning and redevelopment are now legion.[12] However, much recent development in Mill Creek may produce similar results. Like their predecessors, those responsible for planning Mill Creek often treat symptoms and fail to address the underlying processes that produce them. Planners too often concentrate on narrowly defined problems and fail to see the connections among seemingly unrelated phenomena. Designers tend to focus on physical form and fail to account for the processes that will continue to shape their projects over time. These failings are not limited to planners and designers. To plan a neighborhood is both a spatial and a temporal undertaking, but planners' and designers' maps are usually static snapshots of current conditions, narrowly framed. Grassroots activists often concentrate on a specific local problem or a particular site and overlook how these fit into the larger neighborhood, city, and region. Some problems, though manifest locally, are phenomena set in motion outside the neighborhood and must be resolved in that context. Some features of the built landscape are clues to forces that continue to exert a decisive influence, while others are artifacts of processes now defunct. Some are amenable to change, others are not. Some are themselves dynamic agents that enable or constrain possibilities for subsequent development.[13]

Mill Creek is a place of many puzzles. It is among the poorest neighborhoods in Philadelphia, yet it is home to many well-educated, middle-class residents, almost all African American. Boarded-up storefronts speak of failed ventures, but other institutions, like the numerous community gardens, flourish. Blocks of vacant land and wasted structures border blocks of well-tended houses and gardens. The amount of open land in Mill Creek is striking, especially in contrast to the dense fabric of small row houses. On some blocks, only one house or one small lot is vacant; in other areas, houses have sagging porches and crumbling foundations, and there are almost as many vacant lots as buildings. There are patterns to how and where abandonment occurs. Such patterns reveal the nature of Mill Creek and are key to its future.[14] When those who plan and build the city disregard the significance of these patterns or fail to see them at all, they waste resources, produce dangerous, expensive mistakes, and inflict grave injustice on all who live there.

There is an impulse, particularly among Mill Creek residents and local politicians, to build new homes on vacant land, but there is no housing shortage in the city of Philadelphia, whose relatively stagnant population growth and large proportion of aging homeowners mean there will continue to be a surplus of houses for the foreseeable future.[15] There are also many "heir" houses, homes left vacant after an owner's death, for which there is no clear title. Transfer of ownership and rehabilitation of such homes before they deteriorate beyond repair should be given priority over new construction. There exists substantial investment in the neighborhood by its residents, which could be recognized and strengthened by infill construction on vacant land within and adjacent to well-maintained blocks of homes. Certain vacant lots are appropriate candidates for new construction. There are, for example, many individual, scattered vacant properties, "missing teeth" in otherwise intact blocks of homes, the consequences of isolated events such as fire and death. Vacant corner lots are also common, the remains of the many corner stores that once served the neighborhood. They are artifacts of changing scales and modes of merchandising and the failure of new businesses to fill the gap. However, socioeconomic processes alone did not produce all of Mill Creek's vacant land. Some are the byproduct of natural processes and should not be built on.

The single feature of the Mill Creek landscape that has had the most significant, persistent, and devastating effect is the least recognized: the buried floodplain of the former creek (from which the neighborhood takes its name) and the hydrological processes that continue to shape it. And yet the strong pattern—the band of open land and deteriorating buildings–created by those processes is striking once recognized. This pattern extends throughout the entire length of the stream's former course. It is most prevalent in Mill Creek and adjacent neighborhoods to the north, where poverty is rife, but even in more affluent neighborhoods to the south and farther north. Although the former creek bed is buried, the valley bottom still functions as a floodplain, where the soil is sometimes saturated.

The Mill Creek once drained about two-thirds of West Philadelphia, and its sewer still does. The creek itself once flowed above ground, and the water's erosive force cut valleys from its tributaries in the north to its mouth at the Schuylkill River. Mills powered by water operated along Mill Creek by 1711, and in the mid-nineteenth century, steam-powered textile mills were prominent. In the eighteenth-century, wealthy Philadelphians built country estates on the outskirts of the city, such as Woodlands at the mouth of Mill Creek and Paul Busti's Blockley Retreat of 240 acres, established in 1794, which overlooked the creek upstream. Busti's estate was purchased in 1836 to create a hospital in the country for psychiatric patients. Mill Creek formed the boundary between the male and female wards and was an integral part of the grounds, which were designed as a pastoral landscape intended to provide a soothing environment for patients.[16]

The Hopkins Atlas of 1872 shows the creek, hospital, and mills within a grid of streets, houses, and platted (but undeveloped) properties. This is a landscape undergoing rapid change from countryside to street-car suburb. With picks and shovels and horse-drawn carts, armies of men leveled hills, filled in valleys, and buried streams in sewers. The surface of new streets was twenty to thirty feet below the former hilltops and thirty to fifty feet above the old streambeds.[17] The Bromley Atlas of 1895 no longer shows the creek, and rowhouses have replaced the mill buildings at Forty-Sixth Street and Haverford. In 1923, Mill Creek Playground and Sulzberger Middle School, an imposing brick structure on Forty-Eighth Street between Aspen and Fairmount, took up two of the last remaining open blocks. In the Bromley Atlas of 1927, almost all the land north of Haverford had been developed, and the sinuous line of the sewer beneath blocks of row houses is the only visible trace of Mill Creek.

Today, the seventeenth-century forest and the eighteenth- and nineteenth-century pastoral and industrial landscapes seem obliterated, but abundant traces remain. From the corner of Forty-Sixth and Haverford, one can read several hundred years of history. A large block slopes upward toward the northeast. Once divided by streets and covered by homes, it was for many years a grassy meadow with a grove of ash and ailanthus trees, and is now a ball field, church, and apartment complex. On the north-west corner is an open lawn—the site of the Blundin Mill; one block to the south was the location of another mill, now also demolished. A high stone wall runs for seven blocks along the south side of Haverford Avenue; it was built in the mid-nineteenth century to enclose Pennsylvania Hospital's buildings, gardens, and inmates. The western branch of the hospital still functions as a psychiatric facility, but the eastern property was sold and its buildings demolished in 1959 to make way for the towers of West Park, a public housing project. Uphill to the east, behind the stone wall of the old hospital, the roof of the Busti mansion is visible. It is now the Lee Cul-tural Center, where basketball courts and a playground occupy the former gardens. Downslope, in the valley where the creek once flowed through the Blockley Retreat and hospital grounds, is a school that was built over the buried floodplain in the 1960s and an enclave of townhouses that was constructed in the 1990s.

By the late nineteenth century, wastes from slaughterhouses, tanneries, and households had polluted the creek. In the 1880s, it was buried in a sewer, its floodplain filled in and built upon, but it still drains the storm water and carries all the wastes from half of West Philadelphia and from suburbs upstream. Each new suburb built in the watershed poured more sewage and storm water into the sewer. The size of the pipe—about twenty feet in diameter—is now too small for the quantity of combined sewage and storm water it must convey after major rainstorms.

Over the course of the twentieth century, the ground fell in, here and there, along the line of the sewer. The creek undermined buildings and streets and slashed meandering diagonals of shifting foundations and vacant land across the urban landscape. Local newspapers chronicled the long series of broken pipes and cave-ins.[18] In the 1940s, forty-seven homes were demol-ished because they were "plagued with rats and filled with sewer vapor."[19] In 1945, a neighborhood of small row homes built above the sewer on the site of the former Blundin Mill was destroyed when the sewer collapsed. In 1952, a thirty-five-foot deep cave-in on Sansom Street swallowed two cars, and porches of three homes crumbled into the crater. On July 17,

1961, the sewer caved in beneath Funston Street near Fiftieth. Initially, four houses were destroyed and three people killed; ultimately 111 homes were condemned and demolished, leaving hundreds homeless and many others fearful of further collapse. "We haven't been ordered to leave. We're just too frightened to stay here," one person told a reporter.[20] Months later, Philadelphia's *Evening Bulletin* described residents' complaints of sewer odors and their frustration at the city's slow response in repairing the thirty-foot chasm.[21] By 1980 entire city blocks lay open within the buried floodplain. Young woodlands of ailanthus, sumac, and ash grew up on older lots, urban meadows on lots vacated more recently. Many community gardens in this part of West Philadelphia lie above the buried floodplain of Mill Creek; older gardeners remember when buildings sank, their foundations undermined by subsiding fill.

In 1945 Pennsylvania enacted enabling legislation for federally funded redevelopment under the Urban Redevelopment Law. Three years later, the city designated the Mill Creek neighborhood as a redevelopment area and hired architect Louis Kahn to produce a plan. In 1950, following a sewer collapse near Forty-Seventh and Fairmount Streets, Kahn was also commissioned to design the Mill Creek Housing Project on several square blocks near the cave-in. Newspaper articles from the 1950s through the 1960s record protests by residents who opposed public housing, particularly the high-rise apartment blocks. The public housing was built, as were play fields and ball courts on other blocks that had fallen in. Land directly over the sewer pipe was maintained as open lawn or turned into parking lots, but much of the public housing was built on the buried floodplain. There have been no major cave-ins in recent years, but sinking streets, playgrounds, and parking lots and shifting building foundations continue to plague the area. The school built on the corner of Forty-Sixth and Haverford in the 1960s, for example, sustained structural damage in the 1990s.

Between 1950 and 1970, the overall population of the Mill Creek neighborhood declined by 27 percent. Although the neighborhood's nineteenth-century residents had been predominantly Caucasian, "Blacks" and "Mulattos" lived side by side with "White" families in 1880.[22] By 1950, however, its population was about 27 percent Caucasian and 73 percent African American, and by 1960, the white population had dropped to about 13 percent, to 4 percent in 1970, and to less than 2 percent in 1990. There were local reasons for these demographic changes, but they are also part

of a much larger story. The city of Philadelphia, as a whole, lost population during this period. While six suburban counties around Philadelphia
grew by as much as 12 percent in the 1990s, Philadelphia lost 9 percent of
its population during the same period.[23] This is a local manifestation of a
national phenomenon, a massive migration from central cities to suburbs
and exurban areas, which reshaped American rural and urban landscapes,
consuming farmland and forests and destroying urban communities in the
process.[24]

Given the outward flow of population and capital and the inward flow
of sewage and groundwater, the abundance of vacant land and deteriorating or abandoned properties in Mill Creek is not surprising. Burying the
creek in a "combined" sewer that carries both sanitary sewage from homes
and business and stormwater runoff caused another problem: combined
sewer overflows. Normally, as rain falls, it flows quickly off roofs and across
pavement to the sewer, then on to a sewage treatment plant for cleans-
ing before discharge into the Schuylkill River. After a heavy rain, there is
too much runoff, and a mixture of sanitary sewage and storm water flows
directly into the river—a combined sewer overflow. Such overflows are a
significant source of water pollution, and, by the 1990s, the US Environmental Protection Agency threatened to fine the city of Philadelphia if they
were not eliminated.

To read the landscape of Mill Creek permits the reader to see what is
not immediate: the former store in a vacant corner lot; the future forest in
today's meadow; water underground in the cracks of a building's foundation, the slumps in pavement. To read landscape is also to anticipate the
possible, to envision, choose, and shape the future: to see, for example,
the connections between buried, sewered stream, vacant land, and polluted
river, and to imagine rebuilding a community while purifying its water.

The West Philadelphia Landscape Project

For more than thirty years, I have worked in and studied Mill Creek, both
the neighborhood and the larger watershed: first, from 1987 to 1991, as part
of a larger landscape plan and "greening" project for West Philadelphia;
then, since 1994, as the primary focus of my research. A key proposal of the
West Philadelphia Landscape Project from the 1980s on has been to manage Mill Creek's buried floodplain as part of a broad approach to planning

the city's watersheds to reduce combined sewer overflows and restore water quality and as a strategy to secure funds to rebuild the neighborhood.[25] The proposal calls for detaining stormwater runoff on low-lying vacant blocks in Mill Creek in order to eliminate combined sewer overflows from the watershed. It is not feasible to bring the creek back above ground; it is now a sewer that carries waste as well as storm water, but its presence as a green ribbon of parks and play fields would recall the creek, protect houses from flooding, and provide local open space for a variety of public and private uses. Even in 1987, this was not a radical proposal, but an application of well-accepted watershed-planning practice to an urban watershed.

By the end of the first phase of the West Philadelphia Landscape Project in 1991, my students, colleagues, and I had made proposals for the strategic reuse of vacant urban land in the Mill Creek watershed and had designed and built dozens of gardens and blockscapes.[26] *The West Philadelphia Landscape Plan: A Framework for Action* summarized the proposals and advocated a top-down/bottom-up approach where all those whose decisions shape the city, from individuals and businesses to nonprofit organizations and public agencies, would have a role. For each recommendation the report discussed funding, sponsors, actions already taken, next steps, and the cost of inaction.[27] I proposed a series of roundtables that would bring together individuals from diverse perspectives, including residents and public officials, to discuss and critique the WPLP recommendations and to formulate their own actions. The proposal was not funded, but the approach it outlined has guided my work ever since.[28]

During the first phase of the project (1987–1991), and for years following, I had hoped to convince the City Planning Commission and the Philadelphia Water Department that the buried creek was both a force to be reckoned with and a resource to be exploited, but, when the city's *Plan for West Philadelphia* was published in 1994, it failed to mention the buried floodplain and the hazards it posed. That same year, the city donated a large parcel of vacant land for the construction of subsidized housing for first-time, low-income homeowners. This latter project was especially troubling, for the site was on the buried floodplain.

When the West Philadelphia Landscape Project began in 1987, I did not intend a long-term involvement. However, the City Planning Commission's disregard for the health, safety, and welfare of Mill Creek residents renewed my commitment. It also prompted new realizations that both sharpened and enlarged the questions my research sought to answer. Confronted with skepticism about the existence and dangers of the buried floodplain, I began to understand this resistance as a form of illiteracy—an inability on the part of public officials, developers, and even Mill Creek residents themselves to read the landscape.

I organized my teaching and research to explore these issues. From 1994 to 2001, students in my classes at the University of Pennsylvania and at the Massachusetts Institute of Technology analyzed the urban watershed, demonstrated how storm water could be collected in landscape projects that are also stormwater detention facilities, and created designs for wetlands, water gardens, and environmental study areas on vacant land in the Mill Creek neighborhood. When the West Philadelphia Landscape Project website was launched in early 1996, it featured the database, reports, and projects built from 1987–1991. Since then, it has been a showcase for ongoing work.[29]

To reach a broad spectrum of the Mill Creek population, my students and I launched a program with a public school in the Mill Creek neighborhood. What began as a community-based, environmental education program organized around the urban watershed grew into a program on landscape literacy and community development. From 1996 to 2001, hundreds of children at Sulzberger and students at the University of Pennsylvania learned to read the neighborhood's landscape; they traced its past, deciphered its stories, and told their stories about its future, some of which were built. The tools they used were their own eyes and imagination, the place itself, and historical documents such as maps, photographs, newspaper articles, census tables, and redevelopment plans. The program had four parts: reading landscape, proposing landscape change, building landscape improvements, and documenting these proposals and accomplishments. The first two parts were incorporated into university and middle-school curricula during the academic year; all four were integrated in a four-week summer program.

The school's front doors look out on the high ground of the old floodplain terrace and face a small neighborhood of homes around a local community garden. The cafeteria and gym in the lower level are on the buried floodplain; so is the playground and, across the street, the Mill Creek Housing Project (now demolished). I was warned that many teachers in the Philadelphia School District shunned Sulzberger; its reputation seemed to stem from the students' weak performance on standardized tests (among the worst of middle schools in the city) and from the fact that the neighborhood had a dangerous reputation. Like the residents of Mill Creek, all the students (and most teachers) were African American. At the start of the first year of the expanded program in fall 1996, a Sulzberger teacher told me that her students called their neighborhood "The Bottom." So they already know it's in a floodplain? "No, they mean it's at the bottom." Both meanings of the word can be read in the area around the Sulzberger Middle School: standing water after rain; slumping streets and sidewalks; vacant, rubble-strewn house lots; whole square blocks of abandoned land; men standing around street corners on a workday afternoon, jobless.

The school's environmental curriculum treated at length such topics as tropical rain forests and exotic wildlife, while issues of local importance like watersheds and plant succession received scant attention or none at all. One popular science teacher took students once a year to an environmental study center in the suburbs to see and study "Nature." To change the teachers' and students' perceptions that the Mill Creek landscape was divorced from the natural world was quite a challenge. It was equally hard to persuade students that the neighborhood had ever been different or that it might be changed. When my students spoke of designs for change, the children told them all the reasons the proposals would fail. "It won't happen." "Someone will wreck it." Studying the history of the neighborhood proved to be the key that unlocked the students' imagination.

"You mean, there really was a *creek*!?" a thirteen-year-old exclaimed in April 1997 as she examined a photograph from 1880 showing stream, mill, workmen dwarfed by the huge sewer they were building, and new rowhouses in the distance. This breakthrough in her understanding came six months into the Mill Creek Project. The catalyst was a series of weekly classes taught by students in my seminar. Each of my students led a group of six or seven twelve- and thirteen-year-olds in a series of six ninety-minute workshops. The sessions focused on particular time periods. My students brought in texts, tables of statistics, maps, and photographs, and then asked the eighth-graders to describe and compare them. To help the children draw out meanings from the documents, they posed successive questions. By breaking up big questions into smaller questions to which the students could find answers, my students led them to develop a hypothesis and then to find further evidence to support it. Only after the children had identified potential explanations for what they had observed, did my students relate background information that they had gleaned from their own reading and

Figure 4.1
Thirteen-year-old students, nineteenth-century maps in hand, discovered that this
vacant lot in Mill Creek's buried floodplain once contained several blocks of homes
and that the buildings were torn down over time, the result of both disinvestment
and subsiding ground. Photo by Anne Whiston Spirn, 1999.

from our seminar discussions. The idea was to encourage the children to
form the habit of looking for significant detail, framing questions, and rea-
soning out possible answers. The goal was that, after reading these documents describing the history of their neighborhood, the students would
transfer this process to the reading of the landscape itself (figure 4.1).

The Sulzberger students' interest intensified as the time period under
discussion got closer to the present. During one class, they compared maps
from 1872, 1886, 1895, 1910, and 1927, which showed the rapid development of the neighborhood, and looked at photographs of the construction
of the Mill Creek sewer. The class on the period from 1930 to 1970 was a
turning point. My students were apprehensive, for they anticipated that the
Sulzberger students would be angry to learn about the effects of redlining
and urban renewal on the neighborhood. They asked the children to play
the role of a neighborhood council in 1961; each group was a subcommit-
tee charged with investigating an important issue. The groups presented

their findings to the entire class and recommended actions to be taken, which then were discussed and voted on. One group investigated the origins of the 1961 cave-in and what was being done to prevent future catastrophes. They read newspaper articles, studied maps and photographs, and learned that the cave-in was one of many that had occurred along the Mill Creek sewer since the 1930s. A second group reviewed Louis Kahn's *Redevelopment Plan for Mill Creek* and his design for Mill Creek Public Housing.[30] They were particularly impressed to learn that Kahn was a famous architect. The students marked up a copy of Kahn's plan and coded it with different colors to illustrate their recommendations that the neighborhood council should support some features and oppose others, such as the construction of high-rise apartment blocks and the conversion of many through-streets to cul-de-sacs.

A third group looked into how homeowners and small businesses might obtain loans for mortgages and improvements. This group read the Home Owners Loan Corporation (HOLC) criteria for rating neighborhoods and studied the maps of Mill Creek in the *Philadelphia Real Property Survey* of 1934, which showed every block, except for a few occupied by cemeteries and schools, as highest risk, and learned the meaning of redlining. The students' response to the HOLC report, maps, and lending practices surprised me. They showed no anger. Instead, their faces registered surprise, then relief, then determination to come up with an effective response: a city-wide march on city hall, a petition, and the establishment of a community bank.

The students' energy carried over into the next class, which focused on the present and planning for the future. Staff members from the West Philadelphia Empowerment Zone and the City Planning Commission and two gardeners from Aspen Farms Community Garden visited the class. Sulzberger students asked the planners: "Why did you let those new houses be built on the buried floodplain? Did you warn the people who bought them?" "What are you doing about the Mill Creek sewer?" "What have you done about redlining?" "Why haven't you started a community bank?"[31]

Landscape literacy entails more than reading; it means shaping landscape also. Each student made a proposal for how the creek might be transformed from a liability into a neighborhood asset. At the end of the school year the essays and drawings were published in a booklet, along with one-sentence reviews by the mayor of Philadelphia, city councilmen, and others.[32] At the end of April, the Sulzberger students, together with their Penn mentors, gave a public presentation on the history of Mill Creek, illustrated with slides and posters, at a symposium held at the University of Pennsylvania.

At the beginning of the semester, Sulzberger students described their neighborhood in negative terms and said they would not live in Mill Creek if they had a choice. Only one student said she planned to attend college. Two months later, all but one student planned to attend college. The teacher reported that his students' performance in all subjects had improved dramatically. He attributed this to the Mill Creek Project: to the way that primary materials challenged and made history real for the children and to their growing perception of how their own lives and landscape were related to the larger city, region, and nation.

Teaching and studying the history and landscape of Mill Creek also caused learning to become real for my students. Most were unprepared for what they observed: the sheer extent of devastation in the Mill Creek landscape, for example, and the high level of intelligence among the children. My students' weekly journals revealed their evolving understanding of nature, race, and place. After several visits to Sulzberger, some acknowledged their surprise that some of the Sulzberger students were smarter than they, and this led them to reflect on their own prejudice and privilege. They also reported that their experiences in Mill Creek challenged the assumptions and theories asserted by texts that they were reading for other courses.

The culmination of the year was a four-week summer program for Sulzberger students and teachers organized and led by my research assistants. In the mornings, the group met either at the community garden a block away, where they built a water garden and an outdoor classroom, or at Sulzberger, where they constructed a topographic model of the Mill Creek watershed and learned how to create a website. Two Sulzberger students from the eighth-grade class worked as junior counselors in the mornings and, in the afternoons, as research assistants at the university, where they wrote, illustrated, designed, and produced "SMS News," a series of webpages that were posted on the West Philadelphia Landscape Project website.[33] The four Sulzberger teachers also spent afternoons at the university; one research assistant taught them web-authoring and how to use GIS (geographic information systems) software to map the neighborhood. At the end of the summer, one of these teachers was appointed to head the school's new computer program.

The computer teacher created an after-school computer club, and worked with the staff of Penn's Center for Community Partnerships to secure grants for the purchase of equipment and software. Within two years, members of the computer club were taking apart and building computers and writing computer code to adapt commercial software.

From 1998, Sulzberger Middle School and the Mill Creek Project received increasing local, national, and international recognition. The Sulzberger portion of the West Philadelphia Landscape Project website led Pennsylvania's governor to invite students from Sulzberger to make a five-minute presentation as part of his 1998 Budget Speech to the state legislature; the students' presentation was televised, as was the legislature's response, a long, standing ovation. Later that year, the Philadelphia School District named Sulzberger "School of the Month" and produced a television documentary on the Mill Creek Project and the school's innovations. In 1999 Sulzberger was the subject of a report on NBC Evening News, a national television program. In 2000, President Bill Clinton visited the school.

Recognition for the Mill Creek Project and for Sulzberger teachers and students opened doors to other collaborations. In 1999, the Mill Creek Coalition, a group of neighborhood organizations, invited me to speak to their group about the creek and its impact on the community, and we embarked on a series of joint projects, including research on flooded basements and a course for residents on the history of Mill Creek's landscape.[34] From 1996 to 1999, there were over a million visits to the West Philadelphia Landscape Project website from more than ninety countries on six continents. Among those who visited were public officials. In the fall of 1996, staff of the US Environmental Protection Agency's regional water division, who were increasingly concerned about combined sewer overflows in Philadelphia, invited engineers at the Philadelphia Water Department to meet with me to discuss the potential of stormwater detention to reduce this type of pollution. In 1999, staff from the Philadelphia Water Department's newly formed Office of Watersheds asked me to take a group of engineers on a field trip to Mill Creek. With nineteenth-century maps in hand, we walked and drove along the buried floodplain and looked at potential sites for stormwater detention projects. An immediate outcome of this trip was the decision to design and build demonstration projects associated with Sulzberger, which would detain stormwater and also function as an outdoor classroom for the school. The Water Department got a grant to fund the project in 2000 and pledged to work with teachers and students at Sulzberger. They hired one of my research assistants to work on the project and, in 2001, cosponsored the summer program on the urban watershed with Sulzberger Middle School, and met with members of the Mill Creek Coalition.[35] Later that year, the Philadelphia Water Department, the Philadelphia Housing Authority, and the Philadelphia City Planning Commission submitted a proposal for $34.8 million to the US Department of Housing and Urban Development's Hope VI Program in order to redevelop Mill Creek Public Housing as a demonstration project that would provide an environmental study area for the school and integrate stormwater management measures to reduce combined sewer overflows. The proposal was successful, and the city cleared the site in November 2002 and broke ground in August 2003 on the project.

In 2001, I was confident that things were going well for Mill Creek. I had moved from the University of Pennsylvania to the Massachusetts Institute of Technology in the fall of 2000 and continued to work with teachers at Sulzberger. In 2002, the computer teacher at Sulzberger visited MIT in order to lay plans for further collaboration. Then, a few months later, the Commonwealth of Pennsylvania took control of the Philadelphia School District and granted responsibility for the management of Sulzberger, among other schools to Edison, Inc., a corporation headquartered in New York. After trying to work with corporation staff that summer, the computer teacher and the other key teacher in the Mill Creek Program resigned in protest at certain new policies. In 2004, I learned that the water department's demonstration project in Mill Creek would not be built as envisioned. New houses would be built, but the program to integrate "green" infrastructure to manage stormwater and improve water quality was curtailed, as was the collaboration with Sulzberger.

Putting Mill Creek on the map and keeping it there is not easy, whether by "Mill Creek" one means the buried creek itself, the neighborhood, or the people who live there. Confronting these failures, I remembered the children's initial skepticism about prospects for change: "It won't happen. Someone will wreck it." Ten years later, in 2012, the Sulzberger teachers were still angry. "Things were going so well with this project...that we became part of the national spotlight," one teacher remembered. Why then, he reflected, was the school's Mill Creek Project abandoned and not replicated? Why indeed.[36]

Education, poverty, crime, transportation, housing: "There's no money in America in the 21st century to deal with those things," observed Howard Neukrug, who founded the Office of Watersheds in 1999 and was appointed Philadelphia Water Commissioner in 2011. "But, there is this money that we're spending to improve the quality of water. ... For whatever reason, as a nation, we've prioritized combined sewer overflows."[37] With the US Environmental Protection Agency threatening to levy major fines on the city for polluting water, Neukrug persuaded the Philadelphia Water Department to embark on a visionary plan for reducing combined sewer overflows using green infrastructure: *Green City, Clean Waters: Combined Sewer Long Term Control Plan Update* (2009). *Green City, Clean Waters* is now recognized as a national landmark of policy, planning, and engineering. It calls for reducing impervious surfaces in the city by 30 percent by 2020 in order to capture the first inch of rain to fall in a storm. If the plan works, it will save the city billions of dollars and has the potential to provide many other benefits, including jobs, education, and neighborhood development. But will it work (physically), and can it be done (economically, politically)?

To help test and refine Philadelphia's plan, in 2010 and 2011, my MIT students studied the ultra-urban Mill Creek watershed from the headwaters of Mill Creek to its mouth and found that mistakes of the past persist even as this visionary plan is put forward. Ironically, in recent years, the city of Philadelphia built new houses on former vacant land in the Mill Creek neighborhood, including many on the buried floodplain of Mill Creek. The strong pattern of vacant land on the buried floodplain is no longer as clear as it was, and the opportunities for addressing the city's combined sewer overflow problem there have been diminished. Furthermore, few residents of the inner-city neighborhoods along the buried creek know about *Green City, Clean Waters*, and they lack the former Sulzberger students' landscape literacy. They do not read the intertwined stories their landscape tells of buried creek, undermined foundations, abandoned houses, vacant land, and community gardens. Without grasping those stories, it is difficult to envision how new landscapes might rebuild the neighborhood while purifying the city's water. During their fieldwork in the Mill Creek watershed, my students encountered many questions from residents who were curious about what they were doing. When the students described the *Green City, Clean Waters* program, people were skeptical. "No jobs, no hope," one man told them. His response inspired them to propose a program that connects low-income communities with "green-collar" jobs through education, job-training, and the construction of local prototypes.[38]

My Ecological Urbanism class at MIT continues to study the Mill Creek watershed and to make proposals that integrate environmental restoration, community development, and the empowerment of youth, taking a top-down/bottom-up approach that brings together public officials and neighborhood residents and makes education and landscape literacy key ingredients. In 2015, I co-taught the class with Mami Hara, chief of staff at the Philadelphia Water Department. Our students envisioned Philadelphia Green Schools, which integrates three movements—green schoolyards, community schools, and place-based education—to create powerful programs and partnerships, where schools are at the heart of community development.[39]

Landscape Literacy, Environmental Justice, and City Planning and Design

Mill Creek is shaped by all the processes at work in inner-city America. The neighborhood was laid waste by the flow of water and capital and the violence of redevelopment and neglect. The correlation of a buried creek with deteriorated buildings and vacant lands in inner-city neighborhoods is not unique to Philadelphia; similar situations are found in Boston, New York, St. Louis, and many other American cities.[40] Mill Creek is typical of many American inner-city neighborhoods where the residents are predominantly low-income people of color. Known locally as "The Bottom," it is one of many such bottoms, hollows, and flats in the United States.[41] They are at the bottom, economically, socially, and topographically. Here, harsh socioeconomic conditions and racial discrimination are exacerbated by health and safety hazards posed by a high water table and unstable ground.

Despite such conditions, the landscape and population of these communities embody resources as well as problems. In Mill Creek, the resources are many and varied. Flourishing community gardens demonstrate the energy and determination of the gardeners who reclaimed them from abandoned lots; flowers planted along the sidewalk and bags of vegetables offered there express the gardeners' generosity. Blocks of homes with furniture on porches, with identical flower boxes, and with newly planted street trees are signs of existing social networks. Inside local schools, the drawings, models, and essays that decorate the halls speak of young people's intellect and vision. Even vacant blocks and the buried floodplain are potential resources. To recognize resources is not to deny the problems but to see each in the context of the other.

Twenty years ago, I thought that the worst effect of landscape illiteracy was to produce environmental injustice in the form of physical hazards to health and safety. The Sulzberger students showed me that there is an even greater injustice than inequitable exposure to harsh conditions: the internalization of shame for one's neighborhood. This is a particularly destructive form of injustice. To feel both at home in a place and ashamed of it is harmful. It saps self-esteem and can engender a sense of guilt and resignation. Before the students at Sulzberger Middle School learned to read their landscape more fully, they read it partially. Without an understanding of how the neighborhood came to be, many believed that the poor conditions were the fault of those who lived there, a product of either incompetence or lack of care. Learning that there were other reasons sparked a sense of relief. Once they had the knowledge and skill to read the landscape's history, they began to see their home in a more positive light, came to appreciate the effort and vision that places like Aspen Farms represent, and to regard some adults, like the gardeners, as heroes. They came to consider the possibility of alternative futures and brimmed with ideas. Secure in their knowledge and their ability to reason, they challenged public officials with confidence and impressed them with articulate proposals. To read and shape landscape is to learn and teach: to know the world, to express ideas, and to influence others.

Verbal literacy—the ability to read and write—is commonly acknowledged as an essential skill for the citizen to participate fully and effectively in a democratic society. Teaching literacy became a cornerstone of the American civil rights movement of the 1950s and 1960s. The "Citizenship School," which began as a means to increase voter registration through the promotion of literacy, evolved into a forum for discussion and catalyst for political action.[42] When, in 1999, I first read about Myles Horton's work with civil rights activists, and Paolo Freire's with adult literacy programs in Brazil, I was struck by the many parallels to my experience with landscape literacy in Mill Creek.

Freire designed literacy programs that were tailored to what he calls the "word universe" of the learners. To extract the words specific to the universe of particular people and places and as a preparation for *reading* the word, he employed images of the surroundings. He found that "decodifying or reading the situations pictured leads [people] to a critical perception of the meaning of culture by leading them to understand how human practice or work transforms the world."[43] He believes that people should learn to read in the context of the "fundamental moments of their common history" and proposes that texts of local history be created for that purpose from transcripts of taped interviews with older inhabitants.[44] In *Literacy: Reading the Word and the World*, Freier and Donaldo Macedo describe literacy as a form of cultural politics that either "serves to reproduce existing social formations" or "promotes democratic and emancipatory change."[45] They assert that knowledge of the world is a precondition for literacy and that understanding and transforming the world should be the goal of literacy. Reading, they say, "always involves critical perception, interpretation, and the *rewriting* of what is read."[46] Macedo suggests that "emancipatory literacy" has two dimensions: "On the one hand, students have to become literate about their histories, experiences, and the culture of their immediate environments. On the other hand, they must also appropriate those codes and cultures of the dominant spheres so they can transcend their own environments."[47]

Studying their neighborhood's natural and built features brought the place alive for the Sulzberger students. The understanding of their own landscape also opened wider vistas. It introduced them to broader social, political, and environmental issues and promoted other learning. In Freire's terms, it enabled the "students to develop a positive self-image before grappling with the type of knowledge that is outside their immediate world. ... It is only after they have a grasp on their world that they can begin to acquire other knowledge."[48]

Like verbal literacy, landscape literacy is a cultural practice that entails both understanding the world and transforming it. One difference between verbal literacy and landscape literacy, however, is that many professionals responsible for planning, designing, and building the city are not landscape literate. After six weeks' investigation into the history of their neighborhood, the children were more literate than many professionals, and some of their proposals for the neighborhood were more astute. To be literate is to recognize both the problems in a place and its resources, to understand how they came about, by what means they are sustained, and how they are related. Landscape literacy is a prerequisite for what Randolph Hester has called "ecological democracy," which emphasizes people's "direct, hands-on involvement" in building community where "actions are guided by understanding natural processes and social relationships" within their own locality as well as in a larger environmental context.[49]

Landscape literacy should be a cornerstone of community development and of urban planning and design. To plan prudently is to transform problems into opportunities and liabilities into resources, and to intervene at an appropriate scale. To design wisely is to read ongoing dialogues in a place, to distinguish enduring stories from ephemeral ones, and to imagine how to join the conversation. The stakes are high for those who must live in the places professionals help create. Like literacy, urban planning and design are cultural practices that can either serve to perpetuate the inequities of existing social structures or to enable and promote democratic change.

Acknowledgments

This chapter is a substantial revision of two prior publications; each of these essays tells the story of West Philadelphia's Mill Creek with a slightly different emphasis. The first, "Restoring Mill Creek: Landscape Literacy, Environmental Justice, and City Planning and Design," was published in *Landscape Research* (July 2005) and reprinted in *Justice, Power, and the Political Landscape*, edited by Kenneth Olwig and Don Mitchell (Routledge, 2009). The second, "Restoring Mill Creek: Landscape Literacy, Environmental History, and City Planning and Design," expanded on the history of Mill Creek and described developments between 2005 and 2011; it was published in *Nature's Entrepôt: Philadelphia's Urban Sphere and Its Environmental Thresholds*, edited by Brian Black and Michael Chiarappa (University of Pittsburgh, 2012). The current version is shorter and places the Mill Creek work in the context of ideas of nature and with reference to the concept of ecological democracy. The chapter was published in slightly abridged form in Steven Moore, ed., *Pragmatic Sustainability* (Routledge, 2016). I am grateful to Sverker Sörlin and Henrik Ernstson for comments that helped shape the chapter. Many debts are incurred during a project of such long duration, and it is impossible to acknowledge them all here. The West Philadelphia Landscape Project website (http://www.wplp.net) lists sponsors and participants. The initial support of the J. N. Pew Charitable Trust from 1987 to 1991 made possible the foundation from which all later activities grew.

Without the support of the Netter Center for Community Partnerships at the University of Pennsylvania (http://www.nettercenter.upenn.edu), the work with Sulzberger Middle School would not have been possible. For copies of publications about the West Philadelphia Landscape Project and to see photographs, plans, designs, course syllabi, and videos, visit www .annewhistonspirn.com and www.wplp.net.

Notes

1. Williams 1983, p. 219.

2. See Spirn 1997. For more than thirty years, I have asked my students (the majority are North American, with many others from South America, Asia, Europe, and the Middle East) for their personal definition of nature. Their responses have included the following: nature was given as a trust to humans by God; nature is trees and rocks, everything except humans and the things humans make; nature is a place where one cannot see the hand of humans, a place to be alone; nature consists of creative and life-sustaining processes, which connect everything in the physical and biological worlds, including humans; nature is a cultural construct with no meaning or existence outside human society; nature is something that cannot be known; nature is sacred; nature is God.

3. Spirn 1984, 1997.

4. Olwig 1996; Spirn 1998.

5. Spirn 1998.

6. Spirn 1998; Hester 2010.

7. In his discussion of how to identify and select a worthy case, Bent Flyvbjerg (2001) makes a distinction between extreme, critical, and paradigmatic cases (pp. 78–80). An extreme case makes it easier to identify the significance and study the interaction of diverse factors. A critical case "has strategic importance to the general problem" under investigation, while a paradigmatic case is prototypical and metaphorical.

8. The idea of landscape literacy builds upon but is distinctly different from the idea of environmental legibility as developed by Kevin Lynch (1964, 1981) and others. It also differs from ideas of environmental or ecological literacy (Orr 1992), primarily in its emphasis on human as well as natural history, on landscape language as a medium of action and expression, and its relevance to other issues beyond sustainability.

9. Design for ecological democracy, as defined by Hester (2010), combines participatory and ecological approaches to design with the goal of creating places that are memorable, healthy, equitable, and well adapted to their human community and

natural environment. Hester makes no mention of landscape literacy, which, for me, is a prerequisite to ecological design and planning as a democratic enterprise. His approach also focuses on grassroots, hands-on, participatory design and planning, while I advocate the integration of top-down and bottom-up approaches. With those amendments, I find the term "ecological urbanism" useful. Grounded in first-hand experience of place and direct participation in place-making, this concept is distinctly different from Andrew Dobson's (2004) more abstract notion of "ecological citizenship," whose primary goal is the creation of an environmentally sustainable society. Murray Bookchin's (1982, 1986) concept of "ecological freedom" aligns with ecological democracy in certain ways (though Hester does not cite him), as in, for example, the perspective that problems of natural and social ecology are inseparable, an emphasis on the communal and the direct engagement of the individual, and the critique of hierarchy and conventional city planning.

10. This chapter draws from more than three decades of fieldwork and of scholarly and participatory action research associated with the West Philadelphia Landscape Project, which I have directed since 1987. Sources include: historical documents such as census records, maps, plans, photographs, and newspaper articles; GIS maps, including the overlay of diverse data, such as topography, income, and vacant land; photographic documentation; interviews; and direct observation. Given the scope of the project and the limited length of this essay, it is impossible to cite the diverse evidence and many sources for the arguments made here. More detailed citations will be documented in my book-in-progress, with the working title "The Buried River: Restoring Nature, Rebuilding Community, Empowering Youth."

11. Hillier 2003.

12. See, for example, Jane Jacobs (1961), Herbert Gans (1962), and Nathan Glazer (2007). Protests against urban redevelopment in US cities in the 1950s and 1960s gave rise to new approaches to participatory design and planning, from advocacy to consensus building to capacity and knowledge building. For a critique of and alternatives to conventional mapping, see, for example, Mathur and Da Cunha (2001, 2012).

13. Spirn 2011.

14. Spirn, Pollio, and Cameron 1991.

15. Ferrick 1997. Parts of Philadelphia recently experienced a modest population growth, but most neighborhoods in the city continued to lose population between 2000 and 2010.

16. The history of the Mill Creek neighborhood is presented in Spirn and Ott (1998).

17. Levine 2012.

18. These newspaper articles were collected and compiled in the spring of 1997 for my seminar at the University of Pennsylvania, "The Power of Place: Water, Schools, and History" (Hillman 1997).

19. *Evening Bulletin* (date indecipherable), Urban Archives, Temple University.

20. *Evening Bulletin*, July 21, 1961, Urban Archives, Temple University.

21. *Evening Bulletin*, May 1963 (date indecipherable), Urban Archives, Temple University.

22. Based on the US Census of 1880, Enumeration District 504. The census was handwritten with tables for the Mill Creek neighborhood that documented the age, race, occupation, health, and birthplace for all residing at each street address.

23. Diaz 1999. Since 2007, Philadelphia has had a modest increase in population. By 2018, a dramatic shift was evident in the Mill Creek neighborhood. New residential development has attracted Caucasian and Asian students from nearby universities. Aggressive speculation, predatory lending, and tangled deeds have led many low-income African American residents to lose their homes.

24. Jackson 1985; Rome 2001.

25. Spirn 1991.

26. Spirn and Pollio 1990; Spirn, Pollio, and Cameron 1991, Spirn and Marcucci 1991, Spirn and Cameron 1991.

27. Spirn 1991.

28. The proposal was to the J. N. Pew Charitable Trust, which had supported the work from 1987 to 1991.

29. West Philadelphia Landscape Project (WPLP), www.wplp.net.

30. Kahn 1954.

31. All four visitors were African American. The staff person from the empowerment zone was very impressed by the eighth graders proposals, as were the two gardeners. The city planning official, however, was quite defensive. She confronted me after class: "You put them up to that!" I did not.

32. From the report *Power of Place: Essays about Our Mill Creek Neighborhood*. The texts and drawings of this report are on the WPLP website, as are the reflections of Sulzberger teacher Glen Campbell; see http://web.mit.edu/wplp/sms/pub.htm. The name of the course was inspired by Dolores Hayden's book *Power of Place* (1995), which was required reading for the course.

33. West Philadelphia Landscape Project, "SMS News," http://wplp.net/library/2012/projects/millcreekproject/smsnews.html/.

34. A description of these activities is on the WPLP website at http://web.mit.edu/wplp/project/mccoal.htm and http://web.mit.edu/4.243j/www/wplp/s-cornitcher.html.

35. Sarah Williams reflects on that experience fourteen years later in two videos, *Green City, Clean Waters* (2014) and *Coming Full Circle* (2014). In 2012 I began to record oral histories from people who have participated in the West Philadelphia Landscape Project since 1987. Among those interviewed were research assistants, like Sarah, as well as teachers and children (now thirty years old) from Sulzberger Middle School, and the Philadelphia Water Commissioner. What they told me was revelatory. Hear their stories in multimedia videos at www.wplp.net/stories.

36. Donald Armstead, personal communication, August 2012. See three teachers' reflections in the video *When Learning Is Real* (2013) at www.wplp.net/stories. The failure to sustain the successful program at Sulzberger is part of a much larger failure of educational reform in the public school systems of US cities. See, for example, Ravitch (2000) and Payne (2008).

37. Howard Neukrug, personal communication, August 8, 2012. See *Green City, Clean Waters* at www.wplp.net/stories. The Clean Water Act of 1972 (amended in 1977 and 1987) gave the US Environmental Protection Agency the power to enforce water quality standards.

38. *Green City, Clean Waters* flourished under Mayor Michael Nutter. When he reached his two-term limit in 2016, Philadelphia elected a new mayor with different priorities, who appointed a new water commissioner. After 2018, under the Trump administration, the EPA may not be so aggressive in its enforcement of clean water regulations. Despite the program's successes, commitment to its future is unclear.

39. See the 2015 proposals at http://web.mit.edu/nature/PhiladelphiaGreenSchools.html. In 2018, the class focused on the current housing crisis and proposed programs to aid and protect low-income homeowners and secure vacant land on the buried floodplain. Proposals from 2018 and other years are at http://web.mit.edu/nature.

40. Spirn 1986, 2000.

41. Moga 2010.

42. Horton and Freire 1990.

43. Freire and Macedo 1987, p. 36.

44. Ibid., p. 45.

45. Ibid., p. 141.

46. Ibid., p. 36.

47. Ibid., p. 47.

48. Ibid., p. 128.

49. Hester 2010, p. 4.

References

Bookchin, M. 1982. *The Ecology of Freedom*. Palo Alto, CA: Cheshire Books.

Bookchin, M. 1986. *The Limits of the City*, 2nd ed. Montreal: Black Rose Books.

Diaz, M. 1999 "Philadelphia Loses 9% of Its Population." *Philadelphia Inquirer*, July 1.

Dobson, A. 2004. *Citizenship and the Environment*. New York: Oxford University Press.

Ferrick, T. 1997. "Graying Homeowners, a New City Woe." *Philadelphia Inquirer*, September 15.

Flyvbjerg, B. 2001. *Making Social Science Matter*. New York: Cambridge University Press.

Freire, P., and D. Macedo. 1987. *Literacy: Reading the Word and the World*. South Hadley, MA: Bergin & Garvey.

Gans, H. 1962. *The Urban Villagers*. New York: Free Press.

Glazer, N. 2007. *From a Cause to a Style: Modernist Architecture's Encounter with the American City*. Princeton, NJ: Princeton University Press.

Hayden, D. 1995. *The Power of Place: Urban Landscape as Public History*. Cambridge, MA: MIT Press.

Hester, R. 2010. *Design for Ecological Democracy*. Cambridge, MA: MIT Press.

Hillier, A. E. 2003. "Spatial Analysis of the Historical Redlining: A Methodological Approach." *Journal of Housing Research* 14(1): 137–167.

Hillman, H. 1997. "Urban Redevelopment and the Mill Creek Neighborhood: 1930–1975." Unpublished paper for Urban Studies 320, Water, Schools, and History, University of Pennsylvania.

Horton, M., and P. Freire. 1990. *We Make the Road by Walking: Conversations on Education and Social Change*. Philadelphia: Temple University Press.

Jackson, K. 1985. *Crabgrass Frontier*. New York: Oxford University Press.

Jacobs, J. 1961. *Death and Life of Great American Cities*. New York: Random House.

Kahn, L. 1954. *Mill Creek Redevelopment Area Plan*. Philadelphia: Philadelphia City Planning Commission.

Levine, A. 2012. "The Grid versus Nature: The History and Legacy of Topographic Change in Philadelphia." In *Nature's Entrepôt*, edited by Brian Black and Michael Chiarappa, 139–159. Pittsburgh: University of Pittsburgh Press.

Lynch, K. 1964. *Image of the City.* Cambridge, MA: MIT Press.

Lynch, K. 1981. *A Theory of Good City Form.* Cambridge, MA: MIT Press.

Mathur, A., and D. da Cunha. 2001. *Mississippi Floods: Designing a Shifting Landscape.* New Haven, CT: Yale University Press.

Mathur, A., and D. da Cunha. 2009. *Soak: Mumbai in an Estuary.* New Delhi: Rupa.

Moga, S. T. 2010. "Bottoms, Hollows, and Flats: Making and Remaking the Lower Section of the American City." PhD diss., Department of Urban Studies and Planning, Massachusetts Institute of Technology.

Olwig, K. 1996. "Recovering the Substantive Nature of Landscape." *Annals of the Association of American Geographers* 86(4): 630–853.

Orr, D.W. 1992. *Ecological Literacy: Education and the Transition to a Postmodern World.* Albany: State University of New York Press.

Payne, C. 2008. *So Much Reform, So Little Change.* Cambridge, MA: Harvard Education Press.

Ravitch, D. 2000. *Left Back: A Century of Failed School Reforms.* New York: Simon and Schuster.

Rome, A. W. 2001. *The Bulldozer in the Countryside.* New York: Cambridge University Press.

Spirn, A. W. 1984. *The Granite Garden: Urban Nature and Human Design.* New York: Basic Books.

Spirn, A. W. 1986. "Landscape Planning and the City." *Landscape and Urban Planning* 13: 433–441.

Spirn, A. W. 1991. *The West Philadelphia Landscape Plan: A Framework for Action.* Philadelphia: Department of Landscape Architecture, University of Pennsylvania. http://www.annewhistonspirn.com/pdf/spirn-wplp-plan.pdf.

Spirn, A. W. 1997. "The Authority of Nature." In *Nature and Ideology*, edited by J. Wolschke-Bulmahn, 249–261. Washington, DC: Dumbarton Oaks.

Spirn, A. W. 1998. *The Language of Landscape.* New Haven, CT: Yale University Press.

Spirn, A. W. 2000. "Reclaiming Common Ground: Water, Neighborhoods, and Public Spaces." In *The American Planning Tradition*, edited by R. Fishman, 296–313. Baltimore, MD: Johns Hopkins University Press.

Spirn, A. W. 2011. "Ecological Urbanism." In *Routledge Companion to Urban Design*, edited by T. Banerjee and A. Loukaitou-Sideris, 600–610. New York: Routledge. Revised version: http://www.annewhistonspirn.com/pdf/Spirn-EcoUrbanism-2012.pdf.

Spirn, A. W., and M. Cameron. 1991. *Shaping the Block*. Philadelphia: Department of Landscape Architecture, University of Pennsylvania. http://www.annewhistonspirn .com/pdf/spirn-wplp-shaping_block.pdf.

Spirn, A. W., and D. Marcucci. 1991. *Models of Success: Landscape Improvements and Community Development*. Philadelphia: Department of Landscape Architecture, University of Pennsylvania. http://www.annewhistonspirn.com/pdf/spirn-wplp-model _success.pdf.

Spirn A. W., and C. Ott. 1998. "Tracing the Past, Shaping the Future: Urban Redevelopment and West Philadelphia's Mill Creek." Paper presented at the American Historical Association Annual Meeting, January 8, Washington, DC.

Spirn, A. W., and M. Pollio. 1990. *"This Garden Is a Town."* Philadelphia: Department of Landscape Architecture, University of Pennsylvania. http://www.annewhiston spirn.com/pdf/spirn-wplp-garden_town.

Spirn, A. W., M. Pollio, and M. Cameron. 1991. *Vacant Land: A Resource for Reshaping Urban Neighborhoods*. Philadelphia: Department of Landscape Architecture, University of Pennsylvania. http://www.annewhistonspirn.com/pdf/spirn-wplp-vacant_land .pdf.

Williams, R. 1983. *Keywords: A Vocabulary of Culture and Society*. Rev. ed. New York: Oxford University Press.

5 Realms of Exposure: On Design, Material Agency, and Political Ecologies in Córdoba

Martín Ávila and Henrik Ernstson

A nine-year-old child in the Argentinean city of Córdoba is taken to the hospital and is kept breathing through artificial respiration.[1] A scorpion had crept in through the grate of the shower and stung him. Similar human-scorpion encounters have become more common over the last ten years and have prompted a public campaign on how to avoid being stung.

In this chapter we take an interest in more-than-human urban encounters of this kind. We want to understand what it means to share a place, not with cute, cuddly, or majestic animals that are easily visible, but with small animals, insects, and organisms that we instinctively fear will hurt us. The chapter therefore contributes to a growing literature that elaborates methods and frameworks to think about animals as fellow urban inhabitants. This has ranged from following the traces left by water voles and badgers in Birmingham in trying to upset expert ways of knowing the city;[2] to writing accounts that try to sensitize humans to how penguins and flying foxes experience the city of Sydney as "narrative subjects";[3] and, finally, to draw on media accounts of a tiger, an elephant, and a cow, which fled zoos, circuses, and slaughterhouses, to elaborate on the possible political agency of nonhuman animals.[4]

In relation to this literature, our contribution lies in approaching animals that we instinctively fear and, rather than using more traditional ethnographic methods, we use material design as a method of speculating about such more-than-human relations. Design has the advantage of sustaining affective, social, material, and political tensions and possibilities with species that we humans relate to. In this context, the chapter describes and reflects on an alternative shower grate that we designed with the idea of shifting the roles and relations between humans and scorpions toward cohabitation. A central aim is, therefore, to make urban dwellers more aware of the realms of exposure that our everyday living produces among other creatures so as to better understand the political, metabolic, and affective implications of what it means to share a place.[5]

Indeed, the Córdoba situation is telling in that while we are aware of the state of the boy, who is fortunately stable and out of mortal danger, we know little about scorpions and why they increasingly end up in showers. To us, this silence on other-than-human urban dwellers hides fundamental questions regarding the historical distinction between humans and nature. We see in material design and speculation a method to articulate richer notions of urban nature and urban ecology, moving beyond what mainstream policy and scientific methods allow, from biodiversity conservation to the increasingly popular idea of ecosystem services.[6] This chapter focuses on situating our design intervention *between* species, and in particular to do so in Córdoba, and in that way search for a method of grounding urban natures. We will start with a brief historical survey of modern infrastructure in the city and show how this relates to a more-than-human urban politics, which includes not only tiny creatures and intimate feelings of fear, but also citywide metabolic processes. Building on this, we will describe our alternative design of a shower greate, which will help to rethink urban nature and its histories and futures.

Pollution, Appropriation, and Response-Ability

In *Malfeasance*, Michel Serres offers the idea of a "natural contract" in which "appropriation [among living species] takes place through dirt."[7] If somebody spits in the soup, nobody else will eat it. The male tiger marks his territory with stinking piss. Across species, the animal body knows how to leave its mark in order to appropriate, to own.[8] However, with the rise of the sanitarian city and centralized network infrastructure from the late nineteenth and early twentieth centuries in Córdoba and other Western cities, how we view our dirt has changed.[9] In flushing away our bodily excretions—blood, urine, feces, semen—we are not any longer in direct contact with our waste, which still goes on to appropriate wider territories, ecosystems, even the biosphere, in our name.[10] While urban sewage and water networks significantly reduced the incidence of communicable diseases such as cholera from the late nineteenth century onward, these have also operated as a technology of abstraction, separating us from our pollution and its appropriations and carving out the space of our sanitized ordered homes.[11] Through modern technical networks, we became cut off from the effects of our mode of living and how it affects other organisms.

In Córdoba, this history of infrastructural growth intersected with the lack of funds for the upkeep and maintenance of water-borne infrastructure in the older parts of the city. The mundane activities of showering, washing, and toilet-flushing slowly started to build up a fruitful, nutrient-rich habitat for scorpions and other organisms under the city. These organisms not only adapted but thrived in such sewage ecosystems. It is here, at this intersection between the sanitized modern everyday home (for humans), and the underworld habitat of the scorpion (and other organisms) that encounters between humans and scorpion take place, mediated by openings and orifices that connect with our bodily needs to extract dirt. The human-scorpion encounter at the center of our essay brings to the surface—or to put it more strongly, *performs*—how infrastructure is not only material, but also cultural, affective, and involving multiple species—a perspective usually not found in the vast literature on urban infrastructure and its histories.[12]

Our interest expands urban infrastructure studies to include ontological dimensions of urban ecologies and the life of other-than-human urban dwellers. In particular, we take the situation in Córdoba as an opportunity to explore the relations enacted when species meet and interact, and how their modes of being rub against each other. This means recognizing, with Donna Haraway, that a political dimension is inextricably part of any creature's mode of being. To explore the ontological *with* the political—the mode of being *with* how to live together—is, she suggests, "to become worldly and to respond"—that is, to somehow engage, recognize, and enrich our human ability to respond to others, for better or for worse, in what Harraway terms *response-ability*.[13] In this chapter we use design to approach "response-ability," especially focusing on our abilities to engage (or not) in and with the life worlds of other creatures.

Speculating through Design

Design plays a role in creating registers to acknowledge and change how the world "is" and how it "works" and, therefore, what it may become. Particular designs participate in creating *affective ecologies* whereby living creatures (including humans) can establish contact with one another, directly or indirectly. Creatures can be rendered sensible to other life forms in concrete ways through design. In this sense, design can support an exploratoration of the ecological and political aspects of how we become part of the worlds of others, and how they become part of our worlds (while keeping in mind that these worlds are ontologically not identical).

As argued by Isabelle Stengers, in such situations when ontologically different worlds meet, speculation rather than description becomes necessary: "Description...relies upon the naturalistic assumption that there are things generalisable/universal and, hence, transferable and imposable. Rather than focusing on *what is* (as description does), speculation places the emphasis upon *what may become* within different suites of relations (or contexts) and from different standpoints."[14] A descriptive mode tends to assume a script and becomes overly dependent on anthropocentric metaphors, analogies, and narrative, which hamper the exploration (and composition) of more-than-human ecologies.[15] While design is not independent from language and symbols, it carries a certain material autonomy with which other organisms can interact. It is from this (material) interaction that some sort of interspecies communication can occur and a window can be opened to speculate *urban ecologies yet to come.*[16]

Designing with Other Creatures and Matters in Mind: A Design Brief

There are at least three guiding criteria that we applied in designing a device that can intervene in the human-scorpion encounter. First, the device should not remove the fear of the possible encounter between humans and scorpions, but rather stay with the fear and complexities of what it means to live in affective more-than-human ecologies. Second, the device should increase the range of ways that humans can engage with other organisms and their habitats (that is, increase response-ability). And third, the device should be capable of being scaled up from the individual situation to city-level metabolic flows in order to avoid or at least to lower the harm of human activity on other ecosystems. In the following sections we will go through how we think about design in relation to these points, before describing the final design proposal.[17] While we did design a prototype, we should emphasize that the aim of our material speculative approach serves to invite the reader to engage in an alternative reality, a fictive reality, since the design proposal is not a commercial product.

A design process works toward the creation of a *device* (a physical arti-fact, service, or a system) to deal with an identified situation.[18] Any device (etymologically stemming from *to divide*) arranges partitions—that is, it causes inclusions and exclusions in terms of perception, sensations, com-munication, and other possible interactions.[19] A doorknob is designed for the human hand to turn it; the human foot is excluded from interacting functionally with the door knob. Nonetheless, all devices have unintended and often unforeseen effects that arise from their own configuration. When we designed the car, we created not only a way to transport something from A to B, but also the car crash, and at a more global scale, increased carbon emissions in the atmosphere. In the case of Córdoba, its sewage system is part of a centralized design; it is a *strategy* for removing feces from thou-sands of homes that was rolled out by engineers over decades and that per-sists in the present. However, due to the continuous growth of the sewage and water networks and the lack of resources to keep up with maintenance during the last decades, these networks have started to attract species such as mice, cockroaches, and scorpions. One result has been a rise in encounters between scorpions and humans, particularly *Tityus trivittatus*, one of the most common scorpions in Argentina and one of the most dangerous to humans. For instance, during one day in November 2012, medical doc-tors tended to thirty-eight cases of scorpion stings in Córdoba, although the average monthly number is considerably lower.[20] In 2010, two young children tragically died after having been stung by scorpions inside their homes.[21] As a response to this threat, people pour toxic chemicals down their shower grates and toilets, trying to kill the scorpions and destroy their habitat.

If we study this quite nightmarish situation a bit more closely we start understanding the need for a design that does more than simply stopping the scorpions from entering the home. The device we are seeking needs to change relations more fundamentally and in ways that recognize the com-plexities we are part of. That is, the sewers not only perform "as planned," by transporting effluent from buildings, roads, homes, and so on, but also create alternative ecological niches for multiple beings.[22] Cockroaches and mice, two other common sewer inhabitants, find nutrients accumulated on walls, where the sedimentation of discarded food, blood, semen, and feces and other organic and inorganic substances have created possibilities for life, which might be harmful *or* beneficial to the wide variety of organisms that come into contact with these systems. Thus, under the city, and created by the city, there is a thriving habitat with beings that we usually fear and would rather not cohabit with. Furthermore, the scale of their habitat is so vast and these beings are so resilient and pervasive, that we need to contemplate what a responsive cohabitation could mean—not only in a negative sense, as a response to a "threat," but in the positive sense of caring for the liveliness of the environments we inhabit. To try to deny life to these ecosystems by continuously discharging pesticides that kill indiscriminately and poison downstream ecosystems is not sustainable in the long run. Thus, what we need is a device that takes us close to the scorpions and acknowledges their habitat and that of their fellow creatures.

This brings us to the second criterion of the design. It needs to increase the range of available responses between species. In the current system, the fixity and permanence of household shower grates are problematic. Normal shower grates are usually made of metal alloys and screwed in tightly, and in line with a modernist-Promethean logic of humans controlling nature, they not only perform a permanent physical boundary but also fix a cultural boundary between the sanitized home and the underworld of sewage as if the two had nothing in common. But we do have things in common; we know now that there has been harm on both sides. Consequently, due to the material and cultural fixity of the metal grates (as a design, as a device), it partitions, structures, and compels human behavior toward the simplistic response of discharging toxic effluents into the grate in order to kill scorpions, destroy their habitat and, along with them, a variety of other beings. The fixity seems to structure a relation of disgust, or at least one of ignorance of other life-forms and the effects of our human excretion of dirt. Are there alternative devices or designs that can alter this destructive tendency? Can a different device increase the responses by which relevant species can interact and compel a more curious attitude or a different human behavior toward nonhumans of the city? Can it widen the question of "who is here" in the city?

While avoiding the direct encounter between the scorpion and the human is central, the device should also scale up, as part of our third criterion, to address the wider metabolic flow of the city. Each individual household is a productive component of an urban metabolism. Materials and liquids flow through households and affect the city and downstream ecosystems. How can our alternative design support ecological considerations of energy, shelter, nutrition, toxicity, and so on for all humans and nonhumans that participate in these environments? As we will see, this calls for designing an alternative shower grate that involves humans in communal gift-giving as part of a contract of cohabitation. It is simply not enough to protect the human (or the scorpion); there needs to be a two-way relationship in which our actions as humans and scorpions contribute toward our *co*habitation, a recognition of being of the same city.

In this chapter we draw on these three criteria and use this situation of designing with "response-ability" to scorpions in order to reflect more generally on our relations with other beings. Following Haraway, we attempt at "staying with the trouble," not resolving the "problems" or neutralizing what may repel us.[23] "Staying with the complexities," as Haraway writes, "does not mean not acting, not doing research, not engaging in some, indeed many, unequal instrumental relationships; it does mean learning to live and think in practical opening to shared pain and mortality and learning what that living and thinking teach."[24] The central questions to which our method of speculation with design tries to respond to are: What role can design play in enabling us to cohabit with any beings, let alone those we dislike or that pose serious risks to our lives, without taking away the tensions inherent in that relationship? How can we cohabit with animals that we instinctively fear?[25] Before moving on to our alternative grate design, though, we need to engage with the scorpion and its "underworld" of sewage to better understand how they live and form part of food chains and relationships that sustain intricate and wider ecosystems.

Getting to Know the "Underworld": Waste for Some, Food for Others

Some of the oldest neighborhoods of Córdoba are the most affected by the presence of *alacranes*, as scorpions are locally known. The sewers in these areas were built with concrete pipes during the first four decades of the twentieth century. Although some private properties and households in these areas have made upgrades using more modern PVC (polyvinyl chloride) pipes, the public infrastructure connecting to them remains outdated. Over time these older parts of the system have accumulated sediment, and the differences between private (and new) and public (and old) systems are easily visible in online videos produced by sanitation companies that have been filmed inside the sewers using remote-controlled cameras.[26]

Here we find vibrant food webs with decomposers and detritivores such as bacteria, fungi, cockroaches, and other organisms that feed on, and thus break down, the sedimented food sources that have accumulated on the walls. Decomposers find fatty deposits, which they metabolize and convert into proteins and fats to build their own bodies. In the process, the decomposers make available inorganic chemicals, which can be recycled as mineral nutrients for plants at the subsequent trophic level, further increasing the consumption of sediments. In this accidental relationship with decomposers and detritivores, there are positive effects for humans because what is waste for us can become food for them. On the negative side, some detritivores, for instance cockroaches, can become vectors for human disease. Additionally, as cockroaches feed and multiply they attract the top predator of this ecosystem—scorpions.

As scorpions surface from the underworld into human homes, some people get stung. Media coverage addresses the phenomenon each year during the critical summer months.[27] While there are several animals (spiders, snakes, and scorpions) in Córdoba that might threaten human lives with their poison, scorpion stings are the most common cause of hospitalization.[28] Studying the areas of the city most affected by scorpion stinging, we can identify key issues that contribute to their proliferation.[29] Factors include poor hygienic conditions, due mainly to the careless disposal of waste or the lack of infrastructure for its disposal; sewage exposure in public spaces; and the degree of vegetation in contact with sewage, where it encourages the presence of other species. Through interviews with specialists, and through hospital statistics, we have gathered evidence that most accidents with scorpions (more than 80 percent) happen in the bathrooms of private households. As a response to the awareness that household grates are the prime mediator of accidental encounters, people have been advised by the government to place smaller, denser meshes below the fixed grates to obstruct the entry of scorpions and cockroaches into the rooms (see figure 5.1).[30]

However, as we noted in the previous section, the fixed mesh does not decrease the presence of scorpions. Rather, it continues to silence the effect of human dissemination of dirt and noxious chemicals alongside their biological and ecological implications. Our alternative design must try to change this relationship and concretely acknowledge the ecosystem below, which involves taking a closer look at the scorpion.

Getting to Know a Fellow Species: What Is a Scorpion?

To get to know a different species requires the use of all senses—touch, smell, taste, sound, and sight—alongside more conventional studying. As an important part of the design process, for a year and a half the first author

Figure 5.1
A standard grate. Note the smaller plastic mesh placed underneath, recommended by local authorities, to prevent the passage of scorpions. Photo by Martín Ávila.

raised scorpions in multiple terrariums at home.[31] Living with scorpions helped him to study their behavior, but more crucially, in terms of the design process, this allowed him to gain firsthand experience of living with scorpions and to better understand the risks involved in cohabitation.[32] Notes were taken throughout this period, and questions such as *"What is another living being?"* and "What does it do, and how?" were asked with a view toward getting closer to the scorpion and understanding how this species may act and what it is capable of.

Bringing this experience together with more conventional studies, we can start writing a description of this species and how it lives. Scorpions are arthropods, invertebrates with segmented bodies and jointed limbs that form an exoskeleton made mostly of the fibrous substance chitin. They are efficient predators of insects and other small animals; their sting possesses venom, which is usually neurotoxic. To a human being, the sting from most of the existing species of scorpion (about 1,500) would hurt no more than a honeybee. However, twenty-five species of scorpion can be deadly to a human, in some cases capable of killing within seven hours. While the evolutionary history of hominids (our history) dates back 28 million years (and that of primates about 75 million years), scorpions' evolutionary history dates back 425–450 million years.[33] From an evolutionary perspective, they have been quite conservative morphologically, while highly adaptive in their behavior, physiology, and ecology, which explains their ability to thrive in extreme physical conditions. As biologist Gary Polis writes:

> Some [scorpion] species can be supercooled below the freezing point for several weeks and yet return to normal levels of activity within a few hours. Other species can survive total immersion under water for as long as one to two days. Desert species can withstand temperatures several degrees higher than most other desert arthropods are able to tolerate.[34]

That scorpions can live in cities demonstrates such adaptive capabilities, but it also highlights our advance into their ecological niches. From the Spanish conquest to the end of the sixteenth century, the city of Córdoba expanded into the Suquía River, which was the natural habitat of scorpions (and other species).[35]

When it comes to feeding, scorpions use their sting to capture prey. They hunt at night, and although they have vision, vibrations from their prey guide their hunting while they orient and sense with their whole body. Scorpions do not sting unless provoked or if they feel threatened. Interestingly, our very condition as diurnal human animals has made it difficult to study scorpion ecology. It was not until 1954 when the use of ultraviolet light became common in field research that their nocturnal habits could be documented and studied (see figure 5.2).[36]

Given what we have learned, the idea of cohabiting with *Tityus trivittatus* might be discarded automatically because they are potentially deadly for humans. On the other hand, have they not already adapted to our cities? Are we not constantly expanding our habitats and displacing them and pushing them to adapt to a wide variety of artificial systems? Their adaptability and evolutionary history indicate that they are likely to continue to adapt to extremes. Combating them with noxious pesticides might be effective in the short term but ecologically devastating in the long term. Taking the human-scorpion situation of this essay as an example of the tensions involved in cohabitation, we now turn to our alternative design that attempts to acknowledge human and scorpion needs at several trophic levels.

Figure 5.2

Tityus trivittatus in normal daylight (*top*) and with UV light (*bottom*). Photos by Martín Ávila.

Degradable Urbanism: An Alternative Design for a Shower Grate

The following describes our proposal for an alternative shower grate that intervenes in the present situation to speculate on cohabitation. It works in three main ways, which will be elaborated on below: to capture scorpions coming too close to human homes, seeking to change destructive human behavior that destroys habitats for creatures in the sewage, while biodegrading to feed the ecosystem below with nutrients. We first describe its functions and then compare it with present grates.

The photos in figure 5.3 are placed in the order of how the device would be used (see figures 5.3a, 5.3b, 5.3c, and 5.3d). The grate is internally covered with organic material such as bone meal (figure 5.3c). This attracts cockroaches, which, upon entering, get stuck in the adhesive that covers the upper and lower surfaces of the trap. The trapped cockroach sends out vibrations that would attract foraging scorpions that remain too close to the grate. If the scorpion enters the grate, it gets stuck on the same adhesive. In protecting the human home, the design recognizes that scorpions are hunters that do not eat dead insects or animals but are attracted by vibrations from prey.

However, while killing individual scorpions and cockroaches, the grate also operates to nurture and sustain the ecosystem below through altering metabolic and collective dimensions around the grate. When humans use the shower, the water flow will slowly degrade a white mineral layer on the grate's upper and visible side. Successive showers gradually reveal a darker layer underneath, which is made of a clayish mineral compound that becomes increasingly visible (compare figure 5.3a with figure 5.3b). The incremental darkening is a way for the grate to signal decay and transformation, and to warn humans of increasing "exposure," getting in closer and closer connection with the sewer. Thus, in contrast to the fixed metal grate between the "underworld" and us, this device operates to expose the sewer. It makes apparent the need to maintain the system with the intent of transforming our relationship to the "underworld" of sewage. Indeed, while *protecting* humans from dangerous individual scorpions, it also *attracts* humans to interact with the grate to sustain and intensify the relationship of affect and fear between the human home and the underworld of sewage.

In practice, once the orifices of a grate are almost completely dark (visually signaling "connection" to the sewer), it needs to be replaced (see figure 5.3d). This would happen every three to four months if the shower is used regularly. The user could discard the grate, compost it or directly mix it with soil, or just throw it in the garbage bin. Because the grate's materials continue to degrade, it is up to the person discarding it whether it will contribute directly to some metabolic cycle nearby or not. Either way, the nutrients that have accumulated from the insects and arthropods caught on the sticky surface will ultimately contribute to some biophysical process. Meanwhile, during its useful cycle (when operating as a grate), the device complements natural processes by releasing nontoxic organic and inorganic materials and can thereby also increase the sense of connection *with* rather than division *from* those places and systems that we do not see.

Comparing current models of fixed grates with our proposed degradable grate, we note certain differences. The fixed grate expresses an ideology of strict separation between the sanitized home and an underworld that is to be kept at bay. Through it go water and other waste, never to be thought about again. Our alternative grate is less a separator than a "mediator" in Bruno Latour's sense of the word in that it transforms, translates, distorts, and modifies meaning, and, we might add, material relations.[37] It connects the human home and the habitat of others, and translates both into a new (co)habitat, a shared and wider ecosystem. The grate's appearance furthermore signals that it is in a constant state of change and disintegration, reminding us humans that we take part in and relate to other worlds that we might know little about, but that at times intersect with our world. Our grate thus differs from current conventional grates in terms of how it creates and changes relations at different scales and in the way that it changes metabolic cycles. In this sense, the proposal is normative. It seeks to produce a change in behavior in people, to compel the user to participate in a new constellation of relationships that certainly demand more than those relations upheld by a fixed grate. Indeed, users need to make a concerted effort to use the alternative grate for their own benefit, and the benefit of others. It implies a shift in lifestyle and provokes a change in perception of who or what we are living with.

More generally, the alternative grate demonstrates a design approach in contrast from standard anthropocentric practices. Although it aims to benefit humans, the starting and the end point is the condition of the wider ecosystems. Our focus is not only the well-being of individual humans, but also on the way in which the artifact (and the humans engaging with it) may participate in the life (and death) of others, so that the livability

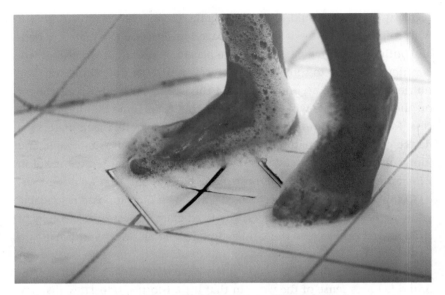

Figure 5.3
(a) Grate while showering (*top*). (b) Opening the protective strip to install a fresh grate and replace the degraded grate (*bottom*). (c) The grate is fitted with a trap for scorpions and cockroaches (*top right*). (d) Taking away the degraded grate (*bottom right*). Photos by Martín Ávila.

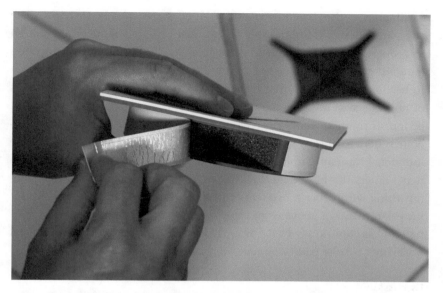

Figure 5.3
(continued)

or vibrancy of the shared cohabitation or ecosystem can be sustained. The alternative design translates this commitment in metabolic terms through its property of being scalable to the whole city. If mass produced, the alternative design would be a basic, simple thing to buy and use. If it were to become popular and installed in thousands, maybe tens of thousands of homes across the city, these thousands of devices, replaced every third or fourth month, would degrade and erode and start shaping the metabolic system at the city scale.[38] Importantly, the design operates beyond the individual human-scorpion encounter in regulating what material components enters the biosphere.[39] It challenges conventional design that does not think with wider ecosystems and more-than-human ecologies. And it provokes thinking about what other designs could be replaced with alternatives that aim to affect the way we engage with beings that we do not normally consider part of our everyday lives.

Discussion

We recognize the playful dimension of our speculative approach. It is also highly situated because the alternative grate design really only makes sense in Córdoba. Therein lies our commitment to grounding urban natures, a practice that seeks situated responses, practices, and sensibilities. However, it is worth rounding off with a discussion of what this approach to intervene in the entanglement between different life forms could say about politics and the politics of urban ecologies.

Our work tries to respond to how the simultaneous artificiality and wildness of urban nature demand a different way of thinking and practicing politics. Our cities, layered with attempts at modernizing and regularizing city life and city folk—and with a great variance across the world—hold in common the creation of quite fantastic ecologies, what some British geographers have eloquently phrased as the "dense comings and goings of urban life," a quickly shape-shifting "recombinant ecology."[40] Cities are unique high-energy environments, with a bundle of unpredictable inputs and fluxes of seeds, animals, and organic matters that are brought together in novel constellations with concrete and clay, with roads, cars, and electronic equipments. This makes for a strange place, and novel encounters are bound to happen. How are we as humans to organize our politics together with such wider, more-than-human communities with which we share the city?

The answer we are developing here attempts to stay localized and sustain dimensions of cohabitation that involve, among others, uneasiness, curiosity, fear, and fascination. Before developing this notion further, we can first contrast it with more mainstream natural scientific approaches that likewise deal with other life forms, in particular biodiversity and urban ecosystem services approaches. During the last decades, such work to change planning and human behavior to safeguard other life forms—often translated into policy tools such as habitat maps, biodiversity networks, or tables with contingency costs and trade-offs—typically reenact a separation of nature from culture.[41] They designate value to other life forms from within a Western and anthropocentric epistemological viewpoint.[42] While expressing care for other life forms, these ways of seeing and registering the nonhuman, risk continuing to mark a line between "nature" and "culture," between "them" and "us," just as the fixed conventional grate did. Here we have tried to move beyond, but also to complement, scientific registers—to make possible, perhaps—a richer, more affective connection between species. In short, to expand a multispecies sensorium of engagement and encounter. We can discuss this in three broader ways.

Affective Urban Ecologies

Mainstream approaches risk erasing or silencing vital dimensions of the ecologies that make up our habitat and worlds. By complementing centralized strategies and develop localized tactics, we have created a situated device that aims to integrate affective more-than-human ecologies as part of everyday urban life.[43] This means, on one hand, and as mentioned already, that the alternative grate in Córdoba would make little sense elsewhere— for instance in Texas, where snakes are the menace, or in Cape Town, where baboons cause problems. However, the practice that we have developed here to think design with (rather scary) nonhumans could still travel and be used to create other alternative designs in other places.

Our proposed grate aims to enact affective ecologies in several ways. To start with, the darkening surface of the grate shows what is normally imperceptible—namely, the degradation and flow of materials from a building. As such it belongs more to the paradigm of food than to that of household fixtures or appliances. It thus helps us to perceive the material flows that are disseminated to the environment and to sense the scale at which other artifacts degrade and how they influence our habitats. This direct relationship contributes to the possibility of increasing awareness of how the chemicals of hygiene products, cleaning products, and other products used at home influence the environments we inhabit by being disposed off into the sewers.

At a time when ecological crises expose the shortsightedness of various modes of human development, paradigms of design need to be disrupted through, for example, a redesign of everyday artifacts so that human exposure to other vital realms and species increases. The result would be a greater understanding of the complex ecological interplay in which humans are involved, including relationships that seem undesirable. In the process, we might also reach a more mature stage of reflection in producing the artificial, so that (design) proposals will consider the life cycles of products in relation to multiple beings.

This type of design practice also facilitates environmental education and participation. Instead of a centralized effort, such as a campaign in schools or workplaces about scorpions, educating becomes the province of nonhuman artifacts, in our case the biodegradable grate. This in turn implies that, as with any design, one would need to follow up on how the grate has been used to understand the different kinds of interactions, learnings, and changes it has, or has not, made possible.

Our proposal could thus be seen as part of recent efforts to reevaluate humanity's place "in nature." These range from scientific versions of Earth System Stewardship, or Gaia, with their associated global-legal regulations and imperatives, to posthumanist interventions to give voice to nonhumans, and further to decolonial thought, for instance through *Pachamama*, the term used by Andean pre-Hispanic cultures to designate human responsibility to all life forms. To various degrees, our mode of design can participate in discussions around efforts to materialize indigenous, postcolonial, feminist, and anticapitalist cosmologies that seek to reconfigure ways to be in the world.[44]

However, it is important to note that our *device* still *divides* and organizes an "above" and "below."[45] It does not try to arrange some kind of flat ontology where all is collaboration and bliss. Rather, it stays with the trouble and tension and actually tries to maintain a separation, an outside to its own relationality.[46] Thus, the grate is not a source of food for all cockroaches, but a trap for some of them and their predators, the scorpions. This can at first glance be viewed as a problematic example of cohabitation because organisms are killed, which is not the case with the fine mesh wire recommended by city officials in Córdoba. However, while the official mesh is structured around (total) safety, our design stays with the tensions of cohabitation as it seeks to participate in rearranging more fundamentally humanity's place in nature. The routine action to replace the grate after it has disseminated its nutrients, after it has become darker and we feel exposed, brings our human collective life closer to the trouble by nurturing the species that threatens us while preventing the possibility of human death (by single individuals of this species of scorpions). The grate thus forms an explicit part of the metabolic flow of the city and operates as what could be called a *biosemiotic threshold*.[47] More plainly put, the alternative grate engages humans and relates them to what is under their feet, creating a connection rather than a disconnection and thereby making us sensitive to ecological interactions that have become invisible through current infrastructure. The device arranges *a higher degree of exposure* to worlds that we humans are not normally in contact with.

Realms of Exposure

Through the particularities of Córdoba, we have now learned about the divisions between the human domestic environment and the "underworld" of sewage. Our work through design has attempted to *expose this lack of contact* with basic processes that are vital to any ecological niche, including our own, which involves acts of killing (some) scorpions and cockroaches, while protecting and nurturing the collective of scorpions and other beings through the release of nutrients. This approach is consistent with Haraway's position that "asymmetrical" multispecies encounters[48] require more than caring and nurturing, but also, as we just noted, dying and killing:

> We are in a knot of species coshaping one another in layers of reciprocating complexity all the way down. Response and respect are possible only in those knots, with actual animals and people looking back at each other, sticky with all their muddled histories. Appreciation of the complexity is, of course, invited. But more is required too. Figuring what that more might be is the work of situated companion species. It is a question of cosmopolitics, of learning to be "polite" in responsible relation to always asymmetrical living and dying, and nurturing and killing.[49]

Our alternative design is a direct attempt at inserting a device into one of these many knots. As a mundane object, it actively participates at various scales along a natural-artificial continuum in the handling of feces, urine, and other forms of (human) pollution to increase response-ability, our human ability to respond to others.[50]

By mediating between different realms of exposure, our work attempts to expose ontological aspects of design (preferences, behavior, and beliefs that seem unconscious and taken for granted) with the intention of increasing our participation in processes that might be difficult but are necessary to negotiate and enhancing our awareness of the (inarticulate) interests of more-than-human collectives. This invites a last speculation on including nonhumans or other-than-humans when thinking politics.

More-than-Human Political Assemblies

The alternative grate device can be said to operate at two levels: a micropolitics, practiced at the singular domestic level and coded with intimate feelings of fear and tensions; and potentially a macro-politics, operating on a massive metabolic and mass educational scale if it installed in thousands of households. These politics are enacted through the maintenance that the device requires, maintenance that is intentionally inscribed into it and that pushes humans to be part of something seemingly other (the life of sewage systems and scorpions, the areas where our bodily effluent is ultimately disposed of). The expiration date makes impossible the strict separation between spheres of dwellings.

These two levels of politics, while important, hide a deeper question of what politics means in a categorically more-than-human world. This question centers on exploring, in Aylon Cohen's words, "the boundary of the political community ... between logical animals (humans) and phonic animals (nonhumans),"[51] and then considering whether our device can affect who or what has a voice in matters of common concern.

Following recent developments of Jacques Rancière's thought, for instance, we could understand the scorpion as participating in "more-than-human political moments" as it breaks out of anonymity and disrupts the sanitized ordered home.[52] While Rancière has argued that political agency cannot be extended to nonhumans,[53] his theory of politics as *aesthetics* (relating to perception by the senses) is nevertheless strictly nonanthropocentric and opens toward more-than-human interpretations of the political.[54] His assertion that a political subject is "an agent of the division of the [political community]" lends itself to understanding the scorpion in political terms. Indeed, politics proper for Rancière means breaking the normalized order of a policed space, one that allows only certain sounds and utterances to be sensed and translated into intelligible speech. If the alternative grate can assist in recognizing the new agent as a new "voice," then we could at least cautiously entertain the possibility that the device is participating in the making of more-than-human political assemblies. And, indeed, there are some indications that the grate could play this role through its own materiality.

It is the material design of the grate that produces accountability on part of humans to maintain the system. The materiality of the device also reformats the modern sanitized home so that the more-than-human "voice" of the underworld can be expressed, "heard," and sensed through the darkening of the (degrading) grate. If these conditions are not heeded, the grate will disappear and maybe the underworld will make itself heard again through a tragic and violent encounter with a scorpion in the bathroom. We here discover that at least part of the complex of living beings of the city's underworld can assert themselves as having, as it were, a palpable presence, which is one of the most basic principles of politics, the making-visible/sensible/hearable of new collectives.

Crucially, nonhuman beings' assertion of existing here among us (as an integral part of the city) bypasses the *representations* that we usually use to understand them (through, for example, scientific investigations, which take them as objects of nature, displayed as "habitat maps" or "ecosystem services," or by civic associations that want to protect wildlife and regard them as stakeholders in society). Rather, the device mediates between humans and the underworld of scorpions in such a way that scorpions' assertion of existing takes place through *their own modes of living*, not through representation by humans. The materiality of design, especially the view of a device as something that *arranges partitions*—that causes inclusions and exclusions in terms of perception, sensations, communications, and possible interactions—resonates strongly with Rancière's theory that political moments is about disrupting the "partition of the sensible."

If Rancière favors anarchistic rupture, liberal parliamentarian theory also provides speculative possibilities for our design approach. In Latour's elaboration of a "Parliament of Things," he writes: "The point...is that we don't assemble because we agree, look alike, feel good, are socially compatible or wish to fuse together, but because *we are brought by divisive matters of concern* into some neutral, isolated place in order to come to some sort of provisional makeshift (dis)agreement."[55] Perhaps our device could be a mediating artifact that could make possible more-than-human political deliberations. However, in contrast to Latour's rather expansive notion of a new Parliament, our speculation on scorpions in peoples' bathrooms has provided a much more intimate, everyday setting to think about more-than-human political assemblies and their constitution through the daily rhythm of life (and death) in the city.

Conclusion

This chapter started with an accidental encounter between a child and a scorpion in a bathroom. We used this situation to elaborate a design approach that opens toward a richer understanding of urban ecology and the natural-artificial continuum. Moving beyond traditional scientific approaches and descriptive social scientific research, we drew upon a speculative mode of research to explore urban ecologies yet to come, which the alternative shower grate materialized. As an artifact, this device invites human dwellers to stay with the tension of cohabitation, enrich their affective connections, and support wider metabolic flows while possibly encouraging the making of new more-than-human political assemblies.

We believe that our design approach to ecology could intervene in the current grave situation of unsustainability. The artifacts that surrounds us, from mass-produced domestic products to high-tech devices and big infra-structure networks, compel us to constantly leave our traces on every part of the planet, disseminating novel chemical combinations that do not take into account any other being but humans, nor any other being's chemical or metabolic flow. Because these chemical combinations have come into use at such a quick pace, the biosphere is unable to process them, leaving new, unknown, and harmful dynamics affecting many species, including our own. Performing as a border, the grate we proposed mediates these passages *between* different worlds (of the "human-home" and the "scorpion-underworld"), and it does so through its material components, with the hope of contributing toward a thinking, sensing, and doing that is life-affirming. Politically, this mediating border, this device, could embody the responsi-bility and *response-ability* that come with the acknowledgment of our part in a more-than-human world under stress.

Acknowledgments

Leonardo López, Mariel Twentyman, Camilo Mattoni, Gabriel Bernardello, and Gerardo Leynaud worked with the first author in contributing in different ways to the development of the alterative design proposal discussed in this chapter. We are also thankful for constructive comments on earlier versions from Sverker Sörlin, Maja Frögård, and Irma Kinga Allen. The first author acknowledges the Swedish Research Council *Vetenskapsrådet* (VR) for its support for the project "Symbiotic Tactics" (Dnr: 438-2013-297). The second author acknowledges the Marcus and Amalia Wallenberg Foundation (MAW) for support alongside the Swedish Research Council Formas through two research grants ("Socioecological Movements in Urban Ecosystems," Dnr: 211-2011-1519, and "Ways of Knowing Urban Ecology," Dnr: 250-2010-1372).

Notes

1. "En el hospital, un nuevo ingreso por picadura de alacrán: El Hospital de Niños recibió este lunes un cuarto internado por escorpionismo. Todos estables," *Día a Día*, May 1, 2015, http://www.diaadia.com.ar/cordoba/en-el-hospital-un-nuevo-ingreso -por-picadura-de-alacran. For all internet sources in this chapter, the last access date was September 18, 2018.

2. Hinchliffe et al. 2005; Hinchliffe and Whatmore 2006.

3. van Dooren and Rose 2012, p. 5.

4. Cohen 2015.

5. We recognize that our account from inner-city Córdoba in Argentina is situated within a Western-planned city and with households mainly connected to centralized infrastructure networks. This needs to be acknowledged in comparative research.

6. Henrik Ernstson and Sverker Sörlin, "Toward Comparative Environmental Urbanism: The Discovery of Urban Natures in a 'World of Cities,'" chapter 1 in this volume.

7. Serres 2010, p. 3. See also Serres's *The Natural Contract* (1995). For a critique of Serres's (2010) treatment of waste as appropriation through pollution, see Reno (2014). Drawing on biosemiotics, Reno foregrounds the *signals* that animals send out through their scat/shit and views waste as "signs of life," rather than waste as "matter out of place," and thereby affirms a nonanthropocentric framework. Our work resonates with his emphasis of the "liveliness of waste" (ibid., p. 19). For more, see note 47 on bio-semiotics.

8. This includes "certain plants," which at times "throw out little invisible jets of acid... and we all know that nothing grows in the frigid shadow of fir trees" (Serres 2010, p. 2).

9. Laporte (2002 [1978]) calls it the "history of shit."

10. For a historical account of infrastructure-led sanitarian transformation of Western cities, see Melosi (2000).

11. For Laporte (2002 [1978]), urban sewage and water infrastructure are tightly bound up with the historical rise in Europe of the bourgeois class with its ideas of home, cleanliness, and morality.

12. In relation to sewage and waste, see Melosi (2000) and Karvonen (2011). For a contrasting context from Dakar, see Fredericks (2014).

13. Haraway 2008, p. 41. See also the early work from the 1930s on "Umwelt" by Estonian biologist Jakob von Uexküll (2010 [1934]).

14. The quotation is from Booth and Williams (2014, p. 183; emphasis added), with explicit reference to Stengers (2010).

15. See Maran and Kull (2014, p. 46), who explain that narrative description is inadequate for the description of ecological semiosis and communication between species: "There are no general purposes that non-human organisms follow, their intentions are local and they do not have the tools for temporal integration or meta-description.... A narrative description of ecological events is [thus] always metaphoric." This could be one critical conversation to have with van Dooren and Rose's (2012) approach to viewing animals as "narrative subjects." For a foundation into Maran and Kull's work, see von Uexküll (2010 [1934]).

16. See Ávila (2012) for several examples of how material designs set up different forms of communication (and symbiotic relations) between humans and other species.

17. We should clarify that the design proposal of the grate was not a commercial commission. Rather, the design was a material configuration and research element in helping to conceive human and other-than-human relations in alternative ways. As such, other socioecological and more-than-human situations had been studied before we choose this particular one with humans and scorpions.

18. As developed in Avila (2012).

19. As we develop in the last section, design can be seen as a device that arranges partitions and opens for an interesting conversation with Rancière's (2010) theory of politics as aesthetics.

20. Varying from year to year, the average number of persons getting stung by scorpions may be around two or three cases per day during the summer, with less

during the winter months. The source for this type of site-specific information comes from interviews we did in Córdoba but can also be found in newspapers and public reports; see, for example, "Se registran 40 picaduras de alacranes por día en Córdoba," *Cadena 3*, January 3, 2018, https://www.cadena3.com/noticias/sociedad /registran-picaduras-alacranes-por-dia-cordoba_110780.

21. See the e-forum Forotarantulas (http://www.forotarantulas.com/foro/index.php ?topic=9659134.0) with links. See also "Una nena de 7 años murió tras ser picada por un alacrán en Córdoba," *Infobae*, January 8, 2017, https://www.infobae.com/sociedad /2017/01/08/una-nena-de-7-anos-murio-tras-ser-picada-por-un-alacran-en-cordoba/.

22. In a similar way, Hinchliffe and Whatmore (2006) observe that "cities are inhabited with and against the grain of expert designs" (p. 124).

23. Haraway 2010, 2016.

24. Haraway 2008, p. 83.

25. These questions form part of a wider project entitled Symbiotic Tactics (2013–2016) carried out by the first author with several designs including the alternative grate on which this chapter is based. These designs resulted from collaborations with many professionals and are based on research developed at the Multidisciplinary Institute of Vegetal Biology and other research groups within the Argentinean Research Council (CONICET). The design proposal part of this chapter was elaborated by Martin Ávila and Leonardo López using the project working title "Doomestics."

26. To view a video of the difference between private and public connections in Córdoba, see "Video inspeccion de conexión cloacal domiciliaria," YouTube, August 15, 2011, https://www.youtube.com/watch?v=59a0lm4TGuU. Note that the video is not from the specific neighborhoods being discussed in the main text. What is clear from the video and other reports is that there is a marked difference between (older) public and (newer) private pipelines, with thicker sediment in the former. From a traditional environmental justice perspective, this could indicate increased risks in terms of which type of household (class, ethnicity, and so on) scorpions are most likely to enter and cause harm in. We have found no secondary material to support such an environmental justice analysis.

27. For government information on scorpions and how to capture them, see "Alacranes: Cómo capturarlos en forma segura," http://prensa.cba.gov.ar/salud/alacranes -como-capturarlos-en-forma-segura/.

28. See Gastón Hernán Pepa, "Especies venenosas en Córdoba: 'No tema pero tome precauciones,'" *Córdoba Times*, November 13, 2013, http://www.cordobatimes.com /sociales/2013/11/13/especies-venenosas-en-cordoba-no-tema-pero-tome-precau ciones/.

29. For editorial reasons we cannot provide the reader with all visual information we have available. For a map of the areas most affected by scorpions in households, see

Natalia Lazzarini, "Alacranes: Más picaduras en el centro y sudeste de Córdoba," *Día a Día*, October 1, 2015, http://www.diaadia.com.ar/cordoba/alacranes-mas-picaduras -en-el-centro-y-sudeste-de-cordoba.

30. See, for example, "Temporada de Alacranes: Consejos para cuidarnos en el hogar," Punto Sanitario, http://puntosanitario.blogspot.com.ar/2014/12/temporada-de -alacranes-consejos-para.html.

31. Martín Ávila and Leonardo López designed the alternative grate.

32. The design experiments were carried out with scorpions of several species (*Urophonyus braquicentus, Tityus trivittatus, Bothriurus bonariensis*), but focusing on the most dangerous for a human being, *Tityus trivittatus*.

33. Polis 1990, p. 2.

34. Ibid., p. 3.

35. The city grew with colonization following a known pattern of Spanish conquistadores killing or forcing away indigenous peoples, including Comechingones, Sanavirones, and other groups. In 2016 the city's population was approximately 1.5 million people.

36. Polis 1990, p. 128.

37. Latour 2005b, p. 38.

38. Keep in mind that this metabolism is also shaped by many materials that lie outside the control of this device, including detergents, chemicals, cleaning implements, flooring and fixtures, and so on. These materials nonetheless participate by harming or benefiting some living systems at some ecosystemic level.

39. This aligns with Reno's (2014) biosemiotic analysis of waste, not as "matter out of place," but as "signs of life."

40. Hinchliffe and Whatmore (2006) quote G. Barker's (2000) notion of "recombinant ecology". For ecologists' treatment of species as urban adapters/avoiders, see the volume edited by Niemelä et al. (2011).

41. See Ernstson (2013) and Ernstson and Sörlin (2013) for studies of the politics of biodiversity mapping and ecosystem services in Cape Town. See Lachmund (2013) on the development of habitat maps in Berlin from the 1960s.

42. See Peder Anker's *Imperial Ecology* (2001) for the origins of ecology as a science that par excellence was developed to control environments and peoples across the British Empire. We also note that there are more bottom-up approaches to biodiversity; see, for example, Arturo Escobar's (1998) early call and useful problematization in the context of indigenous knowledge practices.

43. Compare with Hinchliffe and Whatmore's (2006) argument for a "politics of conviviality," but with more Deleuzian connotations. See Katherine Wolfe's (2006)

reading of how Rancière's notion of politics could communicate productively with Deleuze's idea of the "imperceptible" (in spite of Rancière's reservation of the political potential of Deleuze's philosophy).

44. See, for instance, de la Cadena (2015) and Haraway (2016), as well as Garuba (2012).

45. Note, however, that this is done by materializing an uncertainty principle, not knowing who or what is going to establish contact with the device. More generally the alternative grate is designed to degrade and disseminate organic and inorganic compounds with chemical compositions that are nontoxic to other life forms.

46. See Swyngedouw and Ernstson (2018) for an argument against flat ontologies that risk off-staging political agency.

47. Throughout this chapter, we find several affinities with biosemiotic studies. In relation to how the alternative design fuses semiotics and metabolic flows, biosemiotician Jesper Hoffmeyer (2008, p. 345) suggests what he calls "semiotic fitness," arguing that "the magnitude of the flow of energy and the semiotic controls guiding the utilization of that energy…have constituted the pivotal points in both the historical process of civilization, and in the evolution of life on earth." This provides reasons for why our alternative shower grate can be understood as a form of "attunement" (Ávila 2012), a biosemiotic technology that is useful as a "tool for semiotic activity of every sort," such as for communication between humans, nonhumans, and all their combinations (Hoffmeyer 2008, pp. 343–344). For an explanation of open thermodynamic systems as life processes, see Schneider and Sagan (2005).

48. Haraway 2008, p. 81.

49. Ibid., p. 42.

50. Haraway 2016.

51. Cohen 2015, p. 277.

52. Booth and Williams (2014, p. 45) analyzed Australian wild fires "breaking free of wilderness and burning the settled lands of human habitation" as an example of a "more-than-human political moment."

53. When interviewed by Jane Bennett (2010, p. 106) on whether he "thought that an animal or a plant or a drug or a (nonlinguistic) sound could disrupt the police order [an important philosophical and political distinction in Rancière's thought], Rancière said no: he did not want to extend the concept of the political that far; nonhumans do not qualify as participants in a demos."

54. The authors of this chapter have debated whether Rancière's theory can be extended to include other life forms. The most challenging condition is his axiomatic criterion of *equality* as a condition for politics. Political agents need to rupture the police order *in the name of equality*, uttering sounds that claim equality for all (Rancière 2010, 2014). An opening for an extension lies in Rancière's categorically

aesthetic, and thus nonanthropocentric approach to politics. It is rupture itself as a singular event that brings about a new state of affairs in which new speaking beings become hearable and intelligible, which in theory does not preclude any other life form. However, we have not come to a full agreement or conclusion on this matter. For concrete case studies in extending the political community via Ranciére, see Booth and Williams (2014) and Cohen (2015). For further discussions about Ranciére and political ecology, see de la Cadena (2015) and Swyngedouw and Ernstson (2018). See also Latour (1993) and Stengers (2010).

55. Latour 2005a, 13; emphasis added.

References

Anker, Peder. 2001. *Imperial Ecology: Environmental Order in the British Empire, 1895–1945*. Cambridge, MA: Harvard University Press.

Ávila, Martín. 2012. *Devices: On Hospitality, Hostility and Design*. Gothenburg: ArtMonitor.

Barker, G., ed. 2000. "Ecological Recombination in Urban Areas: Implications for Nature Conservation." Workshop report from meeting at the Centre for Ecology and Hydrology (Monks Wood), July 13. UK Man and Biosphere Committee, Urban Forum, English Nature, Centre for Ecology and Hydrology, Peterborough, UK.

Bennett, Jane. 2010. *Vibrant Matter: A Political Ecology of Things*. Durham, NC: Duke University Press.

Booth, Kate, and Stewart Williams. 2014. "A More-than-Human Political Moment (and Other Natural Catastrophes)." *Space and Polity* 18(2): 182–195.

Cohen, Aylon A. 2015. "'We Support Circus Animals Who Kill Their Captors': Nonhuman Resistance, Animal Subjectivity, and the Politics of Democracy." In *Tiere, Texte, Transformationen: Kritische Perspektiven Der Human-Animal Studies*, edited by Reingrad Spannring, Reinhard Heuberger, Gabriela Kompatscher Gufler, Andreas Oberprantacher, Karin Schachinger, and Alejandro Boucabeille, 277–294. Bielefeld: Transcript.

de la Cadena, Marisol. 2015. "Uncommoning Nature." *E-Flux Journal* 65: 1–8.

Ernstson, Henrik. 2013. "Re-Translating Nature in Post-Apartheid Cape Town: The Material Semiotics of People and Plants at Bottom Road." Actor-Network Theory for Development Working Paper Series, edited by Richard Heeks, no. 4. Manchester: Institute for Development Policy and Management, School of Environment, Education and Development, University of Manchester. http://hummedia.manchester.ac.uk/institutes/cdi/resources/cdi_ant4d/ANT4DWorkingPaper4Ernstson.pdf.

Ernstson, Henrik, and Sverker Sörlin. 2013. "Ecosystem Services as Technology of Globalization: On Articulating Values in Urban Nature." *Ecological Economics* 86: 274–284.

Escobar, Arturo. 1998. "Whose Knowledge, Whose Nature? Biodiversity, Conservation, and the Political Ecology of Social Movements." *Journal of Political Ecology* 5: 53–82.

Fredericks, Rosalind. 2014. "Vital Infrastructures of Trash in Dakar." *Comparative Studies of South Asia, Africa and the Middle East* 34(3): 532–548.

Garuba, Harry. 2012. "On Animism, Modernity/Colonialism, and the African Order of Knowledge: Provisional Reflections." *E-Flux Journal* 36: 1–9.

Haraway, Donna J. 2008. *When Species Meet*. Minneapolis: University of Minnesota Press.

Haraway, Donna J. 2010. "When Species Meet: Staying with the Trouble." *Environment and Planning D: Society and Space* 28(1): 53–55.

Haraway, Donna J. 2016. *Staying with the Trouble. Making Kin in the Chthulucene*. Durham, NC: Duke University Press.

Hinchliffe, Steve, Matthew B. Kearnes, Monica Degen, and Sarah Whatmore. 2005. "Urban Wild Things: A Cosmopolitical Experiment." *Environment and Planning D: Society and Space* 23(5): 643–658.

Hinchliffe, Steve, and Sarah Whatmore. 2006. "Living Cities: Towards a Politics of Conviviality." *Science as Culture* 15(2): 123–138.

Hoffmeyer, Jesper. 2008. *Biosemiotics. An Examination into the Life of Signs and the Signs of Life*. Scranton, PA: University of Scranton Press.

Karvonen, Andrew. 2011. *Politics of Urban Runoff: Nature, Technology, and the Sustainable City*. Cambridge, MA: MIT Press.

Lachmund, Jens. 2013. *Greening Berlin: The Co-production of Science, Politics, and Urban Nature*. Cambridge, MA: MIT Press.

Laporte, Dominque. 2002 [1978]. *History of Shit*. Cambridge, MA: MIT Press.

Latour, Bruno. 1993. *We Have Never Been Modern*. Cambridge, MA: Harvard University Press.

Latour, Bruno. 2005a. "From Realpolitik to Dingpolitik or How to Make Things Public." In *Making Things Public: Atmospheres of Democracy*, edited by Bruno Latour and Peter Weibel, 4–31. Cambridge, MA: MIT Press.

Latour, Bruno. 2005b. *Reassembling the Social: An Introduction to Actor-Network-Theory*. Oxford: Oxford University Press.

Maran, Timo, and Kalevi Kull. 2014. "Ecosemiotics: Main Principles and Current Developments." *Geografiska Annaler, Series B: Human Geography* 96(1): 41–50.

Melosi, Martin V. 2000. *The Sanitary City: Urban Infrastructure in America from Colonial Times to the Present*. Baltimore, MD: Johns Hopkins University Press.

Niemelä, Jari, Jürgen H. Breuste, Glenn R. Guntenspergen, Nancy E. McIntyre, Thomas Elmqvist, and P. James, eds. 2011. *Urban Ecology: Patterns, Processes, and Applications*. Oxford: Oxford University Press.

Polis, Gary A., ed. 1990. *The Biology of Scorpions*. Stanford, CA: Stanford University Press.

Rancière, Jacques. 2010. *Dissensus: On Politics and Aesthetics*. London: Bloomsbury.

Rancière, Jacques. 2014. *Moments Politiques: Interventions 1977–2009*. New York: Seven Stories Press.

Reno, Joshua O. 2014. "Toward a New Theory of Waste: From 'Matter out of Place' to Signs of Life." *Theory, Culture and Society* 31(6): 3–27.

Schneider, Eric D., and Dorian Sagan. 2005. *Into the Cool: Energy Flow, Thermodynamics and Life*. Chicago: University of Chicago Press.

Serres, Michel. 1995. *The Natural Contract*. Ann Arbor: University of Michigan Press.

Serres, Michel. 2010. *Malfeasance: Appropriation through Pollution?* Stanford, CA: Stanford University Press.

Stengers, Isabelle. 2010. "Including Nonhumans in Political Theory: Opening Pandora's Box?" In *Political Matter: Technoscience, Democracy, and Public Life*, edited by Bruce Braun and Sarah J. Whatmore, 3–34. Minneapolis: University of Minnesota Press.

Swyngedouw, Erik, and Henrik Ernstson. 2018. "Interrupting the Anthropo-obScene: Immuno-Biopolitics and Depoliticizing Ontologies in the Anthropocene." *Theory, Culture and Society* 35(6): 3–30.

van Dooren, Thom, and Deborah Bird Rose. 2012. "Storied-Places in a Multispecies City." *Humanimalia* 3: 1–27.

von Uexküll, Jakob. 2010 [1934]. *A Foray into the World of Animals and Humans*. Minneapolis: University of Minnesota Press.

Wolfe, Katherine. 2006. "From Aesthetics to Politics: Rancière, Kant and Deleuze." *Contemporary Aesthetics* 4 (2006): 1–15.

III Popular Natures

6 Nature's Popular Metropolis: The Greening of the San Francisco Bay Area

Richard A. Walker

No study of urban natures can afford to overlook the case of the San Francisco Bay Area, the greenest of cities in the United States. It has earned that title by virtue of over a century of conservation of open space, bay waters, and coastal areas the length and breadth of the metropolitan area. The Bay Area is replete with what might be called "popular urban natures" because the landscape of the region bristles with parks, open spaces, and other protected areas that are the result of widespread mobilization of committed citizens, fierce outbreaks of environmental politics, and thoroughgoing incorporation of green spaces in public life. I have assayed the depth and breadth of this process of popular nature-making in the city elsewhere; I use this opportunity to elaborate on the key ideas in the making of urban natures and show how they must be grounded geographically and politically.[1]

The argument proceeds in three parts. First, the bay metropolis encompasses a huge array of open spaces—loosely called the "greenbelt"—that have become an everyday part of the urban scene, experienced as scenic backdrop, as recreational areas, and as integral to local residents' sense of place. That greenbelt is widely viewed as preserved wildland, in contrast to the artifice of the city, yet it is anything but nature in the raw. It is an urbanized nature—a socionatural hybrid profoundly transformed by the encounter between city and country and between popular ideas and practices and ecological processes. Second, the greenbelt landscape can be understood as popular urban nature in the crucial sense of being the consequence of strenuous political activity by a mobilized citizenry that has been well organized, well led, and well heeled. Popular spaces of urban nature have been achieved through a sustained struggle in counterflow to the dominant logic of profit-making, expressed in terms of the public interest and manifested in publicly accessible open space. Third, the successful fight to naturalize the Bay Area landscape has generated enduring organizations, scientific defenses of nature protection, and legislation enforced by agencies of the state. Popular natures necessarily become governmental, but no less democratic for all that, because they are movement generated (and defended) rather than imposed from above. These three arguments define the three sections of the chapter.

In the conclusion, I put the San Francisco story in broader geographical perspective. It presents an outstanding case of how the experience of one locality with urban natures was the foundation out of which grew a legacy of national environmental leadership and even global impact on conservation efforts from Alaska to the Amazon. It shows that sweeping glosses on global urbanization, urban ecologies, and environmental resilience need to be seen as local-global dialectics, rather than universal processes, precisely because the social ecologies of different cities follow a wide range of pathways. In some cases, like that of the Bay Area, the local is so potent that it *becomes* the global.

Making Nature in the City

Cities are natural, in the sense that they are made up of natural materials, fed by flows of air, water and energy, and alive with living things. That is true, but too minimal to grasp what it means to create a "popular urban nature." Parks and open spaces are natural in being formed from the stuff of nature and unnatural in the sense of being products of human industry, so what kind of unnatural nature are they? One can say that they are *hybrids* of the social and the natural, following Erik Swyngedouw, but how did such hybridization come about?[2] In this section, I build a reciprocal approach to urban natures in the San Francisco Bay Area in four iterations: unnatural blessings, country in the city, culture of nature, and vitality of nature. I call the resulting urban landscapes *metro-natural*: nature thoroughly integrated into urban space and the urban experience.

Unnatural Blessings

Nature has undoubtedly been kind to the Bay Area. The natural setting, hard by the Golden Gate, is very much its trademark. The watery expanse of San Francisco Bay gives the metropolis its centerpiece. The surrounding hills, golden in the summer sun, provide a topographic counterpoint to the bay and are backed up by mountains thick with wooded canyons, oak savanna, and evergreen chaparral. Dramatic fog banks blow in from the Pacific, with its sandy shores and blue-green vistas. And an abundance of sunshine is mixed with highly variable winter rainfall, marking this as one of the handful of Mediterranean climate zones of the world. It is said to be one of the most beautiful cities and agreeable places to abide on earth. Moreover, not far away lie the incomparable California landscapes of redwood forests, Big Sur, and the Sierra Nevada.

The inspirational quality of the local landscape is an article of faith among local environmentalists. As Dorothy Erskine, founder of People for Open Space, put it: "Our surroundings are so dramatic that I think that it has generated a certain emotional drive that led to victory in the battle for the bay, and advanced our region farther than other parts of the United States in consciousness about the environment."[3] While there is an element of truth to this mythology, San Francisco has a horrendous record of environmental destruction. It grew rich by tearing asunder the mountains for gold and silver, laying waste to the rivers and forests, filling and polluting the bay, and paving over magnificent sand dunes.[4] Natural beauty did not, therefore, come with an insurance policy that it would not be filled, fouled, carved up, and cut down. A verdant nature did not grant San Francisco the kind of urban landscape one finds today, replete with parks and hiking trails, second-growth forests and tidy vineyards, or a bay full of sailboats and Chinese mussels. So we have to look to human origins for the kind of naturalized city made up of green and blue open spaces among the built-up zones of the metropolis.

On closer inspection, the naturalized landscape of the Bay Area is a crazy quilt of parks, reserves, refuges, and other kinds of open spaces, protected by a panoply of laws and governments. In this metropolis of 8.5 million people, the fourth largest in the United States, over one-quarter of its territory (1.25 million acres) has been set aside as what local environmentalists call "secure greenbelt." It is not, in fact, a belt at all, but an interwoven patchwork of over two hundred protected areas within fifty miles of San Francisco, which add up to considerably more land than Yosemite National Park—and that does not include the even larger area protected by the Bay Conservation and Development Commission and the California Coastal Commission, or three oceanic reserves off the coast.

Hence, the naturalized Bay Area landscape that locals and visitors visualize as a wonder of nature is a thoroughly socialized and artificially maintained part of the metropolis. The greensward is an act of social engineering. Without that intervention, there might be very little open space left, no beautiful vistas to contemplate, no beaches to swim at, no lovely parks to picnic in. The Marin Headlands, Point Reyes, and the rest of the coast would be lined with houses, Mount San Bruno and Angel Island leveled, the bay filled with rubble, and freeways shooting in all directions. That this did not occur is due to repeated mobilizations, battles, and laws, not just the presence of an inspirational nature. Every inch of open space has been fought for. The metro-natural Bay Area landscape rests firmly on the unnaturally successful accomplishments of popular efforts at conservation.

The Country in the City

While it is commonplace to say that the city is reworked nature and that nature in the city is massively altered, we need to take a closer look at the geography of how that mutual transformation unfolds. The making of urban nature takes place through the encounter between city and country. To begin with, cities demand a countryside to service their metabolic needs for minerals, food, energy, and water, as well as to absorb city refuse, and this creates an urbanized countryside. The urban extraction of rural resources is usually presented as taking place at great distances, but it is, if anything, more intense close by the city, as Von Thünen noted two hundred years ago. The urban periphery is the backyard of the city and fiercely exploited.[5]

Next, the geography of city and country is deeply interdigitated; the city does not just march over rural areas in a "the wall of sprawl," as local environmentalists call it. In fact, the metropolis expands in solar bursts along transportation routes and topographies of least resistance, enveloping rural landscapes. Meanwhile, rural land uses are reconstituted in the interstices, and the countryside never entirely disappears; it becomes interwoven with the city. In the Bay Area, for example, large swaths of land are still reserved as watersheds for domestic water supply and grazing land for dairy cattle. Some rural activities, such as gravel quarries, actually intensify as the suburbs engulf them. A remarkable instance of this is the expansion of the wine industry in Napa and Sonoma counties, sporting vineyards planted with the precision of subdivisions.[6]

In short, city and country coevolve and their boundaries are ever-changing. The green spaces of the metropolis begin not as leftovers of an archaic nature or an agrarian paradise; they are urban-rural hybrids of considerable extent. In the nine-county Bay Area, which consists of roughly 4.5 million acres, only three-quarters of a million acres lie beneath buildings and pavements. By contrast, agricultural, grazing and forest lands occupy about 1.75 million areas, and at the center of it all is the bay, another three-quarters of a million acres. The metropolitan landscape is, thus, a coat of many colors—yellow, green, brown, black, blue, and gold—made up of fields, woods, highways, houses, creeks, and reservoirs.

Moreover, as city and countryside collided in the Bay Area, something entirely different arose, a third kind of space. People like Dorothy Erskine, who cared deeply about local landscapes, were moved to demand the conservation of open spaces as part of the urban experience. From their lead a social movement was born to conserve the metro-natural landscape by reworking former bits of countryside into new elements of the city and reaching out into the working countryside to outflank the exploding metropolis. This movement to create metropolitan open spaces, or popular urban natures, was born of a reaction to the bulldozers of development leveling the familiar bits of the urbanized countryside and the desire to keep hold of ruralized nature as a counterpoint to the city.

A Culture of Metropolitan Nature

Why did Dorothy Erskine and her comrades love local landscapes so much that they were determined to save them? The geographer Yi-Fu Tuan calls the love of familiar landscapes *topophilia*, but it is too static a notion to explain popular views of nature in a dynamic urban setting. The continual mingling of country and city complicates the geography of environmental sentiment, as does the quilting of the protected landscape of the greenbelt. Raymond Williams, looking critically at the English ideology of landscape, showed how the deep connections between the urban and rural in early modern England gave rise to a distinctive "structure of feeling" about that country's green and pleasant land.[7] In the Bay Area, too, a structure of feeling about green and open spaces has emerged out of the encounter of city and country and the protection of urbanized nature.

Bay Area environmentalism is a product neither of an abstract love of nature nor of the elevated values of urban life, but of dreams of rural idylls

Figure 6.1
Mission Peak Regional Park, east side of Silicon Valley, ca. 2004. Photo copyright
Alvin Docktor.

turning into nightmares of urbanization. It was born in the transitional
realm where city and country collide, where housing developments laid
waste to oak savannas, freeways ran roughshod over hill and dale, and garbage dumps encroached on the bay. Contrary to the view that American
conservation arose chiefly from an ideology of wilderness,[8] the most valued
natures have often been the ones nearest the city. In the Bay Area, these
include such cherished venues as Muir Woods, Mt. Tamalpais, and Mt. Diablo, as well as the familiar landscapes of the Palo Alto foothills, Mission
Peak, and Carquinez Straits (see figure 6.1). These are the most accessible,
visible, and threatened of urban natures and the sites of defining fights over
open space in the San Francisco region. They are not a passive backdrop to
the city, but zones of social conflict where a love of hybrid natures has been
acquired through battle. Every inch of protected open space vibrates with
history; the greenbelt is a living landscape redolent with meaning.[9]

A local structure of feeling, or popular culture of nature in the city, has been constructed on the basis of the material achievements of the conservationists and the quilt of naturalized spaces they created. It is inculcated among the general public through experiences of hiking, going to the beach, riding a ferry, or looking at the scenery. Living in and around a protected San Francisco Bay is the keystone of the whole edifice. Schools teach conservation, environmental organizations preach it, and the popular press affirms it. Everyday life and the ordinary practices of residents of the Bay Area lead easily to their becoming "metro-naturals," who share a unified and naturalized sense of the landscape.

Geographers have long grappled with this process of consciousness formation in relation to material landscapes. Kenneth Olwig refers to the sense of identification with local surroundings as an "invisible fellowship of the landscape." Allen Pred has investigated the "everyday world of being and becoming" in reference to modernity. Alex Loftus speaks of an "everyday environmentalism" arising from oppositional practice and class conflict. Henri Lefebvre famously declared the all modern experience has become urban, resonating between landscapes and representations. These ideas surely apply to the naturalized spaces of the urban greenbelt and the culture of nature inculcated in and through it.[10]

Furthermore, the Bay Area culture of nature is an ethical universe. Moral value is placed on the greenbelt, which is seen as the city's saving grace. On the one hand, open space naturalizes the metropolis with greenery, vistas, and wildlife; on the other hand, open space humanizes the city by providing places to play, think and escape. Moreover, a city is rendered more humane because its green lands are as much human- as nature-made and the product of popular action; therein lies their secret pleasure and moral worth.[11]

Resplendent Nature in the City

The story of the metro-natural landscape of the Bay Area does not end with the human achievement of setting aside and learning to love the green quilt of open space. Although there is no longer very much, if any, primal "First Nature" in the city, the metropolis is not undifferentiated "Second Nature," as one might think from some theorizing about modern environments.[12] Urban natures are hybrids in several senses. For one, the metropolis features a wide variety of spaces and ecologies; not only are the streets of San Jose a far cry from the uncut redwoods of Big Basin, they are also different from the backyards, community gardens, and mini-parks tucked into the urban fabric. A second sense of hybridity in urban natures is in how similar background conditions have been worked up into vastly different results: both the rows of boxy houses of the Sunset District and the tree-covered reaches of Golden Gate Park were carved out of enormous sand dunes on the western flank of San Francisco. A third dimension of hybridity is the way urban natures have been reworked over time. This is clear in the built-up areas, which have been reconstructed time and again in the old central cities; but even a place as wild as Point Reyes bears the imprint of successive use for fishing, grazing, second homes, and tourism.[13]

At the same time as we admit the transformed, humanized, and hybrid nature of urban natures, there is more to it than that. We need another term that speaks to the kind of verdant natures that endlessly crop up in the city, from backyard bees in Oakland to feral turkeys in Berkeley to the teeming benthos of San Pablo Bay. I like to think of these resplendent green and blue places as "Third Nature." Urban ecologies have an amazing resilience, an overlooked fact that has been crucial to the success of popular urban natures from Cape Town to Boston. Cut back on pollution, and oysters can get reestablished. Open the dikes on the salt ponds, and marshlands reappear. Stop poisoning coyotes, and they roam the streets of San Francisco (much to the chagrin of pet owners). Of course, some of these revivals require more human intervention than others: clapper rails remain a fragile wetland species, while wild boar run amok in the oak woodlands. In this sense, urban natures are not just social products (Second Nature) or even socionatural hybrids; they are altered natural systems that nonetheless retain a certain autonomy and causal force.[14] That is, they have powers of recuperation that fill up the open, ruralized, and naturalized spaces of the city and alter ideas about city and country and practices of urban living, including conservation efforts. They, too, are metro-natural.

In sum, what we see in the San Francisco case is a long-term spiral of city and country, reservation of green spaces, a culture of nature, and recuperated natures developing synchronously and chronologically. This interplay of nature, social practice, and structures of feeling is the multiple hybrid I am calling the "metro-natural landscape." It is the first step to understanding what is meant by popular urban nature in the Bay Area. But there are two more steps to a full comprehension of the achievement of a metro-natural region.

Politicizing Nature in the City

We can only get so far in coming to grips with the constitution of popular urban natures by resting in the realm of the geographic encounter between people and landscape in the city. We have to move to a different plane of analysis, that of politics, to inquire how a century of environmental activism in the San Francisco region stitched together such an enormous metropolitan greenbelt. One can draw three important lessons from that experience. The first lesson is that the people of the Bay Area became well organized in the defense of open space and succeeded in building a mass environmental movement. Second, the social nature of the Bay Area has been critical to the ability of a mass green movement to prosper in the public realm. Third, green politics in the region developed in a favorable political environment with deep traditions of public interest politics and progressive thought.

Building a Popular Movement

Bay Area environmentalism is a social movement that grew from many seeds and continues to flourish right up to the present. A first step to success was to get organized. Strong green organizations have been essential to bringing people together, mobilizing resources, and providing leadership. They have, moreover, been critical instruments for transmitting the prevailing culture of urban nature. Popular uprisings have generated hundreds of green groups seeking to preserve creeks and tidelands, groves and hillsides, trails and scenic views, beaches and wildlife.[15]

Organizing at different scales has also been vital, given the many levels of US urban politics. Local organization is one leg of the movement, embedding it in everyday experiences and demands; the other leg is regional organization, which has provided a broader perspective and more durable presence. The most important regional organizations are the Marin Conservation League, Save Mount Diablo, Committee for Green Foothills, Save the Bay, and the Greenbelt Alliance—the latter two stretching across the whole Bay Area. The Sierra Club and the Trust for Public Land also maintained a strong regional presence even as they went on to national prominence. Organizations of different scales have allowed the movement to encompass

Figure 6.2
Founders of the Sempervirens Club at Big Basin Redwoods State Park, 1900. Courtesy
of History San Jose.

a range of visions and respond to issues at the appropriate scale or to jump
scale, as needed.[16]

Most of the green organizations of the Bay Area got a leg up thanks to
the initiative of upper-class conservationists. Prominent businessmen and
members of the local elite founded the Sierra Club, Sempervirens Club (see
figure 6.2), and Save the Redwoods League around the turn of the nineteenth century. Wives of bankers and professors established the Marin Conservation League, Save the Bay, and the Committee for Green Foothills at
midcentury. The prominence of the upper classes was especially marked
in both periods. Old monied families, like the Alexanders and Kents, contributed to green causes, while family members from Caroline Livermore
to Sylvia McLaughlin mobilized their networks in support of green organizations. More recently, wealthy philanthropists from Silicon Valley,
such as the Moores and Packards, have poured money into green causes
in the region.[17] Equally important is the upper middle class of educated

professionals, especially around the universities at Berkeley and Stanford, who have provided key leadership for the movement. The movement has drawn on the large pool of intellectuals swimming in the buoyant waters of Bay Area cosmopolitanism, starting with Joseph LeConte and John Muir in the late nineteenth century, through Progressive-Era academics such as David Starr Jordan and William Dudley, to postwar writers like Raymond Dasmann and Ernest Callenbach.

Despite its elite origins, however, environmentalism metamorphosed into a mass movement in the Bay Area—the world's first such popular uprising for nature protection. In the 1960s, the Sierra Club, Save the Bay Association, and Save Our Seashore ballooned from a few hundreds to tens of thousands of members by appealing to the general public to defend San Francisco Bay, Point Reyes, and the Colorado River. The bay, above all, became a wildly popular cause that converted vast numbers of locals (including me) to the legions of green. This mass appeal ultimately drew hundreds of thousands of supporters into green organizations across the region by the late twentieth century. The middle class has been eager to support Bay Area open space, and so has a working class mindful of the need for clean air, energy conservation, and recreational areas. The unions have often lent their voices to conservation causes such as the formation of the East Bay Regional Parks in the 1930s, the Golden Gate National Recreation Area in the 1970s, and urban growth boundaries in Sonoma County in the 1990s. Over the last twenty years, people of color—who make up most of the contemporary California working class—have been prominent in campaigns to control pollution and have voted in large majorities for more parks.

To outsiders, it may be hard to believe that there could be so wide a popular alliance behind conservation in the Bay Area. After all, schisms over environmental issues between workers and elites or between whites and blacks are legion in the United States, and often worse in the global South. I have no wish to deny the reality of social injustice in the bay region, the racial blindness of upper-class whites, or the tensions between greens and environmental justice activists in places like West Oakland and Richmond.[18] Nevertheless, the breadth of the popular movement for nature protection in the Bay Area is striking, and one sees less of the reactionary outlook among the upper classes that open space is to be defended *against* the rabble than one sees in cities like Delhi or Cape Town.[19] The question is, why?

A Favorable Social Environment

Political economy has undoubtedly played an important part in the Bay Area's environmental politics and metro-naturalism. Rapid and repeated growth since the Gold Rush has meant that the region never wallowed in the kind of distress that gives rise to appeals to development at any cost or, worse, the race to the bottom by cutting taxes and neglecting social infrastructure. The Bay Area economy has long been on the high road of economic development via investment, innovation, and entrepreneurship. As Michael Storper argues, the social dimension of political economy is decisive for explaining urban innovation; it requires a rich matrix of formal and informal institutions that bond economic actors together and bridge gaps between disparate economic networks. The Bay Area not only has such a matrix, but has built a strong sense of identity and mobilization around its innovative character. The result is the richest metropolitan area per capita in the United States with the highest percentages of billionaires and millionaires, creating an ample reservoir of funds to support green organizations and causes.[20]

The class structure of the Bay Area has been very favorable to environmentalists. Along with its many wealthy families and prosperous businesses, the area is noted for a high-end employment base in electronics and the internet, war and security, medicine and biotech, higher education, and finance, administration, and business services. These sectors have demanded a well-educated technical, managerial, and professional labor force, which is why the region has the most college graduates per capita of any US metro area and second most PhDs. This large upper middle class has provided many potential adherents to the environmental movement and capable leaders for the green organizations of the metropolis. Furthermore, there has been a substantial white-collar middle class consisting of teachers, nurses, office workers, and the like, as well as a skilled and well-paid blue-collar working class that has fought for its fair share of the pie. There is, of course, a substantial lower working class toiling in menial jobs without protections, made up overwhelmingly of immigrants and their children. Their conditions are often lamentable, but because of continued growth, influx of new recruits and upward mobility, no large, permanent underclass has formed. The result has been a higher average income and lower poverty rate than in any other city in the United States, let alone any of the metropoles of the global South.[21]

Another factor attenuating the effect of class is the cross-cutting influence of gender. The most important group of rebel spirits in the Bay Area has been women, who have served as the shock troops of the conservation movement.[22] Women like Dorothy Erskine, Amy Meyer, and Janet Adams are the unsung heroes of popular environmentalism in the Bay Area. Through the middle of the twentieth century, such women were usually college-educated mothers and housewives married to businessmen and professors. More recently, they have been lawyers, scientists, and managers in their own right, filling the ranks of green nonprofits. Why have women been so prominent? On the one hand, they may be upper class but they are rarely capitalists; the male domination of business and family has always raised questions about how class and gender intersect. Conversely, women's role as prime caregivers and nurturers has meant an intense involvement with human well-being. Their affinity for metro-naturalism has often arisen from such things as the loss of woods where children play, contamination of drinking water, or fumes from nearby factories, not just views of the Golden Gate.[23]

Swimming in Progressive Seas

The green movement in the Bay Area has had a distinctly progressive cast over the last century, a key dimension of the metro-naturalism of the place. On the metric of opposition to capital's unchecked ambitions, Bay Area greens get high marks. Groups like Save the Bay, Committee for Green Foothills, and Save Mount Diablo have consistently taken uncompromising stands against real estate promoters, industrialists, and the state over large scale developments, whether for new towns, research parks, or highways. Similarly, regional environmental organizations like the Greenbelt Alliance, Communities for a Better Environment, and the Sierra Club have been among the strongest opponents of forms of production, transportation, and suburbanization that increase energy use and poison the city—and people of color—with refinery emissions, diesel fumes, and other air pollution.

From its origins in the Progressive Era, conservation politics in the Bay Area took a more militant, preservationist turn, and its organizations maintained a greater degree of commitment to public parks than contemporaries such as the Boone and Crockett Club in New York. Berkeley graduates Stephen Mather and Horace Albright created the National Park Service in the 1910s. Save the Redwoods League started out believing in private parks and ended up as the chief advocate for the state parks system in the 1920s, behind realtor Duncan McDuffie. In the 1930s, the Marin Conservation League was already demanding (and winning) local land use planning to control urban growth. In the postwar era, the Sierra Club kept going down a road less traveled behind the likes of Dave Brower, Martin Litton, and Dwight Steele, as they turned against mainstream conservation on issues like nuclear power, multiple use, and clear-cutting. In the 1960s, San Franciscans led the first revolt against freeway mania, pushed for regional greenbelt planning, and froze development of the bay and the coast. Following that, the first popular opposition to dams and pesticides came out of Northern California in the 1970s. And so it has continued to the present, whether in the Greenbelt Alliance's demand for full protection of another million acres of open space in the region or Silicon Valley Toxic Coalition's campaigns to control global electronic waste.

Why this progressive cast to the popular green politics of the Bay Area? The political coloration of popular social movements is by no means a given of mass mobilization nor of a favorable social structure. Populist movements have often taken a conservative turn, and environmentalists have frequently demonstrated a weak commitment to environmental justice across class and race lines.[24] Bay Area metro-naturalism derives from a distinctive political environment and trajectory of conservation politics.

First, given the well-heeled character of so many Bay Area greens, there is a strong element of class interest in guarding metropolitan open space; the bourgeoisie are prodigious consumers of space, with large properties, a capacious sense of entitlement, and a love of scenic views (what Williams called "pleasing prospects"). Nonetheless, many of the elite have gone against the grain of class interest to question the profit-making that provided their family fortunes and elevated incomes. One reason is that they have so often been forced to defend the redoubts of privilege from the unrelenting onslaught of industry, commerce, and land development. The Bay Area's dynamic economy has provided plenty of grist for the conservationist mill, from clear-cutting redwoods in Marin to filling the bay to create Foster City to covering the foothills behind Stanford with industrial parks.[25] But there is more to why Bay Area conservationists came to question untrammeled profit-making from land and to stand "in opposition to blind progress," as they have often put it.

A second element of a progressive green movement is the strong legacy of public lands that resulted from federal ownership of large portions of the western states. While in states like Nevada the federal presence evokes resentment, in California, where much more land was privatized in the nineteenth century, continuing federal stewardship has been a foundation for conservationists to protect vast acreages in national parks, wilderness areas, and national forests. This notion of public lands has carried over to the state parks system and, aided by state control of coastal waters up to the high tide mark, to the establishment of many state beaches, the protection of the coast and of San Francisco Bay, and the creation of offshore state and federal oceanic reserves.[26]

A third source is a commitment to the "public interest," a legacy of the Progressive reform tradition in California. Popular revolts marked by the Second Constitutional Convention of 1879, the victory of Hiram Johnson and the Progressive Republicans in 1911, and the New Deal era of the late 1930s and 1940s unleashed waves of reform of politics, government, and the use of natural resources. The postwar environmental movement renewed that tradition, with Bay Area metro-naturals firmly committed to the idea of *public* space: parks, reserves, and offshore waters dedicated to public use, open to all, and treated as common property. Even in wealthy Marin County, vast tracts are readily accessible and widely used by people from other counties. The East Bay Regional Parks are well stocked with public swimming lakes, picnic areas, and playing fields enjoyed by millions of working-class families. Save the Bay not only fought against fill, it demanded public access to the waterfront, and the same is true of coastal campaigners; as a result, piers, paths, and beaches are packed with folks from all walks of life. This is quite at odds with the experience in places like Westchester County, New York, or the shores of Chesapeake Bay, which have lots of wildlife reserves but little public land or public access.[27]

Last, Bay Area environmentalism has drawn on many radical currents prevalent in the region. Such ideological cross-dressing includes socialism, anarchism, antimodernism, eastern religions, gay and women's liberation, and lifestyle countercultures. For example, Gary Snyder, an inspirational writer of deep green persuasion, combines Zen, bioregionalism, and Wobbly sentiments in a seamless whole. Kenneth Rexroth, whose bohemian soirees launched the Beat movement in San Francisco, loved backpacking in the Sierra as much as anarchism and Chinese poetry. Robert Walker, whose powerful photographs played a key role in saving Mount Diablo, founded the Gay Sierrans within the Sierra Club. In short, green is one of the colors on the rainbow flag of the Left Coast, where politics and cultures have long been out of step with the rest of America.[28]

To summarize, the success of popular movements for nature conservation in the San Francisco region has been a broad-based political achievement, made possible by a wide array of green organizations, leadership and funds from the upper classes, hard work by dedicated women and men, appeals to the public interest that cross class and race lines, and fight after fight against the unrelenting forces of development.

Governing Nature in the City

Beyond the urban encounters with nature discussed in the first section of this chapter and the elements of political style analyzed in the second, a third arena has been vital to the creation of the metro-natures of the San Francisco Bay Area. The triumph of popular conservation could not have been realized without three key facets of urban government: planning, regulation, and science. These speak to the idea of "technological natures" in the urban field and the influence of planners, administrators, and intellectuals. While supporters of popular urban natures such as Henrik Ernstson take a suspicious view of expertise and top-down approaches to governing urban natures, popular mobilization is rarely sufficient by itself. Without the state, planning, and expertise, opposition to the machinery of capitalist growth and urban expansion would rest on weak reeds; the people are wise and strong in many ways, but they have to mobilize higher powers to instantiate their vision of metro-naturalism.[29]

Planning and Regional Vision

Like so many social movements, Bay Area conservation has all too frequently involved defensive, piecemeal actions by local groups feeling the hot breath of the bulldozers on their neck of the woods. Nonetheless, an overarching vision of containment of the city emerged to provide some guidance to the swirling battles all around the metropolitan area. This has been the function of one organization above all, People for Open Space, founded by Dorothy Erskine and Jack Kent in the 1950s to bring recreation planning to the metropolitan region, and transformed into the Greenbelt Alliance by

William Evers and Larry Orman in the 1980s to provide a regional vision for proliferating local antigrowth movements. The story of Bay Area environmentalism cannot be told without the influence of planning and planners, who were crucial in turning the fight from one of conserving natural areas to battling the juggernaut of urban expansion. Land-use conflicts have shown, time and again, the need to tackle the logics of sprawl, housing supply, and local land use regulation. Conservationists have had to join forces with urban planners to rewrite the rules of the game of urban growth and land use controls. In the process, urbanization stopped being taken as an unquestioned good or unchallenged rule of economics, as in so much of the United States, and was rethought, reconfigured, and redirected.[30]

Several strategies have been tried in the effort for urban containment. One was to seek metropolitan government. It has been a planning mantra going back to the Progressive Era that if government can be rationalized, good land use will follow. As postwar US cities flew apart into thousands of suburban pieces, municipal fragmentation came under heavy fire from planners and political scientists, with the Bay Area a center of government reform agitation in the 1950s. Metropolitan government never got far, however, given the American faith in "home rule."[31] Nonetheless, planning reformers got the California legislature to require local general plans with open space elements and conforming zoning regulations, which green activists have used to good effect ever since.

The legislature even gave the toothless Association of Bay Area Governments (ABAG) the job of preparing a regional growth plan in 1970. ABAG's planners were emboldened to produce a document calling for city-centered development and a greenbelt covering one-third of the region. As Kent observed, "There is no other metropolitan region in the USA that has ever said there ought to be a big permanent greenbelt around its existing system of central cities."[32] Local politicians and developers killed the official plan, but the greens were not daunted. They used the plan as a guidebook for a Greenbelt Action Program that would marry comprehensive planning for housing, employment, transportation, and open space with popular mobilization along the lines of Save the Bay. Forty years later, they have achieved most of what the regional plan called for.

Local communities aided the greenbelt planners by an upsurge of municipal struggles against untrammeled urban development in the 1970s, which came to be called the Growth Control movement. The little city of Petaluma shocked the world of planning law by establishing a maximum number of housing units per year, keeping the 101 highway strip under rein, protecting its historic downtown, and maintaining a visual break between the urban and the rural. San Jose—the poster child of post-war sprawl—did an about-face to adopt an urban service limit line, development fees on subdividers, and a strong general plan, becoming denser than any other Sunbelt city, as a result. The most far-reaching change came to Marin County, which imposed a general plan that put the entire west county off limits to development.[33]

Meanwhile, the Greenbelt Alliance started putting staff in the suburbs to work with local growth-control groups to provide planning expertise and a regional vision. It thereby helped build a regional greenbelt from *both* the bottom up *and* the top down. As a result, the movement to harness city growth in the Bay Area did not degenerate into a grab bag of local turf fights, but became a collective project greater than the sum of its parts. This was exactly the kind of popular movement consolidation that Raymond Williams envisioned in his concept of "militant particularism."[34]

Greening the State

The regulatory and administrative powers of the state have been absolutely necessary to the success of the metro-naturals of the Bay Area. Law and government are the solid reef that the conservation movement built out of its political victories, one that has grown piece by piece to make the greenbelt a permanent feature of the urban landscape and city life in the region. Contemporary social theory has difficulty with the dialectics of social movements and state power: the Right dismisses state action as useless interference with the "free market"; the liberal center denatures the state by speaking only of "governance" not of the hard structures of government; and the Foucaldian Left focuses on "governmentality," or the state's efforts to shape social subjects. In the struggle over urban space, however, the role of law and state power cannot be overlooked in the people's struggles for a "right to the city," as Don Mitchell and James Holston have observed.[35]

The Bay Area greenbelt is made up of a multitude of government-owned parks, reserves, and open spaces at every scale—national, state, county, regional, and city. The first such urban parks were created in the nineteenth century, but the modern chains of parks took shape only in the 1930s with

New Deal support. After World War II, money flowed briskly from state and local governments, which enjoyed ample tax revenues and easy sale of government bonds. Hundreds of thousands of acres were put aside around the Bay Area during the high tide of park making. The wolf came to the door in 1978 with the tax revolt in California, which cut government revenues dramatically and dried up acquisition funds.[36] Yet a strange thing happened on the way to ruin: people in the Bay Area kept voting for bond issues and special taxes to enlarge the parks system.

Most parks were created for recreation, even as they protected some of California's prime scenery and natural wonders. Recreational parks and excursions were vital to the development of mass environmentalism in the postwar era because they taught large numbers of people the pleasures of outdoor activity and inculcated a love of forests, beaches, and rivers. At the same time, the parks demanded rangers and other administrators, who developed the arts of managing these naturalized spaces in and around the city; the necessary managerial, ecological, and public relations expertise was by no means self-evident and had to be learned through trial and error.[37]

Meanwhile, powerful regulatory bodies were established to defend San Francisco Bay and the California coast, as well as to control air and water pollution. The bay and coast are essential to San Francisco's famously scenic setting, but their destruction was assured had not the greens won permanent protections from the state in 1965 and 1972, respectively. The Bay Conservation and Development Commission has been spectacularly successful and was cited by the first United Nations Conference on the Human Environment as a model of citizens' initiatives. The creation of the California Coastal Commission, the Coastal Conservancy, and offshore state and federal marine reserves followed in short order.[38]

Science for the People

Popular organizations and state officials have all depended on the expertise of scientists and the spread of scientific insights in their efforts to build and manage the Bay Area greenbelt. The region has a particularly sophisticated public and many well-educated activists, so the level of environmental knowledge has been high going back to the late nineteenth century. Scientific research and education have gone hand in hand with public mobilizations on behalf of urban natures, and the Bay Area has often been a fountainhead of environmental science as part of its leading role in land and water conservation.[39]

The local environmental movement has been bolstered repeatedly by Bay Area scientists trained in ecology, geography, and forestry, who have questioned everything from pesticide abuse to the viability of high dams. They have been crucial in providing the green organizations with technical expertise, speaking to councils of government, and infusing the movement with new ideas. The same has been true of the development of planning theory in the Bay Area, backed up by some of the first sophisticated critiques of suburban sprawl and New Urbanist theories of high density development.[40]

One important advance is the growth of knowledge about San Francisco Bay, including the earliest extensive research on estuarine systems, which has been followed up by years of research on the fiercely contested Sacramento River and Delta system. The San Francisco Estuary Institute studies invasive species in the continent's most altered estuarine ecosystem, while research on ocean upwelling, phytoplankton, and marine productivity has flourished, especially around the Farallon Islands and Monterey Bay. Wetlands restoration science is more advanced here than anywhere else, as is wildlife rescue at the Marine Mammal Center.[41]

Another highly developed arena of knowledge construction about urban natures in the Bay Area is that of toxic pollution and health. Some of the earliest studies of radiation poisoning, chemical toxicity, electronics dumping, and body-burden were done here in conjunction with the activist work of groups like Communities for a Better Environment, Breast Cancer Action, the Silicon Valley Toxics Coalition, and the Natural Resources Defense Council. Environmental health science has been advanced thanks to the region's large medical research complex and hefty funding from the socially oriented California Wellness Foundation, the HealthCare Foundation, and the Kaiser Foundation.[42]

In order to instantiate popular demands for nature in the urban landscape, it is not enough to have great green ideas and political movements. It is necessary to build solid frameworks of planning, science, and government. Without this, we end up romanticizing popular struggles that have little long-term impact on cities. The imprint of popular natures in the San Francisco Bay Area has been grounded in the durability of green governance in this environmentally minded region.

Conclusion: Beyond the Bay

San Francisco is only one of many global metropoles, and the development of popular natures in the Bay Area has to be seen in relation to geographies at multiple scales from the local to the global; the metropolitan is only one such scale.[43] No place in the modern world stands alone, least of all a crossroads of technology, finance, and commerce such as the Bay Area. The region's environmentalism has always been informed by dialogue with national and worldwide visions of nature, politics, and government. But more than that, San Francisco has a distinctive place in the history of environmentalism because the force of its local popular urban nature has carried far beyond the boundaries of the metropolis.[44]

In fact, the Bay Area has been a leader in US conservation ideas, organizations, and politics from the outset. It fought for what was effectively first national park (Yosemite Valley) in the 1860s and the second and third (Yosemite and Sequoia) in the 1890s, created the first land trust to protect redwoods in 1901, gave birth to the National Park Service in the 1910s, and led the way in the movement for state parks in the 1920s. In the postwar era, it was a force in promoting car camping and outdoor recreation, developing rock climbing and backpacking, and agitating for wilderness and wild river protection nationally. In the 1960s, it was the first place to stop the US freeway mania in its tracks, create mass environmental organizations, and protect agricultural areas with conservation reserves. By the early 1970s, it had achieved an unprecedented level of protection for the surrounding bay, coastal zone, and ocean waters, becoming a model for the country. It created the first national seashore and the first urban national park, as well as leading the drive to double the size of the national park system through the Alaska Lands Act. By the 1980s, the Bay Area was well ahead of the pack in using land trusts and conservation easements, instituting local growth controls, and requiring energy and water conservation.

Yet, the influence of the San Francisco metropole goes even farther. Bay Area greens did more than "Think globally, act locally" (a slogan coined in Berkeley in the 1960s); they went on to enact their visions on the global stage, after laying down solid foundations in the region. In Neil Smith's term they "jumped scales," taking their experiences worldwide and showing a concern for global natures in advance of most places.[45] A student leader at Stanford, David Harris, came up with the idea of Earth Day in 1970. In the 1980s, David Brower established the Earth Island Institute to incubate dozens of environmental groups worldwide, such as Baikal Watch and the International Marine Mammal Project. Friends of the River, formed to fight dams in California (where high-dam engineering originated), became the International Rivers Network operating in sixty countries. The Pesticide Action Network, created to fight California's chemically saturated agriculture, quickly went global and now counts six hundred partners organized in five continental groups. Rainforest Action Network based by the bay has been a key defender of the Amazon and Southeast Asian tropical ecosystems. The Goldman Prize, funded by San Francisco philanthropists, salutes environmental activists around the world. Critical Mass, the bicyclists' monthly challenge to car-dominated cities, has spread from San Francisco to cities around the globe. In other words, Bay Area green politics have impacted the rest of the world by virtue of an abundance of ideas, leaders, organizations, knowledge, funders, and alliances. It has been a fount of innovation in the realm of environmental policy, just as it has in the world of electronics and the internet.

The Bay Area's success in defending popular urban natures stands on three pillars. It begins with a metro-naturalism, or love of naturalized urban landscapes, rooted in a virtuous circle of saving open spaces and learning through everyday experience. Just as important, San Francisco built a popular green politics that featured strong organizations and dedicated leaders with a commitment to public access; in the process, green became one among many colors of the Left Coast's progressive flag because of its opposition to mindless growth and dedication to the public good. Finally, green sentiments have translated into a solid framework of law and regulation, land use planning and environmental science that maintain the Bay Area's hard-won endowment of protected land and waters.

In all this, time matters as well as space and place. Ideas and practices change with new challenges, as seen in the epochal shifts in conservation policies in the Progressive, New Deal, Postwar and Neoliberal eras. Today is an entirely new epoch for the environmental movement, one that presents severe new challenges to which popular forces and state policies must rise if any number of disasters are to be averted. Given the menace of global climate change, merely saving urban green spaces can seem as archaic as creating picturesque gardens in eighteenth-century century Britain. California is being hit by shrinking snowpack, more erratic rainfall, hotter summers, raging wildfires, and rising sea levels, to which people and governments must now respond. In the twenty-first century, the Bay Area is once more leading the way on a range of policies for renewable energy, carbon emissions reduction, and green building strategies to combat climate change.[46] That far-sighted approach to new challenges owes thanks to the legacy of environmentalism in the region, a citizenry well informed on the dangers of unbridled growth, and a state habituated to the need to regulate and plan for a sustainable future. A local culture of popular natures with deep roots and a strong political base is once again sending forth new green shoots.

Acknowledgments

Thanks to Henrik Ernstson and James Evans for their helpful comments.

Notes

1. This chapter draws on my in-depth study of conservation in the bay region, *The Country in the City: The Greening of the San Francisco Bay Area* (Walker 2007). Sources for all factual claims can be found in that book.

2. On the city as hybrid, see Swyngedouw (2006) and Heynen, Kaika, and Swyngedouw (2006).

3. Erskine 1976, p. 141.

4. Brechin 1999; Dreyfus 2008; Booker 2013.

5. Von Thünen 1826; Cronon 1991; Brechin 1999. On urban metabolism, see Wolman (1965).

6. On Bay Area land use, see Santos et al. (2014). On protecting Napa Valley, see Conaway (2002). On its landscape, see Grossinger (2012).

7. Williams 1973; Tuan 1974.

8. Nash 1967; Cronon 1995.

9. Stroud (2012) makes a similar argument about New England's forests.

10. Lefebvre 1970; Pred 1995; Olwig 2002.

11. On the ethical dimension of practice and protest, see Jasper (1997) and Sayer (2011).

12. On Second Nature, see Smith (1984) and Loftus (2012).

13. Watt 2016.

14. Davis 1998; Pollan 1991; Falck 2010; Stroud 2012.

15. For overviews of social movement theory, see Caniglia and Carmin (2005) and Davis et al. (2005). On organizations and social movements, see Minkoff and McCarthy (2005).

16. On scale and politics, see Walker and Heiman (1981), Smith (1992), and Herod (2010).

17. On movement resources and networking, see Diani and McAdam (2003). On elites in US conservation, see Hays (1959), Hurley (1995), and Rothman (1998).

18. On the schisms, see Bullard (1990), Hurley (1995), and White (1996). On continuing racial divides in the Bay Area, see Schafran (2013) and Walker (2018).

19. Contrast the story told by Baviskar in chapter 8 of this volume or by Kosek (2006) for New Mexico.

20. Storper 2013; Storper et al. 2015. Also see Walker (2001, 2008, 2018) and Walker and Lodha (2013). On the importance of resources for social movements, see Davis et al. (2005).

21. Storper et al. (2015). Being the world's greatest center of information technology has meant the amassing of huge fortunes at the top, and this has made the current Bay Area one of the most unequal cities in the United States; Walker (2018).

22. Curiously, women have been all but invisible in US environmental history, until recently. See Musil (2014) and Ungar (2014).

23. On male dominance of business in California, see Walker and Lodha (2013). On the development of women's political consciousness from the domestic outward, see Bookman and Morgan (1988) and Spencer-Wood (1994).

24. On American populism, see Postel (2007). On Southern California populism, see Davis (1990) and McGirr (2001). On environmental justice movements elsewhere, see Bullard (1990) and Hurley (1995).

25. On elite landscape tastes, see Williams (1973) and Heiman (1988). On the contrarian and even radical nature of the Bay Area's elite conservationists, see Erskine (1976), Thiessen (2010), Brower (2012), and Hart and Kittle (2006). For similar observations on New England's gentry, see Stroud (2012).

26. California has more acreage in federal parks than any state except Alaska—and the latter's huge national parks were the brainchild of Sierra Club president and

San Francisco resident, Edgar Weyburn. On battles over western public lands, see Langston (1995), Kosek (2006) and Nie (2008).

27. On the public interest idea in American politics of the Progressive and New Deal eras, see Rogers (2008). For a spirited defense of environmental law as public trust, see Wood (2014). On conservation in Westchester, see Duncan and Duncan (2004).

28. On the Bay Area's left tilt, see DeLeon (1992), Ashbolt (2012), and Walker (2018).

29. See Ernstson (2013), Ernstson and Sörlin (2013), and Lewis and Ernstson (2019). Contentious popular movements are neither ordinary politics nor governance, nor are they entirely outside the state (Tarrow 2012).

30. For a similar view, see Angotti (2008); what he calls "community planning" is a fertile combination of popular activism and guided government action.

31. Scott 1985; Dyble 2009.

32. Kent 1983, p. 59.

33. On the national debate unleashed by Petaluma and other growth control ordinances, see, e.g., Burrows (1978) and Brower, Godschalk, and Porter (1989).

34. Contrast this with the conservative nature of the 1980s "Homeground Revolution" in Los Angeles, portrayed by Davis (1990). On militant particularism, see Harvey (2001).

35. Mitchell 2003; Holston 2008.

36. On local government finances in the twentieth century, see Teaford (1984) and Sbragia (1996). On Proposition 13 and its aftermath, see Martin (2008).

37. On the growth of outdoor recreation, see Hays (1987) and Young (2017). On the difficulties of park and resource management, see Hirt (1994) and Langston (1995).

38. On the Bay Conservation and Development Commission, see Bodowitz (1985). On the Coastal Commission, see Healy (1978).

39. On early environmental science in California, see Smith (1987).

40. For example, Livingston and Blaney (1970); Fellmeth (1973); Van der Ryn and Calthorpe (1986).

41. Nichols et al. 1986; Cohen 1994; Williams Associates and Faber 2004. See also Booker (2013).

42. Belliveau 1981; Szasz 1994; Dillon 2017.

43. On geographic scale, see Massey (1994), Swyngedouw (1997), and Herod (2010).

44. Traditional histories of American conservation were always cast at a national scale; see, e.g., Hays (1969), Nash (1967), and Rothman (1998). That has changed; see, e.g., Klingle (2007) and Stroud (2012).

45. Smith 1992. On the way policies travel internationally, see Rogers (2008).

46. On California's energy and climate policies, see Walker and Lodha (2013), Knuth (2014), and Walker (2018).

References

Angotti, Thomas. 2008. *New York for Sale: Community Planning Confronts Global Real Estate*. Cambridge, MA: MIT Press.

Ashbolt, Anthony. 2012. *A Cultural History of the Radical Sixties in the San Francisco Bay Area*. London: Pickering and Chatto.

Belliveau, Mike. 1981. *Toxics in the Bay*. Oakland: Citizens for a Better Environment.

Bodovitz, Joseph. 1985. "The Shrinking of San Francisco Bay and How It Was Stopped." *California Waterfront Age* 1(4): 21–27.

Booker, Matthew. 2013. *Down by the Bay: San Francisco's History between the Tides*. Berkeley: University of California Press.

Bookman, Ann, and Sandra Morgan, eds. 1988. *Women and the Politics of Empowerment*. Philadelphia: Temple University Press.

Brechin, Gray. 1999. *Imperial San Francisco: Urban Power, Earthly Ruin*. Berkeley: University of California Press.

Brower, David, David Godschalk, and Douglas Porter, eds. 1989. *Understanding Growth Management*. Washington, DC: The Urban Institute.

Brower, Kenneth. 2012. *The Wildness Within: Remembering David Brower*. Berkeley, CA: Heyday Press.

Bullard, Robert. 1990. *Dumping in Dixie: Race, Class and Environmental Quality*. Boulder, CO: Westview Press.

Burrows, Lawrence. 1978. *Growth Management*. New Brunswick, NJ: Center for Urban Policy Research, Rutgers University.

Caniglia, Beth, and JoAnn Carmin. 2005. "Scholarship on Social Movement Organzations: Classic Views and Emerging Trends." *Mobilization* 10(2): 201–212.

Conaway, James. 2002. *The Far Side of Eden: New Money, Old Land, and the Battle for Napa Valley*. Boston: Houghton Mifflin.

Cronon, William. 1991. *Nature's Metropolis: Chicago and the Great West*. New York: Norton.

Cronon, William. 1995. "The Trouble with Wilderness; or, Getting Back to the Wrong Nature." In *Uncommon Ground: Toward Reinventing Nature*, edited by William Cronon, 69–90. New York: W. W. Norton.

Davis, Gerald, Doug McAdam, W. Richard Scott, and Mayer Zald, eds. 2005. *Social Movements and Organizations*. New York: Cambridge University Press.

Davis, Mike. 1990. *City of Quartz: Excavating the Future in Los Angeles*. London: Verso.

Davis, Mike. 1998. *Ecology of Fear: Los Angeles and the Imagination of Disaster*. New York: Metropolitan/Henry Holt.

DeLeon, Richard. 1992. *Left Coast City: Progressive Politics in San Francisco, 1975–1991*. Lawrence: University of Kansas Press.

Diani, Mario, and Doug McAdam, eds. 2003. *Social Movements and Networks: Relational Approaches to Collective Action*. New York: Oxford University Press.

Dillon, Lindsey. 2017. "Pandemonium on the Bay: Naval Station Treasure Island and the Toxic Legacies of Atomic Defense." In *Urban Reinventions: San Francisco's Treasure Island*, edited by Lynne Horiuchi and Tanu Sankalia, 140–158. Honolulu: University of Hawai'i Press.

Dreyfus, Philip. 2008. *Our Better Nature: Environment and the Making of San Francisco*. Norman: University of Oklahoma Press.

Duncan, James, and Nancy Duncan. 2004. *Landscapes of Privilege: The Politics of the Aesthetic in an American Suburb*. New York: Routledge.

Dyble, Louise. 2009. *Paying the Toll: Local Power, Regional Politics and the Golden Gate Bridge*. Philadelphia: University of Pennsylvania Press.

Erskine, Dorothy. 1976. "Environmental Quality and Planning: Continuity of Volunteer Leadership." In *Bay Area Foundation History Series*, vol. 3, Gabrielle Morris and John Jacobs, interviewers, 121–162. Berkeley: Regional Oral History Office, Bancroft Library, University of California.

Ernstson, Henrik. 2013. "Re-Translating Nature in Post-Apartheid Cape Town: The Material Semiotics of People and Plants at Bottom Road." Actor-Network Theory for Development Working Paper Series, edited by Richard Heeks, no. 4. Manchester: Institute for Development Policy and Management, School of Environment, Education and Development, University of Manchester. http://hummedia.manchester.ac.uk/institutes/cdi/resources/cdi_ant4d/ANT4DWorkingPaper4Ernstson.pdf.

Ernstson, Henrik, and Sverker Sörlin. 2013. "Ecosystem Services as Technology of Globalization: On Articulating Values in Urban Nature." *Ecological Economics* 86: 274–284.

Falck, Zachary. 2010. *Weeds: An Environmental History of Metropolitan America*. Pittsburgh: University of Pittsburgh Press.

Fellmeth, Robert. 1973. *The Politics of Land*. New York: Grossman.

Grossinger, Robin. 2012. *Napa Valley Historical Ecology Atlas: Exploring a Hidden Landscape of Transformation and Resilience*. Berkeley: University of California Press.

Hart, John, and Nancy Kittle. 2006. *Legacy: Portraits of 50 Bay Area Environmental Elders*. Photographs by Nancy Kittle; text by John Hart. San Francisco: Sierra Club Books.

Harvey, David. 2001. *Spaces of Hope*. Berkeley: University of California Press.

Harvey, David. 2012. *Rebel Cities: From the Right to the City to the Urban Revolution*. London: Verso.

Hays, Samuel. 1959. *Conservation and the Gospel of Efficiency: The Progressive Conservation Movement, 1890–1920*. Cambridge, MA: Harvard University Press.

Hays, Samuel. 1987. *Beauty, Health and Permanence: Environmental Politics in the United States, 1955–85*. New York: Cambridge University Press.

Healy, Robert, ed. 1978. *Protecting the Golden Shore: Lessons from the California Coastal Commission*. Washington, DC: Conservation Foundation.

Heiman, Michael. 1988. *The Quiet Evolution: Power, Planning and Profits in New York State*. New York: Praeger.

Herod, Andrew. 2010. *Scale*. London: Routledge.

Heynen, Nik, Maria Kaika, and Erik Swyngedouw, eds. 2006. *In the Nature of Cities: Urban Political Ecology and the Politics of Urban Metabolism*. London: Routledge.

Hirt, Paul. 1994. *A Conspiracy of Optimism: Management of the National Forests since World War Two*. Lincoln: University of Nebraska Press.

Holston, James. 2008. *Insurgent Citizenship: Disjunctions of Democracy and Citizenship in Brazil*. Princeton, NJ: Princeton University Press.

Hurley, Andrew. 1995. *Environmental Inequalities: Class, Race, and Industrial Pollution in Gary, Indiana, 1945–1980*. Chapel Hill: University of North Carolina Press.

Jasper, James. 1997. *The Art of Moral Protest*. Chicago: University of Chicago Press.

Kent, T. J. 1983. "T. J. Kent, Jr., Professor and Political Activist: A Career in City and Regional Planning in the San Francisco Bay Area." In *Project on the History of Statewide and Regional Land Use Planning in California, 1950–1980*, vol. 2, 1–125. Berkeley: Regional Oral History Office, Bancroft Library, University of California.

Klingle, Matthew. 2007. *Emerald City: An Environmental History of Seattle*. New Haven, CT: Yale University Press.

Knuth, Sarah. 2014. "Speculating on the Green City: Property and Finance in the Clean Energy Economy." PhD diss., Department of Geography, University of California, Berkeley.

Kosek, Jake. 2006. *Understories: The Political Life of Forests in Northern New Mexico*. Durham, NC: Duke University Press.

Langston, Nancy. 1995. *Forest Dreams, Forest Nightmares: The Paradox of Old Growth in the Inland West.* Seattle: University of Washington Press.

Lefebvre, Henri. 1970. *La revolution urbaine.* Paris: Gallimard.

Lewis, Joshua A., and Henrik Ernstson. 2019. "Contesting the Coast: Ecosystems as Infrastructure in the Mississippi River Delta." *Progress in Planning* 129: 1–30.

Livingston and Blayney. 1970. *Foothills Environmental Design Study: Report No. 3 to the City of Palo Alto.* With assistance of Lawrence Halprin and Associates. San Francisco: Livingston and Blayney.

Loftus, Alex. 2012. *Everyday Environmentalism: Creating an Urban Political Economy.* Minneapolis: University of Minnesota Press.

Martin, Isaac. 2008. *The Permanent Tax Revolt: How the Property Tax Transformed American Politics.* Stanford, CA: Stanford University Press.

Massey, Doreen. 1994. *Space, Place and Gender.* Minneapolis: University of Minnesota Press.

McGirr, Lisa. 2001. *Suburban Warriors: The Origins of the New American Right.* Princeton, NJ: Princeton University Press.

Minkoff, Debra, and John McCarthy. 2005. "Reinvigorating the Study of Organizational Processes in Social Movements." *Mobilization* 10(2): 289–308.

Mitchell, Don. 2003. *The Right to the City: Social Justice and the Fight for Public Space.* New York: Guilford Press.

Musil, Michael. 2014. *Rachel Carson and Her Sisters.* New Brunswick, NJ: Rutgers University Press.

Nash, Roderick. 1967. *Wilderness and the American Mind.* New Haven, CT: Yale University Press.

Nichols, Fred, James Cloern, Samuel Luoma, and David Peterson. 1986. "The Modification of an Estuary." *Science* 231(4738): 567–573.

Nie, Martin. 2008. *The Governance of Western Public Lands: Mapping Its Present and Future.* Lawrence: University of Kansas Press.

Olwig, Kenneth. 2002. *Landscape, Nature and the Body Politic: From Britain's Renaissance to America's New World.* Madison: University of Wisconsin Press.

Pollan, Michael. 1991. *Second Nature: A Gardener's Education.* New York: Grove Press.

Postel, Charles. 2007. *The Populist Vision.* New York: Oxford University Press.

Pred, Allan. 1995. *Recognizing European Modernities: A Montage of the Present.* New York: Routledge.

Rogers, Daniel. 2008. *Atlantic Crossings: Social Politics in a Progressive Era*. Cambridge, MA: Belknap Press of Harvard University Press.

Rothman, Hal. 1998. *The Greening of a Nation? Environmentalism in the United States since 1945*. Fort Worth, TX: Harcourt Brace College Publishers.

Santos, Maria, James Thorne, Jon Christensen, and Zephyr Frank. 2014. "An Historical Land Conservation Analysis in the San Francisco Bay Area: 1850–2010." *Landscape and Urban Planning* 127: 114–123.

Sayer, Andrew. 2011. *Why Things Matter to People: Social Science, Values and Ethical Life*. Cambridge: Cambridge University Press.

Sbragia, Alberta. 1996. *Debt Wish: Entrepreneurial Cities, U.S. Federalism and Economic Development*. Pittsburgh, PA: University of Pittsburgh Press.

Schafran, Alex. 2013. "Origins of an Urban Crisis: The Restructuring of the San Francisco Bay Area and the Geography of Foreclosure." *International Journal of Urban and Regional Research* 37(3): 663–688.

Scott, Mel. 1985. *The San Francisco Bay Area: A Metropolis in Perspective*, rev. ed. Berkeley: University of California Press.

Smith, Michael. 1987. *Pacific Visions: California Scientists and the Environment, 1850–1915*. New Haven, CT: Yale University Press.

Smith, Neil. 1984. *Uneven Development*. Oxford: Basil Blackwell.

Smith, Neil. 1992. "Contours of a Spatialized Politics: Homeless Vehicles and the Production of Geographical Scale." *Social Text* 33: 54–81.

Spencer-Wood, Suzanne. 1994. "Turn of the Century Women's Organizations, Urban Design, and the Origin of the American Playground Movement." *Landscape Journal* 13(2): 125–137.

Storper, Michael. 2013. *The Keys to the City*. Princeton, NJ: Princeton University Press.

Storper, Michael, Thomas Kemeny, Naji Makarem, and Taner Osman. 2015. *The Rise and Fall of Urban Economies: Los Angeles and San Francisco since 1970*. Stanford, CA: Stanford University Press.

Stroud, Ellen. 2012. *Nature Next Door: Cities and Trees in the American Northeast*. Seattle: University of Washington Press.

Swyngedouw, Eric. 1997. "Neither Global nor Local: 'Glocalization' and the Politics of Scale." In *Spaces of Globalization: Reasserting the Power of the Local*, edited by Kevin Cox, 137–166. New York: Guildford Press.

Swyngedouw, Erik. 2006. "Circulations and Metabolisms: (Hybrid) Natures and (Cyborg) Cities." *Science as Culture* 15(2): 105–121.

Szasz, Andrew. 1994. *Ecopopulism: Toxic Waste and the Movement for Environmental Justice*. Minneapolis: University of Minnesota Press.

Tarrow, Sidney. 2012. *Strangers at the Gates: Movements and States in Contentious Politics*. New York: Cambridge University Press.

Teaford, Jon. 1984. *The Unheralded Triumph: City Government in America, 1870–1900*. Baltimore, MD: Johns Hopkins University Press.

Thiessen, Janet. 2010. *Dorothy Erskine: Graceful Crusader for Our Environment*. San Francisco: Dorothy Erskine Biography LLC.

Tuan, Yi-Fu. 1974. *Topophilia: A Study of Environmental Perception, Attitudes and Values*. Englewood Cliffs, NJ: Prentice-Hall.

Unger, Nancy. 2014. *Beyond Nature's Housekeepers: American Women in Environmental History*. Oxford: Oxford University Press.

Van der Ryn, Sim, and Peter Calthorpe. 1986. *Sustainable Communities*. San Francisco: Sierra Club Books.

Von Thünen, Johann. 1826. *Der Isolierte Staat in Beziehung auf Landwirtschaft und Nationalöekonomie*. Hamburg: Perthes: English version: *The Frontier Wage*. Translated by B. Dempsey. Chicago: Loyola University Press, 1960.

Walker, Richard. 2001. "California's Golden Road to Riches: Natural Resources and Regional Capitalism, 1848–1940." *Annals of the Association of American Geographers* 91(1): 167–199.

Walker, Richard. 2007. *The Country in the City: The Greening of the San Francisco Bay Area*. Seattle: University of Washington Press.

Walker, Richard. 2008. "At the Crossroads: Defining California through the Global Economy." In *A Companion to California History*, edited by David Igler and William Deneven, 75–96. Hoboken, NJ: Wiley-Blackwell.

Walker, Richard. 2018. *Pictures of a Gone City: Tech and the Dark Side of Prosperity in the San Francisco Bay Area*. Oakland: PM Press.

Walker, Richard, and Michael Heiman. 1981. "Quiet Revolution for Whom?" *Annals of the Association of American Geographers* 71: 67–83.

Walker, Richard, and Suresh Lodha. 2013. *The Atlas of California: Mapping the Challenge of a New Era*. Berkeley: University of California Press.

Watt, Laura. 2016. *The Paradox of Preservation: Wilderness and Working Landscapes at Point Reyes National Seashore*. Oakland: University of California Press.

White, Richard. 1996. "Are You an Environmentalist, or Do You Work for a Living? Work and Nature." In *Uncommon Ground: Toward Reinventing Nature*, edited by William Cronon, 171–185. New York: W. W. Norton.

Williams Associates and Phyllis Faber. 2004. *Design Guidelines for Tidal Wetland Restoration in San Francisco Bay*. San Francisco: The Bay Institute and the California Coastal Conservancy.

Williams, Raymond. 1973. *The Country and the City*. London: Chatto and Windus.

Wolman, Abel. 1965. "The Metabolism of Cities." *Scientific American* (September): 178–190.

Wood, Mary. 2014. *Nature's Trust: Environmental Law for a New Ecological Age*. New York: Cambridge University Press.

Young, Terence. 2017. *Heading Out: A History of American Camping*. Ithaca, NY: Cornell University Press.

7 Invasion and Citizen Mobilization: Urban Natures in Dalian

Lisa M. Hoffman

It was a warm summer Saturday morning in August 2013 when the group of volunteers met to pull invasive plants in Dalian, a major port city in northeast China. Participants included recent high school graduates and individuals who had been retired for years, men and women, regular activists and new participants. All had gone through training provided by a well-established environmental organization about the targeted plant and its damage to the local ecosystem. After driving to the roadside not far from the universities where the work was to be done, the volunteers pulled protective clothing out of their bags—long sleeved shirts, long pants, gloves, and scarves for their heads and mouths—to ward off scratches and insects (see figure 7.1, *top*). They also shared machetes, clippers, and shovels, and tossed water bottles to each other because of the heat. When I attended another outing with the same organization in the summer of 2011, about twenty-five people congregated to listen to the director describe the invasive weeds and insects that had been introduced with imported plants and were impacting the local ecosystem. They passed around a sample leaf for everyone to see and touch, and then asked participants to pull them, which they did for about an hour before sitting together for lunch, chatting, and taking photos (see figure 7.1, *bottom*).

The physicality and materiality of such volunteering seem to be critical aspects of these experiences—the heat; the chopping, cutting and pulling of the plants; the backs bent and gloved-hands grabbing; the protective clothes; and the shared water, and often shared snacks. The plants themselves, described as invasive, indicative of things out of place and problematic, may be understood as active parts of the social processes of volunteering, which intertwines the work of nongovernmental organizations

Figure 7.1
Top: An environmental volunteer with clothing to protect herself from scratches and insects. *Bottom*: A group of volunteers learning about an invasive plant before setting to work to eradicate it from a local park. Photos by Lisa Hoffman.

(NGOs) with transnational border-crossing politics of exchange gone awry. Rather than taking plant and human as separated, this chapter thus aims to think of them together, as plant-human. It thus asks what we gain by thinking across and through distinctions that typically frame ecological discussions (such as plant/human) rather than focusing on the break between them. As citizens are mobilized to pull these plants out of the ground and engage in ecosystem support, social worlds and collectivities are being constituted; norms of governing are being established; and urban natures are being understood as sites to negotiate government responsibility, individual contributions, natural beauty, economic development, and geopolitics. These voluntary, nongovernmental efforts to dispose of an "alien" species shape both our understandings of responsible urban citizenship and our knowledge of urban natures.

The material here is based on fieldwork in 2011, 2013, and 2014 in Dalian city, a large port and metropolitan region in northeast China with a population of over six million. It draws on participant observation with a large environmental NGO (ENGO) that has multiple projects for cleaning marine areas, educating people about leading low carbon lives, and addressing foreign invasive species. Fieldwork also included interviews with other urban residents about these issues.

In addition to participating in the invasive species activities, I accompanied this organization on another project in 2014. This was a campaign to reduce air pollution by convincing drivers to volunteer to stay off of the roads one day every ten days. According to the last digit of their license plate number, for example "5," the drivers would commit to taking public or other transit on the fifth, the fifteenth, and the twenty-fifth of every month. When I attended an event promoting this campaign in a shopping area parking lot hosted by the organization, the volunteers approached drivers when they exited their cars and told them about the project (see figure 7.2). Most were quite willing and thought it was an important thing to do since air pollution was such a serious health and environmental problem. In such a campaign, nature was there, but it was not healthy, they knew it, and it was through these citizen-to-citizen interactions, supported by the city government, but led by this social organization, that environmental health and well-being would be addressed. Nature—and here specifically the air—was a site of citizen-led regulatory intervention.

Figure 7.2
An environmental volunteer (*center*) approaches a driver about limiting his vehicle use to help reduce air pollution. Photo by Lisa Hoffman.

As argued in this chapter, it is notable that these efforts were led by a society-based NGO and not the city government, even as it worked with the city on various projects, and the leader of this organization was a former government official. Such collaborations and citizen mobilizations signify important shifts in the way urban governance in China is enacted. While such activation of society and individual participants is specific to contemporary China, these efforts also highlight the place of urban natures in negotiating shifting governmental relations more broadly. Thus, within this volume's project of comparative urban environmentalism, this chapter also argues that the case of environmental volunteering in China offers the opportunity to think not only about new governmental rationalities, which include the promotion of nongovernmental/social organizations and citizen volunteering, but also about what is at stake in terms of the mutual constitution of "urban natures" and "sustainable citizens" in the process. In a rapidly changing and increasingly urbanized and worlding China, such analysis demonstrates the role that urban natures play in the quotidian coconstitution of state and society. To lead us into this analysis, I will begin with a brief overview of contemporary practices of citizen mobilization in China.

Citizen Mobilizations

Volunteering with NGOs in spaces previously dominated by state management—such as poverty relief, disaster assistance, and environmental work—has become increasingly common in contemporary China. This space of social action and citizen mobilization is critical in our world of cities. In China, it is a contemporary state of being that sits between ambitious plans to urbanize 250 million more people, political campaigns to build a harmonious society, and goals of realizing national rejuvenation along with personal well-being (the so-called Chinese Dream), in all of which social stability and security are prominent themes. The nongovernmental organizations, known as social organizations (*shehui tuanti/shehui zuzhi*), and citizen-led (*minjian*) efforts broadly, have become increasingly important in these processes, especially in addressing social issues related to urbanization. This role is directly related to the formal recognition of social organizations by the government, encoded in a series of directives about how they should register and how volunteers should be organized. To be official, social organizations had to have a government sponsor and register through the Ministry of Civil Affairs,[1] although a 2016 law regarding charitable organizations allowed organizations to register directly with the ministry. Nevertheless, many do not register and instead either exist on the fringes of legality or register as enterprises.[2] The outings described above were organized by a local social organization that was registered formally and often liaised and collaborated with the government—what may be called a GONGO, a government organized nongovernmental organization at the time of fieldwork. It received government funding (the director's salary was paid by the city government), but the organization's work was done by volunteers and was supported primarily through member dues.

While citizens understand the notion of social responsibility and active participation in organized activities (*huodong*) through reference points in Maoist socialism as well as Confucian ethics and even Christianity, the fact that these are charitable activities (*cishan huodong*) is important. An official desire for citizens to "voluntarily" step up and participate in a range of issues, to help strangers and in cross-class relationships, and to donate their private time and resources to the public good make these modes of social activity qualitatively distinct in the contemporary moment. "I don't do this because the government told me to," one regular volunteer explained to me. "This is all voluntary and spontaneous (*zifa*)." The outpouring of volunteer efforts after the 2008 earthquake in Sichuan Province also must be noted as significant in the popularization of volunteering, with some estimating that as many as three million people volunteered in some manner at that time, many for the first time.[3] Moreover, following the earthquake, the central government passed regulations that recognized the importance of social organizations' efforts, particularly in disaster relief, and published a white paper suggesting "that the government should strengthen 'social mobilization mechanisms' in order to 'give full play to the functions of non-governmental organizations and organizations at the grassroots level as well as volunteers in the sphere of disaster relief.'"[4] Such declarations further opened up the space for social organizations, and more specifically, for new kinds of *collaborations* (as opposed to conflicts) between government agencies, nongovernmental entities, and individual citizens, and thereby shaped subjectivity as well.[5]

Although much volunteer activity involves helping those in need, a particularly active sector of citizen volunteering focuses on environmental protection (*huanbao*). This kind of activity has been accepted by many, in both rural and urban areas, as reasonable in contemporary China. In Dalian, like other major urban centers, people can participate in volunteer efforts aimed at the environment in numerous ways. There are, for instance, regular trash pick-up, weeding, and educational opportunities, all of which may be organized by social organizations, residential developments, community (*shequ*) administrations, or university students.[6]

In addition, a white paper on human rights published in 2012 by the central government included, for the first time, a full chapter on environmental protection, which covered the importance of air pollution, sewage systems, and the right to enjoy a "healthy environment."[7] This formal attention to environmental problems is linked with the production of knowledge about the "environment" as a site of governmental intervention,[8] with national development discourses, and with an increase in the number of citizen-initiated environmental groups, or ENGOs, which are defined as groups whose "primary goal is protecting the environment by either curbing pollution or protecting nature, or both."[9] One study conducted in 2008 indicated China had a total of 3,539 ENGOs, including those that were formally registered with the government, those that were citizen-based, and those that were embedded in schools.[10] While ENGO growth is related to serious environmental degradation resulting from new industrial processes and fulfillment of resource demands, public reactions to limited enforcement of existing regulations, and the advocacy of international environmental groups, it also has to do with a new attitude toward collective action that developed in the late 1980s and early 1990s. This attitude, what has been called "liberation" for environmentalists, occurred when the environmental leaders "became aware that collective action could improve the quality of the environment."[11] This awareness was supported by state-level decisions in 1996 that encouraged "public reporting on, and exposing of" environmental violations.[12] Moreover, it has been argued that the decentralization of decision-making to localities has in fact made it more difficult for the central government to manage environmental issues. Support for nongovernmental actors is then a way for "non-state actors to carry some of the environmental protection burden."[13]

A focus on the environment and nature have thus created distinct spaces of governmental intervention that in our contemporary moment rely both on direct state policy and regulation and, significantly, on citizen mobilization and social organization efforts. These mobilization efforts are embedded in the globally prominent "ecological framework" and fit well with China's specific concern for population and national quality development (*suzhi*), which "focus[es] on the ways that external conditions impede or foster human development."[14] The ecological framework, as Hsu has argued, "taught that each person's 'quality of life' was shaped by the 'quality' of his or her local environment."[15] Hubbert, moreover, has underscored that the embrace of environmentalism in China is often equated with being modern and educated, signifying higher *suzhi* levels.[16]

In summary, we may understand the formal acceptance of social organizations, including ENGOs, and support for their efforts (in politically acceptable realms) as new governmental technologies. All sectors recognize that with economic reforms, global trade, and more recent campaigns to urbanize the population, China faces new kinds of social and environmental problems that require new ways of doing things. Methods of centralized planning and distribution from the high socialist era were no longer feasible or effective; the government thus called on other sectors, such as society and the market, to do their share. These ways of doing things—by volunteers and social organizations and through citizen-led efforts—may be understood as specific solutions to contemporary governmental problems, which, when brought together in more stabilized patterns, may be called "strategic assemblages"—a term used to explain how "groupings of heterogeneous elements" may come together in a more stable way and be "deployed for specific purposes at a particular historical conjuncture."[17] In this case, we see a rapidly urbanizing country that is also undergoing governmental shifts from high socialist central planning and authority to more diverse governmental technologies, such as the use of social organizations, individual citizen mobilization, and even market incentives to address specific problems of pollution and invasive plants, as well as poverty and human suffering. Volunteering and NGOs, in other words, help to release social anxieties about ecological, social, and health concerns.

Greening Campaigns and Species Invasion

Dalian is an interesting site for investigating environmental volunteering and the ways such social practices and relations help produce urban natures. The city is known as a clean and green city, and under the leadership of Mayor Bo Xilai (1993–2000) it undertook an official greening campaign and marketed itself, and has been recognized domestically and internationally, as an environmental model city. Two volunteer events I described above, however, both targeted the now invasive *Sicyos angulatus*, also known as the burr or star cucumber (*ciguogua*).[18] It is an annual vine that winds around the native plants and trees in China. It is native to the eastern United States and in some parts of the country it is identified as invasive. While much transfer of invasive species happens through regular international trade, and Dalian is a major port city, the volunteers I met linked the arrival of *ciguogua* with the urban greening policies of the early 2000s. Importing plant materials for greening projects is a fairly common strategy in cities across China and has led some scholars to argue that "China needs to fully utilize its substantial native phytodiversity…in the creation of urban green spaces" precisely to avoid "plant invasions."[19] In 2005 the volunteers said they saw some indications of the invasive character of *ciguogua*, but it was not so serious. Between 2006 and 2008 it became a larger issue and was identified in multiple locations, making these plant eradication projects one of the major issues for the social organization. Paralleling this process and increasing global trade overall is the "exponentially growing number" of scientific studies in China on invasive species, which underscores a broad recognition of the issues across the country according to one study,[20] while another states that "China's biodiversity is threatened by the invasion of alien species, due to the expansion of global trade and international transport and tourism."[21] In addition, as the middle class grows and has more funds to supply its own landscapes, more "exotics" have been imported, further supporting the argument that China urgently needs public education campaigns on the "great economic and environmental risks posed by invasive plants."[22]

Dalian has also made headlines for other forms of environmental "public participation,"[23] including large anti-pollution protests that led to the (temporary) closing of a major factory using toxic chemicals,[24] and regular critique by citizens of the extensive coastal land reclamation for development. Marching against the chemicals, driving less, and uprooting invasive plants on weekends are framed by participants both in terms of individual health and in terms of landscape beauty, which, in turn, is closely linked with tourism and economic development. Those involved in environmental issues in the city expressed the sense that while the municipal government was interested in being a green city, it neither paid attention to these kinds of secondary consequences, nor was it developing long-term sustainable practices. Participation with social organizations thus not only linked government responsibility and individual citizen mobilization in new ways, but volunteering for the environment also connected people with other actants—such as "invasive" species—in new ways as well.

The notion of invasion is important for understanding the way people relate to nature around them for it implies some kind of harm or disturbance—underscored in the phrase "invasive alien species." The volunteers emphasized that this vine was not in its correct place and thus was not in harmony with its surroundings, but that it was indeed native somewhere. In contrast to experiences of the "invasion" of indigenous vegetation by "alien" species in post-apartheid South Africa in terms of "civic terror and moral alarm,"[25] in Dalian it is more about the correct or incorrect place for a plant and less about a general commentary on the state of the moral order of the nation. An environmental activist explained, for instance, that some new species are introduced without a problem: "But there are others that impact the local ecosystem. You can see these plants killing our plants." Introduction of new species did not necessarily mean invasion and destabilization of the local conditions. To him it was about understanding the correct and harmonious place for these species, and how, when they are moved somewhere else, they may become a problem. This did not mean, however, that they were inherently problematic. Rather, it was *the relation and not the object* that was problematic. Nature in the city, then, may emerge in contested and complex ways, intersecting other governmental rationalities and categories of health, beauty, progress, quality life, economic development, social responsibility, and foreign invasion.[26]

Such complexity and understandings of urban natures were apparent in interviews with participants in the invasive weed pulling event I attended in 2011. The volunteers ranged in age from high school students to those who had retired. Their explanations for why they were participating in the activity on a Saturday referenced the key governmental categories of health, beauty, conservation, and economic and population development. Comments from participants included: "If I can help society and help others, then I am happy"; "Dalian is a pretty coastal city and the environment is important. Dalian citizens should do something to keep the city beautiful"; "I do many of these activities. Every Saturday there is trash pick-up at local parks, and I am active in a group that helps protect land because there is less and less agricultural space"; and "We have to use these opportunities to talk about how economic development and the environment are related." One high school student explained that his school did not have an environmental group, so he came to this organization. After training at the organization for two to three hours, he and several classmates came to participate. "The water used to be clean," he said by way of explanation, "but now the pollution in the sea is very serious." Notions of the city beautiful, a green and clean environment, and citizen responsibility merge in these practices. Caring for the environment in the contemporary moment was considered an appropriate way to show one's concern for the public good and to express one's social responsibility. It also hinged on the intersection of humans and plants, as in the physical work of the eradication efforts. Participation was polysemous—incorporating modernity, the good life, citizen responsibility, and nature in harmony.

One man brought his son and explained that he volunteered because he believed environmental safety was important. He had been volunteering with this group for many years, which he justified in terms of the city's history. Dalian was known for its oil and chemical production, which, he explained, had produced many serious environmental issues. Yet his understanding of the role of the individual—and his or her family—highlights the expanded notion of citizen action. "There are many things the government cannot do, so the people must do it with their own abilities," he explained. "Some things the government must do, and individuals cannot do, such as policies. But we need to be responsible for the environment for many years, not just one year. I feel this is the responsibility of society. The government won't necessarily care for this, so we must do these things." His son chimed in, saying that "this is our home and our responsibility. We should do it ourselves."[27] Reinforcing the idea that ordinary volunteers could have an impact, an environmental leader noted that volunteers were particularly useful because "they are the common people [laobaixing] and can do things that the government cannot do." He elaborated that volunteers did work that "the government in fact wants done" and that this shaped the "relations between the volunteers and the government."

Of note, this father-son pair also was connected with a large group (sevety-nine people) of volunteers from a state-owned company located outside of the central city in the Economic and Technical Development Zone. This company required its workers to participate in some kind of charitable activity (cishan huodong)—a particularly contemporary understanding of volunteer work and exhibition of one's social responsibility. All of the lower-level managers (and party members) in the finance department from the father's company were participating that day, as well as the director. "The company is very busy," he said "but as a citizen of the city we should do this.... In the past we have cleaned up the garbage near our company, and this is the first time we have done an activity like this [with this ENGO]." Like other associations or workplaces, this state-owned unit brought red banners with the name of the unit written across it, echoing the displays and mobilization efforts and referencing symbols of collective action of the Cultural Revolution as well as the 1989 student movement.[28] It is also noteworthy that, when institutions such as this work-unit came to participate, they did so in the interests of "their city," known for its "natural beauty"—a local rather than national identity and concern with a more bourgeois aesthetic feature that would have been problematic in the high socialist era. One participant described this effort as a dual process of simultaneously "raising up" the level of the city and the level of the people. At the same time, their organized volunteer activity was a response to the lack of government attention. Public expressions of environmentalism may be understood as an acceptable way to show one's concern for the public good—a practice that brought disparate notions of social responsibility and organized work together. Other interviewees described volunteer work as a "supplement" to government projects in spaces the government was not able to manage fully. If someone had skills and the resources (that is, their own economic security), explained one volunteer, then it would be okay for him or her to participate in these activities.

The Making of Urban Natures

In these activities the site of intervention is understood as "nature"—to be saved, preserved, and made harmonious again. Protecting nature sits then at the intersection of new social spaces and practices of community-based volunteering, even what we could call a "consciousness" of environmental protection in urban China, and a sense that some people have their own time (perhaps understood as leisure time) to participate in such activities. These intersections are reflective of the subjects and forms of governance emerging in urban China—shaping not only those who participate, but also the landscapes themselves as people label them healthy, polluted, natural, and/or urban. Hence, the constitution of "urban nature" as a field of action, knowledge about it, understandings of its health, and identification of interventions that will help it are intimately connected with the contemporary subjectivities and collectivities emerging to do the intervening. The mechanisms, practices, and norms that produced a field of governmental action also shaped the very subjects active in that arena. The production of urban natures, in other words, is necessarily linked with the emergence of environmental volunteers.

We should also consider what is at stake (materially, socially, politically) in the kinds of collectivities and socialities these processes produce. For instance, what socialities emerge through collective physical activity of cutting plants; the sharing of snacks, water, and time with other citizens; identifying something as out of place and dangerous (invasive); and engaging in communal unpaid, leisure weekend activities? In these eradication efforts, the plants are enrolled in these social processes such that plant/human actants emerge, potentially shaping the politics of volunteering in contemporary China. The state/nonstate spaces of social action in these volunteering efforts also matter, as such intermediary social spaces are indicative not only of citizen-subjects who volunteer responsibly, but also of changing relations between citizens and the state.[29] This case thus underscores that analyses of governing and governmental technologies should also include conversations about urban natures, and that urban natures may in fact be productive sites for understanding how governing produces fields of governmental action.

In addition to thinking about what is at stake in the collectives and subjectivities that enroll both humans and plants, this chapter also aims to make a conceptual contribution by thinking *through* and *across* categories that are typically conceptualized as distinct. Much work on NGOs in China asks, for instance, if China has a civil society, and if so, what degree of "autonomy" this space has from the government. Such research questions conceive of a split between state and society and understand agency to be embedded in particular, often opposed, social actors in each field (that is, either in the state or in society). As such, state and society are set up against each other, with power residing in one or the other, and autonomy conceptualized as a naturally existing state of being rather than a form of governing. Moreover, views built on this kind of universalizing, binary state-society split often assume a clear distinction between other foundational (Western) categorizations, like culture and nature, where nature is considered an a priori category that exists outside of human action yet can be protected, cleaned, weeded, and conserved, and culture is the human-created space of ritual, religion, art, and so on. Here, however, I wish to think across and through, rather than *about* such distinctions, and in terms of both/ and rather than either/or, to understand better the way urban natures are socially formed.[30] In particular, this approach may help us understand what is at stake not only in the kinds of collectivities and subject forms we see, but also in notions of urban nature that view plants, albeit invasive species, as enrolled in human social action. Both the volunteering subjects who learned collectively about the invasive species, donned protective gloves, and used machetes and other tools to remove the plant, and the object of their intervention, a natural world being saved and put back into a more harmonious state, emerged in relation to profound urbanization trends and governmental shifts.

Environmental volunteering did not just appear in China in response to identifiable environmental problems in the city,[31] or with the emergence of a civil society, in other words. Rather, such practices materialized alongside changing relations between subjects and the state, relations that are embedded in complex assemblages and networks of subjects, things, and political rationalities, including the work unit participants, plants identified as out of harmony and thus invasive, and discourses of citizen responsibility. These assemblages may be understood, as Marcus and Saka argue, as the "result of the intersection of two open systems," such as humans and nature. This means that the social form of urban nature unfolding in this instance is "only discernible as a result of the intersection of both such systems."[32] A grounded approach thus highlights the enrollment of invasive plants into social worlds, the bent backs of weeding, volunteer participants, nongovernmental/social organizations, and even global politics of trade, exchange, and migration. The intersection of open systems, and the way various entities are pulled into the practice of environmental volunteering also encourages us to "rethink" how agency itself may be "distributed" across systems of humans and things, such that the *ciguogua* plant and volunteer coexist and even share agency across them.[33] Thinking *through* intersections—rather than thinking in terms of an either/or—offers a way to conceive of plants, people, government directives, and nongovernmental entities together in the constitution of nature and natural spaces in Dalian.[34]

This invasive plant, out of sync with the local environment, is enrolled in, and thus a part of, father-son participation in plant-pulling activities, official greening campaigns that imported new species, government documents legalizing NGOs, efforts to increase the number of citizen volunteers in China, and transnational politics of invasion and national sovereignty. It is through all of these points of reference that the practice of volunteering for the environment becomes thinkable and commonplace for urban residents in China. In these activities, the site of intervention is understood as nature—to be saved, preserved, and made harmonious again. This space—nature in the urban, local ecosystems—is threatened by plants, plastics, and insects that are considered out of place and inharmonious. Such volunteer work is "something the citizens have to do," as one volunteer activity leader in Dalian explained. "The local government doesn't care about this yet." Thus, work units, schools, and individuals mobilize and find their own citizenship entangled with plants, building new communities and social networks in the city as well.

Conclusion

In conclusion, I wish to emphasize that shifting assemblages of state and nongovernmental actors, of invasive species and state regulations for registering social organizations, and of local volunteers and brochures advertising their city as beautiful, green, and modern do stabilize in more formalized approaches to governmental problems (such as those concerning economic development, urban planning, and environmental protection). These formalized approaches also shape objects of governmental intervention, such as "the environment" and its "well-being," as well as "urban natures" more specifically. The constitution of such a field of action is intimately connected with the emergence of those expected to intervene and be active, "voluntarily," in this domain. The government official who became the leader of the Dalian ENGO and the young man who sought out this organization because his school did not offer volunteering opportunities such as this may be identified as "responsible" citizens, part of the growing middle classes, and willing to take action in nongovernmental/social spaces. The mechanisms, practices, and norms that produce a field of governmental action thus shape the very subjects active in that arena. In Dalian, the production of urban natures, in other words, is necessarily linked with the emergence of environmental volunteers. In addition, the enrollment of plants into the social practice of volunteering suggests agency itself may be distributed across humans and plants, potentially shaping the politics of volunteering in contemporary China. Much then is at stake in *thinking across and through* categories and intersections, rather than using either/or approaches.

Thus, thinking about the *grounding of urban natures* has offered an opportunity to think more about what is at stake in the emergence of a world of cities where *urban spaces* are being reformulated as fields of governmental intervention and where wider social problems are identified, classified, and solved. More specifically, I grounded this analysis in Dalian, with a naturally deep and ice-free harbor, a beautiful coastline, a history of heavy industry, and a national and international reputation as a model environmental and green city, and in this contemporary moment when the state-society relationship in China is being reworked, cities are experiencing greater decentralization of authority, and citizens are being encouraged to be more independent, self-enterprising, and individually responsible after years of state centralized planning. The world of cities in which we all live, and the urban world being created at breakneck speed in China, is our laboratory for understanding power, politics, and how we come to be the people we are, in the spaces we inhabit.

Acknowledgments

The research for this chapter was supported by the Urban Studies Program at the University of Washington, Tacoma, as part of a larger project of volunteering in urban China. I am grateful to the environmental organization with which I did fieldwork for allowing me to participate and interview people, and especially to the leaders and organizers. In the interests of anonymity, I will not name you, and hope you understand. Gratitude also to Henrik Ernstson, Sverker Sörlin, and the other participants in the Grounding Urban Natures workshop, as well as to participants in "The Future of NGO Studies" conference in Chicago, 2013, where I presented an earlier version of this chapter. Special thanks to Henrik for his continued engagement with this chapter and to Monica DeHart and Jennifer Hubbert for reading an early draft. I take responsibility for all failings of the chapter.

Notes

1. Friends of Nature, an environmental organization founded by Liang Congjie, was one of the first to register formally in 1994—as a "national level membership organization"—and now has thousands of members (Knup 1997, 12; Schwartz 2004, 39).

2. Lee 2009, 352; Shieh and Deng 2011. See also Knup (1997); Estes (1998); Ma (2002); Zhu (2005); Lee (2009); Simon (2013); and Hsu (2017). A 2016 law also restricted foreign NGO activities in the country.

3. Roney 2012, p. 88; Zhang 2012, p. 228.

4. Cited in Roney (2012, p. 85).

5. Hoffman 2013, 2015.

6. Many of the environmental groups in Shanghai, for instance, were started by university students and are not officially registered (Lee 2007).

7. An 2013.

8. The "natural" environment has been targeted as a site of governmental intervention through market logics, mechanisms that measure and quantify, and through the decentralization of decision-making to local authorities. Consequently, sustainable city-building has been mobilized as a new source of value and field of action, producing particular kinds of city spaces and shaping the conditions of possibility for place-making (Hoffman 2009).

9. Ru and Ortolano 2009, p. 149.

10. Kang 2010.

11. Ru and Ortolano 2009, p. 155.

12. Schwartz 2004, p. 35.

13. Ibid., p. 28.

14. Hsu 2017, p. 125. Carolyn Hsu (2017) argues that not only did *suzhi* discourses and ideologies of personal and population improvement align well with the global ecological framework, but also that the environmental activism that arose in China suggests the emergence of a new mode of citizenship: social entrepreneurship.

15. Hsu 2017, p. 128.

16. Hubbert 2014.

17. Rabinow and Rose 1994, p. xvi; Ong and Collier 2004.

18. See Zhang and Han (1997); Zhang et al. (2007); Qu et al. (2010); and Xu et al. (2012).

19. Axmacher and Sang 2013.

20. Liu et al. 2012.

21. Zhao 2005.

22. Axmacher and Sang 2013; see also Liu and Diamond (2005).

23. See Martens (2006).

24. BBC 2011.

25. See Comaroff and Comaroff (2001, p. 630).

26. See also Hubbert (2014).

27. Several surveys indicate that environmental awareness is limited in urban China. For instance, a survey from 2000 in Shanghai found that while people had strong "environmental attitudes," the "environmental knowledge" was weak. In questions about the impact of heavy metals and used batteries, 18 percent were aware of the

impact and 34 percent "were entirely unaware of such a hazard" (Lee 2007, p. 287). See also Hubbert (2014).

28. Esherick and Wasserstrom 1990.

29. Hoffman 2015.

30. Allan Pred's (1995, 2000) work on situated practices is helpful in thinking in nonbinary ways. See also Merrill (2015) on the use of Pred's both/and approach, and Merrill and Hoffman (2015) on Pred's contributions, particularly how situated analyses help to make that which is taken for granted visible.

31. Ru and Ortolano (2009) examine the marked increase in the number of "citizen-organized environmental nongovernmental organizations (ENGOs)" since the 1990s.

32. Marcus and Saka 2006, p. 103.

33. Ernstson 2013.

34. See Ong (2004) on incorporating multiple actors, norms, and institutions into understandings of space-making. See also Dierwechter (2004) on thinking about urban planning across scales and domains.

References

An, Baijie. 2013. "Healthy Environment Vital, Says White Paper." *ChinaDaily*, May 15. www.chinadaily.com.cn/china/2013-05/15/content_16499504.htm.

Axmacher, Jan, and Weiguo Sang. 2013. "Plant Invasions in China—Challenges and Chances." *PloS One* 8(5). www.plosone.org/article/info%3Adoi%2F10.1371%2F journal.pone.0064173.

BBC. 2011. "China Protest Closes Toxic Chemical Plant in Dalian." BBC News Asia-Pacific, April 29. www.bbc.co.uk/news/world-asia-pacific-14520438?print=true.

Comaroff, Jean, and John Comaroff. 2001. "Naturing the Nation: Aliens, Apocalypse and the Postcolonial State." *Journal of Southern African Studies* 27(3): 627–651.

Dierwechter, Yonn. 2004. "Dreams, Bricks, and Bodies: Mapping 'Neglected Spatialities' in African Cape Town." *Environment and Planning A* 36: 959–981.

Ernstson, Henrik. 2013. "Re-Translating Nature in Post-Apartheid Cape Town: The Material Semiotics of People and Plants at Bottom Road." Actor-Network Theory for Development Working Paper Series, edited by Richard Heeks, no. 4. Manchester: Institute for Development Policy and Management, School of Environment, Education and Development, University of Manchester. http://hummedia.manchester.ac .uk/institutes/cdi/resources/cdi_ant4d/ANT4DWorkingPaper4Ernstson.pdf.

Esherick, Joseph W., and Jeffrey N. Wasserstrom. 1990. "Acting Out Democracy: Political Theater in Modern China." *Journal of Asian Studies* 49(4): 835–865.

Hoffman, Lisa. 2009. "Governmental Rationalities of Environmental City-Building in Contemporary China." In *China's Governmentalities: Governing Change, Changing Government*, edited by Elaine Jeffreys, 107–124. New York: Routledge.

Hoffman, Lisa. 2013. "Decentralization as a Mode of Governing the Urban: Reforms in Welfare Provisioning and the Rise of Volunteerism." *Pacific Affairs* 86(4): 835–855.

Hoffman, Lisa. 2015. "Serving and Providing for Those 'In Need': 'Intermediary' Spaces and Practices of Liaising, Collaborating, and Mobilizing in Urban China." In *New Mentalities of Government in China*, edited by Elaine Jeffreys and David Bray, 141–158. New York: Routledge.

Hsu, Carolyn. 2017. *Social Entrepreneurship and Citizenship in China: The Rise of NGOs in the PRC*. London: Routledge.

Hubbert, Jennifer. 2014. "'We're Not THAT Kind of Developing Country': Environmental Awareness in Contemporary China." In *Sustainability in the Global City: Myth and Practice*, edited by Gary McConogh, Melissa Checker, and Cindy Isenhour, 29–53. New York: Cambridge University Press.

Kang, Shi-Hao. 2010. Review of Hong Dayong et al., *Zhongguo minjian huanbao liliang de chengzhang* [The growing nongovernmental forces for environmental protection in China]. *East Asian Science, Technology and Society: An International Journal* 4(3): 457–460.

Knup, Elizabeth. 1997. "Environmental NGOs in China: An Overview." *China Environment Series* 1: 9–15.

Lee, Rebecca. 2009. "Modernizing Charity Law in China." *Pacific Rim Law and Policy Journal* 18(2): 347–372.

Lee, Seungho. 2007. "Environmental Movements and Social Organizations in Shanghai." *China Information* 21(2): 269–297.

Liu, Jian, Hua Chen, Ingo Kowarik, Yiran Zhang, and Renqing Wang. 2012. "Plant Invasions in China: An Emerging Hot Topic in Invasion Science." *Neobiota* 15: 27–51.

Liu, Jianguo, and Jared Diamond. 2005. "China's Environment in a Globalizing World: How China and the Rest of the World Affect Each Other." *Nature* 435(30): 1179–1186.

Ma, Qiusha. 2002. "Defining Chinese Nongovernmental Organizations." *Voluntas: International Journal of Voluntary and Nonprofit Organizations* 13(2): 113–130.

Marcus, George E., and Erkan Saka. 2006. "Assemblage." *Theory, Culture and Society* 23(2–3): 101–109.

Martens, Susan. 2006. "Public Participation with Chinese Characteristics: Citizen Consumers in China's Environmental Management." *Environmental Politics* 15(2): 211–230.

Merrill, Heather. 2015. "In Other Wor(l)ds: Situated Intersectionality in Italy." In *Spaces of Danger: Culture and Power in the Everyday*, edited by Heather Merrill and Lisa M. Hoffman, 77–100. Athens: University of Georgia Press.

Merrill, Heather, and Lisa M. Hoffman. 2015. "Introduction: Making Sense of Our Contemporary Moment of Danger." In *Spaces of Danger: Culture and Power in the Everyday*, edited by Heather Merrill and Lisa M. Hoffman, 1–18. Athens: University of Georgia Press.

Ong, Aihwa. 2004. "Urban Assemblages: An Ecological Sense of the Knowledge Economy." In *Cyber China: Reshaping National Identities in the Age of Information*, edited by Francoise Mengin, 237–253. New York: Palgrave Macmillan.

Ong, Aihwa, and Stephen J. Collier. 2004. *Global Assemblages: Technology, Politics and Ethics as Anthropological Problems*. Malden, MA: Wiley-Blackwell.

Pred, Allan. 1995. "Out of Bounds and Undisciplined: Social Inquiry and the Current Moment of Danger." *Social Research* 62(4): 1065–1091.

Pred, Allan. 2000. *Even in Sweden: Racisms, Racialized Spaces, and the Popular Geographical Imagination*. Berkeley: University of California Press.

Qu, Bo, Wei Zhang, Qiang Zhai, Nan Li, Li-xia Wang, Yan Lu, and Tian-lai Li. 2010. "Preliminary Analysis on Invasive Species in Liaoning Province." *Pratacultural Science* 9: 009.

Rabinow, Paul, and Nikolas Rose. 1994. "Introduction: Foucault Today." In *The Essential Foucault: Selections from Essential Works of Foucault, 1954–1984*, edited by P. Rabinow and N. Rose, vii–xxxv. New York: The New Press.

Roney, Britton. 2012. "Earthquakes and Civil Society: A Comparative Study of the Response of China's Nongovernment Organizations to the Wenchuan Earthquake." *China Information* 25(1): 83–104.

Ru, Jiang, and Leonard Ortolano. 2009. "Development of Citizen-Organized Environmental NGOs in China." *Voluntas* 20: 141–168.

Schwartz, Jonathan. 2004. "Environmental NGOs in China: Roles and Limits." *Pacific Affairs* 77(1): 28–49.

Shieh, Shawn, and Guosheng Deng. 2011. "An Emerging Civil Society: The Impact of the 2008 Sichuan Earthquake on Grass-Roots Associations in China." *China Journal* 65: 181–194.

Simon, Karla. 2013. *Civil Society in China: The Legal Framework from Ancient Times to the New Reform Era*. Oxford: Oxford University Press.

Wessells, Anne. 2013. "The Working Waterfront as Enacted Assemblage: Urban Blue Space in Tacoma." Paper presented at the Association of American Geographers Annual Meeting, Los Angeles, CA, April 9–13.

Xu, Haigen, Sheng Qiang, Piero Genovesi, Hui Ding, Jun Wu, Ling Meng, Zhengmin Han, et al. 2012. "An Inventory of Invasive Alien Species in China." *NeoBiota* 15: 1–26.

Zhang, Ning 2012 "The Wenchuan Earthquake, Social Organizations, and the Chinese State." *Urban Anthropology* 41(2–4): 211–246.

Zhang, Shumei, and Han Quanzhong. 1997. "Preliminary Study on the Foreign Plants in Dalian." *Journal of Liaoning Normal University, Natural Science Edition* 20(4): 323–330.

Zhang, Shumei, Wang Qing, Jiang Xuepin, Luan Shujun, Li Dongliang, and Wang Yunsuo. 2007. "Further Study on Exotic Plants in Dalian, Alien Invasive Plant— *Sicoyos angulatus L.* in Dalian: Damage and Prevention Strategies." *Journal of Liaoning Normal University*, March.

Zhao, Yuhong. 2005. "The War against Biotic Invasion—A New Challenge of Biodiversity Conservation for China." *UCLA Journal of Environmental Law and Policy* 24(2): 459–496.

8 Urban Nature and Its Publics: Shades of Green in the Remaking of Delhi

Amita Baviskar

Nothing prepares you for the first view of Mangarbani. There's the Gurgaon-Faridabad toll road, your standard highway on Delhi's outskirts, rolling through a landscape where dusty scrub vegetation is being rapidly replaced by dustier high-rise construction sites. There's an eyesore called the Gurgaon Faridabad Combined Solid Waste Management facility, with acres of open garbage, some scrawny cows, and flapping crows. Beside the *kachcha* (unpaved) road along the dump's broken boundary wall, there are deep, jagged-edged craters, relicts from the stone quarrying that was done here until ten years ago. The land is rocky and open, dotted about with trees and shrubs, one of those ennui-inducing views where your mind begins to wander to more interesting things like the grocery shopping list or reminding yourself to call the plumber when you get home.

In the middle of this nowhere, Pradip Krishen, author of *Trees of Delhi*,[1] whom I am accompanying, stops the car. We walk for about ten minutes, winding our way past rocks hugged by stunted plants, between trees twisted by hot dry winds. It is 8:00 in the morning in late March, and it already feels like summer. And then, suddenly, we arrive at the lip of a cliff. The ground drops away and so does my jaw. Spread out below us is a deep wooded valley, densely yet delicately green, the expanse of its tree canopy broken only by the whitewashed domed tower of a small shrine in the distance. Besides the shrine, the only other sign of human presence is a boundary pillar on the far end of the valley. That's it; the rest is undisturbed forest. The only sound is the plaintive call of peafowl, the only movement their ponderous glide from one tree to another. Oh, there's also the racket of parakeets arrowing across the sky. Some grasses wave as the breeze catches the outcrop of rocks below our feet. Everything else is still. We could be two hundred kilometers away in the middle of Sariska National Park except that we are not. We're in Delhi National Capital Region (NCR), twenty minutes away from the wall-to-wall carpeting of tarmac-glass-concrete-stone, twenty minutes from traffic jams, crowds, noise, dust, and smoke. Yet it feels like we have landed on a different planet.

By weaving two interrelated narratives of urban natures—Mangarbani, where we started, a sacred grove on the periphery of the metropolis that faces conversion into real estate, and the Delhi Ridge, a natural and naturalized "wilderness" that has been domesticated for recreational use—this chapter addresses the cultural politics of urban nature. It focuses on how green spaces and urban publics are mutually constituted in Delhi, India. It delineates the social transformations through which the cultural meanings that inhere in urban natures are reimagined, and the ecological transformations that give rise to new social relations around the use and protection of green spaces. In particular, the chapter shows how the move to create and preserve specific forms of urban nature can be closely related to the rise of a middle class that has consolidated its power in the period of economic liberalization since the 1990s and has appointed itself as the vanguard of public environmental causes. However, instead of improving the urban environment for all citizens, this "bourgeois environmentalism" has had far-reaching adverse ecological and social effects. Moreover, the urban order that middle-class environmentalists seek to impose does not go unchallenged, but is undermined by other users of public green areas, ranging from poor migrant workers foraging for firewood to young lovers seeking anonymity. After foraging in Mangarbani and visiting the Delhi Ridge, the chapter closes by showing that, although the meanings and practices around urban natures are contested, they also give rise to new alliances and understandings that are mutually fruitful.

Mangarbani

What's so special about Mangarbani? It's not as if Delhi lacks large green spaces. Besides numerous parks and gardens, there is the densely wooded expanse of the Ridge, the northern-most spur of the Aravalli range which stretches all the way to Rajasthan. However, from the ecological point of view, the Ridge is seriously compromised. A lot of it has been spruced up for human use, the undergrowth cleared and exotic species planted. Among these imports, the most pernicious has been Central American mesquite (*vilayati keekar,* or *Prosopis juliflora*), which has established itself by suppressing indigenous plant species and the life forms they support.[2] Because it is hardy and propagates easily, *P. juliflora* has been a favorite of forest departments looking for a quick-fix for greening India since colonial times. So in most large green areas in Delhi and its environs today, *P. juliflora* dominates over native species, to the detriment of local biodiversity.

Mangarbani has managed to remain remarkably free of the *vilayati keekar* curse. Even more miraculous, it has undergone virtually *no* human interference or exploitation for several hundred years. The surrounding villages have protected the grove as sacred to the memory of Gudariya Baba, a hermit whose shrine stands at the base of the valley. They believe that anyone who cuts wood or grazes their animals in this one-hundred-hectare forest invites the Baba's wrath and retribution. So Mangarbani stands out in the Delhi region for being an unspoiled old growth forest of a kind unique to the Aravalli range, a startling vision of what these ancient hills would look like if they were protected from biotic pressure.

And what a vision it is! The top of the valley and its steep sides are thickly covered with *dhau,* a medium-sized tree with pretty leaves that go from pale green to purple brown (see figure 8.1). Such a profusion of *dhau* is typical of the climax vegetation of some tropical dry deciduous forests. According to Krishen, whose *Trees of Delhi* brought Mangarbani to the notice of a wider public, the tree used to be found all over the Ridge but now is in danger of disappearing in Delhi. Two other beautiful trees that grew in the forests that have vanished from the Ridge—*kala siris* and *salai* with its fragrant resin—survive only in Mangarbani in the Delhi region. The valley includes some dry and sandy patches where plants typical of arid regions—trees like *kareel* (the *kair* of the famous Rajasthani vegetable dish *kair-sangri*) and *roheda* with its flamboyant orange flowers—can be found. The moist valley floor is shadowed by tall *kaim*—the original *kadamba* of Krishna's Vrindavan[3]—and *kanju* with its fruit encased in translucent papery discs. Along with these are the more common trees of the Ridge: *ronjh, bistendu, hingot,* and *doodhi.* During the spring, *doodhi ki bel* is laden with sweet-smelling creamy flowers; its perfume escorts us down to Gudariya Baba's shrine.[4]

On the path to the shrine is a nasty surprise. There is a temple, a large building with a courtyard and pond, which is being expanded to double its size. The land has already been cleared of its vegetation. The temple is the site of an annual fair and other religious events, and the crowds that

Figure 8.1
Mangarbani's *dhau* forest with Gudariya Baba's shrine. Photo by Pradip Krishen.

descended on it most recently have left behind smelly heaps of dirty Sty-
rofoam plates. Although the temple's growing precincts pose a problem in
this pristine area, there is an even bigger issue at stake, one that threatens
the very existence of Mangarbani.

Mangarbani and its surrounding land used to be the *shamilat deh*
(commons) of Mangar, Bandhwari, and Baliawas villages,[5] settlements
dominated by the Gujjar caste, with about three thousand landowning
households. Since precolonial times, the *malikan deh* (proprietary body
of a village), which consisted of all landowning households represented
through village *panchayats* (local councils), controlled these forests, grazing
lands, and ponds. In revenue records, the commons were classified as *ghair
mumkin zameen* (uncultivable land) and therefore exempt from agricultural
tax. Landless households in the village belonging to the Scheduled Castes
(former Untouchable castes who cleaned and disposed of human waste
and animal carcasses) had rights to collect firewood and fodder from these
commons only at the pleasure of their upper-caste landowning patrons,
as did agricultural tenants. In the late 1970s, the governments of Haryana
and Uttar Pradesh states and the Union Territory of Delhi began carving

out plots of the land in the commons to give to landless Scheduled Caste households for cultivation. This was ostensibly a relatively painless program of "land reforms" since it did not expropriate any cultivatable land from existing landowners, but only allocated a portion of their shared "uncultivatable" commons. However, the landowners were not willing to allow even this limited curtailment of their rights and managed to successfully block it.[6]

Fearing that the government would try again to wrest control of their commons, landowning villagers across Haryana state mobilized politically to get the Punjab Village Common Lands Regulation Act of 1961 amended. From being collectively owned by the village *panchayat*, the commons were partitioned such that individual owners of agricultural land received titles to common lands in proportion to the size of their private holdings. This partition remained notional until 1986, when individual claims were demarcated on the ground. This privatization of the commons facilitated their commodification. Several villagers sold their titles to real estate developers and speculators who have fenced and walled in their plots, preparatory to clearing and building on them. This activity is so far confined to the area surrounding Mangarbani but may soon encroach into the forest if the real estate lobby in the Haryana government has its way. Many individual titles have been sold and resold to a "powerful business- politico- bureaucratic-police nexus with ostensibly no interest in agricultural activities."[7]

The actors who collaborate in this nexus include influential local men who persuade their fellow villagers to sell their land; some of them have set up small offices along the main road advertising their business as property brokers. They receive financial backing and enforcement muscle from local politicians who bribe and intimidate lower-level officials to legitimize and expedite transactions. Bigger real estate firms either buy land through these brokers or appoint them as their agents on the ground, getting capital from investors who include not only people seeking homes and offices for their own use, but also speculators looking to gain from the rise in property prices. Corrupt politicians and bureaucrats are an essential part of this real estate economy. As owners of huge unaccounted wealth, real estate—with its large gap between the declared and actual value of property and its undocumented cash transactions—is a convenient way to invest black money. Bureaucrats and politicians help developers negotiate the regulatory hurdles required to secure building permissions, in return for a share in the profits. The glue of kinship holds this tight-knit network together: a number of leading politicians have immediate relatives in the real estate business.

It is this political economy of land transformation, extending from the village to the state's topmost leaders, that led in 2011 to the Draft Development Plan 2031 for Mangar, which zoned the area for commercial and residential use—a designation that is a death sentence for Mangarbani. From 1991, developers started using the Consolidation Act, a law meant to redress the fragmentation of agricultural fields and village commons, to accumulate land holdings in violation of the Haryana Ceiling on Land Holdings Act of 1972.[8] Since the holdings are *benami* (under assumed names), it is difficult to track and prosecute the actual owners. With the help of political leaders, corrupt revenue department officials, land brokers, and complicit villagers, Mangarbani is on the verge of going the same way as the rest of the Aravalli landscape—denuded, buried under concrete, its ancient forest gone forever.

One would think that it requires a sea change in values for villagers who have protected Mangarbani for centuries to now be willing to see it destroyed. But this change did not happen overnight. Quartzite quarrying in the Aravalli hills in Delhi, Haryana, and Rajasthan states accelerated when Delhi underwent a construction boom before the Asian Games 1982, and struck deeper and wider to meet demand over next two decades as the NCR witnessed unprecedented growth. Some quarries were on private lands, but most were on village commons, and *panchayat* (village council) leaders were quick to seize the chance to make money, even though farmers reported that the blasting of rocks and their removal was causing groundwater to become scarce. In places, the landscape was visibly altered as entire chunks of tall hills disappeared over the course of months. It was only in 2002 that, acting on a public interest petition, the Supreme Court of India ordered a ban on mining in the entire Aravalli range. However, by this time, farming in this semi-arid terrain was already dwindling as a remunerative livelihood. Once the money from mining stopped coming in, villagers were left high and dry and altogether willing to consider other options for their land. The Mangarbani forest, however, remained intact over the last three decades even as the surrounding landscape and people's relationships to land were changing rapidly.

What tipped the scales against the collective protection of Mangarbani as a sacred grove was the tide of real estate development sweeping in from Gurgaon and Faridabad, two "satellite towns" planned as magnets to reduce congestion in Delhi, which afforded real estate developers favorable terms since they were not hampered by the Urban Land Ceiling Act, which prohibited private firms from undertaking large-scale projects in the capital city. Selling to developers made landowners cash rich beyond their imagination; farming was a subsistence activity at best, so villagers were only too willing to give it up in exchange for substantial sums of money. The value of land in the area around Mangarbani remained low until about 2010, when the road connecting Gurgaon and Faridabad began to be upgraded in anticipation of the eventual merging of the boundaries of these two expanding cities. The villagers in this area who sold their lands, including their claim to the Mangarbani forest, were doing only what most of Haryana's villagers have done or are waiting to do.[9]

But what of the religious significance of Mangarbani? How could Gudariya Baba's prohibition be defied? When asked about this, some villagers reiterated their commitment to him. *"Baba ne kahaa ki yahaan koi lakdi nahin kaatega, pashu nahin charayega. Hum barson se unke kahe ko maante aa rahen hain"* [Baba said that no one will cut wood or graze animals here. We have been abiding by his words for ages], said Jairam Harsana of Mangar village. He also described what happened to those who violated the Baba's injunction: their livestock died; their wooden houses burst into flame. But by selling his title to the forest he is at a remove from these acts of retribution since he will not be the one doing the actual cutting of trees. He has regrets, though, about selling the sacred grove and, in 2011, signed a petition along with other elderly villagers asking the government to protect the forest. When asked how that would affect the rights of those who had purchased the titles to Mangarbani's land intending to develop it, he expressed his helplessness: "It was thirty years ago. We didn't know. It was only on paper. No one knew who owned which piece of land. We didn't think it would come to this."

If there is regret in some quarters about losing the forest, other villagers seem to be taking Gudariya Baba's legacy in a different direction altogether. Near the Baba's simple whitewashed shrine is a newly built temple, painted stand-out saffron and all set to expand its precincts, adding more area and deities to the Shiva-led pantheon currently installed for worship. With the temple attracting more devotees and visitors, Mangarbani's spiritual center seems to be shifting away from Gudariya Baba to the standard Hindu multi-god multipurpose buffet and bringing a commercial element that was earlier absent from the forest. The temple is both a salve to the conscience that rues selling out the Baba—"*Hum is dharmik sthal ko sudhaar rahein hain*" [We are improving this religious place]—and a sign that the Baba's spirit may soon be superseded by the all-too-familiar process of temple-led land grab.[10]

Perhaps a clearer consensus about protecting Mangarbani would have been more likely if the forest had remained a common. If individual titles had not been allotted to landowners, it would have been harder to sell the undivided land. But this is speculation. What is evident is that although the village no longer functions as a collective body in deciding the fate of the forest, another collective entity has stepped into the picture to save Mangarbani. A group of environmentalists, most of them upper-middle-class residents of Gurgaon, who have an interest in water conservation,[11] started a campaign to save Mangarbani by publicizing its ecological richness and by pressurizing the government to fulfil its environmental mandate. The campaigners point out that any attempt to change land use in Mangarbani is in clear violation of a 1996 Supreme Court order that, regardless of ownership, such densely wooded areas be legally designated as forests and protected accordingly. They argue that the Draft Development Plan of Mangar, which zones the area for residential and commercial use, should be scrapped. The campaign has received favorable media coverage and, in January 2013, succeeded in getting the National Green Tribunal to order the Haryana government to stop all nonforest activities in the forests around Mangar village.[12] In May 2014, it received a further boost when the NCR Planning Board decided that 250 hectares in Mangarbani, as well as a 500-meter buffer radius around the forest, would be earmarked as a "no-construction zone."[13] This addresses the campaigners' demand that about 500 hectares around the forest should be regulated as a buffer zone with restricted activities and, especially, that construction and water-intensive land use be banned. The area forms the watershed of a seasonal stream that runs through Mangarbani and helps create its distinctive habitat, while also recharging groundwater in the area and supplying water to nearby Dhauj Lake. Haryana state has already done plenty to deplete its scarce water sources; destroying this particular catchment would be another act of development folly.

Most of the buffer has scattered and stunted trees that are indigenous to the Aravalli hills. Although *P. juliflora* has spread here, *dhau*, *ronjh*, the flame-flowered *palash*, blazing yellow-flowered *amaltas* and other natives still predominate.[14] Conservationists argue that there is great potential for restoring the original forest that existed here, for giving the *nilgai* (*Bose-laphus tragocamelus*) and jackals an undivided landscape to roam, and for recreating a habitat for indigenous flora and fauna in a geologically dramatic setting. They would like Mangarbani to be integrated as part of a continuous biodiversity corridor in the Aravalli hills, stretching from Asola Wildlife Sanctuary in Delhi to Kot in Rajasthan. The campaign demands that the Haryana government not only comply with the Supreme Court and National Green Tribunal's orders but also take the initiative to protect the larger landscape of which Mangarbani is part. However, given the state government's complicity in shady real estate development deals, it seems unlikely that it will sort out and settle property rights in the area and make villagers partners in future conservation. Only continued pressure from the conservationists, working through the courts and media, may compel the government to protect Mangarbani.

Although Mangarbani is in some ways a special case in being a sacred grove on the periphery of a modern metropolis, it highlights some significant processes at work in how urban India acquires or loses green spaces, as well as the political economy of land ownership and use. It also delineates the social transformations through which the cultural meanings that inhere in green spaces are reconfigured. The Mangarbani forest came out of obscurity in the last decade because it was featured in a naturalist's handbook.[15] The weekend visitors it attracted were wilderness lovers, affluent residents of Delhi and Gurgaon, many of whom became homeowners thanks to real estate development facilitated by the "political-bureaucratic nexus" that took over village lands. Now that this process threatens Mangarbani, in an ironic twist, some beneficiaries of land commodification have turned "environmentalist," ranging themselves against the "builder Mafia" from whom they bought their luxury apartments and bungalows and seeking to protect a green space that is not only perceived to be ecologically valuable but also an enhancement of their quality of life. From a mutually advantageous relationship with builders, sections of the elite have shifted their allegiance to a new axis, aligning with the older generation of Mangar villagers.

Thus, even as the corporate identity and power of the village is broken down into individual fragments that hasten the commodification of land, another collective group constitutes itself as the guardian of the forest. The environmentalists do not replace the villagers, nor are they in conflict with them. In fact, it would seem that by talking to villagers about the biodiversity of the forest and reminding them that it is their protection that has sustained this grove over the centuries, the environmentalists hope to revive a collective sentiment that will enable them to fight together for the future of Mangarbani. Even as the Baba's spiritual hold on the villagers seems to be becoming more tenuous, environmentalists have stepped in with ecological arguments about respecting all life forms, the interconnectedness of trees, soil, water, and air, and living in harmony with nature—arguments that at times resemble the tenets of a secular religion.

The Delhi Ridge

The sensibility that underlies the environmentalists' efforts—their appreciation of Mangarbani as an original ecological place worthy of protection—is both modern and recent. Although many of the cities that flourished at the site of present-day Delhi over the last two millennia had established systems to harness water and to source timber and fuel from the hinterland, as well as having designated land use based on topography and soil, they did not set aside any area for its ecological importance. Delhi's two major natural features—the river Yamuna and the hilly Ridge—went virtually unregarded until the 1970s, even though they together defined the catchment that watered the wells and ponds crucial for the city's existence.[16] The idea that these landscapes are valuable and demand special attention emerged only when Delhi's expansion had decimated them or severely damaged their ecological integrity. Ironically, as is often the case, the champions of these beleaguered urban ecologies emerged from the very middle classes that were the beneficiaries of urban growth.[17] That is, the changing Ridge and the burgeoning middle classes evolved together, each giving shape to the other.

"The Ridge" is the colonial term for the area locally known as *pahaadi* (hilly land), a series of undulations that begin close to the river in north Delhi and stretch to the southwest, where they are increasingly distant from the river. Images from the nineteenth century depict the Ridge as an open, unpopulated wilderness, with barely a tree in sight. Perhaps such a view was a product of perspective: British and Indian eyes would have passed over the thorny scrub forest as a wasteland because it lacked useful or imposing trees. The Ridge may also have been laid bare over the years as trees were cut to provide city dwellers with fuel and livestock with land for grazing.[18] However, its barren contours were to turn green in the next century.

When New Delhi, the imperial capital, was being built (1911–1931) at the foot of what is now known as the Central Ridge, the viceroy, Lord Hardinge, initiated plans for extensive afforestation, imagining a dense evergreen curtain behind a "splendid…Government House" placed at the top of Raisina hill, "commanding the most lovely views over the city of Delhi and over the whole plain, both east and west" and "dominating the whole of the country round," with the slope down to the plain "covered with terraces and fountains like a miniature Versailles."[19] To create this arboreal backdrop for the principal seat of imperial government, Hardinge drew upon the expertise of P. H. Clutterbuck, a forester from the United Provinces, who suggested a number of indigenous trees from the drier parts of the Himalayan foothills. His advice was endorsed by W. M. Hailey, who inspected the early experimental plantings in 1916: "I would not extend the plantation of exotics. They should only come after we have established indigenous trees."[20] Planting proceeded slowly and on a small scale, limited by wartime budget constraints. The results were not satisfactory. Trees died off as soon as watering was stopped; few species could withstand the rigors of Ridge conditions, its thin soils and exposure to extreme summer and winter temperatures. Over the next twenty years, the government struggled with this uphill task. Although some native trees such as *ronjh*, *palash*, and *siris* managed to survive,[21] it was the Central American mesquite (*Prosopis juliflora* or *vilayati keekar*) that proved to be the most tenacious. As the *Annual Report of Government Gardens 1935–1936* noted, "Prosopis juliflora, one of the hardiest of drought resisting trees, forms the main base of useful, evergreen vegetation[;] and trees raised from seed a few years ago are now well developed and gradually extending in to fresh ground."[22] This exotic had a strong champion in William Mustoe, director of horticulture, who is reported to have personally tucked individual seeds into the ground.[23] Mustoe's diligence and *P. juliflora*'s persistence left a lasting legacy. The "useful evergreen" tree became an invasive species, crowding out the natives. *P. juliflora* now rules the Ridge, as it does across much of the subcontinent's drylands.

Although the Ridge was designated as a "Reserve Forest" by the colonial government in 1933,[24] its legal status did not offer watertight protection. When land was needed for other purposes, portions of the wooded Ridge were made available. As the Delhi Improvement Trust expanded the city to the west to accommodate the "Depressed Castes" from the congested Walled City and those displaced by the construction of New Delhi,[25] the central section of the Ridge around Jhandewalan was cleared and leveled, thereby widening the gap between the northern and southern parts. Independence and the Partition of India in 1947 brought half a million Hindu and Sikh refugees to the city, and many of them were resettled by clearing the central and southern parts of the Ridge. The Southern Ridge was further eaten into to establish the large campus of the Jawaharlal Nehru University and other institutional and residential areas in the 1950s. At around the same time, a section of the wooded parts along the hilly spine of the Central Ridge was transferred to the army, which later illegally expanded its territory; another chunk was grabbed in the 1980s by the ashram of Asaram Bapu, a popular *sant* (holy man).[26] Numerous other encroachments over the last three decades have nibbled away at the Ridge until its death by a thousand cuts seems imminent.[27]

Not only did the forested area of the Ridge shrink because of land diversion and encroachment, but from the 1980s the character of the forest also began to change. Until then, the wooded Ridge was regarded as a wilderness and duly ignored. It was not trespassed upon except by poor men and women who collected wood from the area for cooking and heating, bribing or cajoling the rarely encountered *chaukidar* (guard). In 1978, however, the Central Ridge was the scene of a gruesome crime, filed in popular memory as the Billa-Ranga case.[28] Geeta and Sanjay Chopra, the teenage daughter and son of a naval officer, were abducted when they hitched a ride on the Ridge Road. The car was driven into the woods; Geeta Chopra was raped; she and her brother were murdered. The incident shook middle-class newspaper-reading Delhi: Geeta and Sanjay could have been their children. As the hunt for the culprits began, the Ridge came into focus as a place of danger, the locus of criminal activities. Efforts to bring law and order to the Ridge took a physical form: from being an overlooked, overgrown space, the unruly Ridge was to be disciplined.

On the Northern Ridge, the domestication of wilderness took the form of clearing the dense understorey of shrubs and creepers such as *bansa*, *heens, gondni, jangli karaunda, bilangada*, and *kankera* and replacing it with grass.[29] Ornamental plants and shrubs were planted in neat beds. Graveled walking paths were cut through the forest. A small pond was spanned by a bridge, picturesque reeds planted on its banks, and benches placed so that visitors could gaze upon the pretty scene. A badminton court was created in a depression near the Flagstaff Tower, which had been built by the British in 1828. The ruins of Pir Ghaib, a fourteenth-century Tughlaq hunting lodge, and Chauburja, a mausoleum from the same period, were spruced up. The Ridge was now accessible and inviting to middle-class citizens.[30]

Once manicured, sections of the Ridge were enthusiastically incorporated into the social geography of residents of well-to-do neighborhoods in the vicinity. Morning walks—the quintessential quotidian practice of urban Indians with sedentary lifestyles—bring cars to the gates of the Ridge, from which middle-aged men (and some women) alight, all wearing the sports shoes that declare their commitment to their fitness regime. They stride briskly along the paths, swinging their arms, breathing deeply to fill their lungs with the clean morning air. Some stop to stretch, a few jog; groups do yoga and laughter therapy. Others carry small packets of grain which they scatter at designated spots, charitably feeding flocks of parakeets and pigeons. Still others carry bananas to feed the rhesus macaques that infest the Ridge, their numbers proliferating on food offerings from Hindus who consider them a *roop* (incarnate form) of god Hanuman. After their vigorous exercise, many morning walkers head for the fruit vendors standing near the parked cars to drink coconut water and eat nutritious fruit such as papaya. Then they get back into their cars and drive home to bathe and start the work day.

While the crowds of morning walkers attest to the success of the project of taming the Ridge and encompassing it within the ordered realm of the city, a different facet of this accessibility becomes apparent later in the day. By late morning, well after the fitness enthusiasts have departed from the scene, the rows of parked cars outside the gates are replaced by motorcycles. Walking up the now-deserted paths, one encounters only hopeful families of macaques looking for handouts. But on the lawns, under shady trees and behind sheltering shrubs, there is a discreet but nonetheless palpable buzz of activity. Each semiconcealed spot that offers some privacy harbors a pair of young lovers looking for solitude. In a city where young women are subject to family surveillance, and escaping the censorious public eye is difficult for romancing couples, the gardens of the Ridge offer refuge. As Radhika Chandiramani writes: "There's safety in the park. The park sets limits.[31] They hold hands, press palms together, play with each other's fingers. ... Privacy lurks in public spaces; pleasure lies in the palm of a hand."[32] Paradoxically, the public park, where visibility is coupled with anonymity, allows a retreat from the public into a realm of privacy for partners of various sexual persuasions. Rendering the Ridge safer for citizens by converting the forest into a wooded park created a space that enables romantic and sexual practices that would otherwise have been stifled; it allows youth to express themselves as lovers, desiring and desired subjects who can more fully participate in the increasingly influential discourse of romantic love and courtship.

The domestication of the Ridge thus not only created new bourgeois forms of recreation and caring for the self, but also enabled romantic and sexual practices in public spaces, pushing against the limits of what is considered culturally tolerable and gradually widening them. Making the Ridge safer for ordinary and elite citizens had another unintended effect. Some of those who came to the park for morning walks were drawn to the area that was still wilderness. Sanjeev Khanna remembers when his dog darted into the undergrowth, chasing a Grey Partridge or some exciting scent.[33] "When I followed him, pushing through the bushes, I found myself alone. There was nothing but the sound of birds. It was cooler and the air was sweet and clear. It was gorgeous. Really wild. Other people wouldn't go into this part of the Ridge, but I loved it." Khanna was a teenager in the late 1970s, when he literally stumbled into a fascination with the wilderness of the Ridge. Later, he met a few other school and college students who were interested in bird-watching and began to go on nature rambles with them, learning about the flora and fauna of the Ridge and how it had changed over the last one hundred years and coming to understand the ecological importance of the forest. In 1979, on reading that a section of the Central Ridge had been demarcated for constructing schools, the students decided to organize a protest rally in which they were joined by the residents of Rajendra Nagar, the neighborhood next to the proposed clearance. A year later, the students went on to form Kalpavriksh, an "environmental action group" that campaigned against the diversion of the forest to other land use and the conversion of wilderness into parks.[34]

Over the next two decades, Kalpavriksh continued to monitor the Ridge's biodiversity by conducting annual bird counts and mapping the vegetation. Hoping to ignite the same spark of understanding and appreciation of the wilderness in others, members guided school and college students on "nature walks."[35] It published a booklet about the Ridge and its threatened status.[36] It petitioned the lieutenant-governor of Delhi and other officials to prevent the destruction of the Ridge. Even as Kalpavriksh went on to study and campaign about a range of emerging conflicts between ecology and economic development, traveling farther afield into rural India, the organization's early involvement with the Ridge remained a defining moment in its biography, when Khanna and others realized that it was wilderness that they loved, not a park. How this sensibility set them apart from other upper-middle-class people, and how it evolved into a critique of industrial capitalism and its consumerist culture, leading to a stand against "destructive development" in rural India, is a complex story.[37] But central to it is the sensual experience of the Ridge in the early morning, its tangled wildness a contrast to the ordered, populated park.

Since the 1980s, the Ridge has faced new threats and recruited new champions. Kalpavriksh has shifted base from Delhi to Pune, but other organizations and alliances, formal as well as improvised, have taken up the cause, focusing primarily on preventing further construction on the Southern Ridge, an area now surrounded by affluent neighborhoods, where residents have become concerned about dwindling greenery and aquifers.[38] One such campaign highlights the unintended ironies of the situation. During the lead up to the Commonwealth Games in 2010, the Delhi government planned to expand the sports facilities that it had constructed for the Asian Games in 1982 by clearing an adjacent section of the Ridge. They encountered vehement opposition, including a public-interest petition filed in court, from residents of nearby Siri Fort Village, a low-key yet luxurious haven in a prestigious location inhabited by members of the elite. As the residents denounced the Delhi government for its callous destruction of greenery, they chose to forget that the spacious bungalows in which they lived had been built less than twenty years ago by exactly the same process—clearing the Ridge.[39] Siri Fort Village was carved out of the Southern Ridge to house visiting athletes and sports officials during Asiad '82. After the games were over, the houses were sold at well below market rate to senior bureaucrats and their cronies and relatives. Beneficiaries of that process now reinvented themselves as saviors of the city's green areas.

Conclusion

As Mangarbani and the Delhi Ridge change and are threatened with change, they bring into being new allegiances and alliances.[40] These green spaces and the urban publics who cohere around them have shaped and transformed each other. Reconfigured relations in the ecological and social landscape have had uneven effects. The domestication of the wilderness of the Northern Ridge for recreational use has squeezed out the native flora and fauna; jackals, hares, and monitor lizards have now disappeared. Poor people who collect firewood and grass find it much harder to do so; vigilant middle-class walkers and patroling *chaukidars* are quick to pounce on them. The Ridge is now closed off from its past use as an urban common that provisioned those who lived by the sweat of their brow; they have been replaced by those who sweat in order to keep their bodies fit. Yet the concerns of the laboring classes have not figured in the debate over urban conservation.

In other parts of the city, the conflict over urban nature has been even more violent. Early one morning in January 1995, residents of the well-to-do neighborhood of Ashok Vihar caught and beat young Dilip to death for defecating in the open area that they regarded as their "park."[41] The opposition between different views of urban nature and its commons could not be starker. Dilip was from an adjoining *jhuggi basti* (squatter settlement), where more than ten thousand households had only twenty-four latrines between them, forcing people to use any open space, under cover of dark, as a place to defecate. The more affluent residents of the area tried to discourage this practice by building a wall between the dirty, unsightly *jhuggis* and their own homes, but the wall was soon broken to allow the daily traffic of domestic workers who lived in the *jhuggis* but worked to clean the homes and cars of the rich, as well as the nighttime passage of clandestine defecators. Dilip's death was thus the culmination of a long-standing battle over a contested space that, to one set of residents embodied their sense of gracious urban living, a place of trees and grass devoted to leisure and recreation, and that to another set of residents, was the only available space that could be used as a toilet. When a group of people from the *jhuggis* gathered to protest against this killing, the police opened fire and killed four more people.[42]

The social geography of urban nature in Delhi is a deeply riven, shifting landscape. As the villagers of Mangarbani showed by their alacrity in selling their share of the sacred forest, green spaces can become taken for granted and traded for more tangible gains. Yet other social groups have intervened to evoke a sense of loss and a renewed appreciation of the forest, leading to a new determination to save it from developers. The domesticated sections of the Delhi Ridge now accommodate morning walkers and trysting couples, members of the middle-aged middle classes and their subversive offspring. And, at the same time, for a handful of people, the park opened up a path into the wilderness as an aesthetically and ecologically superior form of urban nature.

While these are unexpected twists produced by the coming together of disparate elements and contingencies, there are expected patterns and continuities as well. More than sixty years after Independence, Viceroy's Lord Hardinge's urban forests command the higher ground close to the centers of power; the Versailles-style gardens that he envisaged grace affluent parts of the city. Greenery is a good index of a neighborhood's prestige and wealth, while its lack is a sign of social exclusion and impoverishment. Most poor, working-class areas of Delhi are massed boxes of brick and cement broken only by narrow streets. There are no trees to sit under, no grass on which to run or play or take a nap in the winter sun. The government's proud slogan of a "clean and green" city dies away once one leaves elite and middle-class areas. When green is confined to the solitary tree that has survived in a wasteland or a densely packed settlement, or the *tulsi* (sacred basil) plant growing in a recycled tin, urban nature is conspicuous by its absence.

Green is not a primary color; it is the result of mixing blue and yellow. So, too, the shades of green that are found in Delhi. Parks, wilderness, wasteland—each is streaked by social character, by ways of knowing and valuing nature that vary with the city's sharp hierarchies and shifting alliances.

Acknowledgments

Thanks to Henrik Ernstson for his close and enthusiastic engagement with this work.

Notes

1. Krishen 2006.

2. Gold and Gujar (2002) have analyzed how villagers in Rajasthan differently value *vilayati* (foreign or imported) *keekar*—*Prosopis juliflora* (mesquite) is a native of Mexico—and *desi* (native or indigenous) *keekar* (*Acacia nilotica*), also called *babool*. *P. juliflora*'s thorns and inedible leaves keep browsing animals away, making it useless for pastoralists seeking fodder, whereas *Acacia nilotica* yields fodder as well as an edible gum. Gold and Gujar argue that *desi* and *vilayati*—native and foreign—are binary categories that organize perceptions of modernity in rural India, especially with respect to agrarian environments and species.

3. Vrindavan, also known as Braj, is an area in present-day Mathura district, Uttar Pradesh, sacred to Krishna, the Hindu deity. In legend, Vrindavan was an ancient forest on the banks of the river Yamuna where the young Krishna lived, grazed cows, sported with village maids, and fought demons. It became a place of pilgrimage for Hindus of the Vaishnava sects from the seventeenth century onward, and several temples were built there. The forest was gradually destroyed over the last two centuries. The *kadamba* tree is associated with Krishna's life in Vrindavan: in an episode made famous in songs and paintings, Krishna stole the clothes of bathing *gopis* (girl cowherds) and hid them in a *kadamba* tree.

4. The scientific name of *dhau* is *Anogeissus pendula*. *Kala siris* is *Albizia odoratissima*, and *salai* is *Boswellia serrata*. *Kareel* is *Capparis decidua*; *roheda* is *Tecomella undulata*; *kaim* is *Mitragyna parvifolia*; and *kanju* is *Holoptelea integrifolia*. *Ronjh* is *Acacia leucophloea*; *bistendu* is *Diospyros cordifolia*; *hingot* is *Balanites roxburghi*, and *doodhi* is *Wrightia tinctoria*. *Doodhi ki bel* is *Vallaris solanacea*. For a complete list of the flora of Mangarbani, see Shahabuddin, Yadav, and Krishen (2013).

5. "Bani" means "little forest."

6. See Chakravarty-Kaul (1996) for a finely observed account of a similar conflict over the commons in North West Delhi. Her analysis includes a detailed examination of the case law on disputes around rights to the commons from the colonial period onwards.

7. This term was used by Ashok Khemka, former director general of Consolidation of Land Holdings in Haryana, an Indian Administrative Service officer turned whistle-blower, who was soon transferred out of this post (see Dogra 2013).

8. To prevent the concentration of land in the hands of a few, the law stipulates that no one can own more than 7.5 hectares of irrigated land or 18 hectares of rain-fed land.

9. This is not to suggest that there has been no farmers' opposition to land acquisition for real estate development in Haryana. In 2008, a *mahapanchayat* (super-panchayat of several villages) declared that it would not allow the government to acquire twenty-five thousand acres of land from twenty-two villages in Jhajjar district and eighteen villages in Gurgaon district for a Special Economic Zone to be set up by Reliance Industries, India's biggest private company (see Deswal 2008). However, such instances of resistance in Haryana and neighboring Uttar Pradesh are primarily tactics for negotiating better terms, not stopping land transactions. Landowners are not unwilling to sell; they just don't want to get a pittance from the government, which then hands over the land to a private company, which makes a killing from the rise in its value. Michael Levien's (2012, 2013) research on land acquisition in Rajasthan shows that land prices rose eight to twelve times after such a transfer, an escalation that the original landowners did not benefit from.

10. Temples sprout up almost overnight on city pavements, in the crevices of *peepal* (*Ficus religiosa*) trees, as kiosks set into walls, on abandoned plots of land, and in squatter settlements as a bid to stake claim to land that a state soft on "hurting religious sentiments" is reluctant to act against. From a small icon, to tiled and cemented surrounds, to concrete canopies and domes is usually a series of quick steps, as is the emergence of a thriving spiritual economy of patrons, priests, vendors of ritual offerings, and worshippers. However recent their vintage, temples tend to announce themselves as *pracheen* (ancient) from the get-go.

11. Boosters style Gurgaon as the "Millennium City," a destination for corporate offices and high-end residential projects with names like Belvedere Towers and Malibu Towne, but first among the basic infrastructural amenities absent in the city is water. Overexploitation has depleted the aquifer; groundwater is brackish. The more Gurgaon's affluent population grows, the worse its water problems (Soni 2000). Environmentalists have so far not been successful in either regulating groundwater extraction in Gurgaon or instituting rainwater harvesting on a significant scale. For an account of unregulated urbanization and the creation of landscapes of inequality on Delhi's periphery, see Soni (2000) and Chatterji (2013).

12. Shrivastava 2013.

13. "No Tourism Activity" 2014.

14. Palash is *Butea monosperma*; amaltas is *Cassia fistula*.

15. Krishen 2006.

16. For an account of the changing place of the Yamuna floodplain in urban political economy and ecology, see Baviskar (2011b).

17. Cf. Williams (1972).

18. According to forester R. N. Parker (1920, p. 25), this is likely to have occurred after the 1857 mutiny because, at that time, the vegetation was thick enough for "the attacking [British] force [to] advance 'concealed in the brushwood stretching up to within musket shot of the walls' [of the Mughal city of Shahjehanabad]." It is also reported that Firoz Shah Tughlaq, sultan of Delhi from 1351 to 1388, planted trees on the northern Ridge and used the area for hunting.

19. Letter from Hardinge to Edwin Lutyens, August 19, 1912, quoted in Krishen (2006, p. 37).

20. Letter from Hailey, Secretary, Notified Area Committee, January 13, 1916. Hailey went on to become the chief commissioner of Delhi (1918–1924). Delhi State Archives.

21. The scientific name of *siris* is *Albizzia lebbek*.

22. Department of Horticulture of Government Gardens 1936, p. 8.

23. George 1958, p. 86.

24. It had been fenced off from grazing earlier, in the late 1910s.

25. Hosagrahar 2005; Legg 2007.

26. The establishment of the ashram was challenged in a 1985 public interest petition, but in 1996 the Supreme Court allowed it to be regularized, despite opposition from forest officials. However, the recent fall from grace of Asaram Bapu, now facing trial for raping a minor at his Jodhpur ashram, may mean that action will finally be taken to close the ashram (Shrangi 2014).

27. For details of the area of the Ridge and its current land status, see Delhi Forest Department (2017). See also Kothari (1988).

28. Billa and Ranga were the two men who were eventually convicted of the crime.

29. Bansa is *Adathoda vasica*; heens is *Capparis sepiaria*; gondni is *Grewia tenax*; jangli karaunda is *Carissa spinarum*; bilangada is *Flacourtia indica*; and kankera is *Maytenus senegalensis*.

30. The process of "beautifying" the Ridge in the 1970s and 1980s was less pronounced in the Central Ridge (where a large section had already been carved out as the Buddha Jayanti Park in the 1960s) and the Southern Ridge (which was not yet surrounded by the upper-middle-class residential neighborhoods that came up in the late 1980s).

31. Here, Chandiramani (2001, pp. 197–198) is referring to young women who, while willing to engage romantically with their partners, want to be able to control what they do. Sexual coercion, including rape, by one's companion is less likely when there are other people around and where a chaukidar or itinerant vendor is a shout away. The "wild" part of the Ridge would not be safe (or comfortable) in this respect.

32. The discussion of contestations over public spaces focuses mainly on the tensions between bourgeois notions of spatial order and public conduct and their defiance by the poor (cf. Kaviraj 1997) and, to a lesser extent, on how this patriarchal spatial order marginalizes women (cf. Ranade 2007). The use of public parks by young men and women seeking privacy and the social disapproval that they face, which can even take the form of humiliating remarks and physical harassment by Hindu nationalist "moral police" vigilante groups, suggests that age-based discrimination is as much a part of the conflict over parks as are class and gender-based orientations.

33. Name changed.

34. Kalpavriksh has gone on to become a well-known research and advocacy NGO, working on issues of ecological sustainability and social equity. It was a pioneer in

developing a broad-based critique of large dams, and has worked extensively to promote community-based natural resource management (see Kalpavriksh n.d.).

35. For a survey of Kalpavriksh's engagement with the Ridge by one of the organization's founder-members, narrated as the account of a nature walk, see Kothari (1988). For an analysis of how activities such as hiking foster a "love for nature" among students in Indonesia, see Tsing (2005).

36. Kalpavriksh 1991.

37. The history of the wilderness movement in India has been sketched by Ramachandra Guha (1989) and Mahesh Rangarajan (1996). Their analysis has focused on the ideological strands of the movement, which range from the socially conservative, demanding "inviolate areas" for megafauna, to the more human rights–oriented "community based management." However, a social history that examines the class background of "wilderness lovers" and relates it to their ways of being in the world and 'structures of feeling' remains to be done (cf. Bourdieu 1984). A small beginning has been made by Mawdsley (2004) and Baviskar (2011a).

38. See Ghertner (2011) for a discussion of one such controversy near Vasant Kunj, where the Delhi Development Authority violated its own master plan to allow the construction of shopping malls and a luxury hotel on a remaining section of the Ridge, a move that was retrospectively legalized by the court.

39. Baviskar 2010.

40. Walker (2007) provides a superb, richly detailed account of this process in the San Francisco Bay Area of California. See also his chapter in this volume.

41. See Baviskar (2003) for other instances of bourgeois environmentalist campaigns to create a "clean and green Delhi," which target the city's working-class occupations and neighborhoods as prime offenders.

42. See report from People's Union for Democratic Rights (1995).

References

Baviskar, Amita. 2003. "Between Violence and Desire: Space, Power and Identity in the Making of Metropolitan Delhi." *International Social Science Journal* 175: 89–98.

Baviskar, Amita. 2010. "Spectacular Events, City Spaces and Citizenship: The Commonwealth Games in Delhi." In *Urban Navigations: Politics, Space and the City in South Asia*, edited by Jonathan Shapiro Anjaria and Colin McFarlane, 138–161. New Delhi: Routledge.

Baviskar, Amita. 2011a. "Cows, Cars and Cycle-Rickshaws: Bourgeois Environmentalism and the Battle for Delhi's Streets." In *Elite and Everyman: The Cultural Politics of the Indian Middle Classes*, edited by Amita Baviskar and Raka Ray, 391–418. New Delhi: Routledge.

Baviskar, Amita. 2011b. "What the Eye Does Not See: River Yamuna in the Imagination of Delhi." In "Review of Urban Affairs," special issue, *Economic and Political Weekly* 46(50): 45–53.

Bourdieu, Pierre. 1984. *Distinction: A Social Critique of the Judgment of Taste.* Translated by Richard Nice. Cambridge, MA: Harvard University Press.

Chakravarty-Kaul, Minati. 1996. *Common Lands and Customary Law: Institutional Change in North India over the Past Two Centuries.* Delhi: Oxford University Press.

Chandiramani, Radhika. 2001. "Lovers, They Are Everywhere." In *City Improbable: Writings on Delhi*, edited by Khushwant Singh, 194–198. New Delhi: Penguin India.

Chatterji, Tathagata. 2013. "The Micro-Politics of Urban Transformation in the Context of Globalisation: A Case Study of Gurgaon, India." *South Asia: Journal of South Asian Studies* 36(2): 273–287.

Delhi Forest Department. 2017. "Recorded Forest," by the Forest Department of the Government of National Capital Territory of Delhi. http://www.delhi.gov.in/wps/wcm/connect/doit_forest/Forest/Home/Forests+of+Delhi/Recorded+Forest.

Department of Horticulture of Government Gardens. 1936. *Annual Report of Government Gardens 1935–1936.* Delhi: Government of India.

Deswal, Deepender. 2008. "Mahapanchayat Decides against Having SEZ [Special Economic Zones]." *Times of India*, May 12. http://articles.timesofindia.indiatimes.com/2008-05-12/chandigarh/27778469_1_sez-policy-sez-issue-pelpa.

Dogra, Chander Suta. 2013. "How Village Common Property along the Aravallis Is Grabbed." *Hindu*, February 9. http://www.thehindu.com/news/how-village-common-property-along-the-aravallis-is-grabbed/article4394445.ece.

George, Walter. 1958. "The Roadside Planting of Lutyens' Delhi." *Urban and Rural Planning Thought*, April, 78–94.

Ghertner, D. Asher. 2011. "Rule by Aesthetics: World-Class City Making in Delhi." In *Worlding Cities: Asian Experiments and the Art of Being Global*, edited by Ananya Roy and Aihwa Ong, 279–306. Oxford: Blackwell.

Gold, Ann Grodzins, and Bhoju Ram Gujar. 2002. *In the Time of Trees and Sorrows: Nature, Power, and Memory in Rajasthan.* Durham, NC: Duke University Press.

Guha, Ramachandra. 1989. "Radical American Environmentalism and Wilderness Preservation: A Third World Critique." *Environmental Ethics* 11(1): 71–83.

Hosagrahar, Jyoti. 2005. *Indigenous Modernities: Negotiating Architecture and Urbanism.* London: Routledge.

Kalpavriksh. 1991. *The Delhi Ridge Forest: Decline and Conservation*. Delhi: Kalpavriksh.

Kalpavriksh. n.d. "About Us." http://kalpavriksh.org/index.php/about-us. Accessed December 4, 2017.

Kaviraj, Sudipto. 1997. "Filth and the Public Sphere: Concepts and Practices about Space in Calcutta." *Public Culture* 10(1): 83–113.

Kothari, Ashish. 1988. "The Delhi Ridge." *The India Magazine*, July, 28–30.

Krishen, Pradip. 2006. *Trees of Delhi: A Field Guide*. Delhi: Dorling Kindersley.

Legg, Stephen. 2007. *Spaces of Colonialism: Delhi's Urban Governmentalities*. Malden, MA: Blackwell.

Levien, Michael. 2012. "The Land Question: Special Economic Zones and the Political Economy of Dispossession in India." *Journal of Peasant Studies* 39(3–4): 933–969.

Levien, Michael. 2013. "Regimes of Dispossession: From Steel Towns to Special Economic Zones." *Development and Change* 44(2): 381–407.

Mawdsley, Emma. 2004. "India's Middle Classes and the Environment." *Development and Change* 35(1): 79–103.

"No Tourism Activity, Construction in Mangar Bani." 2014. *The Hindu*, May 16. http://www.thehindu.com/todays-paper/tp-national/tp-newdelhi/no-tourism-activity -construction-in-mangar-bani/article6014393.ece.

Parker, R. N. 1920. "Afforestation of the Ridge at Delhi." *Indian Forester*, January, 21–28.

People's Union for Democratic Rights (PUDR). 1995. *A Tale of Two Cities: Custodial Death and Police Firing in Ashok Vihar*. Delhi: PUDR.

Ranade, Shilpa. 2007. "The Way She Moves: Mapping the Everyday Production of Gender-Space." *Economic and Political Weekly* 42(17): 1519–1526.

Rangarajan, Mahesh. 1996. "The Politics of Ecology: The Debate on Wildlife and People in India, 1970–95." *Economic and Political Weekly* 31(35–37): 2391–2409.

Shahabuddin, Ghazala, Archana Yadav, and Pradip Krishen. 2013. "Botanical Survey of Mangar Bani Sacred Grove and Adjacent Areas: A Report on Vegetation Diversity, Threats and Management." Delhi: Unpublished report.

Shrangi, Vatsala. 2014. "Probe Likely into Land Encroachment Complaint against Asaram Bapu." *Guardian*, May 24. http://www.sunday-guardian.com/news/probe -likely-into-land-encroachment-complaint-against-asaram-bapu.

Shrivastava, Kumar Sambhav. 2013. "Green Tribunal Orders Halt on All Non-Forest Activities in the Aravallis in Faridabad." Down to Earth, January 25. http://www

.downtoearth.org.in/content/green-tribunal-orders-halt-all-non-forest-activities
-aravallis-faridabad.

Soni, Anita. 2000. "Urban Conquest of Outer Delhi: Beneficiaries, Intermediaries
and Victims, The Case of the Mehrauli Countryside." In *Delhi: Urban Space and
Human Destinies*, edited by Veronique Dupont, Emma Tarlo, and Denis Vidal, 75–94.
New Delhi: Manohar.

Tsing, Anna L. 2005. *Friction: An Ethnography of Global Connection*. Princeton, NJ:
Princeton University Press.

Walker, Richard. 2007. *The Country in the City: The Greening of the San Francisco Bay
Area*. Seattle: University of Washington Press.

Williams, Raymond. 1972. "Ideas of Nature." In *Problems in Materialism and Culture*,
67–85. London: Verso.

9 Regimes of Urban Nature: Organic Urbanism, Biotope Protection, and Civic Gardening in Berlin

Jens Lachmund

In the early 1960s, the Berlin writer Irmgard Wirth called attention to the widespread existence of parks, gardens, and various pieces of the rural landscape within or in the close vicinity of her city:

> Ranging from the small square the size of a block with lawns, flowerbeds and shadowing trees and bench to rest for the air hungry city dweller, to the extended people's park [*Volkspark*]…, to the remaining villages with their old churches, estates, farm houses, meadows and fields, to the distinguished mansion districts with their gardens, or the residential areas from the 1920s that are pervaded with green, to the Grunewald or the vast Spandau- and Tegel-forest in West Berlin, which are almost deserted during the week,—about one fourth of the total surface of this city is "nature," before and beyond the wall it consists of water, forest, and heath![1]

This characterization of Berlin as an extraordinary "green" city in which "nature" abounds has been a constant feature of public discourse in the post–World War II period.[2] More than just a description of the actual cityscape, imaginings of urban nature guided urban policy and contributed to the city's identity. Already, since the late nineteenth century, urbanists, nature conservationists, and large parts of the urban public had been convinced that "green" or "nature" was a necessary antidote to the anonymity, density, and fast pace of the modern metropolis, the poor living conditions of industrial workers, and the traffic, noise, and air pollution that pervaded the city. Many of the basic worries that motivated planners in that period to create public parks, to plant trees, and to protect the urban forests on the fringe of the urban area persist in more recent attempts to "green" the city. At a more concrete level, however, there are considerable differences between the ways that nature has been identified and framed, what kind of problems of the city it has been supposed to mitigate, and how the concern for nature was to be integrated into the planning and managing of urban space. In this chapter I use post–World War II Berlin as a case study to shed light on the political, discursive, and practical processeses through which different models of urban nature took shape in a local context and how these both differed and, at the same time, built on each other. Following my earlier work on urban nature in Berlin,[3] this chapter conceives each of these models as a historically situated "urban nature regime," that is, a set of problematizations, imaginations, and strategic practices that are anchored in and developed through sites or objects of nonhuman nature (such as parks, species, air quality, and so on), which are deemed valuable and therefore supposed to require public attention or care.[4] By tracing how such regimes emerged and achieved relative coherence and stability, the chapter seeks to explore the entanglement of nature and politics in the urban context, as well as to look at the tensions and dilemmas that have existed within and between each of these regimes. My focus is thereby both on the continuity of the preoccupation with "greening the city" as an overarching rationale that connects Berlin's urban nature regimes and on the different ways in which nature has been framed and imagined in each of them. At the same time, I also want to highlight the specific ways in which in each of these regimes, the framing of urban nature has been articulated with changing definitions of how citizenship and expertise should matter in the governing of urban space.

Until the unification of Germany in 1990, the city on which this study focuses was divided into two parts: East Berlin, which was the capital of the German Democratic Republic, and West Berlin, a walled (as of 1961) city-island, which, although formerly under the control of the Western Allies, formed a de facto exclave of West Germany's Federal Republic. I will focus specifically on three different nature regimes between the postwar era and the present. A substantial discussion of the green policy in East Berlin would require a systematic engagement with the theme of socialist urban planning. Besides some cursory remarks I will restrict myself therefore to the development in West Berlin, and, more recently, unified Berlin.

As a first regime I discuss the attempt of planners and city gardeners in the 1950s and early 1960s to transform urbanized space into an "urban landscape" that united the physical features of the landscape and the material outline and architecture of the city into an "organic" whole. The second is the politics of "species and biotope protection" in the 1970s and 1980s in West Berlin and its discursive framing on the basis of urban ecological research. The third is the more recent movement of "urban civic gardening," as I call it here, which involves the active appropriation of green spaces as sites of urban sociability and food production. These three regimes were not confined to distinct periods. Rather, discourses and practices of earlier regimes continued to exist in later ones, resulting in tensions that this chapter will touch on as well.

The Quest for an Organic Landscape

The showpiece of the International Construction Exposition Interbau, which took place in Berlin in 1957, was the Hansaviertel, a central neighborhood that had been destroyed during the war and had been rebuilt according to the ideal of so-called organic urbanism,[5] a nature regime that took shape in the discourses and practices of city- and green planners in the two decades after World War II in West Germany. The guiding rationale of this regime was to transform cities into *Stadtlandschaften*, literally urban landscapes.[6] In contrast to later nature regimes, organic urbanism operated almost exclusively through top-down planning schemes for the rebuilding of cities or even for the design of new towns, such as Sennestadt in the North Rhine–Westphalian region. Citizens figured only as the downstream targets of public campaigns, such as exhibitions that sought to garner support for the new planning ideal. They did not, as we will see with the later regimes, engage citizens as active co-agents of knowledge- and city-making.[7]

According to the proponents of *Stadtlandschaft*, the destruction of German cities during the war offered a unique chance to create an alternative to the classic European city with its dense and highly populated inner districts.[8] In Berlin the rapid growth of the city in the late nineteenth century had resulted in densely developed areas with five-storey tenements with rear buildings and tiny courtyards. These so-called *Mietskasernen* (rental barracks) were criticized not only on aesthetic grounds. The labyrinth of dark rear buildings in which mainly working-class people lived were considered to be breeding grounds of disease and moral deprivation in the view of urbanists and the wider urban bourgeoisie in Germany.[9] Once infamous as the "largest *Mietskasernenstadt* of the world,"[10] bombed Berlin became the target of far-reaching proposals for transformation.

As Hans Bernhard Reichow put it in a trendsetting textbook, the creation of *Stadtlandschaft* would allow "combining the advantages of the big metropolis with those of a simple, close-to-nature countryside life."[11] The concept showed many parallels with the garden city ideal as well as with the program of modernist urbanism of the Athens Charta.[12] It shared with the latter a preoccupation with a spatial separation of urban functions and the call for vast open spaces that would connect the city to its surrounding landscape. The core idea was to shape an "organic" morphology of the city, which itself was an attempt to engineer an equally organic form of social life.[13] In this respect the approach has similarities with *Landschaftspflege* (landscape care), which had earlier attempted to integrate traffic and industrial infrastructures "organically" into the natural landscape. Although the longing for organic forms was not restricted to Germany, it was especially here that it gained in popularity in the Weimar years and notably under National Socialism, when planning for postwar reconstruction embraced the city landscape ideal.[14] The term "organic" received its rhetorical punch through its semantic opposition to the "mechanical," which was associated with density, right angles, disconnection from surrounding landscapes, and a supposed lack of social bonds among the inhabitants. In a trendsetting textbook on "organic urbanism" from 1948, Hans Bernhard Reichow portrayed the city as a machine, alienating its residents from nature.[15] In contrast, an organic city would consist of a hierarchy of nested units: cells, neighborhoods, districts. In 1950 the conservative garden designer Gustav Allinger dreamed of Berlin as a "new city," one that would be a "living organism that is connected to nature."[16] In the same vein, Johannes Göderitz, Roland Rainer, and Hubert Hoffmann characterized their ideal of an "articulated and low-density city" as a "spatially loosened, yet functionally closely entangled texture of single cells of human size."[17] The term "organic" pointed mainly to the morphology of the city as conceived from the bird's-eye perspective of the planner's table. The city should extend smoothly into the surrounding landscape and its material design should imitate natural forms. By structuring the city into small "organic" segments of neighborhoods, planners also wanted to reconstitute close community bonds within the modern metropolis.[18]

The concept of organic urbanism was the basis of the 1946 Kollektivplan for the rebuilding of Berlin, developed by a planning team led by the architect Hans Scharoun.[19] It envisioned a radically restructured city, consisting of dispersed modernist buildings, clustered into homogenous neighborhoods, and cut through by highways and green spaces. Whereas the plan ignored the existing historical development, it fitted the city neatly into the geomorphology of the basin of the river Spree and thereby translated the idea of organic city planning into a locally specific urban vision.

The division of Germany made the realization of a master plan for the entire city impossible. The "16 principles of urbanism" launched by the East German government in 1950 rejected the idea of a synthesis of town and country, and instead called for a compactly structured "socialist" city with monumental centers. Such a city was also seen as "organic," but only in the sense that its components formed a functional whole, not because of its visual morphology.[20] In West Berlin, actual development proceeded through a pragmatic and piecemeal approach of clearing rubble and renovating and rebuilding existing property.[21] The 1948 Bonatz-plan and the subsequent land-use plan for West Berlin (issued in 1950) refrained from radical changes to the city layout. In the end, it was only the reconstruction of the destroyed Hansaviertel that resulted in a coherent architectural ensemble that corresponded to the ideas of the *Stadtlandschaft*. The project was actually a propagandist landmark of Western urbanism to demonstrate a "free-world" alternative to the monumental projects being realized at that time at the East Berlin Stalinallee.[22] In the late 1960s, East Berlin saw the spread of modernist housing projects, made with precast concrete slabs (*Plattenbauten*), on the outskirts and in destroyed inner-city areas.[23] Although these settlements were loosely structured with green spaces, they were meant not to realize an organic *Stadtlandschaft*, but to technically and economically rationalize housing construction.

At least in West Berlin, the term *Stadtlandschaft* remained a guiding principle of green planning. Directly after the division of the city in 1949, the West Berlin municipality launched its "Green Emergency Program" to reconstruct green spaces, playing fields, and sports grounds. Here specific local politics mattered to the way in which urban nature was articulated. Greening was meant to reconstruct some sense of order in the chaos of the damaged city, and with the sharpening of the Cold War—notably the Russian blockade during the winter of 1948–1949—to demonstrate political assertiveness against the East. In line with the ideals of organic urbanism, Berlin garden director Witte argued that urban planning in his city should consider the "connections and circumstances of the natural landscape."[24] This orientation manifested itself in the creation of extended green belts such as the promenades along the natural waters and urban canals.[25] In 1960 the West Berlin parliament decided to create a comprehensive framework (*Hauptgrünflächenplan*) for the further development of a network of green space. The concept also inspired attempts to preserve green areas on the fringe of the city, for example by turning them into protected "landscape reserves." Another way in which organic planning left its mark on the city's material ecology was in the treatment of the various rubble mounds that resulted from the clearance of bombed quarters and mushroomed in both East and West Berlin.[26] In the latter, these could become landscape opportunities. Thus, for example, rubble that accumulated north of the Grunewald forest, the so-called Teufelsberg, was shaped as a natural-looking hill planted with dense vegetation and connected to surrounding parks and forests.

As we have seen, the organic nature regime implied a quite far-reaching attempt to transform the natural, and indirectly also the social, characteristics of the city. The focus thereby, however, was mainly on urban form. This meant that the discursive ownership of the regime remained largely in the hands of planners, not nature conservationists, civic activists, or ecologists. This only changed with the emergence of biotope protection as a focus of a novel urban nature regime.

Protecting and Promoting Urban Biotopes

The Südgelände (literally, southern area) is the site of a former railroad marshaling yard in the former West Berlin district of Schöneberg. Since the railroad yard had been abandoned in 1948, it had become overgrown with an impressive wood-like wilderness. When in the 1980s plans for a new railway station at this site became public, nature conservationists, ecologists, and activists campaigned for the preservation of what they considered a valuable piece of urban nature. The campaign was successful, and in 2000 a nature park was opened in the Südgelände, both to protect the biodiversity of the site and to allow residents to enjoy its scenery (see figure 9.1).

As in the earlier attempts to create organic landscapes, the nature park was meant to improve the quality of the city through the promotion of nonhuman nature. At the same time, however, the understanding of nature and of its supposed place in the city differed considerably. Already since the 1970s, the concern for urban nature had shifted from matters of urban

Figure 9.1
The Südgelände. Photo by Jens Lachmund.

form to the protection of plant and animal species and their biotopes. Around this concern a quite distinct set of practices and discourses assembled, which I call the *biotope protection regime*. It included diverse actors ranging from academic ecologists to amateur naturalists and conservationists, middle-class neighborhood activists, and representatives of the left-alternative counterculture that flourished in West Berlin at this time. Although these actors and their political strategies differed considerably, they all achieved their political self-definition and their goal orientation at least partly through their sustained engagement with the urban spaces that they framed as biotopes. As with organic urbanism, state-centered planning schemes remained a main policy instrument within this regime. Its content and political momentum, however, were largely the result of contestations and negotiations that extended into the domains of scientific practice as well as civic activism.

In the wake of the international consolidation of ecology in the 1960s and 1970s,[27] some researchers had developed formalized ecosystem models to represent the throughput of energy and materials in exemplary cities.[28] West Berlin soon became recognized as one of the main local centers of this urban turn in ecology. It was not so much the application of formal ecosystem models, however, that characterized Berlin's ecology, but systematic botanical (and to a smaller extent, faunistic) fieldwork within and about the spaces of the city. A central role was played by Herbert Sukopp, a botanist who in 1969 became professor at the Technical University (TU Berlin) and who in 1972/1973, together with two other professors, established a distinct department for ecology.[29] Within a few years Sukopp and a growing number of students and assistant professors had become the most renowned representatives of German urban ecology.

This urban turn can be partly explained by the geopolitical situation of West Berlin and its deprivation of its hinterland, which meant that many ecologists tended to concentrate on the city when doing practical fieldwork. Another factor is that from the late nineteenth century, Berlin had a strong local natural history tradition, and this meant that in the postwar era, local naturalists were able to provide ecologists with an extended historical record against which they could measure the ongoing development of flora and fauna. Moreover, having themselves been cut off from their former rural observation grounds, the naturalists became important collaborators of ecologists in surveying West Berlin's flora and fauna. A third factor was the long-lasting impact of the bombardments of Berlin during World War II. The vast wastelands of bombed plots and the rubble heaps that mushroomed in the outskirts made the city a particularly exciting place for ecologists. The plant species that grew in these places constituted a ruderal vegetation, which differed considerably from the ordinary vegetation of that region. Next to various urban parks and the few nature reserves that had been left intact on the outskirts of West Berlin, such wastelands become a favored site for ecologists' studies.

Sukopp's work in Berlin revolved around the question of how the impact of human land use influenced the composition of the vegetation. He noted particularly the high amount of neophyte species, as well as the absence of many original species that had existed in the area.[30] Although the influence of human land use was pervasive in the Berlin environment, Sukopp argued that its extent depended on the specific use of land and thus varied accordingly.[31]

In the late 1970s, ecological knowledge practices began to coalesce with administrative practices and the city's emerging civic environmental activism to form a politically significant nature regime. Ecologists themselves, notably Sukopp, promoted urban ecology as a practically oriented planning science. He posited that urban spaces were living spaces or biotopes, which hosted various plant and animal species, often even more than rural landscapes. At the same time, however, he warned that nature in the city was endangered by intensifying urban development and that measures should be taken to integrate nature promotion systematically into the planning process. He and other ecologists argued that nature in the city should be preserved not only for its own sake, but also to create better conditions of life for urban citizens.[32] Regular contact with natural environments was considered necessary for city dwellers and even a prerequisite for the healthy development of children. Equally important, the existence of nature in the city was also considered as a means to strengthen other components of the urban ecosystem, such as the quality of the air, soil, and water supply. Although similar arguments had been presented in earlier writings on urban green spaces and garden cities, the argument was now reframed in bio-ecological terms. In particular, since the 1970s, the term "biotope," which denotes a topographical area in which specific biological populations live, has become a political catchword that has penetrated deeply into public consciousness.

Among the allies who sponsored ecologists' agenda, landscape planners and urban environmental activist groups were salient.[33] Evolving from the traditional field of *Landespflege* (landscape care), which had been based largely on a horticultural approach, the new field of landscape planning established itself as a problem-solving discipline, based on ecological research. The profession expanded through the provision of new academic education programs, the largest of which was at TU Berlin. The department of ecology provided teaching for this program. Hence, the new generation of landscape planners passed Sukopp's courses, acquired theoretical and practical skills in urban ecology, and largely adopted a commitment to protecting urban biotopes. Often these planners found jobs in Berlin's public administration or as independent consultants, and thereby became important multipliers of ecology's tenets in urban politics.

A notable difference between the biotope protection regime and the earlier organic one is the convergence of expert-based policymaking with an actively participating citizenship. The spectrum of civic activism in West Berlin ranged from traditional, often politically conservative nature conservation organizations, to middle-class neighborhood activist groups—the so-called *Bürgerinitiativen*—to a colorful counterculture that flourished in some urban quarters. Although the political agenda differed considerably among these groups, they all opposed the various traffic infrastructure projects (highways, canal reconstruction, new power plant) that the Berlin Senate planned at that time, and they all drew at least partly on ecological arguments and research results to bolster their claims against related land-use changes. In such a way they also appropriated the biotope and the plant and animal species of the city as political categories and objects.[34]

The biotope protection regime gained momentum through the Biotope Protection Program, an ecological masterplan for West Berlin, which was publically presented in 1984.[35] The proposal had been prepared by a working group under Sukopp's directorship. Sukopp and his collaborators divided the city into fifty-seven ecological units, or "biotope-types," and assigned different meanings and functions to these spaces. Areas that were "close to nature," such as the few remaining fens, were seen as refuges for original species that were declining in the region. Proposed measures therefore consisted mainly of the minimization of human impact, so that at least the most valuable of these biotopes could survive in the surroundings of the city. For rubble areas and other vacant lots, ecologists emphasized the value of the flora and fauna. They also saw parks and other urban greeneries not only in terms of their aesthetic qualities or recreational functions, but also as biotopes, and they made suggestions for how greeneries should be planted and kept in order to optimize their ecological qualities. For example, whereas the constant removal of weeds is a conventional gardening practice, ecologists considered weeds to be "spontaneous" vegetation that contributed to the flora of the park and that therefore should be tolerated as much as possible. Another focus of ecologists' attention was abandoned railroad tracks and stations where astonishingly rich vegetation had developed. Even in those parts of the city that had been completely built up and paved over, ecologists recognized spaces in which plant and animal species existed and which could be enhanced by means of such practices as the greening of courtyards and roofs.

Although the biotope protection regime remained a relatively stable element of the political landscape of West Berlin and after 1990 was extended over the reunified city, its ability to actually steer urban development remained limited. This was partly due to the conflict of its guiding rationale with the urban development interests that dominated the city. The Species

Protection Program that entered into force in 1988 was harmonized with a development-oriented land-use plan that represented only a modest version of the original proposal for a Biotope Protection Program. Moreover, the legal status of the earlier program was rather weak so that its provisions could easily be sacrificed when they were in conflict with "overarching public interests." The pressure to develop was particularly strong in the aftermath of unification, when the urban railway system was extended and many former wastelands in the central area were rebuilt with shopping centers and governmental buildings of the newly designated German capital. It was only due to the legal requirement of compensation planning that claims for biotope protection could be realized. Thus, the two landmark projects of biotope protection in post-unification Berlin, the nature parks created at the former marshaling yard of Südgelände and at the abandoned airport of Johannisthal, were actually meant to compensate for the loss of nature that was caused by two major urban development projects.

Other limitations arose from the clash between practices and discourses of the biotope protection regime with those of other nature regimes. Notably, traditional forms of shaping green spaces according to horticultural aesthetics or for promoting the recreation of citizens remained deeply entrenched in the practice of administering and managing public space. Thus, the actual spatial design of the aforementioned nature parks was the result of painstaking negotiations between promoters of concerns for biotope protection with garden architects who wanted to "put nature on stage" through horticultural design.[36]

Finally, the regime was not free from internal tensions and dilemmas. Although ecologists claimed that biotopes should be protected to allow citizens to enjoy direct contact with nature, and although activists drew on ecological categories and arguments to defend open spaces in their neighborhood, in the day-to-day practice of planning these often turned out to be conflicting goals. Thus planning ideas for the Südgelände-park show a constant move away from a biotope-protection policy that would have massively restricted public access to the area. Eventually, a pathway system was constructed that allowed visitors to stroll through the area. Similar conflicts became apparent when management measures meant moving or eradicating abundant plants and thereby clashed with activists' framing of the site as unregulated "urban wilderness."

The Rise of Civic Urban Gardening

In 2009 up to 150 residents followed the call of two community activists to clear a small abandoned lot next to the busy Mortizplatz in the urban neighborhood of Kreuzberg. On various collective working days, they cleaned the area of litter and removed about one hundred black locust trees and various shrubs. Subsequently they created beds (mostly in the form of containers that could be relocated if the user agreement that the activist had negotiated with the local council expired), which were planted with vegetables and kitchen herbs. Run by a core group of project leaders and a heterogeneous set of volunteers, the Prinzessinengarten (Garden of the princess), as the site is called, has become a landmark project of civic urban agriculture in Berlin.[37]

As an attempt to improve the city and its environment by means of gardening, rather than protecting preexisting vegetation, the Prinzessinengarten can be seen as a manifestation of a third nature regime, which I call the regime of *civic urban gardening*.

This regime began taking shape around the year 2000, when Berlin and other metropolises around the world started seeing an increasing involvement of citizens in public gardening, often promoted under names such as "guerrilla gardening," "community gardening," or "urban agriculture."[38] In addition to the cultivation of ornamental and edible plants in permanent community gardens, such activities include throwing flower seeds, so-called seed bombs, on public lawns and planting roadsides, tree pits, and abandoned lots. All these activities share a preoccupation with gardening as a pathway to a more livable, sustainable, and closer-to-nature urban order. In contrast to earlier forms of green planning or organic urbanism, which operated through the use of public authority and the expertise of planners and ecologists, civic gardening evokes the figure of the active citizen as the main agent of urban greening.[39]

Some of the characteristics of civic urban gardening evolved from urban nature education projects such as children's farms (*Kinderbauernhöfe*) and school gardens in the 1980s.[40] By actively involving children in the hands-on experience of caring for plants and animals, these projects sought to contribute to their social development and well-being. Extended from children to ordinary adult citizens, this educational motive remained an important motive to the legitimization and operative organization of community

gardens. On the other hand, a different kind of forerunner of civic gardening can be seen in the interventions of Berlin artist Ben Wagin, who planted
Ginko trees—for example, his famous "Parliament of Trees"—at abandoned
areas along the former Berlin Wall.

Such activites gained momentum and started to form a distinct nature
regime also by their programmatic framing with buzzwords such as "community" or "guerrilla" gardening. The phrase "guerrilla gardening" entered
public parlance as an English loanword, after it had been promoted by the
London activist Richard Reynolds, and refered to illicit, and therefore supposedly subversive, activities of greening.[41] The concept of *Gemeinschaftsgärten* (community gardens) was a direct reference to the community garden
concept in New York. The founders of the Prinzessinnengärten took their
main inspiration from Cuba.[42] Its promoters have touted urban gardening
for many reasons: to enable contact with nature, to maintain community
life, to empower women or immigrants, and to promote local food production as an aspect of a sustainable lifestyle. Although translocal exchange
also characterized earlier nature regimes, urban gardening can be seen as
worldwide trend with a special cosmopolitan flair. Often community gardens are conceived as "intercultural gardens" and are meant to provide a
place for immigrant communities and their specific gardening practices,
including cultivating plants from their countries of origin.[43]

Notwithstanding the rhetoric of insurgency that accompanies many of
these activities, civic gardening has found acceptance and even support
from municipal councils and administrations.[44] Thus, whereas local district administrations had for some time rejected such encroachments of
residents into public space (also because they feared that such plantations
could damage the trees), most Berlin districts now have defined rules of
good pratice and offer sponsorship agreements that allow citizens to maintain such plots.[45] They are usually run by an informal network of friends, an
association or—as it is the case of the Prinzessinengarten in Kreuzberg—by
social entrepreneurs. By contrast, when some small temporary community
gardens were established in 2002 on abandoned plots in a neighborhood of
the district Kreuzberg-Friedrichshain, it was an urban renewal agency that
served as a broker, paving the way for agreements regarding the gardens
with the landowners.[46] Even if officially embraced, however, the existence
of community gardens can always be called into question by the municipal
council or by investors. Ensuing public campaigns are rarely able to prevent

alternative projects from being realized at these sites.[47] Moreover, although local government has come to play a facilitating role in civic gardening, it has not developed a coherent planning strategy, as had come together under the earlier regimes. Thus citizens who had been configured as passive residents under the first regime and allies of scientific ecologists and landscape planners under the second became the core actors around whom the civic gardening regime assembled. This is also the case in terms of the guiding knowledge on which civic gardening thrives: although various professional and semiprofessional mediators assume the role of advocates, facilitators and knowledge brokers, the cultivation of competencies by the engaged citizen is regarded as the main way in which knowledge should be produced and circulated in this regime.[48]

Community gardens are projects involving food production, sociability, political resistance, and sociotechnical learning and experimentation.[49] At the same time they are productive of new spatial formations of nature in the city, which differ as much from the parks and green zones of organic urbanists as from the biotopes that formed the focus of urban nature conservation policies. Like ecologists, civic gardeners tend to focus on the marginal spaces of the city, such as wastelands and vacant lots. But in contrast to the positive framing of wastelands as urban nature areas in the biotope protection regimes, civic gardeners tend to see wastelands as empty, ugly, and in need of occupation and maintenance so that they can be turned into productive and useful spaces to grow both food and community. As the founders of the Prinzessinnengarten described their project, it was meant to "transform a wasteland into a garden."[50]

Thus, the first symbolic act of appropriating such spaces tends to involve an outcry against their being used as dump sites. Once a community garden is under cultivation, while some community gardeners value the presence of some wildflowers in their plots, gardening inevitably implies the removal of existing vegetation to make room for their own use of the land. For example in a blogpost about the Rosa-Rose Garten we see pictures of a woman who, according to the subtitle, is proudly "removing weeds."[51] The spatial order of a fully operating community garden generally consists of arrays of beds (often elevated to prevent contact with soil contamination), filled with containers or rice sacks in which edible or ornamental plants are grown and surrounded by patches of unmaintained vegetation and pathways. Garden furniture and storage huts can be further elements.

The Prinzessinnengarten even includes a bike repair station, a café, and an information center, all of which are accommodated in used containers or wooden huts.

Tree pits present a very different kind of opportunity for urban gardening (see figure 9.2). Unlike wastelands, tree pits belong to the formally maintained and regulated parts of the built-up environment. In the nineteenth century, planners planted trees along urban streets in order to embellish neighborhoods and to improve air quality; thus, tree plantating, like park construction, was a strategy through which classic green planners sought to remedy the supposed ills of the city.[52] The trees were placed into square openings in sidewalks, and these pits were dug out to make space for the stems and roots of trees, keep the soil loose, and provide the trees with sufficient water. Public authorities kept these spaces free from weeds, waste, and any other disfigurement. Current civic gardening efforts have reversed official criteria of public order and framed these pits as sterile and boring, as well as attracting litter and dog excrement. Initiatives to plant these areas have come from residents of nearby houses and from shop and restaurant owners who seek to embellish their sidewalks, as well as occasionally from official neighborhood initiatives.[53] Renovating tree pits can range from decorating them with a few flowers to creating minigardens that are sometimes even fenced in to keep dogs out. In contrast to community gardens these plantations usually have a purely ornamental function and represent a wide variety of visual tastes, whether for the naturalistic or the manicured. Either way, such gardens require regular care, especially when the plants are not ecologically adapted to the site and need regular watering.

Celebrations of the new gardening activities as a "search for quietness, earthing, and encounter with nature" echo earlier calls for mobilizing nature as a counterbalance to urban life and modernity.[54] The participation in the very activity of gardening tends to count at least as much for these citizens as the visual or ecological qualities of the resulting plantations. In a promotional video of the Rosa-Rose community garden, one protagonist cherishes the experience of "putting one's hands into the soil" and having a chance "to unwind from this crazy modern life behind the computer."[55] More specifically such bodily involvement with nature is supposed to create a "personal relationship with one's food,"[56] to counterbalance individualization, and to open the eyes to injustices in urban land-use development.[57] Moreover, in deliberate contrast to conventional farming practices, community gardens

Figure 9.2
Tree-pit plantation in Berlin. Photo by Jens Lachmund.

tend to restrain from the use of herbicides and artificial fertilizers and instead embrace small-scale ecologically inspired forms of cultivation. For example, the Prinzessinnengarten claims to "follow the example of free nature"[58] in its decision to grow vegetables in "mixed cultures" instead of the monocultures of industrial farming.

Like urban ecologists with their concern for a specific urban kind of nature, spokespeople of civic gardening also refrain from simply imposing a pastoral imaginary on the city. For example, not only is the widespread practice of using urban-industrial materials such as plastic bags, tires, or bins as flower pots an innovative form of waste recycling, but the combination of natural and industrial elements also subverts entrenched oppositions between nature and city. Moreover, the gardens are understood and styled as elements of a specifically urban culture. Intercultural gardens translate the heterogeneity of multicultural districts into the mixing of gardening and cooking practices. For example the Pyramidengarten in the largely Turkish neighborhood Neukölln offers an Anatolian clay furnace in which, out of respect for Islamic food practices, the cooking of pork is not permitted.

For all of its heterogeneity, the new nature regime is not free from tensions with respect to the other regimes. Thus, the new regime of cultivating wastelands clearly differs from the regime of biotope protection, with its aims of protecting spontaneous ruderal vegetation and its insistence that gardening practices should be adapted to the ecology of the site and refrain from the use of purely ornamental plants. Indeed already in the 1980s, a conservationist had criticized left-wing squatters who had planted beets in a ruderal wasteland for damaging what they considered to be a valuable biotope.[59] But so far there have not been any serious conflicts, particularly since ecologists have been concerned mainly with larger wasteland areas with variegated vegetation whereas civic gardening tends to focus on small plots in densely built districts.

Internally, however, the broader civic gardening regime has its own contradictions and dilemmas. One involves its uneasy mixture of public openness and individual responsibility. Thus, on the one hand, public gardening strives to open up hidden spaces for public appropriation in ways that subvert, minimize, or even conflict with existing private property rights and administrative powers. On the other hand, the practice of civic gardening operates through informal systems that distribute responsibility to individuals or groups and thus lends itself to the creation of informal pieces of quasi-property, such as manicured, fenced-in tree pits and individually "owned" flower beds in some community gardens.

Another dilemma is that while the rhetoric of insurgency underpins the political identity of the regime's participants, they themselves need to cooperate with local governments to realize the benefits of civic gardening. Some commentators have cherished community gardens as seedbeds of alternative economies and social relations that would contradict neoliberal hegemony,[60] but as Marit Rosol has recently argued, the devolution of public responsibility to citizen gardeners falls squarely into the logic of neoliberalism. As she posits, the increasing involvement of the local state as a facilitator of civic gardening activities tends to undermine the politically transgressive motives of these civic gardening activities.

In a similar vein, there is a tension between the tendency of urban gardening to subvert urban order and the performativity of its own practices in creating an alternative urban order. As much as civic gardening diverges from the official order of green planning and sidewalk management, it nevertheless embodies cultural criteria of order that mark places as either well maintained or derelict and are performative of socially exclusive models of citizenship. Nonhuman entities that might be accepted in other places, such as weeds, do not "belong" to a proper community garden. But also, homeless people or dog walkers who have often used the same areas no longer fit with the new spatial order of civic gardening. Moreover, many gardens have become signifiers of a young educated middle-class milieu, vaguely resonating with the recent hype of urban "creativity," and thereby tending to create socially exclusive atmospheres.

Conclusion

The comparison of the three urban nature regimes over time has revealed both continuity in the mobilization of nature as a means of urban change and considerable differences between the ways in which urban nature has been framed and imagined. It is striking that some discursive motives—such as the idea of healing urban problems through enabling contact to nature—have persisted from the nineteenth century to the present. As we have seen, however, terms like "city" and "nature" meant very different things at different times, and hence led to rather distinct regimes. For organic planners, the formation of landscapes was the main focus; for ecologists nature has consisted of the plant and animal species that could be experienced in a city, and for proponents of civic gardening, nature is a worksite that gains personal, social, and political significance through its engagement in embodied practices. As Macnaghten and Urry have said of nature in general, we can talk only in the plural about urban nature, as actually or potentially contested formations.[61]

Nature in all of these regimes has served as an anchor for political imaginaries. Different ideas of nature have served as precepts for critical judgment about urban development as well as a guidelines for decision-making about how spaces should be designed and used or in some cases exempted from human usage. The discourses of these regimes are not free from romantic allusions to nature as the "other" to the city. Nonetheless, nature in these different contexts has been both conceptually and practically urbanized. This process is most evident in the regime of civic gardening and its attempt to frame nature as the nexus of an explicitly urban and cosmopolitan lifestyle. In urban ecology, urbanization of nature is apparent in the valuation of humanly influenced vegetation such as the weeds and neophyte species growing on wastelands, which does not fit with the more ruralist and nativist imaginary of traditional nature conservation. In organic urbanism, the process arose from the experience of the spectator in the landscape as well as from the planner's synoptic gaze on the drafting table. Form, conceived of as organic, was the uniting principle that was supposed to bridge and smooth the differences between nature and the city. At the same time each of the regimes implies different positionings of citizens: as targets and passive recipients of urbanist planning ideas, as political activists who form alliances with ecologists, or as participants in civic greening action and as active holders of urban environmental knowledge. Thus, each of these regimes manifest rationalities and practices that are distinct from and even in conflict with the others.

Although this chapter has focused on only one city, it is clear that none of these regimes has developed in isolation. In some cases, nature politics in Berlin preceded similar developments in other cities, while in others it incorporated ideas and practices that had already been articulated elsewhere. As historians of technology Mikael Hård and Thomas Misa have put it, urbanist ideas and practices not only "circulate" between different cities; they are also appropriated—selected, tuned, transformed—in ways that reflect and sustain the particularities of different places.[62] In Berlin, ideas of the city landscape chimed with general trends in urbanism but gave it a special organic tint and translated it in new ways of green space planning during the postwar reconstruction process. Biodiversity conservation and the search for new ecological planning practices were worldwide trends in the 1980s, but due to the specific conditions of postwar Germany, Berlin was one of the first places where such concerns were systematically implemented in city planning. Notably the emergence of the wasteland as a major research object of ecologists, which then also turned into a conservation object, gave these initiatives its specific local emphasis. Urban gardening in Berlin has been inspired by development in North American cities and in the global South, but has drawn equally on local traditions such as children's farms and earlier concerns with urban nature. Moreover, as in many other European metropolises, urban gardening has become an aspect of a middle-class green lifestyle instead of a resistance movement of socially disadvantaged groups. Therefore, it would be misleading to consider Berlin as an exemplary case of an overarching global master trend. The timing and the concrete pathways through which each of the regimes took shape in Berlin was enabled by, and articulated in close interaction with, the local constellation of Berlin's politico-cultural milieu and the concrete materialities of its parks, forests, and wastelands.

Acknowledgments

I want to thank the editors and the participants of the Grounding Urban Natures meeting in Stockholm for the many comments and suggestions on the earlier drafts of this chapter.

Notes

1. Wirth n.d. [1964?], n.p.

2. For a recent example see the Berlin Senate's "Natürlich Berlin" [Naturally Berlin], an overview of the city's nature reserves (Senatsverwaltung für Stadtentwicklung, Berlin 2008).

3. Lachmund 2013.

4. My concept of "nature regimes" draws loosely on Arturo Escobar (1999) and is defined as "a dynamic set of relations that include (1) the portions of the non-human world that are claimed to represent valuable forms of nature and that

therefore are supposed to require public attention or care, (2) the practices and discourses through which such claims are produced, promoted, and incorporated into public policies, and (3) the individuals, collectives, and institutions that assemble around and actively sponsor these claims" (Lachmund 2013, p. 5). In *Greening Berlin* I presented an in-depth analysis of the "biotope-protection regime" and also dealt briefly with some preceding regimes, including organic urbanism. In this chapter I draw on findings of this book and combine them with more recent work on emerging forms of urban gardening in Berlin.

5. Wagner-Conzelmann 2007.

6. Durth and Gutschow 1988.

7. Wagner-Conzelmann 2007, pp. 17–21.

8. Taut 1946; Allinger 1950, p. 6; Hentzen 1950. See also Bodenschatz (1987, p. 63).

9. See Ladd (1990) for a detailed analysis of this urban imaginary and its dominance in the German planning world.

10. Hegemann 1992 [1930].

11. Reichow 1948, p. 32.

12. The 1933 "Athens Charta" of CIAM (Congrès Internationaux d'Architecture Moderne) reflected mainly the modernist ideas of the Swiss-French architect Le Corbusier. On CIAM's modernism, see Misa (2008).

13. Durth and Gutschow 1988.

14. See ibid. The justification of landscape-oriented urbanism resonated quite well with the nativism of the Nazi ideology. For example, Hentzen (1950, p. 339) claimed that Germans had a more intimate relationship to living things than other peoples. The quest for organic forms, however, was a much broader phenomenon of the period and could also be found outside of Germany; for example, in France Le Corbusier embraced the "organic" structure of Algiers and other non-Western cities as a more lively an alternative to the Western metropolis (see Haffner 2013, pp. 47–48).

15. Reichow 1948.

16. Allinger 1950, p. 154.

17. Göderitz, Rainer, and Hoffmann 1957, p. 8.

18. See Durth and Gutschow (1988).

19. Bodenschatz 1987.

20. Michel and Schulz 2006.

21. Bodenschatz 1987.

22. Ibid., pp. 165–170; Wagner-Conzelmann 2007, pp. 54–95.

23. Michel and Schulz 2006.

24. Witte 1960, p. 216.

25. Witte 1960, p. 218.

26. Fichtner 1977.

27. Söderqvist 1986; Kwa 1989; Kingsland 2005.

28. For example, Duvigneaud 1974.

29. The following section is largely based on chapters 2 and 3 of Lachmund (2013), where a detailed analysis of this approach of urban ecology can be found.

30. Sukopp 1968.

31. Sukopp 1973, pp. 91–92.

32. Ibid.; Brunner et al. 1979; Auhagen and Sukopp 1983.

33. The term "ally" is here used as in Latour (1987), as referring to somebody or something that is enrolled as a supporter of, or participant in, a collective project or network, and who or which thereby contributes to its formation and stablization.

34. For a similar analysis, albeit from a later time period in Stockholm, see Ernstson and Sörlin (2009).

35. Arbeitsgruppe Artenschutzprogramm Berlin 1984.

36. See Lachmund (2013, chap. 5).

37. Robert Shaw, interview with author, May 3, 2015. For a description of the project see also Nomadisch Grün (2012).

38. For example, Reynolds 2008; Müller 2011; Kotte 2012; Nomadisch Grün 2012; Rasper 2012.

39. New urban gardening and agriculture have also become the focus of social science analysis. See, for example, the special issue of *Local Environment* and its introduction by Certomá and Tornaghi (2015). Studies that have focused on Berlin are Jahnke (2007), Rosol (2006, 2012), and Bendt, Barthel, and Colding (2013).

40. Meyer-Renschhausen 2011; see also Kahlki (2008).

41. Reynolds 2008. For an empirical analysis of guerrilla gardening in action see Adams and Hardman (2014).

42. Nomadisch Grün 2012.

43. In this section I rely partly on observations made during visits to these urban gardening spaces in the summers of 2013 and 2014.

44. The 2010 "Strategy Urban Landscape Berlin" refers to "community gardens," "intercultural gardens," and "guerrilla gardens" as valuable elements of urban green in Berlin. Strategie Stadtlandschaft Berlin, http://www.stadtentwicklung.berlin.de /umwelt/landschaftsplanung/strategie_stadtlandschaft/download/Strategie-Stadt landschaft-Berlin.pdf (accessed September 30, 2018).

45. See, for example, the rules and conditions for tree pit plantations in the district Kreuzberg-Friederichshain: "Baumscheibenbegrünung" [Tree pit planting], http:// www.berlin.de/ba-friedrichshain-kreuzberg/verwaltung/org/natur/baumscheiben begrnung.html (accessed September 30, 2018).

46. Stattbau n.d.

47. A notable exception was the campaign against the abandoning of the "Prinz- essinengärten" in 2012. See "Wachsen Lassen: Die Kampagne" [Letting grow: The campaign], Prinzessinengarten, http://prinzessinnengarten.net/de/der-garten-und-die -stadt/kampagne-wachsen-lassen/ (accessed September 30, 2018).

48. An example of how activists promote their gardens explicitly as a means to cultivate citizen knowledge is their collective book project *Wissen wuchern lassen* [Letting knowledge sprawl] (Halder et al. 2014), which covers learning processes and their results from various Berlin gardening projects. For an empirical analysis of knowledge acquisition in Berlin community gardens, see Bendt, Barthel, and Cold- ing (2013).

49. Bendt, Barthel, and Colding 2013.

50. Nomadisch Grün 2012, p. 25.

51. June 20, 2011, "Gartenalltag Archiv," Rosa Rose Garten, http://rosarose.twoday .net/topics/Gartenalltag/ (accessed September 30, 2018).

52. See Lachmund (2013, chap. 2).

53. For example, as part of the various district management schemes (*Quartierman- agement*) which seek to activate residents to participate in such projects. See, for example, "Neu bepflanzte Baumscheibe" [Newly planted tree-pit], Quartiersman- agement (District Management) Brunnenviertel-Ackerstrasse, http://brunnenviertel -ackerstrasse.de/Baumscheibe (accessed September 30, 2018).

54. Müller 2011, p. 9.

55. Video, "Gartenbewegungen in Berlin" [Gardening movements in Berlin] at Rosa Rose Garten, http://www.rosarose-garten.net/videos/ (accessed September 30, 2018).

56. Ibid.

57. All points mentioned in ibid.

58. Nomadisch Grün 2012, p. 122.

59. Anonymous 1990.

60. For example, Müller (2011).

61. Macnaghten and Urry 1998.

62. Hård and Misa 2008.

References

Adams, David, and Michael Hardman. 2014. "Observing Guerrillas in the Wild: Reinterpreting Practices of Urban Guerrilla Gardening." *Urban Studies* 51(6): 1103–1119.

Allinger, Gustav. 1950. *Der deutsche Garten* [The German garden]. Munich: Bruckmann.

Anonymous. 1990. "Unsere Meinung" [Our opinion]. *Berliner Naturschutzblätter* 34(2): 3–5.

Arbeitsgruppe Artenschutzprogramm Berlin [Working Group Species Protection Program Berlin]. 1984. *Grundlagen für das Artenschutzprogramm Berlin* [Fundamentals for a Species Protection Program Berlin], vol. 2. Berlin: Technical University Berlin.

Auhagen, Axel, and Herbert Sukopp. 1983. "Ziel, Begründungen und Methoden des Naturschutzes der Stadtentwicklungspolitik von Berlin" [Aims, rationales, and methods of nature conservation in urban development in Berlin]. *Natur und Landschaft* 58(1): 9–15.

Bendt, Pim, Stephan Barthel, and Johan Colding. 2013. "Civic Greening and Environmental Learning in Public-Access Community Gardens in Berlin." *Landscape and Urban Planning* 109(1): 18–30.

Bodenschatz, Harald. 1987. *Platz frei für das neue Berlin! Geschichte der Stadterneuerung seit 1871* [Space for the new Berlin! History of urban renewal since 1871]. Berlin: Transit.

Brunner, Manfred, Friedrich Duhme, Hermann Mück, Johann Patsch, and Elmar Wenisch. 1979. "Kartierung erhaltenswerter Lebensräume in der Stadt" [Mapping biotopes worthy of protection]. *Das Gartenamt* 28: 72–78.

Certomá, Chiara, and Chiara Tornaghi. 2015. "Political Gardening: Transforming Cities and Political Agency." *Local Environment* 20(10): 1123–1131.

Durth, Werner, and Niels Gutschow. 1988. *Träume in Trümmern: Planungen zum Wiederaufbau zerstörter Städte im Westen Deutschlands 1940–1950* [Rubble of earlier dreams: Plans for rebuilding destroyed cities in Germany's west 1940–1950]. Braunschweig: Vieweg.

Duvigneaud, P. 1974. "L'ècosysteme 'urbs'" [Ecosystem "urbs"]. *Mémoire de la Societé Botanique Belgique* 6: 5–35.

Ernstson, Henrik, and Sverker Sörlin. 2009. "Weaving Protective Stories: Connective Practices to Articulate Holistic Values in the Stockholm National Urban Park." *Environment and Planning A* 41(6): 1460–1479.

Escobar, Arturo. 1999. "After Nature: Steps to an Antiessentialist Political Ecology." *Current Ecology* 40(1): 1–30.

Fichtner, Volkmar. 1977. *Die anthropogen bedingte Umwandlung des Reliefs durch Trümmeraufschüttungen in Berlin (West) seit 1945* [The anthropogeneous transformation of the relief through rubble heaps in Berlin (West) since 1945]. Berlin: Geographisches Institut der Freien Universität Berlin.

Göderitz, Johannes, Roland Rainer, and Hubert Hoffmann. 1957. *Die gegliederte und aufgelockerte Stadt* [The structured and loosend city]. Tubingen: Wasmuth.

Haffner, Jeanne. 2013. *The View from Above: The Science of Social Space.* Cambridge, MA: MIT Press.

Halder, Severin, Dörte Martens, Gerda Münich, Andrea Lassalle, Thomas Aenis, and Eckhard Schäfer, eds. 2014. *Wissen wuchern lassen: Ein Handbuch zum Lernen in urbanen Gärten* [Letting knowledge sprawl: A handbook for learning in urban gardens]. Berlin: AG Spak.

Hård, Mikael, and Thomas J. Misa, eds.. 2008. *Urban Machineries: Inside European Cities.* Cambridge, MA: MIT Press.

Hegemann, Werner. 1992 [1930]. *Das steinerne Berlin: Geschichte der größten Mietskasernenstadt der Welt* [The Berlin of stone: The history of the world's largest city of rental barracks]. Braunschweig: Vieweg.

Hentzen, Kurt. 1950. "Über die Landschaft Gross-Berlins vor den Zerstörungen des letzten Weltkrieges" [On the landscape of greater Berlin before the destruction during the previous World War]. Berlin: unpublished manuscript.

Jahnke, Julia. 2007. "Eine Bestandsaufnahme zum globalen Phänomen Guerrilla Gardening anhand von Beispielen in New York, London und Berlin" [An inventory of the global phenomenon Guerrilla Gardening using examples in New York, London and Berlin]. Magisterarbeit, Humboldt-Universität zu Berlin. https://www.scribd.com/document/3859296/Julia-Jahnke-Guerrilla-Gardening-Master-Thesis-german (accessed September 30, 2018).

Kahlki, Reinhold. 2008. "Kinder- und Jugendbauernhöfe am Beispiel Berlin" [Berlin examples of children and youth farms]. In *Natur erleben und Raum inszenieren* [Experiencing nature and putting space on stage], edited by Tobias Releh and Gerhard Ströhlein, 118–124. Göttingen: Universitätsverlag.

Kingsland, Sharon E. 2005. *The Evolution of American Ecology, 1890–2000.* Baltimore, MD: Johns Hopkins University Press.

Kotte, Jana, ed. 2012. *Berlin gärtnert: Kübel, Beet und Samenbombe* [Berlin is gardening: Planter, bed, and seedbomb]. Berlin: Edition Terra.

Kwa, Chung Lin. 1989. "Mimicking Nature. The Development of Systems Ecology in the United States, 1950–1975." PhD thesis, University of Amsterdam.

Lachmund, Jens. 2013. *Greening Berlin: The Co-Production of Science, Politics, and Urban Nature.* Cambridge, MA: MIT Press.

Ladd, Brian. 1990. *Urban Planning and Civic Order in Germany, 1860–1914.* Cambridge, MA: Harvard University Press.

Latour, Bruno. 1987. *Science in Action.* Cambridge, MA: Harvard University Press.

Macnaghten, Phil, and John Urry. 1998. *Contested Natures.* London: Sage.

Meyer-Renschhausen, Elisabeth. 2011. "Von Pflanzerkolonien zum nomadisierenden Junggemüse: Zur Geschichte des Community Gardenings in Berlin" [From allotment gardens to the nomadic youth: The history of community gardening in Berlin]. In *Urban Gardening: Über die Rückkehr der Gärten in die Stadt* [Urban gardening: On the revival of gardens in the city], edited by Christa Müller, 319–332. Munich: Oekom.

Michel, Harald, and Volker Schulz. 2006. "Von der 'Stalin-Allee' zur DDR Plattenbausiedlung: Anmerkungen zur Wohn- und Siedlungspolitik in Berlin-Brandenburg seit 1949" [From "Stalin-Allee" to GDR settlements of precast concrete slabs: Comments on housing and settlement policy in Berlin-Brandenburg since 1949]. In *Schaufenster der Systemkonkurrenz: Die Region Berlin-Brandenburg im Kalten Krieg* [Showcase of the competition of the systems: The region of Berlin-Brandenburg during the Cold War period], edited by Michael Lembke, 207–224. Cologne: Böhlau.

Misa, Thomas J. 2008. "Appropriating the International Style: Modernism in East and West." In *Urban Machineries: Inside European Cities,* edited by Mikael Hård and Thomas J. Misa, 71–97. Cambridge, MA: MIT Press.

Müller, Christa. 2011. *Urban Gardening: Über die Rückkehr der Gärten in die Stadt* [Urban gardening: On the revival of gardens in the city]. Munich: Oekom.

Nomadisch Grün [Nomadic Green], ed. 2012. *Prinzessinnengärten: Anders gärtnern in der Stadt* [Garden of the princess: Gardening differently in the city]. Cologne: DuMont.

Rasper, Martin. 2012. *Vom Gärtnern in der Stadt: Die neue Landlust zwischen Beton und Asphalt* [On gardening in the city: New rural pleasures between concrete and tarmac]. Munich: Oekom.

Reichow, Hans Bernhard. 1948. *Organische Stadtbaukunst: Von der Grosstadt zur Stadtlandschaft* [Organic urbanism: From metropolis to urban landscape]. Braunschweig: Westermann.

Reynolds, Richard. 2008. *On Guerrilla Gardening: A Handbook for Gardening without Boundaries*. London: Bloomsbury.

Rosol, Marit. 2006. *Gemeinschaftsgärten in Berlin: Eine qualitative Untersuchung zu Potentialen und Riskien bürgerschaftlichen Engagements im Grünflächenbereich vor dem Hintergrund des Wandels von Staat und Planung* [Community gardens in Berlin: A qualitative study of the potentials and risks of civic engagement in the sector of urban green, seen in the context of the transformation of state and planning]. Berlin: Mensch & Buch.

Rosol, Margit. 2012. "Community Volunteering as Neoliberal Strategy? Green Space Production in Berlin." *Antipode* 44(1): 239–257.

Senatsverwaltung für Stadtentwicklung, Berlin. 2008. *Natürlich Berlin* [Naturally Berlin]. Berlin.

Söderqvist, Thomas. 1986. *The Ecologists: From Merry Naturalists to Saviours of the Nation*. Stockholm: Almqvist & Wiksell.

Stattbau. n.d. *Brache: Und danach; Ein Brachenprojekt im Berliner Samarterviertel* [Wasteland: And after; A wasteland-project in the Berlin neighboorhood Sameriterviertel]. Berlin.

Sukopp, Herbert. 1968. "Der Einfluss des Menschen auf die Vegetation und zur Terminologie anthropogener Vegetationstypen" [Human influence on vegetation and on the terminology for antropogeneous types of vegetation]. In *Pflanzensoziologie und Landschaftsökologie: Bericht über das 7. Internationale Symposium in Stolzenau/ Weser der Internationalen Vereinigung für Vegetationskunde* [Plant sociology and landscape ecology: Report from the 7th International Symposium of the International Society for Vegetation Studies in Stolzenau/Weser], edited by Reinhold Tüxen, 65–74. The Hague: Junk.

Sukopp, Herbert. 1973. "Die Großstadt als Gegenstand ökologischer Forschung" [The metropolis as an object of ecological research]. *Schriften zur Verbreitung naturwissenschaftlicher Kenntnisse* 113: 90–140.

Taut, Max. 1946. *Berlin im Aufbau* [Berlin under reconstruction]. Berlin: Aufbau-Verlag.

Wagner-Conzelmann, Sandra. 2007. *Die Interbau 1957 in Berlin: Stadt von heute—Stadt von morgen, Städtebau und Gesellschaftskritik in den 50er Jahren*. [The *Interbau* (architecture exhibition of) 1957 in Berlin: City today—city tomorrow, urban planning and social criticism in the (19)50s]. Petersberg, Germany: Michael Imhoff Verlag.

Wirth, Irmgard. n.d. [1964?]. *Berliner Landschaft* [Berlin landscape]. Berlin: Hans Schwarz.

Witte, Fritz. 1960. "Grünplanung und Natur- und Landschaftsschutz in Berlin" [Green planning and nature and landscape preservation in Berlin]. *Das Gartenamt* 9: 216–218.

IV Technological Natures

10 Elbows over the Fence: Rondevlei and the Invention of Community-Based Conservation in Apartheid Cape Town

Lance van Sittert

Sites of landscape preservation, by virtue of their artificial maintenance in states of suspended animation over long periods of time, act as cultural middens, concentrating and condensing the changing ideas, actions, and conflicts of the surrounding society into deep layered archives from whose stratigraphies different histories can be read. Historians in South Africa have focused almost exclusively on such rural preservation sites.[1] The few who have looked at urban sites have concentrated on mountain prospects.[2] Rondevlei (Round Lake) on Cape Town's False Bay shore offers a corrective to the rural and urban montaine biases of the extant scholarship.

More importantly, Rondevlei was the site where the practice of what became known post-apartheid as community-based conservation was invented. This represented a dramatic departure from the old established practice (inherited from the colonial period) of the complete exclusion of communities surrounding protected areas by means of fencing and paramilitary policing (fortress conservation) and sought to win popular acceptance of reserve areas by integrating the surrounding underclass communities through a combination of controlled access, managed exploitation, and environmental education.[3] The long-term sustainability of fortress conservation was a ratio between the size of the protected area and that of the surrounding underclass population: the smaller the former and larger the latter, the greater the pressure on the fence and its defenders. This ratio was least favorable in urban areas and nowhere more so than at Rondevlei, 290 hectares embedded in a ghetto population of fifty thousand people by the 1970s.

The reserve area to abutting proletariat ratio was a necessary but not sufficient condition for the reform of fortress conservation. Most often the urban fortresses were abolished when the ratio shifted decisively in the latter's favor. To avoid this looming fate, the new warden appointed in 1974, Howard Langley, who had trained as a field ecologist in Zimbabwe at the height of the liberation war and had seen firsthand the logical end point and futility of fortress conservation, decided to open his fortress to the surrounding proletariat. He was able to make this radical break with the practice of fortress conservation only because of the already terminal nature of his small, marginal, urban reserve, but the success of his initiatives saw them exported across the national reserve system after the end of apartheid.

The remnant urban nature enclosed at Rondevlei, located as it was in the midst of apartheid Cape Town's emerging ghetto archipelago, modeled the conditions that would face all protected areas post-apartheid. It was thus an accidental laboratory for the subsequent reform of fortress conservation more than two decades later, when the end of apartheid disarmed it and generalized Rondevlei's conditions to the system as a whole. At that point the philosophy and practices Langley developed at Rondevlei were energetically exported and eagerly adopted throughout the national system, and Langley was elevated to the very highest levels of national conservation management. Rondevlei is thus a corrective to the prevailing view of urban nature as of only aesthetic or ironic interest. While it is certainly true that urban nature reflects the class composition of the city, it also often prefigures future challenges to the inherited colonial system of "nature reserves" as a whole and in that way serves, just as Grove argued island colonies did during the period of European colonial expansion, as laboratory sites in which new strategies and tactics can be developed in the war of position that is conservation.[4]

Preserving the Cape Flats

At its moment of preservation in the mid-twentieth century the Rondevlei Bird Sanctuary was located on the frontier between the expanding city and its rural hinterland on the sandy isthmus called the Cape Flats (see figure 10.1).

The eastern wild edge of the city had already been extensively re-engineered over the previous half century in a Clementsian succession toward urban space first by state foresters and then municipal road builders and property speculators. The colonial state forestry department was also engaged in extensive urban "drift sand operations" to arrest coastal dune

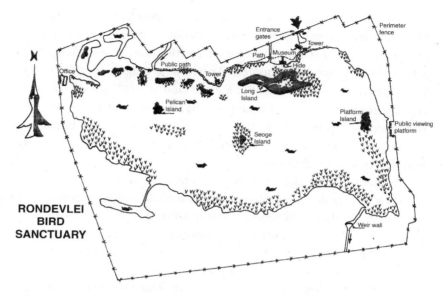

Figure 10.1

Rondevlei Bird Sanctuary, ca. 1978. The map is from C. H. Langley, *Rondevlei Bird Sanctuary: An Introduction to the Rondevlei Bird Sanctuary with Check Lists of Birds and Other Animals Recorded since 1952* (Cape Town: Divisional Council, 1978, p. 1). Rondevlei is located on Cape Flats, some twenty kilometers southeast from the historical city center of Cape Town, an extensive flat sheet of aeolian sand to which the Apartheid regime forcefully moved non-White classified people from the 1950s to the early 1990s.

fields around major coastal centers preparatory to settlement. The Cape Town municipality initiated the process on the Cape Flats in the 1880s to protect its transport infrastructure and open up the area for settlement, and by the beginning of World War I the department of forestry had planted more than twenty-five square kilometers with exotic pines, wattles, and eucalypts.[5] At its Strandfontein plantation on the city's False Bay shore, begun in 1898, some ninety hectares of drift sands had been "fixed" in this way, tripling to 280 hectares by 1950.[6]

Road builders and property speculators came in the wake of the foresters. The city council constructed Prince George's Drive to open up the area for settlement. Two speculators, John Marshall Joyce and Alexander McGregor, trading as Marshall and McGregor, developed townships along the main road across the Cape Flats in the 1900s.[7] In 1916 they established the Cape and Transvaal Land Finance Company to do the same along Prince George's

Drive on the city's reclaimed False Bay shore. To enlarge its landholding, the company aggressively reclaimed wetlands in its domain by infilling, except where the wetlands provided a recreational attraction conducive to residential development. Thus at Zeekoevlei adjoining Rondevlei the company assisted the establishment of a yacht club in 1932 and sold land to a growing community of yachtsmen. In this way the land around the vleis was gradually transformed in the interwar period into a combination of residential and small-scale agriculture, with a growing number of the latter engaging in squatter farming.[8]

This was the Cape Flats that the promoters of a sanctuary at Rondevlei and their first warden sought to preserve in the mid-twentieth century. The best way to do this, they believed, was to fence the vlei and then leave it more or less alone. The purpose of conservation was to keep all outside influences to a bare minimum, freezing the vlei at a point in time when it was imagined to still be more of a natural than a cultural artefact and human traces were light enough to be effaced over time by what were imagined as the inherent restorative capacities of a stable and unchanging nature. This view was informed by nineteenth-century romantic sensibility, natural history, and biological cosmopolitanism, which also influenced white amateur ornithology in the city, with its innate appreciation of a summer sunset over a lake, obsession with collecting personal sightings of every member of the local avifauna, and particular affection for exotic migrants.[9]

Alongside its better known affinity for the city's indigenous flora, Cape Town's urban Anglo middle class also harbored an abiding affection for "the feathered tribe of the Peninsula."[10] A member of parliament from the city, Henry Juta, was instrumental in the passing of a Wild Bird Protection Act in 1899, fully five years before an act to protect indigenous flora, and from the turn of the twentieth century on, all wild birds were protected within Cape Town.[11] A quarter of a century later another Cape Town parliamentarian, J. W. Close, was the prime mover behind the first national legislation protecting wild birds.[12] Without an institutional base or cause such as that provided to botany by the South African College and the Kirstenbosch National Botanical Garden, popular ornithology in the city did not take an organizational form until midcentury.[13]

Anglo middle-class ornithology did, however, inform the activities of the city's Mountain Club and its Botanical Society, and it benefited too from the introduction of biology as a subject in the school curriculum by

the provincial education department in 1921.[14] This broad popular interest
inspired the Mancunian Leonard Gill, appointed director of the city's South
African Museum in 1924, to produce his *First Guide to South African Birds*,
lavishly illustrated by his sister, in 1936.[15] As he explained in the preface,
"Year after year, one of the commonest inquiries addressed to us at the
South African Museum has been for an introductory work on the country's birds. Something small in compass, at small cost, and with abundant
coloured figures seems always to be the desideratum."[16] Gill's book, which
went through five editions over the next twenty years, followed in 1940 by
Austin Robert's *The Birds of South Africa*, unleashed a "quite startling...flood
tide of interest in bird life."[17] This "flood tide" also floated new popular
ornithological organizations in the immediate aftermath of the World War
II, including the Witwatersrand Bird Club in 1947 and the Cape Bird Club
(CBC) the following year, both of which became branches of the professional South African Ornithological Society (SAOS) in 1950.[18]

It was no accident that the CBC was conceived on "the lonely and rugged
Swartklip dune landscape on the False Bay shore...sitting on a huge dune,
overlooking a peaceful small vlei."[19] The Cape Flats had been the focus of
Anglo middle-class popular ornithology in the city throughout the interwar
period. In 1918 Gill's predecessor as director of the South African Museum
had pointed the city's amateur ornithologists to the eastern "fringe of 'the
Cape Flats,'" which he predicted, "if carefully watched over will doubtless
considerably increase the number of birds...recorded."[20] Gill agreed, deem-
ing the Cape Peninsula itself "almost everywhere poor in bird life" apart
from the seashore and vleis of the Cape Flats.

> The vleis (shallow lakes and marshy ground) provide an exceptionally interest-
> ing feature of the local bird life. Pelicans, Flamingos, Avocets and Stilts are often
> to be found, sometimes in large numbers, on one or more of the vleis. Ducks
> of several kinds are often abundant: Pochard, Yellow-bill and Cape Wigeon the
> commonest; Redbill, White-backed Duck and Shelduck less regularly seen. The
> smaller waders are generally to be seen by the hundred (except during three or
> four months of winter) along the edge of the water, arctic and European species
> like the Curlew Sandpiper, Little Stint and Ringed Plover far out-numbering the
> indigenous kinds.[21]

The founders of the CBC were among the many who followed the direction
of the city's professional ornithologists and by 1948 were alarmed at the wartime transformation of the area. To enable the construction of a new military

airfield, a large swath of the Cape Flats along the False Bay shore was drained, thereby also desiccating many vleis and altering the water level and flow in those that remained.[22] The city's booming wartime economy also lead to a massive influx of rural migrants, many of whom squatted on the Cape Flats and supplemented their wages or subsisted by keeping livestock and harvesting wood, flowers, game, and wild birds.[23] The resulting rapid disappearance of wetlands, flora, and fauna from the Cape Flats during the war spurred white middle-class amateur and professional ornithologists newly organized in the CBC-SAOS to take urgent action.

The now retired septuagenarian Leonard Gill, newly elected honorary president of the CBC, lamented that, "nature has to go down before man nearly everywhere; it is only here and there that a bit is set aside to show later generations what the world was once like."[24] Rondevlei was one such fragment, he declared, "a splendid natural feature of the neighbourhood of Cape Town," whose "complete disappearance would be highly regrettable—in fact a tragedy in natural history."[25] In addition to the vlei, Gill urged that what was required was a "buffer zone" around it "to keep the ever-multiplying buildings from coming so near as to spoil it," a fence "to check the ever increasing disturbance which is gradually driving the best birds away," and "a permanent watcher to exercise a general protection."[26] The resort to fortress conservation in the classic colonial mode reflected the extensive imperial service of professional ornithologists in the city in the third quarter of the twentieth century.[27]

The same model informed the "nature reserves" that had proliferated in the city and its hinterland in the 1930s, with the Table Mountain massif being converted into a nature reserve in 1931–1932, wild flower reserves being proclaimed in five neighboring rural towns in 1933–1935, and the city and divisional councils purchasing farms on the far southern peninsula to create a local facsimile of the Kruger National Park in the Cape of Good Hope Nature Reserve in 1939.[28] These reserves were part of the city's developing tourist economy as configured by the interwar automobile and road-building revolutions and intended to provide middle-class residents and visitors alike with convenient access to remnant iconic natural landscapes and species on the city's doorstep. They were protected by location either in middle-class areas of the city or in places far removed from public transport. Rondevlei did not fit this purpose, given its location on the Cape Flats among black squatters and adjacent to one of the city's sewerage works and its harboring birds that, unlike the flowers and game conserved in the city's other nature reserves, were highly mobile, making it impossible to guarantee their presence for visitors. Instead of a tourist attraction, the CBC leadership of professional ornithologists presented Rondevlei as an "ornithological field station" and picked Ernest Middlemiss as their first "permanent watcher" over the vlei.

Fortress Conservation: Rondevlei, 1952–1974

Ernest Middlemiss is a forgotten figure in the annals of Cape amateur and professional ornithology, but in the third quarter of the twentieth century he was the embodiment of its guiding ideas and aims.[29] English-born Middlemiss, a self-taught naturalist, artist, journalist, and minor literary figure, epitomized the amateur tradition of both Cape Town popular and professional ornithology at midcentury.[30] This tradition valued practical experience over professional training. Middlemiss with his wife moved in as warden of Rondevlei in January 1952, together with a black patrolman as their Man Friday.

The barbed wire "security fence" erected in 1951 was Middlemiss's abiding concern owing to the rumored resentment of the surrounding black population at Rondevlei's enclosure.[31] They were, he claimed, people "of a type to which the concepts and practices of protection of animal and floral life is enexpressibly [sic] alien, and probably incomprehensible" and who had before "systematically plundered" the sanctuary.[32]

> Horses and cows tramped and grazed the veld, woodcutters made inroads into the stands of acacia trees and both adults and children exploited the area for its flowers and decorative foliage. Nests were robbed particularly those of wildfowl (one resident commented on "sackfuls of duck eggs" being taken), birds were trapped, fish were speared and illegal shooting took place....Dogs roamed the area at will.[33]

Middlemiss and his black retainer thus maintained a "never-ceasing vigilance" in order to keep the sanctuary "inviolate" against invasion by the neighboring "pondokkie population," the patrolman making daily and the warden monthly "close inspection" of the fence to check and repair its integrity.[34] In the first year Middlemiss reported that the fence had been opened twice and some of its barbed wire stolen, and that "though exceptionally well fenced, the Sanctuary is extremely vulnerable" because, "it is impossible to keep a constant watch over the entire area and, owing to the dense bush trespassers could climb the fence unseen at only a few hundred yards."[35]

Trespass in the sanctuary increased with the increase in the area's poor black population. The development of a low income housing scheme on the sanctuary's northeastern boundary in 1956 increased the surrounding population and created "an insatiable demand for firewood and consequent devastation of all nearby trees."[36] Similar development followed over the next two decades as the municipality reorganized the city into apartheid "group areas" and used the Rondevlei area as a dumping ground for "coloureds" who were forcibly removed from "white group areas" of the city. By the early 1970s Middlemiss estimated that "the density within a one-mile radius has, since 1952, increased many hundredfold" and that thirty-thousand "coloured[s] of a low standard" were now living along the sanctuary's fence line "figuratively standing with their elbows over the fence."[37]

While flower-picking and wood-cutting were at most a "nuisance," arson posed a direct threat to the sanctuary. "A planned act of vandalism could destroy by burning, the vegetation over the greater part of the sanctuary," Middlemiss warned.[38] The southern boundary, being uninhabited and directly in the path of the prevailing summer winds, was particularly vulnerable.

> The dunes south of the Sanctuary…seem to hold an irresistible appeal to vagrant persons and especially on Saturdays and Sundays. In this quiet area drinking, drug smoking and hunting with dogs takes place and, almost inevitably the starting of veld fires. During the dry summer months, when the south-east wind blows in over False Bay, a weekend seldom passes without a fire burning in the five kilometre stretch between the fence and the sea.[39]

Twice during Middlemiss's tenure, in 1959 and again in 1973, weekend arsonists' summer fires breached his fence line and burned substantial tracts of the reserve.[40]

To counter the growing threats of trespass and arson, Middlemiss sought to improve surveillance within the sanctuary by clearing bush along the fence and cutting paths encircling the vlei.[41] In 1954, two twenty-five-foot "observation towers" and a "bird observation hut" were added, providing aerial and concealed vantage points from which to watch for human trespassers and fires as well as birds (see figure 10.2). The following year

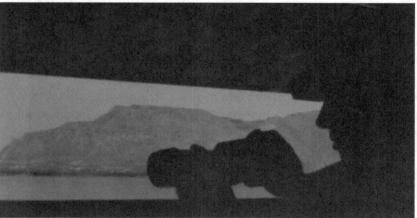

Figure 10.2
Fortress conservation. The observation tower (*top*) and the observation hut (*bottom*) at
Rondevlei, ca. 1954. Photos are from the Cape Divisional Council's *3rd Annual Report
on the Rondevlei Bird Sanctuary for the Year Ended 1954* (Cape Town: Cape Divisional
Council, 1954), pp. 3 and 8.

the divisional council cut a fire break inside the southern, eastern, and western boundary fences. By the mid-1960s the "pressure from illegal woodcutters...especially during the winter months" necessitated "night patrols" of the sanctuary, and when these failed to apprehend the culprits, Middlemiss acquired a "trained guard dog" to assist in "maintaining security in the Sanctuary." He noted with satisfaction that "the local people knew of its presence and were reporting among themselves that the dog roamed the sanctuary at will at night."[42]

When the divisional council allowed the public free entry to the sanctuary on weekends starting in 1970, Middlemiss reported that "the promise of untold delights—all illusory—to be found within the Sanctuary's fence attracted hordes of local youth. After one or two sad and sobering experiences they were turned away and well before they were able to show their only interest in birdlife...as to whether it was edible or not."[43] Thereafter Middlemiss instituted a practice of "judicious thinning out of would-be juvenile visitors" on weekends to ensure that local black youth were "sent back down the road" rather than admitted to the sanctuary.[44]

The purpose of the sanctuary's fortress of fences, paths, observation towers, hides, fire breaks, and patrols was to create an environment free of "disturbance" or "interference" within which "to study the birds in relation to the environment." "It is only under such conditions," Middlemiss declared, "that observations on birdlife can reflect natural habits, rhythms and behaviour."[45] He accordingly initiated a wide-ranging program of daily environmental measurements and "census work" in 1952.[46] To enhance the visibility of the sanctuary's bird population to surveillance, Middlemiss interfered extensively in its natural environment. In addition to bush-clearing, path-making, and the construction of observation towers and a hide, he erected perching platforms, anchored a raft, cleared sedge beds, and bulldozed artificial islands and bays in the vlei to make the waterbird population more "legible" to his census work.

Most dramatically in 1958 the water level in the vlei was lowered to increase the available environment for migrant waders and the availability of all water birds for Middlemiss's "census work." Ironically, the re-engineering of the water level initiated a cascading regime change in the vlei; the collapse of algae, sedge, fish, and dominant waterbird populations (herons, ducks, and migrant waders) in the 1960s and the advance of bulrush and an invasive alien marsh grass, *Paspalum vaginatum* into the vlei led to its accelerated silting up in the 1970s. As Rondevlei disappeared around him, Middlemiss took refuge in his longstanding ambition, the sanctuary's own field museum, named in honor of the CBC's first president and his patron, Leonard Gill, and opened in 1966. Here at least, if nowhere else in the sanctuary, Middlemiss had complete control over Rondevlei's birdlife and, through the taxidermist's art, was able to put on permanent display inside species that were rapidly disappearing in the sanctuary outside. He doggedly refused to take any responsibility for the crisis in the sanctuary, and instead deflected blame onto the public in general and the surrounding black population in particular.

Middlemiss was always reluctant to allow public access to his sanctuary, and Rondevlei was opened only in 1955, five years after it was established. Would-be visitors were required to apply for a permit to visit, which Middlemiss limited to fifteen a day.[47] He further restricted public access to just half the year and to one kilometer of the north shore.[48] In this way he was able to keep "sightseer" numbers under a thousand a year until the 1970s (see figure 10.2). In 1970, however, the divisional council decided to allow free public access on weekends during the open season, and the number of visitors quadrupled to an average of four thousand per annum in the first half of the 1970s.[49] While Middlemiss was able to limit the white public's growing "disturbance" to the north shore and exclude the local black population entirely, he nonetheless claimed that the latter, in addition to trespass and arson in the inner sanctum, were also responsible for "toxic substances...being carried into Rondevlei by polluted waters from the neighbourhood." Regular testing of the vlei water began in the early 1970s, but failed to find Middlemiss's mystery toxin.[50]

Middlemiss's fortress conservation demonstrated his obsession with protecting the vlei against any and all forms of human "disturbance":

> It is an area where the fauna and flora have been left untouched; where the insects, reptiles, amphibians, the birds and the mammals live a life undistorted or disturbed by any interference, which could be of a destructive nature or cause discord. It is a true Sanctuary in every meaning of the word where one is conscious of nature's harmony and congruence.[51]

To maintain this "harmony and congruence," Middlemiss regarded it as "imperative...to step exceedingly warily" and accordingly followed what he deemed "the most valuable and wise policy...to wait and see, and to let nature shake off the past influences and see what it could do for itself." This manifested in an "obdurate policy of non-disturbance and non-intervention" and innate hostility toward any form of "management" of the vlei. The latter antipathy was shaped by his experience of the "ill-advised and disadvantageous" lowering of the vlei's water level in 1958.[52] "Man's attention and actions are more often than not confined to a solitary facet of the Sanctuary and they cannot, in pursuing a programme, see and distinguish the hundreds of other facets, all equally or more important than the one they are planning to alter. Aims, including those of the technical professions, are not always united with reason."[53]

By the 1970s, as he watched the "natural history" of his generation being supplanted by the "technical profession" of "conservation management" based on "the magic word ecology," Middlemiss feared a new determination to "interfere" with "nature" at Rondevlei. The latter he stressed was now "a relict, a record of the past and one struggling to retain its character and the life it holds" and for this reason, "will rely ... , more than ever, on remaining untouched, unimproved, and without any form of interference."[54] "There should be no tendency to favour or to concentrate exclusively on any one of the systems which build up the ecosystem of this supremely valuable environment."[55] Faced, contrary to his romantic imagining, with nature's manifest "disharmony" and "incongruence" at Rondevlei, Middlemiss proposed to do nothing in the hope that the vlei would regenerate itself. By the mid-1970s it was clear to everyone except the warden that his "obdurate ... non-intervention and non-disturbance" were authoring the destruction not the regeneration of Rondevlei.

Community-Based Conservation: Rondevlei, 1975–1994

Middlemiss finally retired as warden of Rondevlei in mid-1975, along with the rest of the generation of nascent professional ornithologists who organized and lead popular ornithology in postwar Cape Town and presided over the collapse of Rondevlei.[56] He was replaced by a twenty-six-year-old "game ranger," Howard Langley.[57] Langley had grown up in the Fish Hoek valley near the southern tip of the Cape Peninsula and was appointed a ranger in the city's flagship Cape of Good Hope Nature Reserve in 1968 straight out of high school. In the early 1970s Langley successfully completed a two-year field ecology course at the then University of Rhodesia in Harare; it was designed for the elite rangers of the then Rhodesian Parks Board who were directly involved in fighting a counterinsurgency war against Zimbabwe's black nationalist movement.[58] Langley's youth, innate rebelliousness, and practical ecology training soon led to an escalating conflict with his superior at Cape Point over the management of the reserve, and the divisional council transferred him to Rondevlei to resolve this problem.

Langley, a self-described "futurist" and avid science fiction reader, had no time for Middlemiss's sentimental nostalgia for the lost Cape Flats of his youth. "I think the past can't be undone. I know people say you can learn from the past, but I don't believe that too much. But we can learn from now and we actually really have to know what's going to happen and try and predict what's going to happen...because it's the future we're going to leave behind, not the past—its already left behind."[59] Looking to the future, Langley saw the absolute necessity of "public buy-in" to Rondevlei if it was to survive the accelerating urbanization of Cape Town. "Grassy Park was just growing like you cannot believe—roads and new buildings and the Regional Council of the Cape [sic] was just building and it was just going crazy....I said Rondevlei's got no future; unless we change what these places are and make them of much greater value to communities...we're going to lose them!"[60]

Langley thus broke decisively with his predecessor in actively encouraging public entry to Rondevlei. Middlemiss was a misanthrope, who at best tolerated and worst despised the "spectacle-hungry crowds quite unashamedly seeking something to see" as a "disturbance" and doggedly restricted their access to the sanctuary.[61] As Langley observed in 1980, "Rondevlei is located within a metropolitan area populated by some one and a half million people, yet only just over 4,000 persons visited the sanctuary this year, many of these being upcountry visitors."[62] In addition to a range of logistical obstacles, Langley attributed this "disturbing lack of interest...by the local population" to Middlemiss's quarter-century policy of restrictions "aimed at almost discouraging public use of Rondevlei...which did much to harm...[its] public image."[63] Langley believed that the construction of a new freeway skirting the sanctuary as the main access route from the city to the False Bay beach resorts would obviate many of the logistical constraints on its public use and so set about enhancing "the general appeal of the Sanctuary to the man in the street."[64]

To this end the permit system, the half-year closed season, and the restrictions on photography were scrapped, an information booklet produced, and the reception area landscaped, including a pond stocked with pinioned water birds "to give the visiting public an opportunity of seeing and photographing at close quarters, many species of birds that they would normally only see at a distance in the Sanctuary."[65] Langley understood the public demand for spectacle and, unlike Middlemiss, actively sought to encourage and accommodate it at Rondevlei. He constructed new islands, bird hides (including one where birds were fed), artificial roosts, and another observation tower to guarantee sightings for visitors. His determination to curtail the bulrush invasion was also largely an aesthetic concern about its screening of the vlei from visitors.

These many innovations, coupled with the rehabilitation of the vlei's bird population, produced a spectacular growth in visitor numbers after 1980 (see figure 10.3). In addition to the general improvements, two specific strategies underpinned the spectacular growth in visitor numbers under Langley's tenure: the introduction of charismatic species and targeting of schools for "environmental education." The reintroduction of hippo in 1981 generated "vast public interest" through press, radio, and television and guaranteed enduring media publicity thereafter (as discussed further

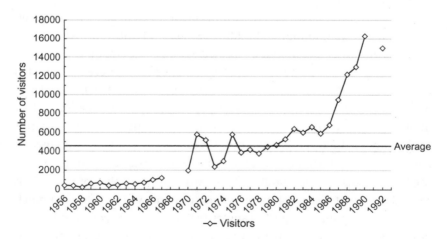

Figure 10.3

Rondevlei public visitors, 1956–1994, compiled from data contained in all twenty-four existing annual reports on the Rondevlei Bird Sanctuary from 1952 to 1988 (Cape Town: Cape Divisional Council, 1952–1988), with no visitor's data for the first four years, and complemented with data from 1990 and 1992 from the Western Cape Regional Services Council (n.d.).

below).[66] More important, though, in sustaining long-term growth was Langley's development of Rondevlei as a centre of "environmental education" for city schools.

Noting in the mid-1980s that "most schools that visit the Sanctuary use it simply as a recreational outing, with pupils learning little about the ecology or purpose of such a nature reserve," Langley set about remedying the situation through the complete renovation of Middlemiss's field museum.[67] Critical of the displays of "large groups of birds mounted on boards with their names below, which serve only as an aid to identification," he supplemented them with "educational displays" in "the form of natural habitats, with each bird or animal displayed in its natural setting and carrying out some function" to enable visitors to "identify the bird in the field but also to see to some extent what role it fulfils in the ecosystem."[68] He also renovated and extended the museum building, added a lecture theater, and developed a series of "audio-visual lectures" on the sanctuary in both English and Afrikaans and an educational guide with worksheets for schools.[69] The captive school audiences were critical to sustaining the sanctuary's growth in visitor numbers particularly in the late 1980s, when "political unrest" and the imposition of a state of emergency in the area led to a sharp decline in adult visitors.[70]

The other barrier to entry at Rondevlei that Langley removed was the fence erected to exclude the burgeoning ghetto population in its immediate neighborhood from the reserve. To Langley, "as soon as you make a rule, you're putting up a fence—that's what you're doing. It doesn't matter if it's a barbed wire fence or a rule or something. And rules don't create compliance, we know that; this country is one of the most lawless countries in the world and we're full of laws and everybody breaks them all the time. You have to manage them and manage the process."[71] The ghetto public's primary interest in the reserve was economic. Instead of suppressing their firewood poaching, as Middlemiss had done, Langley harnessed it to his cash-strapped rehabilitation effort as free labor:

> So I had no money and no budget so I thought, well I've got all these guys coming in illegally and climbing over and trashing our fence, climbing through the fence and cutting the fence to come and cut our firewood. I'm going to organise them and tell them they can come and cut up the firewood, but I will manage the process. I'll even put in a gate for you, I'll give you a bloody key and you can come in and you can cut the firewood where I tell you in blocks. And when you've

finished this section, I'll let you go into the next block, the next block, the next block—because I want you to clear the reserve of invasive trees—so that's how I did it—and I managed to clear the whole reserve of alien vegetation just using locals; they all became my friends, because then they in the end were protecting their own resources—Some of the woodcutters there were like the mafia....They were stopping people coming in and trashing—because it was their resource—which was a serious lesson for me to learn, because I learned in the process. And by the way I had to go through a sifting process because some people just didn't comply, so we said, you lose your permit—if you don't want to comply with the privilege we give you of coming to harvest firewood here, I'm sorry you're going to lose it. And we would give them a third warning and that's it gone. And then these guys would stop those guys coming in; I didn't need to police them, so it worked really well.[72]

It took Langley a decade to clear the reserve of alien acacia this way, and by removing the main incentive for local poaching, he secured a new peace between the reserve and its neighbors. Langley claims that he would have gone further and put styles over the fence or removed it altogether, but his importation of hippo to Rondevlei necessitated its enhanced armoring with cable and then welded mesh to prevent the animals from escaping.[73] The presence of a growing herd of large, aggressive nocturnal herbivores also acted as a powerful deterrent on local bush meat hunters and their dogs, while Langley's reduction in the resident grysbok and porcupine populations in the late 1980s removed their main quarry.[74]

Within the reserve Langley dismissed his predecessor's practice of "allow[ing] nature to run its course," as "no longer valid or practical" because Rondevlei was "no longer...a natural system."[75] Instead he sought to rehabilitate as much of the natural system as possible by reintroducing two key elements deliberately excluded by Middlemiss's fortress conservation, fire and grazing, in order to control the *Paspalum* and bulrush invasions that were converting the vlei into a marsh. Langley estimated that the vlei would take just thirty years to silt up and completely disappear in summer, thereby and so "bringing about the final end of Rondevlei as a Bird Sanctuary."[76] The "cancerous spread" of *Paspalum* had, by the mid-1970s, "claimed the entire shore of the vlei, spread out into the shallower areas forming dense carpets and destroyed all available sand and mud areas that are vital to water birds" and constituted "the greatest single threat to the Sanctuary's future."[77] After all attempts at manual, mechanical, and chemical eradication of the "thick carpets of...virile grass" had failed, Langley proposed what he called "the last hope," the reintroduction of hippo-potami to Rondevlei:[78]

> It is hoped that when introduced to Rondevlei, they will not only control the spread of P vaginatum, but will generally improve the area for birds, by creating channels in the dense reedbeds that are rapidly becoming established in the vlei and create mud banks and wallows, that could be utilised by a wide variety of water-birds.[79]

Langley's first hippos, two young bulls donated by the Natal Parks Board, arrived at Rondevlei in 1981, "the first of their kind to set foot in the Cape Peninsula in over three hundred years."[80] They were followed by two hippo cows in 1983, and the first hippo calf at Rondevlei was born the following year.[81] The hippo re-engineered the vlei in exactly the way Langley predicted they would. "The extent to which they are grazing back the encroaching grass…is greater than was thought possible for only two animals," Langley reported within a year of the first arrivals. "There is now no doubt that…the hippo will in the long term bring about and maintain suitable wader habitat at Rondevlei."[82] They were in fact so successful that by the mid-1980s they had eliminated *Paspalum vaginatum*, thus creating a severe shortage of grazing material, which necessitated the sale of two hippos in 1988.[83]

Langley coupled his reintroduction of grazing with that of fire, the human "disturbance" Middlemiss had worked hardest to suppress at Rondevlei.[84] In the second half of the 1970s Langley had all "alien acacia" eradicated from the sanctuary and tethered goats to supplement the resident grysbok in grazing down the vigorous regrowth of seedlings that followed clearance.[85] With the major fire hazard in the sanctuary removed he initiated the selective burning of bulrush beds, "to reduce the density of old well-established reed-beds and to eliminate the annual build-up of decaying reed stems" and thereby opening them up again to use by birds. He also burned *Paspalum* in such a way as to concentrate the hippos' grazing in the public area along the north shore where he most wanted to attract waders for visitors.[86]

As well as rolling back the *Paspalum* and bulrush invasions Langley implemented a suite of other measures to enhance Rondevlei's attractiveness to water birds and hence visitors. He erected some of the largest acacia felled in the sanctuary in the vlei supplemented by brush piles as nesting sites. To the same end he fired and felled the dense vegetation cover on the many islands created by Middlemiss and built more islands of his own. The sanctuary's growing gull and mongoose populations were also aggressively culled to lessen their predation pressure on nests.[87] Langley's bold management interference produced rapid results in the form of a steady and sustained recovery in wader and water bird breeding populations at Rondevlei, including the reestablishment of its renowned heronry in 1981, a quarter century after its disappearance.[88]

The hippopotami also provided Langley with a powerful argument for not only maintaining, but also expanding the sanctuary. By the mid-1980s the hippo grazing crisis had become acute, and Langley warned of an impending "tragedy": the re-extinction of hippo "after returning ... to an area where they had been extinct for over 200 years and where there [sic] presence is essential for the well-being of the aquatic environment."[89] This was a result, he declared, of the "unfortunate mistake" made in 1950 of placing "too much emphasis ... on preserving the vlei itself" and not enough on the "terrestrial environment of the area" even though the two were "closely inter-related ... and one cannot be adequately conserved without the other."[90] As a result, the sanctuary was "of insufficient size to be ecologically viable," and to enhance its viability Langley was allowed annex more than one hundred hectares of public land adjoining the reserve, which had been earmarked for schooling, as grazing land for his hippo, nearly doubling it in size.[91]

Conclusion

Fortress conservation was reinvented at Rondevlei in the final two decades of apartheid in response to the unique urban pressures faced by the sanctuary-cum-reserve. Its location on the Cape Flats exposed it to aggressive invasion by both exotic vegetation and poor blacks, the former the legacy of environmental engineering by foresters and the latter of the social engineering by apartheid urban planners. By the mid-1970s these twin assaults had destroyed Rondevlei as a bird sanctuary and the credibility of the fortress conservation approach of its first warden, Ernest Middlemiss. Faced with the complete failure of conventional conservation, Rondevlei's second warden, Howard Langley, used its "large open air laboratory" to experiment with a new approach that substituted alliance-building for force to win rather than compel popular consent to the reserve. Langley's eclectic and innovative fusion of scientific ecology and pragmatic futurism redefined Rondevlei's purpose away from "birds" to "nature" and from elite recreation to popular education. By broadening his remit and winning popular consent for this expanded mandate, Langley was able to aggressively enlarge the boundaries of the reserve in the late 1980s, thereby successfully enclosing land earmarked for black education and housing as hippo grazing.

The importance of Rondevlei as the laboratory for the invention of a new kind of urban conservation is confirmed both by Langley's subsequent meteoric rise within the local state to head of Cape Nature in 2001 and by the generalization of his approach to massively expand the city's reserve system post-1994.[92] Langley's reintroduction of hippo to Rondevlei, in particular, powerfully demonstrated that the urban environmental clock could be successfully wound back from five past midnight to precolonial dawn and that by doing so conservationists could successfully claim back scarce urban land from the city's burgeoning poor black population. The consent of the latter to their continued dispossession could in turn be secured through their employment and "environmental education" in the enlarged reserves.

Notes

1. Carruthers 1995; Foster 2008.

2. See, for example, Foster (2008, pp. 144–177) for Johannesburg and van Sittert (2003) for Cape Town.

3. See Berkes (2004) for theory on community-based conservation; Cock and Fig (2000) and Ramutsindela (2004) for its practice in Southern Africa; and Graham and Ernstson (2012) and Graham (2015) for its use in Cape Town.

4. Grove 1996.

5. Union of South Africa 1913.

6. Union of South Africa 1913, tables 5 and 15; 1950, tables 3a and 12.

7. Rosenthal 1980, pp. 4–8.

8. See, for example, Middlemiss (1946).

9. Ibid.; Middlemiss 1974, pp. 4–6.

10. The words of those of the director of the South African Museum, Louis Peringuey, cited in Bolus (1918, p. 66).

11. Cape of Good Hope (1899, pp. 644–645) and Wild Bird Protection Act (1899, No. 42).

12. Union of South Africa 1925, pp. 658–665; Union of South Africa 1926, pp. 115–137.

13. See van Sittert (2002) for Cape botany and Gill (1955) and Carruthers (2004) for Cape ornithology. The South African Ornithological Union was founded by the director of the city's South African Museum, W. L. Sclater, in 1904 but disbanded in 1916; it was then revived as the South African Ornithological Society by the director of the Transvaal Museum, Austin Roberts, in 1929.

14. See, for example, Skaife (1963, pp. 57–67) for the introduction of biology into the school curriculum; Skaife (1920) and Skaife (1928) for popular nature study; and L. M. R. (1946), Bolus (1918), Two Bird-Loving Members (1919, 1920, 1921, 1922, 1923, 1925) and Meiklejohn (1940) for the Mountain Club.

15. See the *First Guide to the Birds of South Africa* by Gill (1936). Gill reported having spent seven years compiling this book.

16. Ibid.

17. See Winterbottom (1981, pp. 180–181) for the number of editions and Gill (1948, pp. 605–606) for the quotation.

18. Cape Bird Club 1998, pp. 3–4.

19. Ibid.

20. Bolus 1919, p. 66.

21. See Gill (1940, p. 202).

22. See de Vries (1991, pp. 192–193).

23. See Sayers (1986), Magona (1990), Greenbank (1993), and Meier (1998).

24. Quoted in Middlemiss (1974, p. 23).

25. Quoted in ibid. (pp. 24–25).

26. Quoted in ibid. (p. 25).

27. See Brockington (2002), Neumann (2002a), and Neumann (2002b, pp. 22–47) for the colonial model.

28. See van Sittert (2002, p. 125) and Skaife (1963, pp. 52–56) for the city's white middle-class agitation for a Kruger National Park facsimile on their doorstep.

29. Cape Bird Club 1998. Middlemiss did not even warrant an obituary notice in the Cape Bird Club journal *Promerops* when he died in 1992.

30. See Winterbottom (1981, 1995) and Cape Bird Club (1998). Even the professionals were amateurs, Gill was trained as a palaeontologist, Winterbottom as an educationalist and Broekhuyssen as an entomologist.

31. See Cape Divisional Council (1952, pp. 4–5). I will make frequent use of the council's first thirty-seven annual reports, which are dated from 195 to 1988 and are grouped together in the References list. See also Gill, quoted in Middlemiss (1974, pp. 24–25).

32. Cape Divisional Council 1952, p. 4.

33. Cape Divisional Council 1971, 1972.

34. See Cape Divisional Council (1972, p. 28). Gill quoted in Middlemiss (1974, p. 23); additional quotations in Cape Divisional Council (1952, p. 6).

35. Cape Divisional Council 1952, pp. 5, 11.

36. Cape Divisional Council 1956, p. 1.

37. See Cape Divisional Council (1972, pp. 25, 54). See also Langley (1978, p. 1), who revised the estimate of the neighboring population upward to fifty thousand.

38. Cape Divisional Council 1952, p. 5.

39. Cape Divisional Council 1972, p. 26.

40. See Cape Divisional Council (1959, pp. 1–2); Cape Divisional Council (1973, pp. 4–6).

41. See Cape Divisional Council (1955, p. 3) for the creation of a "fire path" along the reserve's southern boundary.

42. Cape Divisional Council 1965, p. 1.

43. Cape Divisional Council 1970, p. 1.

44. Cape Divisional Council 1973, pp. 1–2.

45. Cape Divisional Council 1952, pp. 6, 13.

46. For details, see ibid., pp. 13–25.

47. See Middlemiss (1974, p. 76) for the opening of the sanctuary to the public only at the insistence of the Cape Divisional Council.

48. Ibid., pp. 76–79.

49. Ibid.

50. Cape Divisional Council 1972, pp. 32–36; Cape Divisional Council 1975, pp. 4–6; Cape Divisional Council 1976, pp. 3–4; Cape Divisional Council 1977, p. 5.

51. Middlemiss 1974, p. 70.

52. Ibid., p. 414.

53. Ibid., p. 4.

54. Ibid., p. 416.

55. Ibid.

56. Jack Winterbottom retired as director of the Percy Fitzpatrick Institute for Ornithology at the University of Cape Town in 1971 and died in 1984; Gerry Broekhuysen retired from the University of Cape Town in 1973 and died two years later.

57. Draper 1998.

58. Duffy 2000.

59. Transcript of interview with C. H. Langley, Clovelly, January 24, 2014, p. 12.

60. Ibid.

61. Ibid. See also Middlemiss (1974, pp. 76–85, 416–419).

62. Cape Divisional Council 1980, p. 2.

63. Ibid., p. 3. Langley listed remoteness from main tourist route, high crime rate in the area, the lack of public transport, signage, facilities, publicity, and public interest in birdlife, and the "elusive nature" of the birds themselves as contributing factors. See Transcript of interview with C. H. Langley.

64. Cape Divisional Council 1980, p. 3.

65. Cape Divisional Council 1982, p. 3.

66. Cape Divisional Council 1981, p. 2.

67. Cape Divisional Council 1984, p. 3.

68. Cape Divisional Council 1976, p. 4. See also Cape Divisional Council (1987, pp. 5–6).

69. Cape Divisional Council 1985, p. 5.

70. Cape Divisional Council 1986, p. 2.

71. Transcript of interview with C. H. Langley, p. 14.

72. Ibid., p. 15.

73. Cape Divisional Council 1983, pp. 2–3.

74. Cape Divisional Council 1986, p. 5; Cape Divisional Council 1987, p. 10; Cape Divisional Council 1988, p. 5.

75. Cape Divisional Council 1976, p. 6.

76. Cape Divisional Council 1977, pp. 11–12.

77. Cape Divisional Council 1975, pp. 6–7; Cape Divisional Council 1976, p. 7.

78. Cape Divisional Council 1975, p. 7; 1976, p. 7. The idea was first mooted by R. G. Atwell in 1964.

79. Cape Divisional Council 1976, p. 7.

80. Cape Divisional Council 1981, p. 9.

81. Cape Divisional Council 1983, p. 6; Cape Divisional Council 1984, p. 9.

82. Cape Divisional Council 1982, p. 8; Cape Divisional Council 1984, p. 9.

83. Cape Divisional Council 1984, p. 9; Cape Divisional Council 1985, pp. 2, 11; Cape Divisional Council 1988, pp. 11–12.

84. See Cape Divisional Council (1952, p. 17) for Middlemiss's report that he had "been given to understand that the [sedge] beds have been burned regularly in the past by local inhabitants" and Middlemiss (1974, pp. 29–31, 87–88) for his defense of his exclusion of fire from the sanctuary.

85. Cape Divisional Council 1978, p. 6. See also Cape Divisional Council (1979, p. 6); Cape Divisional Council (1980, pp. 14–15); Cape Divisional Council (1986, p. 9) for the retention of acacia along the northern and eastern fence lines as "buffers" against the surrounding black township and the removal of these "buffers" in 1980 and the late 1980s.

86. Cape Divisional Council 1981, pp. 10–11.

87. Cape Divisional Council 1978, pp. 12–15; Cape Divisional Council 1979, pp. 13–14; Cape Divisional Council 1980, p. 20.

88. Cape Divisional Council 1981, pp. 13–14.

89. Cape Divisional Council 1985, p. 2.

90. Ibid.

91. Ibid., pp. 2–3; Cape Divisional Council 1986, pp. 2–3.

92. See, for example, Petersen et al. (2012) for the post-apartheid proletarian pressure on the city's reserves, and Graham and Ernstson (2012), Ernstson (2013), and Ernstson and Sörlin (2013) for some community-based conservation responses in Cape Town.

References

Berkes, F. 2004. "Rethinking Community-Based Conservation." *Conservation Biology* 18: 621–630.

Bolus, F. 1918. "List of Birds Occurring on the Cape Peninsula." *Journal of the Mountain Club of South Africa* 21: 66–77.

Brockington, D. 2002. *Fortress Conservation: The Preservation of Mkomazi Game Reserve, Tanzania*. Oxford: James Currey.

Cape Bird Club. 1998. "The Cape Bird Club Jubilee 1948–1998." Supplement to *Promerops* (April): 3–4.

Cape Divisional Council. 1952. *1st Annual Report on the Rondevlei Bird Sanctuary [ARRBS] for the Year Ended 1952*. Cape Town: Cape Divisional Council. Subsequent years and annual report number as follows: 1954, 3rd; 1955. 4th; 1956. 5th; 1959. 8th; 1965, 13th; 1970, 19th; 1971, 20th; 1972, 21st; 1973, 23rd; 1975, 24th; 1976, 25th; 1977, 26th; 1978, 27th; 1979, 28th; 1980, 29th; 1981, 30th; 1982, 31st; 1983, 32nd; 1984, 33rd; 1985, 34th; 1986, 35th; 1987, 36th; and 1988, 37th.

Cape of Good Hope. 1899. *House of Assembly Debates*. 644–645.

Carruthers, J. 1995. *The Kruger National Park: A Social and Political History*. Pietermaritzburg: University of Natal Press.

Carruthers, J. 2004. "Our Beautiful and Useful Allies: Aspects of Ornithology in Twentieth-Century South Africa." *Historia* 49(1): 89–109.

Cock, J., and D. Fig. 2000. "From Colonial to Community Based Conservation: Environmental Justice and the National Parks of South Africa." *Society in Transition* 31: 22–35.

De Vries, G. 1991. *Wingfield, a Pictorial History*. Goodwood, Cape Town: National Book Printers.

Draper, M. 1998. "Zen and the Art of Garden Province Maintenance: The Soft Intimacy of Hard Men in the Wilderness of Kwa-Zulu Natal, South Africa, 1952–1997." *Journal of Southern African Studies* 24: 801–828.

Duffy, R. 2000. *Killing for Conservation: Wildlife Policy in Zimbabwe*. Oxford: James Currey.

Ernstson, H. 2013. "Re-Translating Nature in Post-Apartheid Cape Town: The Material Semiotics of People and Plants at Bottom Road." Actor-Network Theory for Development Working Paper Series, edited by Richard Heeks, no. 4. Manchester: Institute for Development Policy and Management, School of Environment, Education and Development, University of Manchester. http://hummedia.manchester.ac.uk/institutes/cdi/resources/cdi_ant4d/ANT4DWorkingPaper4Ernstson.pdf.

Ernstson, H., and S. Sörlin. 2013. "Ecosystem Services as Technology of Globalization: On Articulating Values in Urban Nature." *Ecological Economics* 86: 274–284.

Foster, J. A. 2008. *Washed with Sun: Landscape and the Making of White South Africa*. Pittsburgh, PA: University of Pittsburgh Press.

Gill, E. L. 1936. *First Guide to the Birds of South Africa*. Cape Town: Maskew Millar.

Gill, E. L. 1940. *First Guide to the Birds of South Africa*. Cape Town: Maskew Millar.

Gill, E. L. 1948. "Obituary Dr Austin Roberts." *Ibis* 90(4): 605–606.

Gill, E. L. 1955. "Fifty Years of South African Ornithology." *Ostrich* 26(1): 4–5.

Graham, M. 2015. "Postcolonial Nature Conservation in Practice: The Everyday Challenges of On-Ground Urban Nature Conservation, Cape Town, South Africa." *GeoJournal* 82(1): 43–62.

Graham, M., and H. Ernstson. 2012. "Comanagement at the Fringes: Examining Stakeholder Perspectives at Macassar Dunes, Cape Town, South Africa—at the Intersection of High Biodiversity, Urban Poverty and Inequality." *Ecology and Society* 17(3): article 34.

Greenbank, K. 1993. "Into the Wild Bushes of Nyanga: The Growth, Control and Relocation of Cape Town's Squatters, 1939–1955." PhD diss., University of Cape Town.

Grove, R. 1996. *Green Imperialism: Colonial Expansion, Tropical Island Edens and the Origins of Environmentalism, 1600–1860*. Cambridge: Cambridge University Press.

L. M. R. 1946. "The Birds of Table Mountain." *Journal of the Mountain Club of South Africa* 11: 40–44.

Langley, C. H. 1978. *Rondevlei Bird Sanctuary: An Introduction to the Rondevlei Bird Sanctuary with Check Lists of Birds and Other Animals recorded since 1952*. Cape Town: Divisional Council.

Magona, S. 1990. *To My Children's Children*. Cape Town: David Philip.

Meier, J. 1998. "Retreat and the Pondokkies Evil, 1939–1960." Paper presented at the Department of History and Institute for Historical Research Seminar, University of the Western Cape, July 30.

Meiklejohn, M. F. M. 1940. "Mountain Birds." *Journal of the Mountain Club of South Africa* 43: 12–18.

Middlemiss, E. 1946. *Cape Country: Informal Sketches in Word and Picture of the Natural Environment of the Cape Peninsula*. Cape Town: African Bookman.

Middlemiss, E. 1974. *The Rondevlei Bird Sanctuary 1952–1974: A Record of an Environment*. Cape Town: Cape Divisional Council.

Neumann, R. 2002a. *Imposing Wilderness: Struggles over Livelihood and Nature Preservation in Africa*. Berkeley: University of California Press.

Neumann, R. 2002b. "The Postwar Conservation Boom in British Colonial Africa." *Environmental History* 7: 22–47.

Petersen, L. M., E. J. Moll, R. Collins, and M. T. Hockings. 2012. "Development of a Compendium of Local, Wild-Harvested Species Used in the Informal Economy Trade, Cape Town, South Africa." *Ecology and Society* 17(2): n.p.

Ramutsindela, M. 2004. *Parks and People in Postcolonial Societies: Experiences in Southern Africa*. Dordrecht: Kluwer.

Rosenthal, E. 1980. *Goodwood and Its History*. Cape Town: National Book Printers.

Sayers, A. 1986. "Aspects of the Economic and Social History of Retreat." Paper presented at the Western Cape Roots and Realities Conference, Centre for African Studies, University of Cape Town, July 16–18.

Skaife, S. H. 1920. *Animal Life in South Africa*. Cape Town: Maskew Miller.

Skaife, S. H. 1928. *The Strange Adventures of John Harmer: A Story Based on Facts of the Wonderful Adventures of a South African Boy among Insects, Birds and the Strange Creatures in the Sea around Our Coast: Part II: Dr Secundus and the Birds*. Cape Town: Maskew Miller.

Skaife, S. H. 1963. *A Naturalist Remembers*. Cape Town: Longmans.

Two Bird-Loving Members (pseud.). 1919. "Birds of the Cape Peninsula I." *Journal of the Mountain Club of South Africa* 22: 40–46. And in subsequent years with same authors, title and journal: 1920, 23: 31–51; 1921, 24: 96–107; 1922, 25: 65–83; 1923, 26: 72–87; 1925, 28: 112–122.

Union of South Africa. 1913. *Report on the Chief Conservator of Forests, 1913*.

Union of South Africa. 1925. *House of Assembly Debates*.

Union of South Africa. 1926. *House of Assembly Debates*.

Union of South Africa. 1950. *Annual Report of the Department of Forestry, 1950*.

van Sittert, L. 2002. "From Mere Weeds and Bosjes to Cape Floral Kingdom: Reimagining Indigenous Flora at the Cape, c. 1890–1950." *Kronos* 28: 102–126.

van Sittert, L. 2003. "The Bourgeois Eye Aloft: Table Mountain in the Anglo Urban Middle Class Imagination, c. 1891–1952." *Kronos* 29: 161–190.

Western Cape Regional Services Council. n.d. *Rondevlei Bird Sanctuary*.

Wild Bird Protection Act, No. 42. 1899.

Winterbottom, J. M. 1981. "Edwin Leonard Gill." In *South African Dictionary of Biography*, vol. 4, edited by W. J. de Kock, 180–181. Pretoria: Human Sciences Research Council.

Winterbottom, J. M. 1995. *Far Away and Not So Long Ago*. Toronto: Private Printing.

11   Ecology in the Urban Century: Power, Place, and the Abstraction of Nature

James Evans

Humans are now an urbanized species, with over half of the global population living in cities—a proportion forecast by the United Nations to rise to 75 percent by 2050. At the same time, the Intergovernmental Panel on Climate Change has claimed with 95 percent certainty that climate change is being driven by human activities, prompting scientists to herald the advent of the Anthropocene, a new era in which humans have become the main drivers of environmental change. The challenge of securing a sustainable global future has become a question of taming the environmental impacts of cities. Within this context, ecology has emerged as a technology of governance, promising a way to manage human relations with nature in more sustainable ways. As in the nineteenth century, when crusading sanitarians and engineers tamed death and disease with modern infrastructures supplying water and energy, so in the current urban century, urban ecology is being herlded as being capable of arresting environmental destruction with closed loop systems and adaptive management. Ecology is the scientific assumption lying behind every rhetorical "eco" preface, providing a compass to navigate safe passage to the promised land of sustainability.

The irony of this redemptive role is that ecology originated as a discipline not primarily concerned with people. Environmental historians have offered compelling accounts of how concepts like *succession* and *ecosystems* embody the specific characteristics of the rural and wilderness areas in which early ecologists worked.[1] Sometimes the parallels are literal: the idea of "pioneer" plant communities was derived from research conducted on the vast plains of the Midwest in early twentieth-century America, across which human pioneers had moved barely a century earlier. One particularly stubborn consequence of this has been the hardwiring of cultural preferences for "wild" environments into the scientific models of ecology itself, which tend to value equilibrium systems.[2] When we come to human-dominated systems this has made life difficult. Urbanization results in extremely disturbed systems, where the creative destruction wrought by capitalism in the form of constant development and redevelopment creates an inherently dynamic landscape. In ecological terms cities make little sense, they fit none of the models, and tend to be cast (traditionally at least) as a form of "anti-life."[3]

Until the 1990s the ecological study of cities was largely confined to a handful of German ecologists trapped on the urban island of West Berlin and to the coffee table publications of a few curious naturalists. The Rio Earth Conference in 1992 changed this dramatically, prompting ecologists to call for a "new ecological paradigm" that places humans within ecosystems rather than separate from them.[4] In this era of urbanization,[5] applying systems ecology to cities to develop technologies of ecological governance holds great appeal as it suggests that they are coherent, knowable, and manageable entities.[6] The prize of managing urban ecosystems more sustainably is substantial: cities consume 70 percent of natural resources and produce 80 percent or carbon emissions. They are home to a growing majority of the world's inhabitants and must increasingly adapt to the consequences of a changing climate. No longer simply a curiosity, urban ecology is supposed to facilitate low carbon transitions and help city dwellers adapt to rising temperatures and increasingly extreme weather events. As if that weren't enough, its proponents highlight significant physical and mental health benefits and property price uplift that accrue from proximity to nature.

Urban ecology has gone from subdisciplinary backwater to hot topic, viewed as a key disciplinary ingredient in the quest for sustainability. But perhaps more than any other science, ecology reflects the places in which it is practiced. This chapter explores how urban ecology dovetails with the rise of ecological governance and the suite of ecological planning and policy tools like ecosystem services, green infrastructure, and resilience that accompany it. These highly mobile global policy discourses increasingly frame debates over urban futures, but are characterized by a series of tensions that hamper their application. This chapter critically examines these tools and the forms of urban ecological research through which they are practised and produced. It identifies a gap between the discursive power of urban ecological governance and the relatively modest transformations wrought in cities on the ground and discusses some of the implications of this gap.

The Rise of Ecological Governance

In 2006 the United Kingdom's Department for Environment, Food and Rural Affairs held a meeting in central London to review its research program to establish an evidence base for the adoption of ecosystem services as the foundation for national policymaking.[7] The ecosystem services approach is typical of an increasingly influential set of ecological policy tools that have emerged in response to ecological crisis. The meeting was memorable not for the bad coffee or for the sterile conference room that seemed at odds with the magnificent Georgian building in which it was housed, but for an exchange between a well-known professor and the senior government official who up until that point had sat in pinstriped silence observing proceedings, content to let his minions remind the academic audience of the desired outcomes from the work. The professor stood up and proclaimed that the ecosystem services approach was unable to provide the kind of comprehensive basis for decision-making that was sought because of the difficulties in determining the subjective values of different environmental goods to different people in different places. His outburst was preceded by a circular discussion about the policy implications of valuing a single plane tree in London at one million pounds on the basis of its positive impact on house prices, as against a Scottish pine forest that is rarely used by humans and is by comparison relatively worthless.[8] Riled into action, the senior government official retorted that the department had already decided to use the ecosystem service approach as the basis for its policymaking. It was their job to "make it work"; that was what they were being paid for.

The episode sticks in the mind as an example of the all-too obvious ways in which power sometimes shapes the types of knowledge that gain wider political traction, in this case through the demand from policymakers for ecologically informed tools to better govern society's relations with nature. But the "just make it work" line belies a disjuncture between the promise of ecosystem services as a policy approach and its realities as a scientific planning tool. Alongside ecosystem services, green infrastructure and resilience have emerged in the last fifteen years as a familiar conceptual lexicon for those working in urban environmental planning. All three offer an idealized and universally applicable form of ecological governance, but are based on highly abstract and stylized models of nature (and the relation of society to it).

Take green infrastructure, for example. Originating as a conservation tool for understanding how habitat patches maintain biodiversity in landscapes fragmented by human land uses (like roads, housing, and so on), it has developed into a fully fledged planning concept that is used to capture the multiple functions of green space, for example absorbing rainfall while also providing recreational space. The idea of infrastructure offers a proactive discourse of green space as "doing something" useful for society, but further it suggests a narrative of necessity.[9] Infrastructure is something that we have to have and fits neatly with established approaches to planning, which are familiar with surveying, analyzing, and planning so-called "grey" infrastructures like roads and sewers. In *The Wealth of Nations* Adam Smith assigns the task of constructing and maintaining infrastructure to "the sovereign," who is responsible for "erecting and maintaining certain public works and certain public institutions, which it can never be the interest of any individual or small number of individuals to erect and maintain."[10] Infrastructure is a collective good and as such implies the need for a collective approach.

The ecosystem service approach is often used to value the services provided by various pieces of green infrastructure, although the two approaches differ critically between advocating individual payment for services and simply using the value of services to justify collective investment in the service provider. Lele's memorable analogy is the difference between paying for a hot dog and investing in a hot dog stand, with the inference that it makes little sense to talk of "investing" in a hot dog.[11] Green infrastructure has been conceived of as a form of ecological modernization that promises a winwin approach to planning whereby environmental improvements lead to social and economic benefits. As Maarten Hajer says, "talking about nature as infrastructure creates a link to the importance of nature as amenity (which is essentially a functional idea), but also allows for an engineering approach to nature. If nature is seen as infrastructure, we can also make a move from conservation to the actual creation of new (and better?) nature."[12] Green infrastructure has become firmly entrenched in actual planning practice. Whereas ecosystem services have been pushed to high level policymakers through international consultants and the UN-backed Millennium Ecosystem Assessment, green infrastructure resonates at local and regional levels and propagates through nongovernmental organizations' (NGO) planning networks.[13] The paucity of critical work on green infrastructure perhaps reflects its politically benign exterior, but the idea of nature as essentially malleable and improvable points to an underlying set of beliefs about the relations between society and the environment that warrants further attention in practice.[14]

By contrast, resilience thinking is more explicitly concerned with the relationships between society and the environment. Originating in the work of North American ecologist "Buzz" Holling, *resilience* is defined as the capacity of a system to absorb disturbance and reorganize while undergoing change so as to retain essentially the same function, structure, identity, and feedbacks.[15] Using the example of budworm outbreaks in the spruce-fir forests of eastern Canada, Holling argued that persistent natural systems are not characterized by stability but by instability.[16] Holling's work influenced the 1999 establishment of the Resilience Alliance, an international collaboration among ecologists and ecosystem management scholars from across the Western world. This group developed the concept of the social-ecological system,[17] which applied resilience thinking to human-dominated systems. Developed in the 1990s and elaborated in two edited volumes with contributors from all over the world,[18] this approach suggested that social and ecological systems are linked through a series of physical feedback mechanisms. Knowledge about the local ecosystem is essential to the functioning of a social-ecological system and must be captured by institutions that can translate it into management practices. The idea of social-ecological systems was subsequently applied to urban contexts,[19] and it became an organizing concept for the Stockholm Resilience Centre, established in 2007.

The lexicon of urban environmental planning is astonishingly consistent. It is hard to find a conservation planning document for an urbanized region that does not use green infrastructure as its basis, justifying its value through general appeals to the ecosystem services that it provides society.[20] Resilience has found its way into numerous policy documents and often appears as a guiding principle.[21] In policy documents about regional resilience again ecosystem services are usually suggested as a way to quantify the value of different socio-ecological processes.[22] Currently these approaches tend to remain confined to conservation strategies and regional planning documents, rather than being deployed as the basis for mainstream decision-making (which remains dominated by economists). In practice the rhetoric is defeated by the difficulties of governing something as complex as a city as an ecosystem; for example, there is simply insufficient environmental data to do so, and traditional institutional arrangements militate against

large-scale landscape interventions. Even a coherent conceptual understanding is lacking—the striking observation from a cursory analysis of the
policy and academic literature is that research teams tend to work with one
approach.[23] An analysis of keywords listed in paper titles and abstracts in
the fields of ecosystem services, green infrastructure, and urban resilience
indicates that 13 percent of green infrastructure papers and 21 percent of
resilience papers mention ecosystem services, whereas only 10 percent of
ecosystem service papers mention resilience. This drops to just 2 percent of
ecosystem service papers mentioning green infrastructure. The relationship
between resilience and green infrastructure is weakest, with 2 percent of
resilience papers focusing on green infrastructure and 4 percent of green
infrastructure papers focusing on resilience.[24]

Despite this unevenness, ecological governance holds strong appeal for
policymakers looking for a more scientific basis for urban environmental
management. The next section considers a large-scale field experiment
underway in Baltimore, which is notable for bringing these three ecological
approaches together to study the city as a coherent system. It is perhaps
unique in being the place where the model of ecologically based governance is being deployed and tested most seriously, and offers a window
onto both the potential and the limits of urban ecology to reshape cities.

Baltimore: Ecological Laboratory for the Urban Century

Funded by the United States National Science Foundation from 1980 up
to the current day, the Long Term Ecological Research (LTER) program
represents the flagship environmental science research programme in the
United States, comprising twenty-four ecologically diverse sites, an annual
direct budget of almost $20 million, and approximately 1,100 scientists
and research students. Two metropolises (Phoenix and Baltimore) were
added to their portfolio of sites in 1997, and both projects were granted
second-phase funding in 2004. Led by influential urban ecologists Nancy
Grimm at Arizona State University and Steward Pickett at Baltimore, respectively, both research teams adopted a large-scale ecosystems approach, both
sold themselves on the potential to use their cities as field laboratories,
and both emphasized the virtues of a comparative approach between cities. The project married shifting scientific funding priorities for large-scale
applied work capable of producing scalable findings with the needs of two

cities (Baltimore and Phoenix) under pressure to deal with growing environmental externalities in more efficient ways. This section focuses on the Baltimore research, which has established the city as a laboratory for the staging of large scale socio-ecological experiments that aim to understand and manage the dynamic processes that give rise to the urban landscape.

Ecologists in Baltimore have been seeking to understand how the city's ecosystems change over time by studying the interaction of a range of factors, from hydrology and biodiversity to patch dynamics and soil studies. The Baltimore project states that "its goal is to develop a thoroughgoing understanding of metropolitan Baltimore as an ecological system, and to share this understanding with educators and decision makers."[25] Baltimore represents the cutting edge of ecological work that seeks to move from seeing human activity purely as an external factor causing disturbance to ecosystems to being a driver and limiter of ecological processes in its own right. The overall project is framed by the concept of resilience, conceiving Baltimore as a linked socio-ecological system. Taking an adaptive approach, the project involves staging experiments by altering the green infrastructure in parts of the city to enhance key ecosystem services.

At the core of the work, in addition to the $20 million annual budget, is a nearly $1 billion, six-year experimental manipulation of nitrogen exports in the watershed to improve drainage infrastructure. Like many cities with a primarily industrial heritage, Baltimore is characterized by aging infrastructure and a decrepit sanitary sewer system, much of which is over one hundred years old. Leaks and gradual seepage, accompanied by the occasional yet spectacular sewage fountain, have caused declining water quality, and in 2002 eventually led to a legal action from the US Environmental Protection Agency under the Clean Water Act. In addition to paying $600,000 in fines stipulated in the resulting agreement, city officials had to agree to invest $900 million in sewer upgrades. The wider Baltimore County settled on a similar agreement in reparation for over six hundred spills between 1997 and 2005, providing further money for environment projects to keep nitrogen and phosphorus out of the Chesapeake Bay. These federal mandates opened up opportunities for ecologists to work closely with urban planners and administrators to undertake experimental planting to manage runoff using green infrastructure.

The most intense experiments took place in Watershed 263, a 930-acre area spread over eleven densely populated neighborhoods of west and southwest Baltimore, which drains to Baltimore Harbor's tidal estuary of the Middle Branch of the Patapsco River, near the mouth of Gwynns Falls. Over three quarters of the area of this entirely urbanized watershed, with its mix of residential, commercial, industrial, institutional, and open-space uses as well as roads, parking lots, and vacant or abandoned properties, is impervious to water. In terms of infrastructure, it includes thirteen miles of storm drains that are over three feet in diameter and that converge into one twenty-five-foot diameter outfall. Public open space associated with schools and parks accounts for approximately 30 percent of the watershed, with trees shading only about 5.5 percent of the area compared to 17.32 percent for the city as a whole. The area is economically depressed and predominantly African American, and the Baltimore LTER and its focus on technologically mediated management have echoes of World Bank–style development initiatives, lending a normative liberal politics to the selection of the Gwynn Falls area as one in need of improvement.

Terming it a "natural experiment," the research team undertook extensive greening to increase canopy cover and decrease impervious surfaces especially on vacant and public land. The project team hardwired monitoring equipment into the green infrastructure to provide a basis for adaptive management, aiming to enhance the reduction of pollution through intervening in specific areas and adapting subsequent policy and regulation in response to the results of infrastructure improvements. If experimenting in situ produces more accurate scientific models,[26] then the idea was that "urban ecologists could use designed experiments as a management tool to predict, monitor, and regulate urban ecological patterns and processes."[27] These interventions are monitored in terms of their effects on pollution and runoff, while long-term species surveys of different plots across the city determine the relationship between patch origin, size, adjacent land-use type, and species composition and abundance.

This long-running ecological research project has led attempts to understand the city as an urban socio-ecological system in order to enhance its resilience, building upon the work of the US Long Term Ecological Research network of which the project is part.[28] Accordingly the project is also researching what it calls "social ecology," or the capacity of people to either damage or enhance the ecological functioning of the urban landscape. Although the concept of the social-ecological system emerged from work conducted at the Stockholm Resilience Centre,[29] it has been used by the

Baltimore project team to understand how the urban mosaic functions at the scale of the city. This point is picked up in Pickett and colleagues' review of urban ecological systems,[30] which argues that urban ecological planning tends to be based on principles and cases rather than data and an understanding of processes. The problem identified is that the former approaches struggle to manage the kinds of "novel ecological circumstances" that cities will experience under a rapidly changing climate. This argument is reminiscent of debates from the first half of the twentieth century over the ability of ecology to generate scientifically valid knowledge about causal processes, given its field-based methods and emphasis on the identification of patterns.[31]

The Baltimore project uses computer modeling to understand how different variables affect one another in the city, and seeks to abstract from the specificities of Baltimore through the idea of *syndromes*, or commonly occurring sets of urban environmental characteristics that have predictable functions. The inference is that cities will then be susceptible to standardized management interventions. In capturing general sets of traits rather than a specific set of rules about function, the notion of syndromes owes more than a passing resemblance to Elinor Ostrom's diagnostic approach to Common Pool Resource Management (perhaps no coincidence as Ostrom worked with resilience scholars in her later career).[32] Within this conceptual framework the diagnosis of "symptoms" enables corrective management. The danger of viewing cities as sick patients, though, is that it reproduces the idea that urban nature is a degraded form of "real" nature, echoing the pathologies of the city—like crime and pollution—identified by the writers of sociological urban ecology in the 1970s. Of course that movement lacked any real empirical or explanatory basis, unlike the large-scale and long-term urban ecology research programs occurring in places like Baltimore, which collect large amounts of data to enable a process-based approach.

As an experimental site Baltimore has become emblematic of a specific brand of urban ecology that seeks to meet the demand for data-driven technologies of conservation to underpin sustainable urban management. That said, how generalizable the findings about urban resilience from Baltimore are remains an "open question for now."[33] Baltimore's modern history of deindustrialisation seems quite extreme, compared for example to Stockholm or an East Asian city. At a deeper level, the kind of complex adaptive systems that inform resilience thinking purports to be general and universal, and yet enrolls researchers into the specific systems that they study. In Baltimore the city is transformed from the object into the subject of research; it is a system or laboratory that is simultaneously altered by research as it is conducted.[34] Within this context there is no distance between scientific work and its practical application—a situation that empowers ecologists, Geographical Information System scientists, and environmental scientists not only to engage with but also to stand in for urban planners and policymakers who are traditionally responsible for managing the city. Seen in this light, ecological research is both an applied mission to transform nature in place and an attempt to discern and abstract a set of universally replicable rules and knowledge for use elsewhere. The next section considers these dynamics.

Place, Power, and the Abstraction of Nature

In Baltimore's Watershed 263 ecologists have directly shaped urban nature, building the indicators, designating the sites, defining what counts as desirable nature, and most importantly, installing it in the urban landscape. Ecology intervenes as a form of delegated power provided by the avoidance (or impossibility) of positive action from traditional urban actors. But while the Gwynn Falls study demonstrates the power of ecological perspectives to shape the urban landscape, it simultaneously highlights the inability of ecological science and policy tools to address the pressing social and spatial rifts that characterize contemporary cities. What does monitoring of nutrient loading and urban resilience have to say about massive unemployment? It would be difficult to imagine a scenario in which someone watches David Simon's television series *The Wire*, set amid the poverty and corruption of West Baltimore, and concludes: "You know what Baltimore could really use? A multimillion-dollar investment in monitoring, research and experimentation with nutrient loading in its urban streams and wastewater system."[35] In this way, such research shares much with other technocratic urban governing techniques, ranging from sustainable development projects to so-called Smart Cities, which are disconnected from everyday life and the wider political and economic structures that shape it.

This disconnect matters on the ground as ecological tools empower some actors and disempower others.[36] Green infrastructure has been promoted by and is enacted largely by landscape architects, planners, and conservationists through a managerial approach. Putting ecosystem services into practice requires different skill sets, ones that empower economists, social scientists, and psychologists to discern financial values from quantitative and qualitative datasets and favoring policymakers and planners with the ability to understand and interpret these kinds of knowledge. Resilience and socio-ecological systems privilege the ecologist, albeit one who can link socio-ecological flows to financial and economic imperatives.[37] Within the technocracy of ecological governance each policy tool empowers subtly distinct groups of actors and types of knowledge. Just as the emergence of the sanitarian city in the nineteenth century required a new cadre of urban planners, engineers, and public health experts, so the shift from the sanitarian to the sustainable city involves a renegotiation of professional roles. The danger of this is that it displaces local voices and actors from the arena of urban transformation.

The adoption of conceptual frames like resilience reflects a desire to lend extra scientific credibility to urban governance, but gives rise to an exertion of power without any formal power being attributed. As any practising urban ecologist will attest, ecologists and their interventions play only a very modest role in directly transforming the cities in which they work. •
The greater effects of their work are to reproduce global discourses of urban ecological governance and the promise of systematic and generalizable knowledge through scientific knowledge production. Ecologists must first *extract* knowledge from cities through intensive, long-term field studies, if they are to subsequently *abstract* it as a generalized body of urban ecological knowledge to sustain the universal approaches of ecological governance. It is precisely the impossibility of ever collecting perfectly representative data and the prohibitive costs of collecting comprehensive data for every city that necessitate the abstraction of general principles for urban governance. Baltimore is the place in which ecologists are trying to explain the trademark functions of urban ecology, translating field studies into generalizable principles of the kind that can underpin the scientific management of the sustainable city.

The inherent tension between ecology as a field science reliant upon particular places and its urge to establish principles explains the slippage when specific approaches are rolled out as general fixes. For example, Stephanie Pincetl's critique of the million-tree initiative to plant large numbers of trees in several major US cities suggests that the ecological services provided by different species in different places vary hugely and are poorly understood. A type of tree that sequesters carbon in the midwestern climate of Chicago may do nothing in Los Angeles.[38] The assumed ecological benefits from widely regarded "good policies," like simply planting lots of trees, are largely a matter of faith. Resilience represents a discursive ecological policy tool, which frames systemic approaches within a model of how society functions. As an umbrella goal for cities and regions it is hard to argue with, but what it means on the ground as a governance tool at the local level is less clear. Its success in penetrating national and international policy networks stands in contrast to the difficulties of implementing it as a meaningful basis for decision-making in local and regional contexts.[39]

Of course the tendency of environmental discourse to trade in global claims, which assume singular conceptions of citizenship and place, is not new. Talking about the emergence of global climate science in the 1990s, Jasanoff and Wynne argue that its establishment involved "not only the international coordination of assessment and policies but also the difficult task of harmonization at the cognitive level."[40] By "cognitive harmonization" they mean the processes by which ways of defining, conceptualizing, and measuring objects of research achieve general acceptance among scientists, funders, and policymakers. Environmentalism has evolved through a series of acceptances that goes something like this: global environment = global environmental problems = global environmental solutions, with each stage corresponding roughly to the 1960/1970s, 1980s/1990s, and 2000/2010s, respectively. The Future Earth program provides a recent example. Established in 2012 by the International Council for Science, an NGO based in Paris, this ten-year international research initiative aims to develop the knowledge for responding effectively to the risks and opportunities of global environmental change and to support the shift toward global sustainability. Mimicking the International Panel for Climate Change, its goal is to mobilize thousands of scientists from around the world to establish a coherent platform from which to engage high-level policymakers and other stakeholders "to provide sustainability options and solutions in the wake of Rio+20 [the United Nations Conference on Sustainable Development, 2012]." Global environmental science since the turn of the millennium has created an industry in global solutions, of which Future Earth reflects a recent and extreme version. This cognitive harmonization is now extended to the management of cities as well. The rational and data-centric approach of this brand of urban ecology shares much with the technocentric discourse of Smart Cities, which increasingly holds sway as the solution to urban sustainability challenges, especially in the context of the construction of new cities in the Far East. In the urban century the boundaries between the urban and the environmental solution industries are becoming increasingly blurred.

Pressure from policymakers to simply "make it work" highlights the disjuncture between abstracted global discourse of urban nature and the embedded and messy realities of ecological research underpinning them. This deficit of scientific understanding is of course cast as a solvable problem, discussed in terms reminiscent of the arguments put forward by climate modelers in the 1990s whereby more money to do more research that will collect more data to produce better models will fix the problem. Ecological governance here runs aground on a familiar shore: the inherent specificity of environmental processes in different places at different times. What is interesting, and it formed the starting point for this chapter, is the way in which urban ecological approaches have spread so rapidly, becoming entrenched in mainstream global discourse (and funding priorities) in spite of their inherent difficulties.

Conclusions: (Dis)Placing Ecology

Almost without anyone noticing, urban ecology has become a foundational ingredient of governance in the Anthropocene. Dovetailing neatly with other technocentric approaches like Smart Cities, technologies of ecological governance are increasingly promoted as approaches to urban management. The appetite of policymakers, funding bodies, and planners for ecologically informed decision-making tools has grown in tandem with the emergence of an increasingly influential set of research institutes and NGO networks that promote different approaches around the world. The growing rhetoric of global solutions finds expression in an increasingly complex mixture of approaches on the ground, nourished by a growing reliance on long-term and large-scale scientific research. There is clearly value in understanding the processes and practices of knowledge generation and translation that underpin urban ecological governance. For example, how do ecological governance models originate and circulate through research and consultancy networks? The knowledge produced by ecological research is "placed" in the sense that it is generated through intensive, long-term field experiments, but it must subsequently be displaced through processes of abstraction that allow it to move around the world as a basis for ecologically informed planning. To study such things means being attentive to the actual practices and concepts of ecologists through which "truth" is squeezed out of field sites.[41]

Initiatives like Future Earth and approaches like resilience resonate with the dream of rational management that underpins the Modernist project, but ecology is an inherently field-based science that resists generalizations of the kind required by scientific management. As Holling stated twenty years ago, "Knowledge of the system we deal with is always incomplete. Surprise is inevitable. Not only is the science incomplete, the system itself is a moving target."[42] Statements like this are almost mystical in their simultaneous recognition and simplification of complexity within an over-arching theory of change, but are typical of what we might call "ecological gurus" who populate an emerging cabal of policy-focused global scientists. What Ernstson and Lewis call the "alchemy of transformation" subsumes geographical difference within a one-size-fits all understanding of how change takes place over time.[43] Here the abstractive urge reduces space to time, subsuming local ecologies under standardized tools and techniques. Politically, abstraction privileges scientific forms of knowledge as the basis for decision-making, thereby insinuating a democratic deficit within current models of urban nature.[44] Practically, the lack of executive power afforded to ecologists means that little changes on the ground anyhow. Returning to the opening anecdote, the problem with "making it work" concerns what is lost in terms of the ability to produce genuinely democratic and local urban transformations. Understanding the abstractive moments and scientific practices through which global claims intersect with local place is necessary to open up the possibility of recognizing and nourishing more multiple and nuanced ecologies. Unfortunately the obsession of national funding bodies and global scientific councils with data, process, and scalability is moving ecology away from heterogeneity rather than toward it. Whether the richness of multiple Earths can be captured by the language of systems, services, and syndromes is the question at hand.

Acknowledgments

Thanks to the urban ecologists around the world who have had the patience to share their insights with me and engage in what are decidedly social scientific conversations concerning power and knowledge in the city. Respect to all the people trying to make the world a better place.

Notes

1. Worster 1994; Kingsland 2005.

2. Cronon 1995.

3. Sukopp 2003, p. 295.

4. Alberti et al. 2003.

5. Ljungkvist et al. 2010.

6. Ernstson et al. 2010.

7. The term "ecosystem service" refers to the delivery, provision, protection, or maintenance of goods and benefits that humans obtain from ecosystem functions (Millennium Ecosystem Assessment 2003).

8. These debates have generated much discussion and research; for example, see Bolund and Hunhammer (1999); Boyd and Banzhaf (2007); Gómez-Baggethun et al. 2010).

9. Lennon 2014.

10. Smith 1976, quoted in O'Neill 2013, p. 443.

11. Lele et al. 2013.

12. Hajer 2003, p. 106.

13. Lennon 2014.

14. Wright 2011.

15. Walker et al. 2004.

16. Budworm is usually controlled by natural predators but is occasionally responsible for major outbreaks that destroy mature fir trees. Between outbreaks the firs tend to out-compete the spruce and birch, which suffer more from crowding, producing a forest dominated by firs. But given the combination of large numbers of fir trees and a succession of dry years, budworm populations can escape the control of their predators and cause another outbreak. The outbreak ends when the budworm

population destroys so much of the fir population that it undermines its own food source and the budworm population collapses. Periodic fluctuations in the form of budworm outbreaks are essential in maintaining the budworm, its predators, and the diversity of trees in the forest.

17. Berkes and Folke (1998) characterize socio-ecological systems as coherent interacting systems of biophysical and social factors, which can be defined at different spatial, temporal, and organizational scales and which form a "dynamic, complex system with continuous adaptation." The socio-ecological systems approach suggests that social and ecological systems are linked by multiple feedbacks and display common properties, such as resilience and complexity.

18. Berkes and Folke 1998; Berkes, Colding, and Folke 2003.

19. Elmqvist et al. 2004; Ernstson et al. 2010.

20. Lennon 2014.

21. For example, ICLEI—Local Governments for Sustainability 2009.

22. Ernstson and Sörlin 2013; Lewis and Ernstson 2019.

23. Exceptions tend to be more focused on urban systems rather than scientific ecology per se (Schäffler and Swilling 2013).

24. This analysis was conducted using the Web of Science, including both scientific and social scientific publications between 1970 and 2012.

25. Pickett, Cadenasso, and Grove 2004, p. 3.

26. Cook et al. 2004, p. 467.

27. Felson and Pickett 2005, p. 555.

28. Grimm et al. 2013.

29. There is an important parallel story to be told about how researchers at the Stockholm Resilience Centre have used the city of Stockholm to develop a related conceptual understanding of the city as socio-ecological system (Henrik Ernstson, pers. comm.), as well as about the relationship between these researchers and those working as part of the LTER projects in the United States developed in the 1990s and 2000s (personal commentary Steward Pickett).

30. Pickett et al. 2011, p. 334.

31. Kohler 2002.

32. Ostrom 2007.

33. Pickett et al. 2011, p. 356.

34. Evans and Karvonen 2011.

35. I am indebted to Joshua Lewis for this observation.

36. Ernstson and Sörlin 2013.

37. Nelson 2014.

38. There is a direct analogy with electric vehicles, which are eco-friendly in California due to the high proportion of clean energy supplying the grid, but produce more carbon than conventional vehicles in Chicago due to the reliance on coal for power generation. When it comes to sustainability, place matters.

39. Resilience thinking has spread rapidly within the environmental policy arena because it promises a way to adapt to the kinds of environmental changes and uncertainty that underpin the Anthropocene (Davoudi 2012). But applying scientific theory to explain the social world is not without its problems. By internalizing crisis, resilience mirrors and reproduces more right-leaning political discourses of individuals (or communities or cities for that matter) fending for themselves in the face of crisis (Evans 2011; Turner 2013).

40. Jasanoff and Wynne 1998, p. 47.

41. See Jens Lachmund's (2013) account of the origins of the Berlin School of urban ecology for an excellent treatment of how place shapes science and vice versa.

42. Holling 1993, p. 553.

43. Ernstson and Lewis 2013. Also see Lawhon, Ernstson, and Silver (2013) for a discussion of how ecology might be "re-localized" from and through the global South.

44. Swyngedouw and Ernstson 2018.

References

Alberti, M., J. M. Marzluff, E. Shulenberger, G. Bradley, C. Ryan, and C. Zumbrunnen. 2003. "Integrating Humans into Ecology: Opportunities and Challenges for Studying Urban Ecosystems." *BioScience* 53(12): 1169–1179.

Berkes, F., J. Colding, and C. Folke, eds. 2003. *Navigating Social-Ecological Systems: Building Resilience for Complexity and Change.* Cambridge: Cambridge University Press.

Berkes, F., and C. Folke, eds., with the editorial assistance of J. Colding. 1998. *Linking Social and Ecological Systems: Management Practices and Social Mechanisms for Building Resilience.* Cambridge: Cambridge University Press.

Bolund, P., and S. Hunhammar. 1999. "Ecosystem Services in Urban Areas." *Ecological Economics* 29(2): 293–301.

Boyd, J., and S. Banzhaf. 2007. "What Are Ecosystem Services? The Need for Standardized Environmental Accounting Units." *Ecological Economics* 63(2): 616–626.

Cook, W., D. Casagrande, D. Hope, P. Groffman, and S. Collins. 2004. "Learning to Roll with the Punches: Adaptive Experimentation in Human-Dominated Systems." *Frontiers in Ecology and the Environment* 2: 467–474.

Cronon, W. 1995. "The Trouble with Wilderness; Or, Getting Back to the Wrong Nature." In *Uncommon Ground: Rethinking the Human Place in Nature*, edited by W. Cronon, 69–90. New York: W. W. Norton.

Davoudi, S. 2012. "Resilience: A Bridging Concept or a Dead End?" *Planning Theory and Practice* 13(2): 299–333.

Elmqvist, T., J. Colding, S. Barthel, S. Borgström, A. Duit, J. Lundberg, H. Ernstson, et al. 2004. "The Dynamics of Social-Ecological Systems in Urban Landscapes: Stockholm and the National Urban Park, Sweden." *Annals of the New York Academy of Sciences* 1023: 308–322.

Ernstson, H., S. Barthel, E. Andersson, and S. T. Borgström. 2010. "Scale-Crossing Brokers and Network Governance of Urban Ecosystem Services: The Case of Stockholm." *Ecology and Society* 15(4): 1–25.

Ernstson, H., and J. Lewis. 2013. "Alchemy of Transformation: On the Impoverishment of Socio-ecological Imaginaries." Unpublished manuscript. KTH Division of History of Science Technology and Environment, Stockholm.

Ernstson, H., S. van der Leeuw, C. Redman, D. Meffert, G. Davis, C. Alfsen, and T. Elmqvist 2010. "Urban Transitions: On Urban Resilience and Human-Dominated Landscapes." *Ambio* 39(8): 531–545.

Ernstson, Henrik, and Sverker Sörlin. 2013. "Ecosystem Services as Technology of Globalization: On Articulating Values in Urban Nature." *Ecological Economics* 86: 274–284.

Evans, J. 2011. "Resilience, Ecology and Adaptation in the Experimental City." *Transactions of the Institute of British Geographers* 36: 223–237.

Evans, J., and A. Karvonen. 2011. "Living Laboratories for Sustainability: Exploring the Politics and Epistemology of Urban Transition." In *Cities and Low Carbon Transitions*, edited by H. Bulkeley, V. Castán Broto, M. Hodson, and S. Marvin, 126–141. London: Routledge.

Felson, A., and S. Pickett. 2005. "Designed Experiments: New Approaches to Studying Urban Ecosystems." *Frontiers in Ecology and the Environment* 3(10): 549–556.

Gómez-Baggethun, E., R. De Groot, P.L. Lomas, and C. Montes. 2010. "The History of Ecosystem Services in Economic Theory and Practice: From Early Notions to Markets and Payment Schemes." *Ecological Economics* 69(6): 1209–1218.

Grimm, N., C. Redman, C. Boone, D. Childers, and S. Harlan. 2013. "Viewing the Urban Socio-ecological System through a Sustainability Lens: Lessons and Prospects from the Central Arizona–Phoenix LTER Programme." In *Long Term Socio-Ecological Research*, edited by S. Singh, H. Haberl, M. Chertow, M. Mirtl, and M. Schmid, 217–246. Dordrecht: Springer Netherlands.

Hajer, M. 2003. "A Frame in the Fields: Policymaking and the Reinvention of Politics." In *Deliberative Policy Analysis: Understanding Governance in the Network Society*, edited by M. Hajer and H. Wagenaar, 88–112. Cambridge: Cambridge University Press.

Holling, C. S. 1993. "Investing in Research for Sustainability." *Ecological Applications* 3(4): 552–555.

ICLEI—Local Governments for Sustainability. 2009. *Resilient Communities and Cities Initiative*. Toronto: ICLEI World Secretariat.

Kingsland, S. 2005. *The Evolution of American Ecology, 1890–2000*. Baltimore, MD: Johns Hopkins University Press.

Kohler, R. 2002. *Landscapes and Labscapes: Exploring the Lab-Field Border in Biology*. Chicago: University of Chicago Press.

Lachmund, J. 2013. *Greening Berlin: The Co-production of Science, Politics, and Urban Nature*. Cambridge, MA: MIT Press.

Lawhon, M., H. Ernstson, and J. D. Silver. 2014. "Provincializing Urban Political Ecology: Towards a Situated UPE through African Urbanism." *Antipode* 46(2): 497–516.

Lele, S., O. Springate-Baginski, R. Lakerveld, D. Deb, and P. Dash. 2013. "Ecosystem Services: Origins, Contributions, Pitfalls, and Alternatives." *Conservation and Society* 11(4): 343–358.

Lennon, M. 2014. "Green Infrastructure and Planning Policy: A Critical Assessment." *Local Environment* 20(8): 957–980.

Lewis, Joshua A., and Henrik Ernstson. 2019. "Contesting the Coast: Ecosystems as Infrastructure in the Mississippi River Delta." *Progress in Planning* 129: 1–30.

Ljungkvist, J., S. Barthel, G. Finnveden, and S. Sörlin. 2010. "The Urban Anthropocene: Lessons for Sustainability from the Environmental History of Constantinople." In *The Urban Mind: Cultural and Environmental Dynamics*, edited by P. Sinclair, G. Nordquist, F. Herschend, and C. Isendahl, 367–390. Uppsala: Uppsala University, Department of Archaeology and Ancient History.

Millennium Ecosystem Assessment. 2003. *Ecosystems and Human Well-Being: A Framework for Assessment*. Washington, DC: Island Press.

Nelson, Sara H. 2014. "Resilience and the Neoliberal Counterrevolution: From Ecologies of Control to Production of the Common." *Resilience* 2(1): 1–17.

O'Neill, P. M. 2013. "The Financialisation of Infrastructure: The Role of Categorisation and Property Relations." *Cambridge Journal of Regions, Economy and Society* 12(6): 441–454.

Ostrom, E. 2007. "A Diagnostic Approach for Going beyond Panaceas." *Proceedings of the National Academy of Sciences* 104(39): 15181–15187.

Pickett, S., M. Cadenasso, and J. Grove. 2004. "Resilient Cities: Meaning, Models, and Metaphor for Integrating the Ecological, Socio-economic, and Planning Realms." *Landscape and Urban Planning* 69: 369–384.

Pickett, S., M. Cadenasso, J. Grove, C. Boone, P. Groffman, E. Irwin, and P. Warren. 2011. "Urban Ecological Systems: Scientific Foundations and a Decade of Progress." *Journal of Environmental Management* 92(3): 331–362.

Schäffler, A., and M. Swilling. 2013. "Valuing Green Infrastructure in an Urban Environment under Pressure—The Johannesburg Case." *Ecological Economics* 86: 246–257.

Sukopp, H. 2003. "Flora and Vegetation Reflecting the Urban History of Berlin." *Die Erde* 134(3): 295–316.

Swyngedouw, Erik, and Henrik Ernstson. 2018. "Interrupting the Anthropo-obScene: Immuno-Biopolitics and Depoliticizing More-than-Human Ontologies in the Anthropocene." *Theory, Culture & Society* 35(6): 3–30.

Turner, M. D. 2013. "Political Ecology I: An Alliance with Resilience?" *Progress in Human Geography* 38(4): 616–623.

Walker, B., C. S. Holling, S. R. Carpenter, and A. Kinzig. 2004. "Resilience, Adaptability and Transformability in Social-Ecological Systems." *Ecology and Society* 9(2): n.p.

Worster, D., ed. 1994. *Nature's Economy: A History of Ecological Ideas*. Cambridge: Cambridge University Press.

Wright, H. 2011. "Understanding Green Infrastructure: The Development of a Contested Concept in England." *Local Environment* 16(10): 1003–1019.

12 Refiguring the Rural: Eco-urbanization in Yixing City

Jia-Ching Chen

> The difficulty of balancing land use and ecological security is great. The intensity of land use in Yixing is very high and ecological environmental protection is already extremely urgent....The optimization of land use structure requires the closure and relocation of Taihu shoreline towns and a considerable number of enterprises and villages, which will transform farmers' traditional cultivation customs. This will be done.
> —Yixing Bureau of Land and Resources, *Yixing Land Use Master Plan (2006–2020)*

> Yixing's Qiting subdistrict has a rainbow-shaped bridge called Tangtian Bridge. Next to the bridge is a completely new residential development called Dongjiao Gardens. The people call it "the evicted households' new paradise."
> —"Yixing Dongjiao Huayuan's Qiaodong Residents' Committee and Relocated Households' New Paradise"

Perched on upended cinder blocks at the entrance to the Dongjiao Gardens relocation settlement, the Zhao brothers greet me from their usual spot on the edge of the entry drive near the complex perimeter wall. Twenty feet behind the septuagenarians, a teal Kobelco backhoe shovels in an oscillating pirouette, removing the dark earth hillock from beneath itself.[1] Beyond the excavator, the widening shoulders of Qingyuan Boulevard unfold behind crews of migrant workers, a level line for the flattening horizon of state-planned green development. Across Qingyuan, the shovels have filled a paddy with rubble from Tangtian village, and the itinerant workers have pitched green canvas tents there against the weather. Told from this uneasy vantage point, the story of the Zhao brothers' displacement from their natal village and resettlement at Dongjiao decodes the churning landscape of the countryside in Yixing, and across China.[2] Their story, and many like it, reveals processes of social and environmental transformation that are typically elided by the terms of "green development" and "eco-urbanization" under which economic growth in the region has been promoted. As this chapter will show, eco-urbanization in Yixing extends practices of rural dispossession and deepens patterns of urban-rural inequality by refiguring the rural as a necessary object of social and environmental transformation (see figure 12.1). It is my broader argument here that in facing its environmental crises, the Chinese party-state has sought to maintain local-level economic growth and competition while balancing agricultural land loss by constructing rural land as a national scale environmental resource.

One of the most striking features of China's state-planned green development is how it refigures rural space and rural society as backward and environmentally irrational at local and national scales. I offer the term "refigure" to refer to the party-state's making "the rural" into a concrete signifier of diverse social-environmental processes, constituting it as an object of governing and a site of transformation.[3] These processes of refiguring—of *re*-counting, molding, modeling, diagraming, personifying, rationalizing— include the multiple dimensions of ideology, planning practice, culture, and landscape change that shape the "norms and forms" of green development.[4] In this chapter, refiguring refers concretely to party-state calculative practices, spatial planning, physical landscape change, and the cultural politics of agrarian transformation. Urban nature is here imbricated with the rural in material and symbolic ways. This is evident in the physical construction of the "eco-city," as farmland is converted into sites for housing and the industrial production of green technologies, including photovoltaic (PV) solar panels for global markets (see figure 12.2). Yet, it must be said that the rural is not simply subsumed by the urban. Rather, the rural is forcibly divided from rural society—previously understood as people inhered to natal places of production and reproduction—and is refigured as a space of national environmental governance.[5] In this, I argue that this emergent figuration of the rural is the sine qua non of the party-state's imaginary of national development as a spatially planned and coordinated project at the scale of the entire national territory.

How is it that such a model of green development by dispossession has gained dominance during a time when there is increasing public and party-state concern over rural land dispossession?[6] In order to examine the construction of green development ideology and its forms of environmental

Figure 12.1
The entrance to Dongjiao Gardens, the demolition resettlement housing development for the Zhao brothers and over 15,000 new neighbors occupying 5,380 units. Photo by Jia-Ching Chen, 2011.

Figure 12.2
The site of the Desheng Solar Technology Company facilities. The Yixing "eco-city"
demands the conversion of farmland to sites for the production of green technologies. This billboard shows one of three adjacent solar PV manufacturing projects
approved for construction in 2010, occupying 13.5 hectares of village land cleared
in 2006–2007, and totaling ¥1.12 billion in investment (US$165.42 million in 2010).
Originally slated for completion in 2012, these projects were only partially completed
due to the collapse of the global PV market caused largely by a crisis of overproduction, which was itself a result of green development by dispossession in Yixing and
other solar special economic zones (SEZs). Photo by Jia-Ching Chen, 2010.

value in China, this chapter focuses on the transformation of rural land and
its social relations. With over 330 square kilometers of rural land enclosed
since 2006, green development and eco-urbanization in Yixing lie explicitly
at the intersection of national land management policies and processes of
urban and industrial expansion at the local level. Below, I will discuss this
intersection in the implementation of the National Farmland Preservation
Policy and the National Land Use Master Plan. These policies constitute
the regulatory framework for rural land allocation, which shapes practices
of "urban-rural integration" (*chengxiang yitihua*) and ecological resource

planning. The chapter analyzes multiple dimensions of green development in Yixing's master-planned urban–rural integration.[7] The following section introduces the case and argues that rural land regulation is at the heart of China's contemporary development. Next, the account turns to the experiences of dispossession and dislocation that green development entails. The subsequent two sections examine the quota allocation mechanisms for governing and rationalizing rural land and document how environmental values are constructed and circulated through the institution of this system. Finally, the chapter provides an analysis of how urban villagers are themselves refigured in the process of eco-urbanization and concludes with a discussion about linking a grounded political ecology of Yixing's transformation and the so-called global green economy.

Refiguring Rural Land for Green Development

Like other cities in the Yangzi delta region, Yixing changed rapidly as urbanization and industrialization accelerated through the Chinese countryside during the 1980s and 1990s. Unlike the rest of its neighbors, however, Yixing has been a site of multiple waves of environmental development policy attention and is a centrally designated "Sustainable Development Experimental Area." In 1993, the State Development Planning Commission created the Yixing Industrial Park for Environmental Science and Technology as the national research and development center for China's Rio Declaration Agenda 21 Program for environmental protection. By 1998, Yixing generated 18 percent of the national total value added in the environmental industry.[8] In 2006, the National Yixing Economic and Technological Development Zone (hereafter, "the Zone") was founded.[9]

The Zone was created to extend these experiences into export industrialization in "greentech" and "cleantech" industries, with special policy attention and incentives given to solar photovoltaics and optoelectronics. These so-called green industry projects form the economic motor for what is conceived of in Yixing's master plan as a larger project of eco-urbanization and rural resource integration—hence, the Zone plan's discursive equivalence of eco-cities as *cities that make green things* and *cities with green environments*.

This vision was prominently supported by Li Yuanchao, then a member of the national Party Central Committee and subsequently the vice president under Xi Jinping (2013–2017). Li proposed Yixing's transformation into a national model "eco-city" (*shengtai chengshi*), extending from the western shore of Taihu Lake across Yixing's chain of lakes. Li's vision of a "water city" provided an aesthetic concept and political support for the *Yixing Eco-City Construction Plan*.[10] In the plan, the concept of the eco-city is defined as a framework for growth through "ecological construction."[11] According to the plan, the Yixing eco-city would provide a model of economic and human development by bridging environmental protection, resource efficiency, air quality, rural village improvements, agricultural modernization, industrial restructuring for cleaner production in key sectors, and landscape beautification. To achieve Yixing's rural transformation via eco-urbanization and the solar industry, the Zone's planning authority was extended to 98.3 square kilometers in late 2006 (see figure 12.3). In order to transform rural landscapes into an "ecological framework" linking Yixing's urban core to Taihu Lake, the Zhao brothers' homes and hundreds of villages were enclosed and subsequently marked for demolition.

In the official discourse of the party-state, such dispossession is justified by idealized relationships between spatial planning, environmental governance, and economic development. This drawing together of multiple dimensions of development into eco-urbanization makes it the model solution to the diverse problems accruing from China's prevalent model of development.[12] At the central government level, the Twelfth Five-Year Plan and the Eighteenth National Congress emphasized the "optimization of national spatial structure as the vehicle for the construction of ecological civilization."[13] The National Development and Reform Commission, the Ministry of Housing, Urban, and Rural Development, the Ministry of Environmental Protection, and the Ministry of Science and Technology have produced complementary policies and standards for establishing model eco-city and sustainable development zone projects. According to the Ministry of Environmental Protection, over 97 percent of prefectural-level cities (284 of 293 total) and 80 percent county-level cities (288 of 363 total) now have state designated eco-city and low-carbon city projects.[14]

Yixing's recent environmentalized land enclosures are certainly not without precedent. Moreover, farmland takings have driven the development of the current land management regime. The Zone's administrative jurisdiction was established by incorporating village lands and township-level industrial parks that had been part of the reform-era wave of rural industrialization that crashed over the Yangtze delta region beginning in

Figure 12.3
These fields of prime farmland and Tangtian village beyond were enclosed into the Zone in 2006. The photo captures the landscape as it was just prior to dispossession and demolition in 2010. Much of this prime farmland was retained in production by contract farmers until it was requisitioned for the later phases of the Dongjiu housing projects, which were completed in 2014. The Zone's eco-city plan, with its integration of nationally supported strategic industries and rural land use optimization, enabled authorities to gain policy exceptions for converting protected prime farmland here and elsewhere in Yixing. Photo by Jia-Ching Chen, 2010.

1978.[15] Without effective regulation of farmland loss, China was faced with the problem of maintaining urban economic growth while simultaneously preserving farmland as a pillar of social stability and food security. In order to address this dilemma, the central government adopted a multipronged farmland preservation and land management regime beginning in 1998 with the promulgation of the amended Land Administration Law. As an explicit effort to address the social, economic, and environmental contradictions of the prevailing model of development, the objective is now to rationalize land use at a national scale and to promote the integration of modernized agriculture with new city building. Under the present regime, land is conceived as a resource to be managed according to two regulatory axes. First, its use and purpose must abide by a nationwide quantification and rationalization of "total land supply" for development (*gongdi zongliang*). Second, rural land is seen as an explicitly environmental resource to be protected and efficiently used.[16]

In the present conjuncture of planned rural transformation and eco-urbanization, the category of farmland (*gengdi*) is critical to both of these regulatory axes. Although the state's environmental valuation of rural land includes place-specific uses such as wildlife habitat and ecological preservation, such "ecological services" are also conceived as attributes that can *and should* be planned under centralized authority. It is this state designation of rural land as fundamentally an environmental resource that produces tensions between ecological preservation, the historical emphasis on maximizing grain production, and the current dominance of land development as a source of local government revenue.[17] This makes rural land a sociospatial Möbius strip: both inside and outside, the figure and the ground, it is topologically a single-boundary object with multiple contradictory dimensions. The making of rural land resources into a calculable economic and environmental object allows it to be mutually intelligible between historically rival logics of socialist productivism and ecological protection, while simultaneously maintaining divergent meanings within each.[18] The intensity of the contradictions contained within it is evidenced by the political justification given to dispossession as necessary for environmental governance and for urban-industrial modernization.

The land regulation regime has been critiqued as riddled with opportunities for arbitrage and institutional failures that are due directly to the dual system of state and collective land ownership.[19] However, this prevalent interpretation implies a one-dimensional hierarchical relationship with the central state, which is "gamed" or "negotiated" by local authorities. In my analysis, the central policy development of "ecological targets" and their implementation at the local level are productive of social-environmental relations in refigured "rural" and "urban" spaces.[20] I argue that the local implementation of such policies through a quota allocation system works to make abstracted quantities—and not the enumerated things themselves—the substantive objects of central governance. Paradoxically, in order to preserve its environmentalized value, rural land in any particular locale is governed as a fungible quantity, divided from its place-specific ecological attributes and "preserved" as an arithmetic constituent of a net sum. Conceptualized by the party-state as an exchangeable resource, rural land can be instilled with different functionalist attributes that are themselves equally divisible and locatable as objects. Thus, environmental resources and services (such as those associated with a wetland) are themselves not taken as intrinsic to any particular locale, but as discrete forms of designated, designed, and built environments.[21] In short, rural land is stripped of its previous social-environmental relations, and fundamental categories of rural sociality—farmers, agrarian production, and villages—are refigured in the process. The following section describes villagers' experience of this process of refiguring the rural—of dividing people, as a biopolitical problem of population, from the land as an environmental problem of resource governance.

Refiguring Villagers through Dispossession

In 2008, the Zhaos were evicted from their natal Fenzhuang village, three kilometers to the northeast of Dongjiao Gardens. Until that time, they had lived through five decades of rural production regimes from collectivization to the Household Responsibility System on through to the present privatized leasehold system. In the previous twenty years, the bachelors had depended largely on subsistence agriculture and occasional daywork for their livelihoods. Since eviction, they also received supplementary income from contract farming lease payments on the remaining village farmland and small payments from the expanded rural pension system since 2009. For two years after their eviction from Fenzhuang, they rented temporary housing in a village just beyond the maw of Qingyuan's eastward extension to Taihu Lake. At the time I first interviewed them, in April 2011, they had been resettled in Dongjiao Gardens for about eight months. Despite the official narrative of the "Dongjiao paradise" described in this chapter's epigraph, the Zhaos and their neighbors experienced years of uncertainty and insecurity as a result of their displacement. "We still aren't used to this place," the elder Zhao Ge commented. "What is there to be accustomed to? This place will never be complete." Raising his chin to the backhoe, Zhao Di finished his statement with an "ahh" that mixed a tone of resignation with a hint of the interrogative. They explained this experience of dislocation in two ways.

First, their resettlement had been fraught with delays, broken promises, and financial difficulties. Although regulations stipulate that resettlement housing for people displaced as a result of land expropriation should be completed before eviction occurs, this has yet to happen in Yixing's eco-urbanization. Rather, the dispossessed receive a cash payment for "transition expenses" (*guodu fei*) such as moving and rent costs. Like most in Yixing, the Zhaos' lump sum payouts were calculated on an eighteen-month transition period and payment for an additional six months of delay were not settled until they moved into Dongjiao. Moreover, the ¥450 (US$65) per month that the Zhaos received would not cover a typical one-hundred-square-meter rental in the area, which averaged ¥500 (US$72) per month by 2009 and ¥650 (US$94) by the end of 2010.[22] Once they received ownership of their apartments, there were further costs as the units were delivered as bare concrete boxes with no finishes. These shortfalls and increased living costs for electricity, cooking fuel, water, and food meant that during the entire period of "transition," the Zhaos had to spend their savings and take up piecework "greening" the roadside landscaping in the Zone for ¥50 (US$7.2) per day.[23] The point here is not merely to convey that the Zhaos and their fellow evictees met hardships and exploitive conditions. Rather, the objective is to show how these conditions are features of Yixing's model eco-urbanization. For many villagers, the compensation scheme has served to enclose and circulate their cash savings, originally intended for retirement and emergencies, as a form of land and real estate development finance.

This leads to the second aspect of the Zhaos' experience of "incompleteness": the literal unmaking of their social-environmental world in the transformation of the rural landscape. Zhao Di's remarks referred not only to the under-constructed environs of Dongjiao Gardens, but to the larger eco-city project and the encompassing special economic zone. While they had been evicted over two years prior, their land had yet to be requisitioned for development. In fact, the Zhaos and their neighbors frequently returned to their former village. Bicycling for an hour, they went back to the site of Fenzhuang once or twice a week to tend the vegetable gardens they still depended on for subsistence. In the evening, they would bring a small harvest back, intended to last the days until they returned. The brothers complained that their vegetables were not as they had been before their eviction. "They don't taste good, they're yellow and they rot quickly." They partially attributed this degradation of their food to intermittent care, but emphasized changes to the soil and water resulting from the demolition of the village and ongoing construction projects. Regardless, the imminent "completion" of post-dispossession transition will leave no access to farmland, and the Zhaos and other ex-villagers still dependent on subsistence activities will almost inevitably be left in a much worse position. In my surveys, evictees without access to gardens or cropland reported that weekly food expenses increased by over ¥70 (US$10) per person.

Different resettlement processes and temporary housing situations led to very uneven access to village plots. Furthermore, the quality of plots after village demolition also varied widely. For example, I met other former residents of Fenzhuang who did not experience crop damage. Others reported that the demolition workers were stealing their vegetables. For their part, workers told me that they only took food from gardens that they tended themselves in plots that they observed were abandoned. Through discussions with evicted residents and observation of villages undergoing demolition, I found that such effects were unevenly distributed as the direct results of constantly shifting changes in the village landscape. Citing how cadres and some families benefited from the process of village eviction and demolition, the Zhaos and other villagers were clear in identifying these evolving landscapes as manifestations of a process of development that was socially uneven and politically determined. For example, the processes of eviction, demolition, compensation, and resettlement are not uniform across all household cases. In anticipation of eviction, some families were allowed to establish separate householder registrations for younger family members who were not technically eligible. This enabled each to collect transition and relocation compensation. Others secured permission to expand the area to their homes in order to maximize compensation. Cadres negotiated their compensation packages in advance. By the time the demolition and relocation company was dispatched to deliver notice and document property for compensation, many well-connected households had already signed their papers and received their settlements.

The timing of resettlement relative to eviction is also critical to the experience and long-term outcomes of individual households. With months of advanced mobility, some of these families actually profited directly from their neighbors and evictees from other villages by becoming landlords. These differences in experience have significant direct impacts on household-level outcomes in relation to the village landscape in that some households benefited from the process of demolition itself. During the course of the demolition process, subcontractors for Beijing Construction staged the sorting of materials on the property of the first homes to be destroyed.[24] Subcontractors used partially demolished village space to cast concrete and process quicklime for road cement. In the process, many irrigation ditches were filled, while others were polluted with alkaline silt and the debris of land development. In this way, the transforming rural landscape became a medium through which the uneven effects of its political economy were *made and distributed as environmental*. Here, I mean to call attention to how social inequalities were unevenly reproduced in the physical environment, and how this process likewise continued to reshape differences in social and environmental experience.

These experiences show that eco-urbanization in Yixing is not merely a transformation of physical environments. Rather, rural residents must endure and take part in a years-long process of becoming urban and becoming green. The Zhaos' story presents basic empirical questions about the temporality of change and development in the region. Why had their land been requisitioned at that particular time? To answer this, it is important to call attention to the multiple dimensions of rural transformation that were underway. I have briefly touched on dimensions evident in the landscape, including road and infrastructure building, as well as changes to subsistence livelihoods. Less visible, however, are state mechanisms for managing rural land, its environmental value, and relationships to official goals of modernization and progress.

The official categories of rural land and rural society have been fundamental to state-society relationships since the 1949 revolution. Historically, the primary axis of this relationship centered on questions of production and national development. In policy, the urban-rural divide was made evident with the household registration system (*hukou*), which tied people to their parents' place of registration and restricted migration from the countryside to cities, and the constitutional bifurcation of urban and rural socialist land ownership. Now, under the logic of green development, the state is refiguring the rural in a process of "integration" with the urban. However, even as the rural takes on new meanings in official policy, the process is reconstituting the historical inequalities and biases that have marked the urban-rural divide. These changes and their immediate effects are the focus of the remaining sections.

Refiguring and "Circulating" the Environmental Value of Rural Land

Classical and contemporary theorists have wrestled with the peculiarities of land.[25] As a resource, land must be "assembled" through various institutions, practices, and fictions.[26] This section provides brief historical context for how contemporary practices of village land dispossession have intensified despite increasing conflict and central government concern. The section then analyzes the work of land management quotas in refiguring the rural from a site of socialist production into one of environmental resource optimization. Here, I argue that the party-state has sought to maintain local-level economic growth and competition while balancing agricultural land loss by making rural land into a nationally governed environmental resource. This balance is accomplished, on one hand, by giving localities de facto authority to reorganize agricultural production and to sever collective land ownership, and, on the other, by accounting for and maintaining the total area of arable land within the country as a whole.

This "dynamic balance" of arable land conversion and protection is maintained through a quota system.[27] Quotas for arable land conversion, replacement arable land, and prime farmland protection are passed down through the vertical hierarchy of the Ministry of Land and Resources.[28] This emphasis on a total area metric has roots in Mao-era efforts to expand farmland through massive landscape transformation projects during the infamous Great Leap Forward. But the reliance on arable land area as the definitive indicator of production capacity has a more recent history embedded in the neo-Malthusian imagination. Calculations of population growth and strains on economic production had been debated in China since the late 1950s.[29] With the 1995 publication of *Who Will Feed China? A Wake-up Call for a Small Planet*, Lester Brown renewed international concern over global "carrying capacity" and called attention to China's rapid loss of farmland.[30] The Chinese central government responded by initiating a land survey that was completed in 1996 and revamping the fragmented land regulation system. The 1998 Land Administration Law produced centrally legible and allocable national land resources. This universalizing grid would also ostensibly protect villages from illegal dispossession by local-level governments by requiring approved plans for farmland protection and conversion.

The limits set on conversion of farmland to other uses have been tied to calculations of grain production and food security since the 1997–1999

national moratorium on farmland conversion.[31] In 2006, this calculation
was codified in the national minimum "redline" of 120 million hectares
of total farmland. The national land regime's main policy instrument for
maintaining this threshold is the centralized and hierarchical distribution
of quotas for planned farmland conversion, preservation, and replacement
mentioned above. Quotas are allocated by the Ministry of Land and
Resources downward to provincial bureaus, which subsequently distribute
targets for preserving prime farmland and *producing* replacement arable land
down through the administrative hierarchy to the township level. Quotas
are then implemented according to yearly city land-use plans.[32] Farmland
conversion must be cleared on a project-level basis by city governments.
Plans and target verifications are passed back up to provincial authorities for reconciliation of a net-zero loss (see figure 12.4).[33] Complicating
matters, the Land Administration Law divides farmland into two general
categories of "prime" and "nonprime."[34] Each jurisdiction must protect a
minimum of 80 percent of its total arable land as designated prime farmland. By law, prime farmland must be delineated for protection in land use
master plans and physically marked so that the public can readily identify the plots. Prime farmland is productive, well-irrigated cultivated land
for crops and vegetables, and cannot be converted to other uses including
aquaculture and orchards. The Land Administration Law further stipulates
that state requisitions of any prime farmland, arable land over thirty-five
hectares, and any land over seventy hectares requires approval by the State
Council. However, because the law allows for exceptions for key infrastructural projects, local governments began to devise methods for maintaining
a surplus amount of farmland that could be designated as prime to balance
conversions. According to law, this practice requires the "construction" of
replacement farmland. In practice, local bureaus account for and "bank"
area quantities of land that can theoretically be designated as replacement
farmland (see figure 12.4). As with compensation housing, replacement
farmland is rarely ever completed before dispossession and land use conversion as stipulated by law. In many cases, prime farmland that is no longer possible to farm due to adjacent land use changes or severed irrigation
systems retains its designation as protected prime farmland (see figure 12.5)
These examples signal that the *designation* of farmland is frequently more
salient—if not actually equivalent to—actually cultivated land.

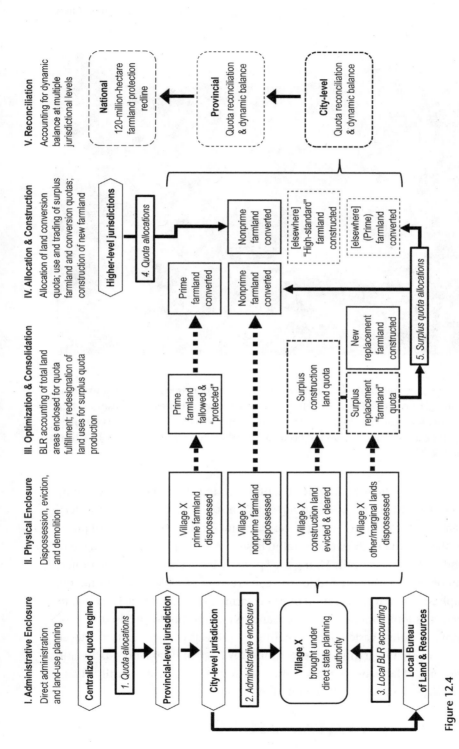

Figure 12.4

Overview of Bureau of Land and Resources Practices of Land Consolidation and Surplus Quota Production and Banking. The figure illustrates how processes of village land dispossession allow land managers to change land use designations and flexibly translate them into various surplus land use quotas for later allocation and maintenance of "dynamic balance." Figure by Jia-Ching Chen.

Figure 12.5
Fallowed "prime farmland." Infrastructure construction frequently leads to prime
farmland being cut off from irrigation and fallowed even before it is requisitioned for
construction projects. The area is still held by the village collective and is classified
as "prime farmland," as it has not been converted to another use. Photo by Jia-Ching
Chen, 2011.

Within the Jiangsu provincial context, Yixing has the lowest per capita
level of farmland at 0.031 hectares per person compared to a provincial
average of 0.064.[35] Yet, Yixing is the main site for the maintenance of prime
farmland quota in the western Taihu basin. The Wuxi Prefectural Bureau of
Land and Resources calls Yixing the "primary battleground" for the protection of prime farmland and for the construction of replacement farmland,
emphasizing that the location of prime farmland should be maintained, its
quantity should not be diminished, and its quality should be raised.[36] These
points all reflect basic policy on farmland protection at the national level.
However, by integrating projects to improve agricultural land quality and
efficiency of land use, eco-city planning efforts have aimed to justify village
land dispossession and the conversion of prime farmland.

In order to skirt the policies on prime farmland protection, the Zone has created projects for constructing "high-standard prime farmland." Developed with engineered soils, the newly produced farmland is designated as equivalent to prime farmland and can therefore be used to justify the "relocation" and "consolidation" of actual prime farmland, which is strictly protected from conversion to other uses.[37] Sun Dian, the director of the Wuxi bureau's agricultural land planning and protection department, states that the construction of such high-standard farmland is aimed at intensifying production and generating economies of scale. He further emphasizes the notion that farmland should be "consolidated."[38] Moreover, Sun's discourse on land use efficiency and productivity links arable land to the health and prosperity of future generations and the problem of "grain security" (liang-shi anquan).

However, rural land consolidation is primarily driven by the imperative of development. The timelines of urbanization and private enterprise development demand predictable quota allocation and farmland replacement. Consolidation enables such smoothing by redesignating village-built spaces and marginal lands as replacement farmland, thereby yielding a "surplus" that exceeds assigned quota targets. In practice, this means that actual agricultural productivity becomes secondary to the availability of a plot of land for use in the production of quota surpluses. For example, Yixing's original high-standard prime farmland project was subsequently canceled when local government appointments shifted in 2012. While it has since been replaced with a project planned in conjunction with the Wuxi prefectural government, the temporal dislocation calls into question what is being "replaced" (buchong). In the operation of the quota regime as a centralized and national quantity, farmland is stripped of specific locational attributes apart from its jurisdiction. This means that features such as cropland productivity or irrigation are discounted. Stripped of its place-specific attributes (such as its history of cultivation, productivity, market or other infrastructures, and so on), land is reduced to a fungible quantity, and its now disembedded environmental value is recorded on paper for "circulation" through the quota system. However, this effort at creating a unified fungible quantity necessarily confronts the reality of the land itself. Even as such a system of state legibility does shape the landscape and material relationships, land as a commodity, as Polanyi asserts, is necessarily a "fictitious" one, as something not originally produced for exchange and whose complete value in social-environmental relationships cannot be captured by a fungible quantity.[39]

This provides us with a new perspective on green development. Yixing's process of eco-urbanization has relied upon an explicit "greening" of rural land that simultaneously upholds goals of agricultural production while denigrating smallholder production and livelihoods as environmentally inefficient. Rural land is refigured as a resource category, requiring active and direct state-led governance. As the producer of the largest share of Jiangsu provincial replacement farmland quota for years, Yixing is pivotal to the implementation of the national quota system and the ultimate accounting in the balance sheets of the central Ministry of Land and Resources. But the work of the local Yixing Bureau of Land and Resources (BLR) in balancing land use conversion requisitions, as well as in recording consolidation and replacement projects, is not limited to fulfilling its quota obligations. Rather, the Yixing BLR plays a much more active role in that it justifies, based on environmental policy, the consolidation of village land in one locale so that farmland elsewhere can be converted into other uses (see figure 12.4). This extends the local governmental role far beyond its implementation of central policy. It means that the work of municipalities in developing and administering the quota system for managing land supply defines the substantive basis of what the central land policy is actually governing.[40] This in turn allows us to understand how quotas for rural land use and farmland conversion enmesh land into an ecological game of net sums.

Observing the politics of land administration, both village residents and government officials readily identified how the work of the Yixing BLR plays two separate roles at the intersection of local jurisdictional and vertical ministerial agendas.[41] At the local level, the BLR accounts for land resources and quotas, facilitating project approval for land conversion. Under the centralized bureaucracy, the BLR ensures that replacement farmland quota obligations are met and that protected prime farmland is not converted to other uses. Rural residents frequently identify the failure of "regulation" of illegal farmland conversion as corruption. Villagers spoke daily about how a good deal of land churning is enabled by collusion between township, subdistrict, and village officials with local bureaus of the Ministry of Land and Resources (MLR), which frequently adapt implementation rules to the specific needs and conditions of local government development projects.

For instance, the BLR and the Yixing municipal authorities failed to notify village collectives of protected prime farmland locations and to clearly mark their boundaries.

Local officials themselves frequently comment, "Above, there is policy; below, there are strategies."[42] For instance, in order to "relocate" and "improve" prime farmland, the Yixing government devised a project to construct "high-standard prime farmland" in conjunction with an "ecological withdrawal of farmland." The high-standard farmland project was to draw large capital investments to construct model demonstration fields for intensive "modern" cultivation methods. Such scientific research applications fall within the designation of prime farmland and led to quick approval. Furthermore, the scheme was approved for implementation in large part because the prime farmland to be "withdrawn" had a nationally recognized environmental function. Over 800 hectares of village agricultural land, the holdings of over 2,500 households, were converted as part of a project to construct a 2,667-hectare buffer and "ecological lifestyle parks" between the Zone and Taihu Lake.[43] The lake ecological lifestyle project, supported by Premier Wen Jiabao, was planned to ring the lake with 200 to 1,000 meters of "recovered" forests, grasslands, and wetlands, with a stated policy goal of constructing a model eco-tourism industry.[44] In other cases, a provincially held conversion quota was allocated to Yixing's special economic zones (SEZs) to facilitate joint venture project timelines. In one instance, this strategy ensured the investment of a German technology company in the construction of a next-generation solar manufacturing facility.[45] Land subsidies, facilitated project approval, and the longer-term infrastructure development presented by the eco-city model also won the establishment of a national solar photovoltaic manufacturing and research base for Guodian, one of the five national state-owned utilities.[46]

The Land Quota System and "Consolidation" of Village Lands

The emergent model of eco-urbanization in China, as we have now seen, is centered on urban-rural integration with ostensible improvements to physical infrastructure and the human environment.[47] Within this context, the Yixing's eco-city project, and its effects on the Zhao brothers and others like them, is only one piece of a larger master plan that includes its two national state-level SEZs, which target the development of environmental industries, the establishment of environmental buffers, and the promotion of intensive nonvillage agriculture by contract farmers and agribusinesses. In order to move such disparate objectives forward, local authorities are given quotas that can be used for construction of housing, public facilities, infrastructure, and industry. Given that the vast majority of land in the region was designated primarily as rural land held by collectives, the Yixing government has had to requisition village construction land and farmland to meet its nonrural land use needs.[48] Because conversion of farmland is more strictly regulated and must conform to farmland preservation regulations, provincial and central government approvals for conversion are increasingly difficult to obtain. Under the quota management regime, sites of "replacement farmland" must be identified before conversion of existing farmland takes place. This leads local governments to rely on the "consolidation" of villages into new urban settlements as a means to rationalize the total land supply within their jurisdictions under a single planning authority. This approach conforms to the national policy of "Three Consolidations" (*san jizhong*), which promotes the movement of rural populations into urbanized settlements, rural industries into industrial zones and cities, and farmland into larger-scale holdings.

The most direct path for local authorities to achieve such "rationalization" entails taking over village-held construction lands and resettling residents into dense housing districts like Dongjiao Gardens. The objective of this process is to allow construction projects to proceed elsewhere. In Yixing (and elsewhere in China) such transfers of village construction land and their subsequent consolidation for producing farmland quota do not follow an observable geographic arithmetic. Xu Fan, a staff member in a subdistrict office of the Yixing BLR who is responsible for handling many of the Zone's land use requisitions, explained that even within a locality, a unit of farmland conversion cannot always be tied to a specific corresponding unit of replacement farmland. Even to local BLR functionaries like Xu, the practice of balancing quota allocations is an opaque matter. In addition to maintaining a set quantity of farmland over a given planning period, local jurisdictions are mandated to maintain a net-zero loss in farmland resulting from conversions. However, the provincial government allocates quotas for construction-land conversion and farmland protection on an unequal basis. This allows the province to maintain its "dynamic balance" of farmland according to the central government plan while optimizing spatial structure for urbanization, industrialization, agricultural production, and environmental protection.

In a place like Yixing, where demand for construction land is high, local staff facilitate the process not only through the transfers of village construction land mentioned above, but also by maintaining an underreported positive balance of quota.[49] To illustrate this to me, Xu Fan hand-annotated a copy of the official spreadsheet for ongoing replacement farmland quota production in seventeen villages. These quotas are also 'produced' by utilizing "consolidated" village lands that become available for reallocation following eviction and demolition. In the car park outside the offices, beneath a sign that read, "Use land frugally and intensively, hold fast to the farmland redline," Xu showed me that the hand-annotated total "production" exceeded the official current tally for those villages by 261.62 hectares. In four other land consolidation projects for completion in 2012, Xu expected to tally 783.56 hectares of village farmland and 376.05 hectares of village construction land off the books. Such "surplus" land allowed the municipal BLR to confirm that construction-land quota was readily available to meet land requisitions without utilizing farmland conversion quota or construction-land quota allocated from above. More importantly, this practice of accounting for "replacement" farmland allows the BLR to facilitate project approval where farmland conversion is occurring. Xu described this as "circulating" (*liudong*) farmland, calling into sharp relief the notion that land could be made fungible.

As I left the BLR compound, I pondered the red character slogan painted on the wall: "All people participate in founding the ecological city."[50] What types of "participation" are elicited by Yixing's eco-city building? Elsewhere in the Zone, dozens of construction projects were in varying stages of being imagined, planned, approved, and built. Among these were three solar photovoltaic cell and panel manufactories that had just been sited on village lands enclosed in 2006–2007 (see figure 12.2).[51] The Zhaos, their village cadre leaders, and workers recently hired into new green industries all have divergent experiences of participation. Read with an imperative overtone, the slogan calls attention to the differential treatment and outcomes experienced by "all people." Moreover, this generalized process of "founding the ecological city" papers over the fact that such differently situated social actors and processes also produce a diverse array of long-term effects and harms. These social-environmental fissures in the foundations of the ecological city are visible in the landscape and have material effects that are yet to be fully understood and accounted for in relationship to the goals of sustainable development.

To return to the issue of farmland, while the delicate geography of "dynamic balance" is not clearly mapped, its uneven spatiotemporality is quite observable in the enclosed but undeveloped village lands piled with rubble and in the proliferation of approved but unconstructed projects for fallowed fields—fields that are designated as "protected" in the operation of the quota system (see figures 12.3, 12.4, and 12.5). This means that though a given parcel may no longer *function* as farmland, it also does not yet require an expenditure of conversion quota. This gap between the land itself and its accounting in the quota system as two distinct aspects of the farmland conversion process highlights the tension arising across the local and national scales of environmental and resource governance. They also serve as clear examples of how the ultimate object of central policy regarding farmland protection is not any given site of farming and livelihood, but a national aggregate indicator of capacity.

Whither Paradise? The Social and Economic Outcomes of Dispossesion and Relocation

Dongjiao Gardens will house over 15,000 dispossessed residents from seven villages within the Zone when construction and resettlement are completed. Almost all of them had resided within the twenty-two square kilometers requisitioned for the first phase of the Zone's eco-city project, dubbed the "Scientific Innovation New City" (*ke chuang xin cheng*).[52] Regardless of official representations such as those in the chapter epigraph, the Zhaos experienced this new "paradise" as remote and incomplete in physical and cultural terms. Dongjiao sits miles beyond the eastern fringe of the urban core. For years after the first two phases were completed and occupied, Dongjiao comprised an isolated grid of residential blocks with almost no planned services. Approximately thirty-five thousand more dispossessed will be housed in three other resettlement districts in the Zone. These projects transpose previous patterns of urban-rural inequality into new spaces of peri-urban segregation.

With the loss of access to land and livelihoods, villagers are forced into a new, more proximate, and yet more explicitly marginalized relationship with the city. In some cases, dispossessed villagers are commonly referred to as a new "underclass" characterized by "three withouts": without land, without work, and without full social benefits. Moreover, a class of "four withouts" is also emerging as some villagers lose permanent housing as an entitlement of collective property. Because Yixing's current compensation system requires dispossessed families to pay for the difference between the "market prices" of their demolished homes and their relocation housing, many families are frequently impoverished in the process. Poor families are frequently unable to pay the fees, and the "compensation" for their demolished homes is diminished in the process as the money is tied to a compulsory mortgage system for the relocation housing and they spend down meager savings on transitional housing. Thus, some families are left with no option other than to attempt to sell the property through a broker. However, as no preestablished market exists for the resettlement housing apart from renting to recently displaced families, this is generally unsuccessful. Many families are forced to purchase a home farther outside of the city. Others move in with relatives as circumstances allow.

In discussing the green development rationales of improved living standards, new clean industries, jobs, grain security, and environmental protection, the Zhaos and other older villagers display a remarkably sanguine view of social progress in spite of a perceived inevitability of dispossession and potential hardships for "us common folk" (laobaixing). Although they have virtually no chance of securing permanent employment in the Zone (even in services, much less in one of the new "greentech" industries), many expect that their children will do better. Nonetheless, in describing the actual processes of eviction, compensation, and resettlement, many expressed outrage over the violation of their property, rights, and dignity, as well as incredulity over the exclusion of farmers from "professional agriculture" as production is reconfigured around large-scale, high-yield cultivation methods.

Illustrating this point, the Zhaos' neighbor, Mrs. Yang, recounted that she was notified of eviction only a month before the harvest season of 2008. As we made our way a kilometer down Qingyuan Boulevard to the site of Sizhuang village, where Mrs. Yang returned every other day, she explained:

> We tried to appeal to the leaders to delay the demolition a few weeks. ... They won't listen to reason. ... Our village chief is a good person, but the cadre at the head of Xuewei [the administrative village]—he doesn't know us and we don't know him. ... Even before we signed [the papers for settling compensation], we were told that they had already contracted our farmland to a woman from Zhejiang.

For leasing her household's farmland, the Yang family receives an annual ¥400 (US$58) from the Yixing government, and ¥250 (US$36) from the contract farmer. However, like many households in the region, they still produced primarily for subsistence and the cash does much less in the face of uncertainty and their rapidly increasing cost of living.

Zhang Ting, the contract farmer, leased paddy fields for wheat and rice from three villages totaling over eight hectares (roughly the holdings of sixty families). In 2010, her market price and contracted procurement price by the State Grain Reserve rose about 30 percent over the previous year with incentives for contract farming. Because of her economies of scale and the spike in prices, she earned 61 percent more per unit area compared to Mrs. Yang and her fellow villagers who harvested in 2008 to 2009. Such a difference cannot be attributed simply to the function of market mechanisms. Rather, the account above shows how the restructuring of grain production has taken place through extra-economic means of force, far outside the ambit of "the dull compulsion" of the market described by Marx.[53]

Retreading her two-year path through the decorative landscaping of flowerbeds and pregrown trees that fringe the rubble of her village, Mrs. Yang and I passed beneath a billboard that proclaimed: "New Talent, New Industry, a New City" (see figure 12.6). Mrs. Yang set a tattered plastic bag with a small trowel and a clipper on the edge of her vegetable patch. Beyond a mound of broken weeded bricks, she pointed and blinked her watering eyes at what appeared almost as a mirage: a bright green-yellow field of mature rice. "Mrs. Zhang will be coming to harvest very soon. She owns tractors and will bring five or six workers to finish it very quickly."

Conclusion: Toward a Grounded Political Ecology of the Global Green Economy

In 2010, prominent billboards featured the exact Kobelco tractors used by Beijing Construction and the local demolition and relocation company to reshape the Yixing countryside (see figure 12.7). The advertisement, also common throughout Shanghai and Beijing in 2010 and 2011, proclaimed, "A green future is deepest in my heart," alongside a picture of a child drawing an idealized natural landscape unfolding incongruously beneath a backhoe. Beyond, a city floats among clouds in a field of white space. The composition recalls traditional Chinese landscape painting, but inverts its

Figure 12.6
The site and remaining rubble of Sizhuang village. Sizhuang village, in the eastern district of the Zone, was demolished in 2008 to make way for Dongjiu Boulevard, which runs along the western edge of the Dongjiao Gardens resettlement estate. A pile of trash and leftover rubble from the village remains. This 2010 billboard reads: "Build the commanding heights of talent, construct the commanding heights of technology, lead in the commanding heights of industry"; on the reverse side, "New Talent, New Industry, a New City." Photo by Jia-Ching Chen, 2010.

usual relationships of a "closed and formal world of man" in the foreground with a "spacious nature…a world of shifting light…fading to infinity" in the background.[54] Here, the white space marks the ambiguous, shifting unity of a metaphysical urban and a closed and formal nature. The imagery suggests a narrative of creative destruction as the sole means to achieve the "green future," and an idea of nature as one that requires physical intervention to be green. It is a visual allegory, highlighting the symbolic and material refigurations wrought by green development by dispossession.

In bringing together the experiences of the Zhao brothers and their loss of land, with the high-level administrative construction of fungible land in China, I hope to ground China's emerging urban nature—a dream world of

Figure 12.7
Kobelco "Green Future" advertisement posted in the Shanghai subway system. Photo by Jia-Ching Chen, 2010.

ecological harmony, industrial innovation, and technocratic efficiency—in the astounding material and symbolic refiguration of the rural people and places upon which it is built. Collectively owned farmland is turned into factories for the production of solar cells for the global market and the emergence of a new middle-class "ecological lifestyle." In these concluding remarks, I would like to raise the question of how these grounded observations connect to global figurations of environmental value and improvement.

The ideology of green development that links rural transformation to the construction of "environmental" industries is tied to the global market for carbon reduction. Starting around 2007, expanding subsidies in the European Union and the United States underpinned the rapid construction of China's solar industry. In China, direct subsidies in land leases and cheap financing (itself bolstered by state-rentier capital) contributed significantly to China's touted "green leap forward."[55] In the course of only a few years, China expanded its solar PV manufacturing capacity nearly fiftyfold from around 1 gigawatt in 2007 to an estimated 49 gigawatts in 2013.[56] Using such means between 2007 and 2011, Yixing built approximately 5 percent of the global manufacturing capacity for PV solar panels. This irruption inserted China's national agenda on green development into global markets for renewables, including carbon credit projects for solar farms certified by the Kyoto Protocol Clean Development Mechanism. However, this success created a crisis of overproduction, and between 2010 and 2013 prices dropped 350 percent faster than predicted. The crash led a crisis of overcapacity, with bankruptcies and the loss of billions in cash as fixed capital as plants were shuttered. In 2012, a report by GTM Research estimated that 180 solar panel manufacturers would go under, 54 of them in China.[57] On the heels of major bankruptcies, including of Solyndra, a company that received US$536 million in federal loan guarantees, American solar companies filed antidumping suits against Chinese suppliers. In its 2012 findings, the United States proposed counter-tariffs of 31 percent on imports of solar panels and solar cells from China. In 2013, the EU imposed an average tariff of 47 percent on Chinese PV cells, panels, and silicon wafers.[58] The two main companies named in the dispute are based in Jiangsu: Wuxi Suntech and Trina Solar. Suntech was the world's largest producer until it declared bankruptcy and defaulted on US$541 million in bonds in March 2013 as a direct result of the global overcapacity crash.[59] The tariffs substantially increased the costs of solar energy and spurred new efforts at international cooperation at the 2015 UN Climate Change Conference in Paris.

These contradictions between national economic development and local environmental and social outcomes in China's environmentalization are indicative of the larger contradictions of China's "green capitalism" in a global context. Briefly, I argue that these contradictions are:

1. *Exporting sustainable development*—the actual environmental sustainability of "green" manufacturing industries is often not weighed in terms of local impacts, and privileges end-of-chain outcomes (such as installed capacity of solar panels).

2. *Legitimation of dispossession and enclosure*—green discourse is used by local government officials as a basis for political legitimacy and to justify ongoing processes of capital accumulation by state force.

3. *Anti-rural bias*—as green discourse is used by developers and government officials to justify land conversion for development and environmental governance, "green" is increasingly equated with a master-planned

optimization of urban-rural space, thus reinforcing previous figurations of the rural as "backward."

4. *International political legitimation*—as China receives increased global recognition for its achievements and potential in greening industrialization and urbanization, perceptions of its authoritarian political system as a means of achieving these ends are normalized. Here, I do not mean to characterize the Chinese state as monolithic and totalitarian. Rather, this point emphasizes the ways that different levels of government and problems of governance (that is, environmental protection, rural urbanization, and green industrialization) are sites of friction or contestation, where social and political dynamics are refigured in relation to green development.

These contradictions suggest potential conflicts between different scales of sustainability objectives. As village fields are plowed for solar farms and forests of carbon credits, tensions between a so-called global green economy and local economic and environmental outcomes are clearly discernable.

China's environmental agenda is not merely a political rationale for justifying dispossession. It is reshaping global resource geographies. Environmental political economies call our attention to how the industrial production of resources takes place and how it entails the construction of new urban natures. If we take for granted that cities have historically been founded for different locational advantages, grow through the slow accumulation of various types of surplus, and subsequently birth new forms of sociality, then China's examples of master planned eco-urbanization circumvent the processes of accretion and change for the amplification of a single agenda. This is an agenda that has broad international support and a mandate underscored by the politics of crisis. At its largest horizons, green development purports to remake the environmental bases of production and, therefore, of value and accumulation. If, as Harvey suggests, the city is the historic place where the world can be "re-imagined and re-made," then that imagination must encompass an understanding of how global environmentalization is producing and connecting new urban and rural natures.[60]

As "green" is increasingly adapted and linked to China's ideology of socialism, I argue that it plays a role in refiguring social values and perceived entitlements, especially rural land tenure and livelihoods. In his analysis of China's agrarian contradictions, Cao Jinqing argues that because village smallholder agriculture cannot compete effectively in global capitalist markets, to which they are nonetheless tied for inputs and sales, smallholder production with land privatization "would lead to rural poverty, unrest, and growing inequality, not agricultural efficiency and smooth urbanization."[61] In attempting to resolve this contradiction, the Chinese state is using a combination of dispossession and the creation of a social safety net for the rural residents who are faced with these rapid and radical changes. This safety net, including the minimum subsistence allowance (*dibao*) and the expanded rural pension championed by Wen Jiabao, helps to secure compliance with forceful dispossession. In this regard, the emerging figuration of the rural may harken early conditions of China's move to a post-socialist political economy and its rise as an environmental leviathan.

Acknowledgments

In addition to valuable comments from all the contributors in this volume, I appreciate insightful suggestions from Amita Baviskar, Ricardo Cardoso, Mona Damluji, Henrik Ernstson, and Hun Kim on various aspects of this chapter.

Notes

1. Kobelco equipment, manufactured in joint venture factories in Sichuan and Hangzhou, is pervasive in demolition and construction sites across the country.

2. Names of people and some places have been modified.

3. I draw on Haraway's (1992) analytical approach to figuration.

4. Rabinow 1989, pp. 7–16.

5. Chen 2013b.

6. Land dispossession is the leading cause of social unrest, with tens of thousands of protests amounting to 65 percent of officially recorded "mass conflicts" each year (Yu 2005; He 2010; Chen 2013a, 2017).

7. See Chen (2017) for a discussion on the institutionalization of these practices.

8. Zhang 2002, p. 62.

9. The Zone was founded under the Yixing municipal authority in April 2006. It was promoted to provincial level status in July of the same year and was designated

a national level economic and technological development zone in March 2013 by the State Council.

10. Yixing Municipal Government 2006; Xu and Ling 2010.

11. The phrase "ecological construction" (*shengtai jianshe*) is a contraction of the slogan "construct an ecological civilization." The party-state has enshrined ecological construction as a pillar of its ideology of socialist development, "merging comprehensively with national economic construction, political construction, cultural construction and all aspects of constructing society" (Xinhua News Agency 2012, n.p.). See also National People's Congress (2016); Central People's Government (2017).

12. See Xinhua News Agency (2012); National People's Congress (2011, 2016); State Council (2010, 2014). For Li, an early proponent of environmental protection evaluation criteria for party officials, eco-urbanization in Yixing and other model cities is also fundamentally about reshaping the party-state itself around the official ideology of ecological civilization; see, for example, Yixing Administrative Bureau (2010).

13. National People's Congress 2011; Xinhua News Agency 2012.

14. As of this writing, online sources for these data under the Ministry of Environmental Protection domain (www.mep.gov.cn) are no longer available. On March 17, 2018, the ministry was reorganized as the Ministry of Ecology and Environment. Since April 2018, the previous site has redirected to a new domain (www.mee.gov .cn) without support for old links. The new ministry has an expanded regulatory purview, notably taking over climate change mitigation from the National Development and Reform Commission; see www.mee.gov.cn.

15. See Bramall (2007); Buck (2012).

16. For examples in national policy, see the opening paragraphs of the National Land Use Master Plan (Ministry of Land and Resources 1997, 2008a; YBLRYixing Bureau of Land and Resources 2010) and the 1998 revision of the Land Management Law, which refers to land management in the context of ecological protection and improvement and the "ecological environment" of agricultural production. These broadened environmental resource concepts are reflected in the 1998 merger of the Ministry of Geology and Mining, the State Administration of National Land, the State Administration of National Oceans, and the State Bureau of Surveying and Mapping to form the Ministry of Land and Resources. See also, the inclusion of land in "environmental resources" in the Ministry of Environmental Protection (2008) guidelines for environmental impact assessment in land use planning.

17. On the latter point, see, e.g., Lin, Tao, and Liu (2006); Hsing (2010).

18. This treatment of "boundary objects" is influenced by Star and Griesemer (1989, p. 393), who, drawing on Michel Callon's and Bruno Latour's critical science studies,

speak of "scientific objects which both inhabit several intersecting social worlds *and* satisfy the informational requirements of each of them."

19. This dual system is based on the socialist ownership of all land enshrined in the constitution, under which all urban land is owned by the state on behalf of the whole people, and rural and suburban land is held directly by collectives. For an overview of the land regulation regime, see Ho and Lin (2003). For a critique of its institutional failures, see, e.g., Lichtenberg and Ding (2008).

20. Over the past two five-year plans, ecological targets (*shengtai zhibiao*, or "ecological quotas") have been developed for a range of environmental and infrastructural goals including resource efficiency, project GDP per unit of converted rural land, wastewater treatment, and afforested green space. These targets and quotas are passed down from the central government to the provinces for fulfillment by local government units. In May 2013 at the Sixth Collective Study Session of the Chinese Communist Party Politburo, Xi Jinping advocated the establishment of "ecological redlines" (*shengtai hongxian*) as a policy translation of an imperative structural limit to development for the assurance of "ecological security" (*shengtai anquan*) and the recovery and growth of ecological service functions (*shengtai fuwu gongneng*). For an example of the application of a broad array of ecological quotas as integral to sustainable development and urbanization in Yixing, see the China Yixing Environmental Science and Technology Park Management Committee (2012) outline of its low-carbon ecological targets system, which includes thirty-six quantitative and nine qualitative targets.

21. Chen 2013a, 2013b.

22. Unless otherwise noted, approximate dollar estimates given at the 2008 average exchange rate, ¥1 = $US0.14.

23. In May 2013, Yixing was named a National Greening Model City for its afforestation work, including a 1,333-hectare "green screen" on the shore of Taihu Lake (see Min 2008).

24. This work took place under the management of Beijing Construction, a major state-owned enterprise. The Zone signed a build-transfer contract with Beijing Construction to complete all of the major infrastructure and much of the architectural construction within the Zone. This financing model is increasingly common in China and directly links local state-led rural land dispossession and speculative urbanization to large construction-finance institutions with strong ties at the central government level. Because such projects are increasingly embedded in the portfolios of large banks, this dynamic raises important questions about the valuation of land development projects and the stability of China's financial system.

25. See, for example, Marx (1906 [1867]); Smith (1976 [1776]); Polanyi (2001 [1944]); Li (2014); Levien (2018).

26. Polanyi 2001 [1944]; Li 2014.

27. In official policy discourse, the relevant phrase is "farmland takings and replacement dynamic balance" (*gengdi zhan bu pingheng dongtai*). This policy is summed up as "take one, replace one" (*zhan yi, bu yi*).

28. Arable land and prime farmland protection quotas: *gengdi baohu yu jiben nongtian baohu zhibiao*; replacement arable land quota: *buchong gengdi zhibiao*. In March 2018, the Ministry of Land and Resources (MLR) was reorganized and its functions were subsumed within the newly established Ministry of Natural Resources. As of this writing, its website homepage (www.mlr.gov.cn) is defunct. While some webpages (currently) persist under the original addresses, much of the data that were previously accessible via MLR homepage menus have not been transferred or linked to the new Ministry of Natural Resources site (see www.mnr.gov.cn).

29. In her definitive ethnography of China's population science and policy, Greenhalgh (2008:41-55) notes that debates on state population control efforts were fraught with autocractic ideological rectitude, with Mao reversing his positions on population growth and control throughout the 1950s. A national dialogue on family planning and individual birth control was sidelined with the eruption of the Great Leap Forward and Mao's 1958 declaration that "for now, a large population is better" (ibid., 53). By the end of his life in 1976, Mao had assented, writing, "it won't do to not control population" (ibid.).

30. Expression of carrying capacity as a function of land area is now prominent in the concept of "ecological footprints" (Wackernagel and Rees 1996). For a review of the difficulties in reducing social-environmental relationships to a single land use metric, see Van den Bergh and Grazi (2013).

31. Further national environmental rationale is also clearly evident in "grain for green" programs that remove farmland and rangeland from production for erosion control and anti-desertification. Grain for green afforestation projects is increasingly monetized, including via global carbon credit markets. From 2006 to 2013, China registered five afforestation projects that will produce 8.8 million metric tons of CO_2-equivalent in Kyoto Protocol Clean Development Mechanism certified emissions reductions (CDM CERs) by 2041.

32. Jurisdictional cities exist at the county, prefectural, and provincial levels of administration.

33. The reconciliation of "dynamic balance" was originally intended to take place within each jurisdicational level. However, administrators in relatively land-scarce Jiangsu and Zhejiang provinces began practices for the banking and trading of quota-allocated land use rights between localities (Wang et al. 2010; Cai 2014). Cai (2014) provides a detailed account of the evolution of the quota system and the subsequent normalization of quota trading. Cai (2014, 2017) unpacks the structural

drivers of such inter-jurisdictional transfers of "flying land," highlighting the issues of local government finance and political tenure.

34. The term for "prime farmland"—*jiben nongtian*—is also frequently translated as "basic farmland." In the MLR translation of the 1999 law, the term is rendered as "capital farmland."

35. Jiangsu People's Government 2009.

36. Wuxi Bureau of Land and Resources 2011. Although Yixing is a county-level unit within the Wuxi prefectural jurisdiction, the prefecture and county territories are not contiguous. This highlights the prevalent practice of inter-locality management of land quotas and farmland dynamic balance.

37. The general process of land use optimization is referred to as land organization (*tudi zhengli*). Land and land use consolidation (*jizhong*) refers to the assembly of land for zoned uses. Farmland reclamation (*fuken*) and remediation (*zhengzhi*) are frequently used to describe projects that consolidate village construction and marginal lands for the flexible accounting of quotas for farmland preservation, construction and conversion, and construction land use.

38. *Ba nonyongdi jizhong* (Wuxi Bureau of Land and Resources 2011).

39. Polanyi 2001 (1944).

40. Wang et al. (2010, 457) cite Jiangsu and Shanghai as the originators in the late 1990s of rural land consolidation practices, which enabled local governments to exceed allocated quotas for construction land. Although the Land Administration Law (National People's Congress 1998) includes broad provisions for converting farmland outside of approved master plans (see Article 58) and encourages rationalization for efficient village land use (see Article 41), these practices still require notification to the State Council. Wang and Bai (2011) cite a 2006 pilot provision by the MLR to allow intra-jurisdiction rural land consolidation to be "transferred" to offset urban demand for construction land quota in Jiangsu, Shandong, Tianjin, Hubei, and Sichuan. This pilot program was extended to the rest of the country in 2008 (Ministry of Land and Resources 2008b; for futher details, see Cai 2014).

41. China's bureaucratic matrix is organized around vertical central government ministries known as "strips" (*tiao*, e.g., the Ministry for Ecology and Environment, the Ministry of Natural Resources, and so on) and horizontal territorial jurisdictions known as "blocks" (*kuai*, e.g., provinces and cities). Theoretically, provincial and local level bureaus report to their respective ministerial hierarchies, while territorial blocks are administered by the people's government of that jurisdiction. Ministry bureaus do not have binding authority over the regional governments within corresponding hierarchical levels. Local governments must also conform to the policies of larger subsuming governments. For instance, Yixing, a county-level city, falls under the jurisdiction of the Wuxi prefecture-level municipality, which is under

Jiangsu province. Local units, such as Yixing's government and its separate SEZs, operate with a great deal of autonomy in pursuing various results-oriented policy goals ranging from GDP growth to farmland preservation.

42. *Shang you zhengce, xia you duice.*

43. Min 2008b; Liu 2010.

44. Wuxi Municipal Party Committee 2009.

45. Interview with Yixing Economic Development Zone Director of Investment and Industrial Planning, Bureau of Foreign Investment, May 21, 2010; from author's fieldwork archives, interview: 20100521.YXZ.1.

46. Through 2012, the three successive phases of the Guodian projects brought over ¥12 billion (US$1.8 billion) of investment to the Zone. The combined manufacturing capacity of the Guodian projects reached 800 megawatts of PV cells and modules in 2012, an increase of 60 percent over 2011, which brought the Zone's total manufacturing capacity to over 3 gigawatts—about 10 percent of the 2012 national total.

47. These physical aspects are frequently conflated under the concepts of ecocity construction in China. A prominent example here is the Shanghai 2010 World Exposition slogan: "Better City, Better Life." There are also distinct cultural terms associated with greening such as "ecological civilization" (*shengtai wenming*) and "ecological living" (*shengtai shenghuo*). These ideas are highly aestheticized and are used to refer to cultural values of environmental consciousness as well as to an improved quality of life.

48. According to the *Yixing Land Use Master Plan (2006–2020)*, the total land area in Yixing in 2005 was 217,742.82 hectares, of which 55 percent was classified as agricultural land. Of 30,831.90 hectares of construction land, nearly 60 percent was held by village collectives, 32 percent was in townships, and less than 8 percent was classified as urban land under the direct planning authority of the municipal government. The plan has the goal of reducing village construction land by half by 2020 (Yixing Bureau of Land and Resources 2010).

49. Interview with Yixing Subdistrict Bureau of Land and Resources Staff, November 11, 2010; from author's fieldwork archives, Interview: 20101111.YBLR.1.

50. *Quanmin canyu chuangjian shengtai shi.*

51. At the peak of solar PV industry expansion in 2010–2012, there were six major cell and module manufacturers operating in the Yixing Zone, including a national state grid enterprise, Guodian, and global top-ten producers Trina and RenaSola. There were also several local state-backed incubator projects.

52. The project name plays on the use of the character for "new" (*xin*) in joining "creation and innovation" (*chuangxin*) to "new city" (*xin cheng*).

53. This often-cited passage comes from the discussion of "so-called primitive accumulation" in *Capital*, volume 1. Marx (1906 [1867], p. 809) describes the process in direct relationship to the social construction of the working class: "The organization of the capitalist process of production, once fully developed, breaks down all resistance.... The dull compulsion of economic relations completes the subjection of the laborer to the capitalist. Direct force, outside economic conditions, is of course still used, but only exceptionally. In the ordinary run of things, the laborer can be left to the 'natural laws of production,' i.e., to his dependence on capital, a dependence springing from, and guaranteed in perpetuity by, the conditions of production themselves."

54. Tuan 1977, p. 57.

55. For a decade now, experts and boosters have been pointing to China's combined economic power and political system as the largest—and perhaps most important—venue for the development of "a clean energy future" (Friedman 2010a; Finamore 2011). See Friedman (2010b) for one of many sanguine references to China's "green leap forward."

56. National manufacturing capacities estimated by Earth Policy Institute (http://www.earth-policy.org/data_center/C26) and Bloomberg (http://www.bloomberg.com/news/2013-09-08/chinese-zombies-emerging-after-years-of-solar-subsidies.htm). A one-gigawatt-capacity thermal power plant would provide electricity to over 700,000 US homes.

57. Analysis by GTM Research, a source of expert analysis on renewables markets, reported by Forbes (http://www.forbes.com/sites/uciliawang/2012/10/16/report-180-solar-panel-makers-will-disappear-by-2015/).

58. In 2018, the United States followed suit and imposed a 30 percent tariff.

59. International Trade Administration 2012.

60. Harvey 2003.

61. Day 2008, p. 56.

References

Bramall, Chris. 2007. *The Industrialization of Rural China*. New York: Oxford University Press.

Brown, Lester. 1995. *Who Will Feed China? Wake-Up Call for a Small Planet*. New York: W. W. Norton.

Buck, Daniel. 2012. *Constructing China's Capitalism: Shanghai and the Nexus of Urban-Rural Industries*. New York: Palgrave Macmillan.

Cai, Meina. 2014. "'Flying Land': Institutional Innovation in Land Management in Contemporary China." In *Local Governance Innovation in China*, edited by Jessica C. Teets and William Hurst, 82–105. London: Routledge.

Cai, Meina. 2017. "Revenue, Time Horizon, and Land Allocation in China." *Land Use Policy* 62: 101–112.

Central People's Government. 2017. "Xi Jinping zhichu, jiakuai shengtaiwenming tizhigaige, jianshe meili Zhongguo" [Xi Jinping advances the acceleration of ecological civilization structural reforms to build abeautiful China]. Xinhua News Agency. http://www.gov.cn/zhuanti/2017-10/18/content_5232657.htm.

Chen, Jia-Ching. 2013a. "Greening Dispossession: Environmental Governance and Sociospatial Transformation in Yixing, China." In *Locating Right to the City in the Global South*, edited by Tony Samara, Shenjing He, and Guo Chen, 81–104. New York: Routledge.

Chen, Jia-Ching. 2013b. "Sustainable Territories: Rural Dispossession, Land Enclosures and the Construction of Environmental Resources in China." *Human Geography* 6(1): 102–118.

Chen, Jia-Ching. 2017. "Social-Environmental Dilemmas of Planning an 'Ecological Civilization' in China." In *Companion to Planning in the Global South*, edited by Vanessa Watson, Gautam Bhan and Smita Srinivas, 180–191. London: Routledge.

China Yixing Environmental Science and Technology Park Management Committee. 2012. "Huankeyuan ditan yindao zhenglüe" [Environmental Science and Technology Park low-carbon leading strategy]. http://www.hky.gov.cn/default.php?mod=article&do=detail&tid=500588.

Day, Alexander F. 2008. "The End of the Peasant? New Rural Reconstruction in China." *boundary 2* 35(2): 49–73.

Finamore, Barbara. 2011. "A Clean Energy Future: A Shared Vision of Presidents Obama and Hu." National Resource Defense Council. http//switchboard.nrdc.org/blogs/bfinamore/a_clean_energy_future_a_shared.html.

Friedman, Thomas L. 2010a. "Aren't We Clever?" *New York Times*, September 19. http://www.nytimes.com/2010/09/19/opinion/19friedman.html.

Friedman, Thomas L. 2010b. "Who's Sleepling Now?" *New York Times*, January 10. http://www.nytimes.com/2010/01/10/opinion/10friedman.html.

Greenhalgh, Susan. 2008. *Just One Child: Science and Policy in Deng's China*. Berkeley: University of California Press.

Haraway, Donna. 1992. "Ecce Homo, Ain't (Ar'n't) I a Woman, and Inappropriate/d Others: The Human in a Post-Humanist Landscape." In *Feminists Theorize the Political*, edited by Judith Butler and Joan W. Scott, 86–100. New York: Routledge.

Harvey, David. 2003. "The Right to the City." *International Journal of Urban and Regional Research* 27(4): 939–941.

He, Dan. 2010. "Land Battles Most Dire Rural Issue: Report." *China Daily*, December 16. http://usa.chinadaily.com.cn/epaper/2010-12/16/content_11713168.htm.

Ho, Samuel P. S., and George C. S. Lin. 2003. "Emerging Land Markets in Rural and Urban China: Policies and Practices." *China Quarterly* 175: 681–707.

Hsing, You-tien. 2010. *The Great Urban Transformation: Politics of Land and Property in China*. Oxford: Oxford University Press.

International Trade Administration. 2012. *Commerce Preliminarily Finds Dumping of Crystalline Silicon Photovoltaic Cells, Whether or Not Assembled into Modules from the People's Republic of China*. Washington, DC: Department of Commerce.

Jiangsu People's Government. 2009. "Jiangsu sheng tudiliyong zongti guihua 2006–2020 nian" [Jiangsu Province Land Use Master Plan (2006–2020)]. Nanjing: Jiangsu People's Government.

Levien, Michael. 2018. *Dispossession without Development: Land Grabs in Neoliberal India*. New York: Oxford University Press.

Li, Tania Murray. 2014. "What Is Land? Assembling a Resource for Global Investment." *Transactions of the Institute of British Geographers* 39(4): 589–602.

Lichtenberg, Erik, and Chengri Ding. 2008. "Assessing Farmland Protection Policy in China." *Land Use Policy* 25: 59–68.

Lin, Justin Yifu, Ran Tao, and Mingxing Liu. 2006. "Decentralization and Local Governance in China's Economic Transition." In *Decentralization and Local Governance in Developing Countries: A Comparative Perspective*, edited by Pranab Bardhan and Dilip Mookherjee, 305–327. Cambridge, MA: MIT Press.

Marx, Karl. 1906 [1867]. *Capital*, vol. 1: *The Process of Production of Capital*. Chicago: Charles H. Kerr.

Min, Deqiang. 2008. "Yixing quanmian tuixing huan Taihu 'tuigeng, tuiyang, taiyü'" [Yixing comprehensively implements Taihu Lake Belt 'withdrawal of farmland, withdrawal of pastures, withdrawal of aquaculture.'" *Wuxi Daily*, June 15. http://www.shuichan.cc/news_view.asp?id=6945.

Ministry of Environmental Protection (MEP). 2008. *Guihua huanjing yingxiang pingjia jishu dao ze tudiliyong zongti guihua* [Technical guidelines for environmental impact assessment in land use planning]. Beijing: MEP.

Ministry of Land and Resources (MLR). 1997. *1997–2010 nian quanguo tudiliyong zongti guihua gangyao* [1997–2010 National Land Use Master Plan]. Beijing: MLR.

Ministry of Land and Resources (MLR). 2008a. *Quanguo tudiliyong zongti guihua gangyao 2006–2020 nian* [National Land Use Master Plan 2006–2020]. Beijing: MLR.

Ministry of Land and Resources (MLR). 2008b. *Chengxiang jiansheyongdi zengjian guagou shidian guanli banfa* [Management methods for the linkage of urban-rural construction land fluctuations]. Beijing: MLR.

National People's Congress (NPC). 1998. *Land Administration Law (1998)*. Beijing: NPC.

National People's Congress (NPC). 2011. *Zhonghua Renmin Gongheguo guomin jingji he shehui fazhan di shier ge wu nian guihua gangyao (quanwen)* [The Twelfth Five-Year National Plan for Economic and Social Development of the People's Republic of China Summary (Complete Text)]. Beijing: NPC.

National People's Congress (NPC). 2016. *Zhonghua Renmin Gongheguo guomin jingji he shehui fazhan di shisan ge wu nian guihua gangyao (quanwen)* [The Thirteenth Five-Year National Plan for Economic and Social Development of the People's Republic of China (Complete Text)]. Beijing: NPC, PRC.

Polanyi, Karl. 2001 [1944]. *The Great Transformation: The Political and Economic Orgins of Our Time*. Boston: Beacon Press.

Rabinow, Paul. 1989. *French Modern: Norms and Forms of the Social Environment*. Cambridge, MA: MIT Press.

Smith, Adam. 1976 [1776]. *An Inquiry into the Nature and Causes of the Wealth of Nations*. Chicago: University of Chicago Press.

Star, Susan Leigh, and James R. Griesemer. 1989. "Institutional Ecology, Translations, and Boundary Objects: Amateurs and Professionals in Berkeley's Museum of Vertebrate Zoology, 1907–39." *Social Studies of Science* 19(3): 387–420.

State Council. 2010. *Quanguo zhuti gongneng qu guihua* [National Major Functional Zones Plan]. Beijing: Central People's Government, December 21. http://www.gov.cn/zwgk/2011-06/08/content_1879180.htm.

State Council. 2014. *Guojia xinxing chengzhenhua guihua (2014–2020)* [National Plan for a New Model of Urbanization (2014–2020)] Xinhua News Agency, March 16. http://www.gov.cn/zhengce/2014-03/16/content_2640075.htm.

Tuan, Yi-Fu. 1977. *Space and Place: The Perspective of Experience*. Minneapolis: University of Minnesota Press.

Van den Bergh, Jeroen, and Fabio Grazi. 2013. "Ecological Footprint Policy? Land Use as an Environmental Indicator." *Journal of Industrial Ecology* 18(1): 10–19.

Wackernagel, M., and W. Rees. 1996. *Our Ecological Footprint: Reducing Human Impact on the Earth*. New Haven, CT: New Society Publishers.

Wang, Tao, and Tiantian Bai. 2011. "Guotu Ziyuan Bu zhengsu chengxiang jianshe yongdi zengjian jiagou" [Ministry of Land and Resources to rectify planned increases of urban construction land through decreases to rural construction land]. *Economic*

Information Daily, Xinhua News Agency, January 10. http://finance.sina.com.cn/roll/20110110/00579224664.shtml.

Wang, Hui, Ran Tao, Lanlan Wang, and Fubing Su. 2010. "Farmland Preservation and Land Development Rights Trading in Zhejiang, China." *Habitat International* 34(4): 454–463.

Wuxi Bureau of Land and Resources. 2011. *Gengdi baohu yu wan qing liangtian jianshe* [Farmland preservation and the construction of vast fertile fields]. Wuxi: Wuxi Municipal Bureau of Land and Resources.

Wuxi Municipal Party Committee. 2009. *Yi Wen Jiabao zongli lianxu san ci shicha Wuxi wei dongli jiakuai jianshe chuang xinxing jingji lingjun* [In order to urge and speed the construction of a leading innovation economy city, Premier Wen Jiabao makes three consecutive inspection visits to Wuxi]. Wuxi: Wuxi People's Government. Author's archives.

Xinhua News Agency. 2012. "Hu Jintao zai zhongguo gongchandang di shiba ci quanguo daibiao dahui shang de baogao (quanwen)" [Full text of Hu Jintao's report to the 18th National Congress of the Communist Party of China]. http://news.xinhuanet.com/18cpcnc/2012–11/17/c_113711665.htm.

Xu, Yuanqiang, and Lin Ling. 2010. "Ba Yixing jianshe cheng 'dongfang shuicheng' nuli zheng chuang quanguo fazhan de shifan" [Make Yixing an "Eastern Water City," diligently vie to create a national model of development]. *Wuxi Daily*, October 9. http://wuxi.people.com.cn/GB/12901554.html.

Yixing Administrative Bureau. 2010. "Shiwei zhaokai changwei (kuoda) huiyi xuexi guanche Li Yuanchao tongzhi lai Yi shicha zhongyao jianghua jingshen" [Municipal standing committee expanded session to study and implement comrade Li Yuanchao's important speech]. Yixing People's Government, December 28. http://www.yxcg.gov.cn/shownews.asp?id=2807.

Yixing Bureau of Land and Resources. 2010. *Yixing shi tudi liyong zongti guihua (2006–2020 nian)* [Yixing Land Use Master Plan (2006–2020)]. Yixing: Yixing People's Government.

"Yixing dongjiao hua yuan qiao dong xia de ju wei hui he chai qian hu de xin le yuan" [Yixing Dongjiao Huayuan's Qiaodong Residents' Committee and Relocated Households' New Paradise]. 2011. *Wuxi Daily*, September 17. Archived at: http://house.wst.cn/News/wuxi/20110917090457_79126.htm.

Yixing Municipal Government. 2006. *Yixing shi shengtaishi chuangjian san nian xingdong jihua* [Yixing City Eco-City Establishment Three-Year Action Plan]. Yixing: Yixing People's Government.

Yu, Jianrong. 2005. "Tudi wenti yi chengwei nongmin weiquan kangzheng de jiaodian—Guanyu dangqian wo guo nongcun shehui xingshi de yi xiang zhuangti diaoyan" [Land problems have already become the focus for farmers' protests to uphold their rights: An investigation of the current situation in China's rural communities]. *Diaoyan Shijie* 18(3): 22–23.

Zhang, Lei. 2002. "Ecologizing Industrialization in Chinese Small Towns." PhD diss., Environmental Sociology, Wageningen University.

V Conclusion

13 Grounding and Worlding Urban Natures: Configuring an Urban Ecology Knowledge Project

Henrik Ernstson and Sverker Sörlin

> There are two ways to lose oneself: walled segregation in the particular or dilution in the universal.
>
> —Aime Césaire, letter to Maurice Thorez, 1956

Central to this book are an urge and a curiosity to multiply the understanding of urban environments by taking in a wider urban experience. Rather than a global model that tries to grasp and decode urban environments in the same way wherever they appear, we have worked with the idea that what is required is an approach that sustains the multiplicity of urban nature, that affords and provides space for various ways of knowing and ways of being within and in relation to urban nature, and that produces an epistemologically and ontologically rich object of study, opening it toward conversations, collaborations, debates, and contestations. In a world that is urbanizing rapidly across a diverse set of cultural and biophysical contexts, it is crucial to open our understanding of urban nature toward a broader urban experience. At the very end of the volume, it is time to reflect on how the growing community who share an interest in urban environmental studies could move on in future work.

One way of taking the project forward would be to engage in a critical and constructive relationship with urban ecology as conceived within the environmental sciences. The meeting between scientific and narrative-based ways of knowing urban environments could focus on *how* knowledge is used in tangible conflicts and controversies. Sara Whatmore and the broader conceptual work built in the field of science and technology studies have opened one practical avenue. In her work on flooding in English towns, Whatmore brought natural and social scientific scholars and representatives from the public together, not because they had an established stake in the matter, but to form a "competency group." The group collectively and transparently elaborated on *ways of knowing* flooding and its many social, environmental, and historical factors with the aim of "redistribut[ing] expertise across the 'scientific'/'vernacular' divide."[1] This put the onus not on *what* is known, but *how* something is known. The grounding and worlding approach of this book would be an important companion in such efforts to contextualize, not discard, scientific ways of knowing.

Another important move forward is to ask not only for in-depth case studies from one city or physical location, which was how we conceived this book project as a first necessary step to gain textured accounts, but to more explicitly design studies that develop comparative "productive geographies," exploring how urban natures are local yet connected to other locations (see also chapter 1 in this volume).[2] Urban scholars have been busy in developing these comparative geographies, including, for instance, studies of "translocal" forms of urban struggles that have followed Slum-Dwellers International, an alliance of marginalized neighborhoods across Asian, African, and Latin American cities;[3] "mobile urbanism" that studies how urban policies, standards, and expertise move and are translated across the world to influence local dynamics;[4] and comparisons across the global South and North of processes that marginalize people from potable water access in Indian and Californian cities.[5] Such comparative work does not seek to find the same variables or factors applicable everywhere, but looks for surprises and possibilities in how differences are played out, and how such differences could be used for theorizing.

Another challenge is how to integrate more-than-human approaches that seek to decenter the anthropocentric perspectives that lie at the heart of most urban and environmental studies. In the humanities and critical social sciences there has been an upswing of thinking that (urban) animals have narrative capacities that can help to open up, rather than pinning down, the anthropocentric view of cities that structures policy and politics.[6] However, while such approaches attend to quite easily identifiable nonhuman subjects, what also seems necessary is to account for wider forms of bio-agency. This could follow how Joshua Lewis approaches the complex coastal ecosystems in Louisiana, where he shows us precisely how humanmade infrastructures, which have been implemented over the course of 150 years, have created a historical-biophysical complex that carries more-than-human agencies beyond simple "nonhumans" and as such shape politics in unpredictable and difficult ways.[7]

Finally—and we will return to this point below—to publish a book today on *grounding urban natures*, which contains studies from across most continents, means to face Western bias in constructive ways. Urban environmental studies, from scientific ecology to critical and poststructuralist geography and on to environmental history, are informed by specific habits of thinking history, city, and nature. We need to draw on postcolonial and decolonial scholarship to develop methods and collaborations to counter such habits and further multiply the ways through which urban natures are understood.

We now continue this chapter by taking our cues from the chapters to suggest a set of heuristics toward a repertoire for comparative urban environmental studies. Our aim is not to articulate a theoretical framework but rather to suggest a scaffold that can support study and collaboration. This aim is connected to William Cronon's edited volume *Uncommon Ground*, which inspired our work with this volume, in which chapters and authors represented a family of attempts that could not easily have been placed under a single rubric or theory but that still made a lot of work for establishing a new ground for critical environmental studies. Our volume also rests on a family of attempts, diverse and inspiring, that aims to explicitly pluralize and rethink urban nature from multiple locations, as well as offering methods and intellectual tools that can be useful in doing so.[8]

Act of Grounding: Articulating, Texturizing, Retrosembling, and Situating

The volume is, overall, an effort to *view urban natures as multiple* through the lenses of *grounding* and *worlding*. These two main heuristics form part of our treatment of comparative environmental urbanism in chapter 1 and they reverberate throughout the book's chapters. While grounding directs attention to how urban nature is reworked in particular places and becomes diverse through situated understandings, worlding tries to capture how places and urban natures are never only local. Instead, through the actions of experts, bureaucrats, activists, and scientists—and animals, vermin, and seeds—together with broader processes such as colonization, land dispossession, and world trade, urban natures are indeed connected from place to place. However, rather than using the meta-frame of globalization, we draw upon how anthropologists, geographers, and historians have tried to address how localities become part of the world, each in its own particular and specific way.[9] On both sides of our analytical effort—the side of the *local* through grounding and on the side of the *extra-local* in worlding—we foreground texture and particularity with the aim of creating a theoretical transaction space for dialogue and contestation wherein the local is not domesticated within the global.

The *act of grounding* translates the unity of "urban nature" as a universal object of science or a backdrop for exploitation, capitalist or otherwise, into multiple social, political, and biophysical relations.[10] Grounding, in this sense, brings material to critique and problematize the simplification of urban nature through taxonomic or ecological scientific frameworks, that is, resisting the idea that urban nature is a stable knowledge object, a thing that can be studied with the same (universal) framework wherever you go. Grounding, on the contrary, goes into the midst of social struggles over how to use, abuse, cohabit, change, understand, and contest urban nature. By tracing or uncovering urban nature through *relations*, urban nature can become pluralized and socialized and include the agency of nonhumans and the vibrancy of matter.[11] What does urban nature mean in different places? How is urban nature composed, contested, and known? What does a given array of social arrangements in-and-through urban natures tell us about the city in question, its people, country, region, and place in the world?

This stance is resonant with how "place" has been thought within relational thinking in human geography. Rather than taking an essentialist approach, we follow Doreen Massey in viewing place as a relational and historical phenomenon, brought about through associated multiple understandings that different social groups might have.[12] This relational and dynamic view, which is akin to what Torsten Hägerstrand termed the "processual landscape" (*förloppslandskapet*), foregrounds a process-driven way to understand the entanglements by which human and nonhumans come together.[13] It also resonates with what Neil Smith called "the production of nature" and what Sverker Sörlin and Paul Warde have referred to as "environing."[14]

At the core of all these efforts, including our own in this volume, lies an urge to differentiate through critical historical and social scientific methods the seemingly basic backdrop categories of "nature," "ecology," and "environment" and to let them emerge as practice-based, contested, and dynamic. Urban natures, hence, are not *other natures*, they are *differently grounded natures located elsewhere* than where we thought not so long ago that nature's conventional place was supposed to be.

Accompanying the act of grounding, we suggest four analytical tactics: *articulating, texturizing, retrosembling,* and *situating.* These are all interlinked and overlapping, but we articulate them separately to demonstrate how they build on a wider literature and gain strength when bundled together.

Articulating refers to making legible certain elements for interpretation, evaluation, debate, or struggle. This is accomplished by scientists and scholars, but also by artists, photographers, landscape architects, and journalists, including activists mobilizing to protect a park, a wetland, or an urban forest. Articulation is thus part of a very general sociomaterial practice that assembles actors, artifacts, and social arenas to construct and provide wider narratives and meanings for particular things and elements.[15] It assigns value (negative or positive) to objects, wetlands, trees, parks, and species, but also operates to define and make visible, and thus contestable, sociomaterial flows such as waste, water, or toxic substances. Articulation is the narrative practice of analyzing and making sense, and a key component of making politics about urban nature at all possible. In this volume we see articulation being used in several chapters. Jens Lachmund (chapter 9) articulates the emergence of urban ecological regimes in Berlin over a one-hundred-year period, placing each within a set of practices and moral ideas of value that shifts with technology, science, and sites—from urban nature as part of an "organic whole," to scientific urban ecology in postwar Berlin, to contemporary popular practices of community gardening. This provides grounds for critiquing what aspects and ways of knowing urban nature that these regimes hide and highlight. Furthermore, Lance van Sittert (chapter 10) narrates the construction of designated natural spaces in apartheid Cape Town, which he shows received their particular meanings within a discourse of white supremacy and racial segregation that highlights certain aspects and values of urban nature instead of others. Similarily, James Evans (chapter 11) articulates how an abstract, mobile, and science-based urban ecology framework emerged in Baltimore, Maryland.

Texturizing means attending to detail and putting effort into acknowledging *how small things matter*—"small" meaning that which may appear small from some mainstream or hegemonic viewpoint. For those building global models of urban ecology this will be a challenge, because if you travel with a strong framework in mind, a ready-made scheme to categorize the world, you will fail to appreciate the subtleties of different situations. The sensibility that comes with texturing in scholarly work is likewise intimately connected to making theory since texturizing could be understood, following James Clifford, as a "a matter of being aware of the difference that makes a difference in concrete situations, of recognizing the various inscriptions, 'places,' or 'histories' that both empower and inhibit the construction of theoretical categories."[16] However, to remain in "the local, 'experiential,' and circumstantial" is not enough; it has to be paired with an effort of working out *why* small things matter through comparative work, "looking beyond the local or experiential to wider, comparative phenomena."[17] This means that theory is not to be produced from lofty heights of abstractions ("global" or universal models, our habitual ways of thinking) but from particular locations and in the midst of detail and texture.

This tension between the assumptions we carry and the backgrounds we come from, on the one hand, and how we respond—as writers, activists, practitioners, citizens—to particular situations, on the other, drives home the productive tension between the local/particular and the global/general that needs to be kept close and explicit, and always needs to be revisited.[18] If this is not the case, the risk is that strong frameworks or concepts, such as social-ecological systems theory, metabolic rift, or biophilic/resilient/ smart cities, can come to create an expectation, a compulsion in the analyst/scholar to reproduce the framework or concept, rather than attending to the texture of place and locality.[19]

Texturizing also has to do with the quality of the analytical approach. With a vast flow of research money now being spent on urban and global environmental problems, thinking seems to be forced through a *generalized* idea of "the urban." With our grounding project being about putting nature in its right(ful) place, we sense a need to resist such nontextured models and return to textured narratives. Or, as Edgar Pieterse insists in relation to understanding new modalities of urbanization proliferating across the world, we need to profoundly revise the categories by which we think cities and politics. Pieterse has suggested that while trend data and demographics are important for responding to urgent developmental needs, we also need "theoretical searching," a space for inventing new categories by which to think cities. This includes, Pieterse continues, novel collaborations with artists, poets, and other urban knowers from outside academia, plus an investment in writing and producing "intimate ethnographies" built upon long-term work in specific urban contexts.[20] We need more textured accounts to theorize the urban anew, accounts such as those developed in this volume and in particular from the emergent cities of the global South. With a recognition of more than a century-long tradition of urban scholarship, from Camillo Sitte and Patrick Geddes to our contemporaries Ananya Roy and Aihwa Ong, we aim to contribute a language of critique, or a "mid-range" theory, that can develop a more circumspect, yet more precise means for developing new sensibilities through which to think urban natures.[21]

In this book we see such work occurring when features of nature move from the emblematic to the agentive. It is when the waste-filled lands of Lagos are subject to thick descriptions that their manifold social, political, and environmental properties can emerge, as Lindsay Sawyer shows in chapter 3. Although the socioecological patterns of reproduced injustice that Anne Whiston Spirn sees in Philadelphia (chapter 4) are not dissimilar from what occurs in many cities, her intricately layered analysis of maps, school projects, and infrastructures has heuristic value in itself. This texturizing approach puts certain demands on scholars because it requires consideration of elements typically drawn from a multiplicity of disciplines. Texturizing is carefully done by Lisa Hoffman (chapter 7) as she allows us to understand the multiple roles that nonindigenous invasive plants play in the making of social relations and roles in Dalian, China. It requires attention to detail in order to appreciate the emergence of not only an object to be managed by volunteers, the "alien plant," but how volunteering itself becomes part of wider state practices of governing spaces and forming subjectivities. Urban nature becomes that lens through which what appears as disparate worlds or projects are interlinked—from the intimate and personal, to nature conservation, to norms of governing, to a site, as Hoffman writes, "to negotiate government responsibility, individual contributions, natural beauty, economic development and geopolitics." A similar connection between the intimate and local, and wider global processes of capital and forms of governing are reached through texture and detail in several of the chapters: in Richard Walker's (chapter 6) account of the San Francisco Bay Area, where urban politics combines with the history of local science and socioeconomic class patterns in a sequence of urban renewal regimes; in

Jia-Ching Chen's (chapter 12) study of the recent history of how local food production and agricultural disposession combine with hyper-fast urbanization, state-run globalizing business models, and associated development ideologies in Yixing City, China; in Amita Baviskar's (chapter 8) delicate account from Delhi about how a present-day urban leisure culture, with couples mating and dating under religious constraints, combines with the imperial planning of parks and urban ornaments to create places that were completely unforeseen and yet are both functional and aesthetic. "Interdisciplinarity" is perhaps not the most appropriate designation for these approaches; rather they make creative use of what is at hand to present the manifold entanglements of urban reality in and through urban nature.

While the two tactics described above are about paying attention to what is visible and ongoing in the present, or the proximate past, *retrosembling* is about the practice of *historicizing urban natures* from a necessarily partial and situated perspective, in contrast to a universal, omniscient framework that by default cannot exist. As such, retrosembling generates histories of urban natures that are admittedly contested and contestable. Indeed, like any historical account, it provides a selective cast of actors, institutions, objects, places, and discourses in telling a particular story.[22] Thus, it understands historicizing as a polyphonic and multiactor process, assembling the views and voices of different social groups rather than those of the single author.[23] Garth Myers's work on the "multi-vocality" of contested urban environments of African cities is instructive as he draws on, and draws in, voices from experts, tribal leaders, hip-hop artists, and novelists and their respective particular framings of cities, places, and nature.[24] The same effect happens in the cinematic ethnography film *One Table Two Elephants* by Jacob von Heland and Henrik Ernstson.[25] Through following botanists, street dancers, and a Khoisan historian, the film problematizes a linear way of narrating history, one that would rely overly on colonial archives and scientific modes of truth making, to allow the subaltern—people from the Cape Flats, the historically marginalized area of the city, and their equally serious practices of making sense of urban nature—to appear and structure the film's account.[26] Such vernacular histories can be seen as elements in a more democratic articulation of *future urban natures not yet known*.

This mode of multipronged analysis helps to dislodge singular, essentialist, and universalist ideas of nature and to emphasize instead, with Jens Lachmund, that "multiple natures are locally embedded in historically specific social practices."[27] In this book this emphasis is demonstrated through particular practices of infrastructure engineering (see Joshua Lewis, chapter 2), the vernacular use of urban parks (Baviskar, chapter 8), processes of rediscovery through work in schools and archives (Spirn, chapter 4), ecological research that redefines the functional properties of ecosystems (Evans, chapter 11), economic-bureaucratic imaginaries (Chen, chapter 12), and social cooperation among amateur and professional "urbanists," or advocates of community (Walker, chapter 6). In these and other chapters in this book, retrosembling work is undertaken to understand, from the bottom up, the formation of urban natures, sometimes intentionally, sometimes unintentionally, sometimes in wildly different ways and with profoundly conflicting functions and politics, and then to situate them into the wider urban fabric.

This process pushes to the fore the quite self-evident point that urban form and urban future cannot be reduced to a given set of standard "solutions" or "policies" that could magically and universally enhance liveability and address environmental, health, and climate challenges. Rather than relying on external or universalist frameworks, the mode of analysis we are advocating contributes to calling attention to the multiple ways through which urban nature has been and will be known, used, protected, destroyed, and reworked.[28]

Finally, we take *situating* to mean the effort to *take each place seriously* for what it offers to theory. But situating, closely connected to the term "situated knowledges" as it has been developed across postcolonial, feminist, and critical science studies, also references a concern to recognize that when we leave universal knowledge claims behind, we embrace, as phrased by Gillian Rose, that "all knowledge [including the knowledge that we make ourselves] is produced in specific circumstances and that those circumstances shape it in some way."[29] This is what James Clifford refers to (in the third epigraph of chapter 1), that when we are are involved in making sense of a wider world, that is, in theorizing, both the places we have visited (our case studies, or archives) *and* ourselves as the traveler, our own positionality (class, race, ability etc.), are involved.[30] While we recognize that the chapters of this volume has developed less critical reflection on how positionality influences the writing of accounts, there is a creative impulse across the volume through taking each place seriously in tracing the active presence of nature in the urban fabric. Urban nature is *not* treated as a backdrop or ornament or something marginal, but central in interpreting wider urban and socioenvironmental processes. Through this *situating* of their account, authors suggest new ways for thinking urban nature that in turn troubles global and universal models of urban ecology.

For instance, in both chapters 2 and 5 this situating involves juxtaposing unexpected appearances of urban nature with different forms of (urban) design. In Louisiana's vast coastal landscape, heavy cypress stumps reappeared when marshlands were dug out during the twentieth century, undermining the "great siphon," an engineering feat to linearize a vast coastal landscape to maximize port and real estate profits and to secure the city from large-scale flooding. Likewise, scorpions in chapter 5 creep up through shower grates in Córdoba to disturb modern dreams of sanitized homes; and in designing an alternative shower grate, Ávila and Ernstson can consider a much wider more-than-human geography that includes children, fear, downstream pollution, and decaying sanitation infrastructure. By situating the cypress stumps and the scorpion in the richness of the details that New Orleans and Córdoba offers, the authors demonstrate the analytical power of *grounding* (situating, articulating, texturizing and retrosembling) in undermining universal and simplistic models of urban ecology.

However, they also invite creative ideas for comparative research. For instance, what are the comparative geographies that we can assemble to explore how Promethean dreams of controlling nature are still haunting our societies today? Or, what *affective ecologies* are in the making across different urban landscapes today, those that move beyond rational, scientistic ways of formulating ecology and that include an appreciation of what binds humans and nonhumans together through fear (of scorpions and flooding) and love (of our children and survival of our city)? The book provides several more such comparative invitations. We could explore how green fields attract multiple groups of residents and experts over time in similar but different ways across the Bay Area (Walker, chapter 6), Delhi (Baviskar, chapter 8), and Berlin (Lachmund, chapter 9). And contemporary Dalian (Hoffman, chapter 7) and post-apartheid Cape Town (van Sittert, chapter 10) offer empirical terrain to think comparatively about how state-supported classifications of indigenous and "alien" plants resonates with the role that urban nature played in upholding white "civility" in apartheid. The book is pregnant with such creative comparative geographies that can inspire future research within comparative urban environmentalism.

Across these interlinked tactics, the act of grounding, consequently, translates urban nature from a simplistic or singular entity—the "urban nature" *qua* "green space" standard—into an open-ended, multifaceted, and plural idea and materiality that is a vibrant, inseparable, constantly changing element of a fluid and extended urbanity. Apart from discovering and unpacking urban natures, and speaking to and about them from various locations, this book has tried to provide examples of how different scholars have responded to the challenge of grounding. They have thus generated multiple historically and geographically specific configurations of urban nature and also demonstrated various methods of how to accomplish this. Situating, articulating, texturizing, and retrosembling are in this respect individually helpful and mutually reinforcing methods for providing historically and empirically valid presentations of the increasingly important "natural" dimensions of the urban.

Act of Worlding: Locatable Practices of Translation

Having proposed an act of grounding, from within and below, we now turn to the act of *worlding*. As an analytical alternative to "globalization" or "the planetary," world*ing* is viewed as those ongoing, continually negotiated, and locatable practices by which thought, things, and places become part of a wider world.[31] For AbdouMaliq Simone it provides a lens to explore the practices through which urban residents access and participate in a "larger world."[32] Similarly, for Ananya Roy and Ahiwa Ong, it represents the "practices that creatively imagine and shape alternative social visions and configurations—i.e. 'worlds'—that are wider than what already exists in a given context."[33] Importantly, for them, the study of the practices of worlding by actors ranging from elites to subalterns invites a mid-range theorizing that "dives below high abstraction to hover over actual human projects and goals unfolding in myriad circumstances of possibility and contingency."[34] For our approach, the worlding of urban natures is about focusing on situated practices that strive to rework socioenvironmental relations in particular places, while at the same time viewing these practices as connected in tangible ways to practices elsewhere.

It is crucial for the understanding of the current phase of urbanization that we see worlding as an empirical—that is, a historical—phenomenon in its own right. Urbanization will not adapt to proclaimed policy or theory, nor will it emulate or imitate previous phases; urbanization will first of all happen and it is essential to insist on its being available in principle for even profound redirection and change. Urbanization, however broad and sweeping, is not planetary in the sense that it is an even force that flows around the world. Nor is it in any simplistic way part of a Western trajectory of globalization or progress, from Babylon to London, Los Angeles and, lately, Lagos, as it is sometimes presented. The concept of worlding works to replace a linear and simplistic arrow of time that moves in rhythm with (European, or today perhaps Chinese) progress, with a much more interconnected, notion of time and space as folded and intertwined where a locatable center is less certain. This decentring of origin uproots a problematic linear understanding of history, tackled head-on by Dipesh Chakrabarty in *Provincializing Europe*: "[Historicism, or the writing of history] consigned Indians, Africans, and other 'rude' nations to an imaginary waiting room of history [in which all nations and cities] were headed for the same destination ... but some people would arrive earlier than others."[35]

We are now in a different world. When Roy and Ong (re)launched the concept within urban studies in 2011, worlding was not only a tool to bring the global South on an ontologically and historically equal footing with the global North, but also the opposite, to equal treatment of the North. The global South is neither "the subaltern" nor an inherently progressive location, but the global South also has, as Roy insists, ideological projects toward world-dominance.[36] In the multipolar world order that has coalesced since the end of the Cold War, Brazilian, Chinese, Arabian, Indian, and other nationalist-cum-geopolitical projects are in formation.[37] It is a world where agency is distributed and effects are, too. Worlding, in this context, provides a theoretical frame in which the old pattern of an evolutionary diffusion of urban norms and standards from the global North to the global South is, if it ever were, unrealistic. Loans and impressions exist, and they are multidirectional.

Historians have contributed constructively in undermining the linear historicist paradigm. From critical studies of the Garden City or Le Corbusier planning ideas, to critiques of "the centralized networked city" in terms of basic infrastructure,[38] they have also provided yet other starting points to multiply understandings of urban natures. For their part, archaeologists and ethnobiologists have excavated what Paul Sinclair calls an "urban mind" that has origins going much farther back than the onset of urbanization in the West. Cities existed outside Europe many thousands of years ago, and urban environments have ever since retained a multiplicity of manifestations across world regions, not only in Asia and Middle East but also including the Americas, where nature was a strong presence in pre-Columbian urban centers in both South and North America.[39] This "urban mind" stretches out in space and time and decenters the place from which "the city" has been thought, providing novel locations and archives to rethink urban natures.[40]

A textured narrative approach thus also acknowledges the *historical* (or idiographic, as conceived by Wilhelm Windelband) character of cities rather than treating them as *phenotypes*, or individual representatives of a common (nomothetic) genotype or standard category.[41] Cities, in this respect, have more in common with nations, or wars, or most other historical phenomena: they do share much in common, but it is their component differences that make a difference—both for people and nonhumans of the city, and for theory construction. These differences are brought about, not through globalization or agglomeration as a "higher" force that structures cities along any simple lawlike formula, but through how ideas, technologies, and policies translate from one place to another and get "inserted" or "accommodated" in very specific ways, each gaining a dialect or flavor of the specific place. The tension between uniqueness *of* place and translation *across* places is what makes a reflective *grounding* and *worlding* comparative approach possible. In this volume, contributors have traced and retraced how apartheid and Western forms of racism were configured into forms of urban nature in Cape Town, New Orleans, and Lagos; how industrial projects linked to certain ideologies have shaped urban natures in Dalian and Yixing; and how scientific methodologies, invented in Berlin and Baltimore, have produced certain conceptions of urban nature, *qua* ecologies, which tended to hide the relational, social, or historical context from where these conceptions originated.

Locating cities in the world and taking their own trajectory and historical tensions and contestations seriously is of central concern to us. This does not mean to suggest that there is no commonality, but that thinking in patterns must constantly be referred back to empirical roots. Cities are simply so *interestingly dissimilar* that the very attempt to bring "the urban" into a formula, as for example in a "science of cities" or a global urban theory, is innately insufficient. Or put differently, urban experiences and urban spatial forms always have a historical baggage *of the world* at the same time as they are part of local politics and society, which affect their worldliness. While being in the world, they are also always unique. Worlding is, in this view, a looser kind of family resemblance, among other equally worldly, nonuniversal, and dissimilar spaces.[42]

A New Urban Narrative in the Making

This book has grown out of a range of fields, from environmental studies, human geography, and anthropology to urban history and urban studies. In our work, however, we have found how such distinctions, while obviously relevant, have failed to capture in full the integrative ambitions of our project to multiply the understandings of urban nature. To move further, we need wider intellectual collaborations—ones that also will have an effect on policy and broader discourse. There are at least four concluding points to make in developing a future agenda for comparative urban environmentalism.

First, through the sheer explosion of urban ecological and environmental studies in the last decades (which we reviewed in chapter 1), "the city" is undergoing a metamorphosis in environmental thought. In the past, naturalists contrasted the Eden of nature with the dark, Satanic mills of the city. In our time, the city has instead come to be increasingly portrayed as a wonderful organ of progress, opportunity, and, ultimately, sustainability. Neither image is realistic. While it is crucial to make "the city" central in discussions about sustainability, the new super narrative of the city—fueled by private-public partnerships high on "smart urbanism" and "green infrastructure," to grand sustainability visions of a city like Masdar City—is, if possible, even more idolized than how the city was vilified by English and North American novelists and poets in protoindustrial times. A grounding and worlding approach can slowly chip away and undermine such idealized, free-floating ideas about the city, building archives of textured accounts that can form the backbone of future scholarly projects and help to tie discussions about the future of cities and urbanization back into real cities and places.

Second, we see a possibility to work more closely with the emergent field of environmental humanities and draw upon its creative way of expanding the humanities to speak eloquently and richly into the environmental question, decentering the authority of the natural sciences. Through mobilizing much wider registers of knowing and engaging the public from the archives of humanist practice, from filmmaking, theater, literature, and art, there is a rapidly evolving set of methods and frameworks that urban environmentalists can draw upon.[43] Our inclusive approach can challenge—and complement—the sciences by partnering with the environmental humanities and use research as a way to attract and co-create publics that matter in public discussions.

Third, even as we have emphasized localized and situated methods of working, we also need to address the growing discourse on *the planetary*. An earthlier geohistorical notion, operating on a wider scale than "the global" or "the world," "the planetary" invites work that crosses the nature/culture divide and speaks to ways that urbanization is intertwined with climate change and ecological upheaval. Such a perspective is exemplified, on the one hand, in the environmental humanities by works like those of Ursula K. Heise (*Sense of Place and Sense of Planet*) and Timothy Morton (*Hyperobjects*).[44] What might it mean for a grounding and worlding approach to take cues from this intellectual terrain? It could mean to draw on eco-critical approaches from literary theory to think planetary living in and through more-than-human city living; or, to follow Bill McKibben in his book *Eaarth,* to trace out what a defamiliarized and already profoundaly changed planet feels like and is understood to be in a world of cities. "The planetary" has also been mobilized within neo-Marxian approaches as the "planetary urbanization" thesis. Developed from Henri Lefebvre by Neil Brenner and Christian Schmid, it, too, undermines the dichotomy of nature and culture, but with an explicit and expansive urban lens.[45] Rightfully critiqued since "the planetary" is too crude a signifier to make sense of the multiplicity of urban politics in a world of cities, which we have argued for here,[46] this analytic is nonetheless able to grasp, as does Martín Arboleda in his study of a Chilean mining town, an urban system that has reached a planetary level never attained before:

> [Planetary urbanization] constitutes an important analytic to understand new forms and scales of urban fetishisation [i.e., how capitalist urbanization hides the sites and networks of its own production]. Indeed, operational landscapes like Huasco, which have been completely engineered to provide low-end energy for the extraction of raw materials destined for consumption in remote corners of the globe, are the geographical imprints of these expanded, wide-sweeping metabolic exchanges [i.e., flows of materials and capital]. Like the sewage and piping networks that feed the life of cities…, Huasco—as a provider of cheap energy—has also been hidden from view [in feeding planetary urbanization].

In comparison to techno-scientific attempts to frame urbanization at a planetary level, from Earth System Science–inspired models to digitial mapping techniques and the now famous nighttime satellite images of Earth often drawn upon in popular discourse, the planetary urbanization thesis insists on the uneven nature of capitalist development, undermining such depoliticizing viewpoints as that of viewing "the planet" as a home for us all, a "spaceship Earth," or associated notions of "Earth Stewardship" and a "good Anthropocene." As Jason W. Moore puts it, "the genius [of capitalism] was to represent time as linear, space as flat, and nature as external."[47] The lesson is that if social relations of power, production, consumption, and so on are not changed, then neither will the conditions that can enable a more sustainable and just urban living on the planet. A grounding and worlding approach to urban nature can certainly stand in a dialectical, and thus productive, relation to the planetary urbanization thesis. The rubbing against each other of a neo-Marxist analysis with and against postcolonial openings, the planetary with and against the textured and the minute, could provide the space for students and activists to think critically and emancipatorily through textured places and unsettle mainstream taken-for-granted ideas on how to tackle "global" or "planetary" environmental challenges.[48]

Finally, it is indeed intriguing to speculate about the possible emergence of a new urban narrative, something that can hold our different projects of research, activism and practices together. Ananya Roy has invited "genres of urban scholarship" to gather a field in an inclusive, yet not cosy consensual way.[49] Surely it will not be a single narrative, but many narratives and imaginaries that can guide how we work, how we think, and what we aim for. Such an enterprise would not only be useful for transformational work on the emerging cities and their environments of tomorrow, but would assist in profoundly rethinking the idea of the city or "the urban" itself. If von Thünen nearly two centuries ago developed a textbook version of "the city" as a concentric distribution of production and consumption, this is now not only a relic, but also the image of a highly hierarchic, nonsustainable, and unequal city.[50] The new models and imaginaries that are now populating urban theory, from "world of cities," to "ordinary" and "worlding" cities, to "mobile"/"rouge"/"black"/"translocal" urbanism, to "cities at the speed of light," or "planetary urbanization," offers new lines of flight to help rethink our urban world, its relation to the environment, politics, and ourselves.

Grounding and worlding as a means for understanding practices and places in textured ways and as connected to multiple elsewheres, offers a possibility of not losing ourselves in either the "walled segregation" of the particular or a "dilution in the universal," as phrased by Aime Césaire.[51] These ideas can carry real weight in the necessary work to question and undermine simplistic models and inherited biases of what the city and the environment represent. They can push for reform in urban thinking in professional education and policy formation. And they can assist in writing from multiple locations to uncover urban natures and their political ecologies past and future.

Notes

1. Quotations from Whatmore (2009, p. 595), with references to Isabelle Stengers and Bruno Latour. See also Lewis and Ernstson's (2019, section 2.4) work on "situational dissensus" in Louisiana coastal landscape.

2. Robinson 2014.

3. McFarlane 2009.

4. See McCann and Ward (2011), who emphasise how this circulation is globally uneven, structured by capital and knowledge production.

5. Ranganathan and Balazs 2015.

6. van Dooren and Rose 2012.

7. Lewis, chapter 2 in this volume; Lewis and Ernstson 2019.

8. Rather than, as Giovanna Di Chiro (1996) writes in the concluding chapter of *Uncommon Ground* (Cronon 1996, p. 452), as "a unified statement [to] reassure 'common ground,'" the commitment was "to develop...a critical discourse about 'nature' and 'environment' that did not attempt to come to final closure [but to] move toward 'uncommon ground.'"

9. Said 1983, pp. 24, 226–235; Simone 2001; Tsing 2005; Roy and Ong 2011.

10. See chapter 1, where we develop our critical, reflective approach based primarily on postcolonial approaches. As we write there in an endnote, we are not building from, nor developing "grounded theory" (Glaser and Strauss 1967).

11. Latour 2005; Bennet 2010.

12. Massey 2005.

13. Hägerstrand 1993.

14. Smith 1984; Sörlin and Warde 2009, pp. 1–19.

15. We have studied social articulation as a key entry point to understanding environmental struggles. See Sörlin (1998); Ernstson and Sörlin (2009, 2013); Ernstson (2013); and Erixon Aalto and Ernstson (2017).

16. Clifford 1989, p. 4.

17. Ibid.

18. See chapter 1 this volume on this point, with reference to Said (1983), Clifford (1989), and postcolonial/Southern urbanism (Parnell and Oldfield 2014).

19. Law 2009; Mol 2010; Ernstson and Lewis 2013.

20. Pieterse and Simone 2012; Pieterse 2014.

21. From a rich literature, including Sitte (1889); Anderson (1923); Geddes (1947) (with a historical critique by Datta 2013); and Geertz (1973).

22. See Cronon (1992), and often emphasized by Swyngedouw (2004).

23. The concept of *retrosembling* can be seen as bringing together a set of words—"resembling," "retrofitting," "assembling," and "reassembling"—that can help in thinking about how to write history. "Resembling" relates to the notion of constructing something that carries validity and truth; "retrofitting" involves going back in time to trace urban natures to their local roots, thus enhancing the practice of urban history; and "assembling" or "reassembling" is a conscious act of responsibly constructing an account that is partial and situated, yet evidence based and creative, as in for instance Bruno Latour's *Reassembling the Social* (2005).

24. See, for instance, Karvonen and Yocom (2011); Myers (2016, 2019); Erixon Aalto and Ernstson (2017).

25. The film (von Heland and Ernstson 2018) interrogates how race, nature, and knowledge are intimately intertwined in Cape Town as a postcolonial city and is inspired by Jean Rouch's (2003) work on "ciné-ethnography," but also on Premesh Lalu's (2009) *The Deaths of Hintsa*, which poses the question on how to write history in the postcolony.

26. The *histories of the margin* are not marginal at all, but rather make way for Dipesh Chakrabarty's (2000) idea of *History 1* (of capital) and *History 2* (of subalterns) as dialectically intertwined.

27. Lachmund 2013, p. 237.

28. McFarlane and Robinson 2012.

29. Rose 1997, p. 305.

30. As concepts, *situating* and *situated knowleges* draw upon the sensibilities developed by Edward Said (1983) and Gayatri Chakravorty Spivak (1988) in postcolonial studies,

and Gillian Rose (1997) and Donna Haraway (1998) and others in eco-feminist and critical science writing. More recently, there have been important developments in this direction of feminist (Truelove 2011; Harcourt and Nelson 2015), embodied (Doshi 2016), and postcolonial/situated urban political ecology (Lawhon, Ernstson, and Silver 2014; see also Ernstson 2013; Silver 2014; Lawhon et al. 2016).

31. Tsing 2005; Roy and Ong 2011. As a concept, worlding has a long tradition; in particular in Edward Said (1983, pp. 21–24, 226–235), who, in discussing "worldiness" and the role of the (literary) critic, emphasized the need to be connected and grounded when one make judgments about the world: "For Said," here quoting from Pal Ahluwalia (2005, p. 141), "theory can be effective only when it is located firmly within the world," meaning that it needs to be connected to real places. Or else we risk "affirming the values of our, that is, European, dominant elite culture" (Said 1983, p. 21).

32. Simone 2001. For an example, see Colin McFarlane's (2009) discussion about "translocal assemblages" in relation to the Slum-Dwellers International social movement to exchange practices, methods, and experiences of resistance and learning across cities of India, South Africa, Zimbabwe, the Philippines, and elsewhere.

33. Roy and Ong 2011, e-book location 662.

34. Ibid., e-book location 656.

35. Chakrabarty 2000, p. 8.

36. Roy 2014.

37. Cardoso 2015.

38. For historical studies, see the edited volume by Bigon and Katz (2014) on *Garden Cities and Colonial Planning* with studies from Africa and Palestine, Glover (2012) on the garden city in India, and Nilsson (2006) on water and sanitation systems in Kampala, Uganda. For recent critique and arguments to move beyond the imaginary of the centralized networked city, see Furlong (2014); Silver (2014); Coutard and Rutherford (2016); Monstadt and Schramm (2017); Lawhon et al. (2018).

39. Fernández-Armesto 1987; Heckenberger 2009; Barthel, Sörlin, and Ljungqvist 2010; Sinclair et al. 2010.

40. *The Urban Mind*, edited by Sinclair et al. (2010) reinterprets ancient forms of urbanization as economy, culture, and ecology and includes studies of Istanbul, the Middle East, and Pre-Colombian civilizations of Latin America.

41. Wilhelm Windelband (1901) developed the Neo-Kantian terms "idiographic" and "nomothetic" to describe two distinct approaches to knowledge: either a tendency to specify and understand the meaning of contingent, unique, and often cultural phenomena (typical for the humanities) or a tendency to generalize and derive laws to explain a phenomena (typical for the natural sciences).

42. Wittgenstein 2001 [1953].

43. Sörlin 2012; Heise, Christensen, and Niemann 2017.

44. Heise 2008; McKibben 2010; Morton 2013.

45. Brenner and Schmid 2012; Arboleda 2016.

46. Leitner and Sheppard 2016; Peake 2015.

47. Moore 2014, quotation from second paragraph.

48. Ernstson and Swyngedouw 2019.

49. See Roy (2014, p. 13), as well as Robinson and Roy (2015, p. 182) on "global urbanisms."

50. von Thünen 1826.

51. Césaire 2010 [1956].

References

Ahluwalia, Pal. 2005. "Out of Africa: Post-Structuralism's Colonial Roots." *Postcolonial Studies* 8(2): 137–154.

Anderson, Nels. 1923. *The Hobo: The Sociology of the Homeless Man*. Chicago: University of Chicago Press.

Arboleda, Martín. 2016. "In the Nature of the Non-City: Expanded Infrastructural Networks and the Political Ecology of Planetary Urbanisation." *Antipode* 48(2): 233–251.

Barthel, Stephan, Sverker Sörlin, and J. Ljungqvist. 2010. "Innovative Memory and Resilient Cities: Echoes from Ancient Constantinople." In *The Urban Mind: Cultural and Environmental Dynamics*, edited by Paul Sinclair, Frands Herschend, Christian Isendahl, and Gullög Nordquist, 391–405. Uppsala: Uppsala University, Department of Archaeology and Ancient History.

Bennet, Jane. 2010. *Vibrant Matter: A Political Ecology of Things*. Durham, NC: Duke University Press.

Bigon, Liora, and Yossi Katz, eds. 2014. *Garden Cities and Colonial Planning: Transnationality and Urban Ideas in Africa and Palestine*. Oxford: Oxford University Press.

Brenner, Neil, and Christian Schmid. 2012. "Planetary Urbanization." In *Urban Constellations*, edited by Matthew Gandy, 10–13. Berlin: Jovis.

Cardoso, Ricardo. 2015. "The Crude Urban Revolution: Land Markets, Planning Forms and the Making of a New Luanda." Unpublished PhD diss., University of California, Berkeley.

Césaire, Aimé. 2010 [1956]. "Letter to Maurice Thorez." Translation by Chike Jeffers. *Social Text* 28(2): 145–152.

Chakrabarty, Dipesh. 2000. *Provincializing Europe: Postcolonial Thought and Historical Difference.* Princeton, NJ: Princeton University Press.

Clifford, James. 1989. "Notes on Travel and Theory." *Inscriptions* 5: 177–188.

Coutard, Olivier, and Jonathan Rutherford, eds. 2016. *Beyond the Networked City: Infrastructure Reconfigurations and Urban Change in the North and South.* London: Routledge.

Cronon, William. 1992. "A Place for Stories: Nature, History, and Narrative." *Journal of American History* 78(4): 1347–1376.

Cronon, William, ed. 1996. *Uncommon Ground: Rethinking the Human Place in Nature.* New York: Norton.

Datta, Partho. 2013. "How Modern Planning Came to Calcutta." *Planning Perspectives* 28(1): 139–147.

Di Chiro, Giovanna. 1996. "Nature as Community: The Convergence of Environment and Social Justice." In *Uncommon Ground: Rethinking the Human Place in Nature*, edited by William Cronon, 298–320. New York: Norton.

Doshi, Sapana. 2017. "Embodied Urban Political Ecology: Five Propositions." *Area* 49(1): 125–128.

Erixon Aalto, Hanna, and Henrik Ernstson. 2017. "Of Plants, High Lines and Horses: Civics and Designers in the Relational Articulation of Values of Urban Natures." *Landscape and Urban Planning* 157: 309–321.

Ernstson, Henrik. 2013. "Re-Translating Nature in Post-Apartheid Cape Town: The Material Semiotics of People and Plants at Bottom Road." Actor-Network Theory for Development Working Paper Series, edited by Richard Heeks, no. 4. Manchester: Institute for Development Policy and Management, School of Environment, Education and Development, University of Manchester. http://hummedia.manchester.ac.uk/institutes/cdi/resources/cdi_ant4d/ANT4DWorkingPaper4Ernstson.pdf.

Ernstson, Henrik, and Joshua A. Lewis. 2013. "The Alchemy of Transformation: On the Impoverishment of Socio-Ecological Imaginaries." Working Paper Series, Division of History of Science, Technology, and Environment, KTH Royal Institute of Technology, Stockholm.

Ernstson, Henrik, and Sverker Sörlin. 2009. "Weaving Protective Stories: Connective Practices to Articulate Holistic Values in the Stockholm National Urban Park." *Environment and Planning A* 41(6): 1460–1479.

Ernstson, Henrik, and Sverker Sörlin. 2013. "Ecosystem Services as Technology of Globalization: On Articulating Values in Urban Nature." *Ecological Economics* 86: 274–284.

Ernstson, Henrik, and Erik Swyngedouw. 2019. *Urban Political Ecology in the Anthropo-Obscene: Interruptions and Possibilities.* Abingdon, UK: Routledge.

Fernández-Armesto, Felipe. 1987. *Before Columbus: Exploration and Colonization from the Mediterranean to the Atlantic, 1229–1492*. Philadelphia: University of Pennsylvania Press.

Furlong, Kathryn. 2014. "STS beyond the 'Modern Infrastructure Ideal': Extending Theory by Engaging with Infrastructure Challenges in the South." *Technology in Society* 38 (August): 139–147.

Geddes, Patrick. 1947. "Town Planning in Kapurthala: A Report to H.H. the Maharaja of Kapurthala, 1917." In *Patrick Geddes in India*, edited by Jacqueline Tyrwhitt, 24–27. London: Lund Humphries.

Geertz, Clifford. 1973. *The Interpretation of Cultures: Selected Essays*. New York: Basic Books.

Glaser, Barney G., and Anselm L. Strauss. 1967. *The Discovery of Grounded Theory*. Routledge: London.

Glover, William J. 2012. "The Troubled Passage from 'Village Communities' to Planned New Town Developments in Mid-Twentieth-Century South Asia." *Urban History* 39(1): 108–127.

Hägerstrand, Torsten. 1993. "Region och miljö—sammanfattning av ett projekt om ekologiska perspektiv på den rumsliga närings-och bosättningsstrukturen" [Region and environment—Summary of a project about ecological perspectives on the spatial structure of production and habitation]. *NordREFO* 5: 229–237.

Haraway, Donna J. 1998. "Situated Knowledges: The Science Question in Feminism and the Privilege of Partial Perspective." *Feminist Studies* 14(3): 575–599.

Harcourt, Wendy, and Ingrid L. Nelson. 2015. "Introduction: Are We 'Green' Yet? And the Violence of Asking Such a Question." In *Practicing Feminist Political Ecologies: Moving beyond the Green Economy*, edited by Wendy Harcourt and Ingrid L. Nelson, 1–26. London: Zed Books.

Heckenberger, Michael. 2009. "Lost Garden Cities: Pre-Columbian Life in the Amazon: The Amazon Tropical Forest Is Not as Wild as It Looks." *Scientific American* 301(4): 64–71.

Heise, Ursula K. 2008. *Sense of Place and Sense of Planet: The Environmental Imagination of the Global*. Oxford: Oxford University Press.

Heise, Ursula K., Jon Christensen, and Michelle Niemann, eds. 2017. *The Routledge Companion to the Environmental Humanities*. London: Routledge.

Karvonen, Andrew, and Ken Yocom. 2011. "The Civics of Urban Nature: Enacting Hybrid Landscapes." *Environment and Planning A* 43(6): 1305–1322.

Lachmund, Jens. 2013. *Greening Berlin: The Co-production of Science, Politics, and Urban Nature*. Cambridge, MA: MIT Press.

Lalu, Premesh. 2009. *The Deaths of Hintsa: Postapartheid South Africa and the Shape of Recurring Pasts.* Cape Town: HSRC Press.

Latour, Bruno. 2005. *Reassembling the Social: An Introduction to Actor-Network Theory.* Oxford: Oxford University Press.

Law, John. 2009. "Actor Network Theory and Material Semiotics." In *The New Blackwell Companion to Social Theory,* edited by Bryan S. Turner, 141–158. Malden, MA: Wiley-Blackwell.

Lawhon, Mary, Henrik Ernstson, and Jonathan D. Silver. 2014. "Provincializing Urban Political Ecology: Towards a Situated UPE through African Urbanism." *Antipode* 46(2): 497–516.

Lawhon, Mary, David Nilsson, Jonathan Silver, Henrik Ernstson, and Shuaib Lwasa. 2018. "Thinking through Heterogeneous Infrastructure Configurations." *Urban Studies* 55(4): 720–732.

Lawhon, Mary, Jonathan D. Silver, Henrik Ernstson, and Joe Pierce. 2016. "Unlearning [Un]Located Ideas in the Provincialization of Urban Theory." *Regional Studies* 50(9): 1611–1622.

Leitner, H., and E. Sheppard. 2016. "Provincializing Critical Urban Theory: Extending the Ecosystem of Possibilities." *International Journal of Urban and Regional Research* 40(1): 228–235.

Lewis, Joshua A., and Henrik Ernstson. 2019. "Contesting the Coast: Ecosystems as Infrastructure in the Mississippi River Delta." *Progress in Planning* 129: 1–30.

Massey, Doreen. 2005. *For Space.* London: Sage.

McCann, Eugene, and Kevin Ward, eds. 2011. *Mobile Urbanism: Cities and Policymaking in the Global Age.* Minneapolis: University of Minnesota Press.

McFarlane, Colin. 2009. "Translocal Assemblages: Space, Power and Social Movements." *Geoforum* 40(4): 561–567.

McFarlane, Colin, and Jennifer Robinson. 2012. "Introduction—Experiments in Comparative Urbanism." *Urban Geography* 33(6): 765–773.

McKibben, Bill. 2010. *Eaarth: Making a Life on a Tough New Planet.* New York: Henry Holt.

Mol, Annemarie. 2010. "Actor-Network Theory: Sensitive Terms and Enduring Tensions." *Kölner Zeitschrift Für Soziologie Und Sozialpshychologie* 50(1): 253–269.

Monstadt, Jochen, and Sophie Schramm. 2017. "Toward the Networked City? Translating Technological Ideals and Planning Models in Water and Sanitation Systems in Dar Es Salaam." *International Journal of Urban and Regional Research* 41(1): 104–125.

Moore, Jason W. 2014. "The Origins of Cheap Nature: From Use-Value to Abstract Social Nature." https://jasonwmoore.wordpress.com/2014/04/07/the-origins-of-cheap-nature-from-use-value-to-abstract-social-nature/.

Morton, Timothy. 2013. *Hyperobjects: Philosophy and Ecology after the End of the World*. Minneapolis: University of Minnesota Press.

Myers, Garth. 2016. *Urban Environments in Africa: A Critical Analysis of Environmental Politics*. Bristol, UK: Policy Press.

Myers, Garth. 2019. "Multi-Vocal Urban Political Ecology: Towards New Sensibilities." In *Urban Political Ecology in the Anthropo-Obscene: Interruptions and Possibilities*, edited by Henrik Ernstson and Erik Swyngedouw, pp. 148–164. Oxford: Routledge.

Nilsson, David. 2006. "A Heritage of Unsustainability? Reviewing the Origin of the Large-Scale Water and Sanitation System in Kampala, Uganda." *Environment and Urbanization* 18(2): 369–385.

Parnell, Susan, and Sophie Oldfield, eds. 2014. *The Routledge Handbook on Cities of the Global South*. London: Routledge.

Peake, L. 2015. "The Twenty-First Century Quest for Feminism and the Global Urban." *International Journal of Urban and Regional Research* 40(1): 219–227.

Pieterse, Edgar. 2014. "Africa's Urban Revolution: Epistemic Adventures." In recorded talk for *Great Texts/Big Questions: GIPCA Lectures Series*, April 30. Cape Town: Gordon Institute for Performing and Creative Arts. http://www.gipca.uct.ac.za/project/great-texts-edgar-pieterse/.

Pieterse, Edgar, and AbdouMaliq Simone. 2012. *Rogue Urbanism: Emergent African Cities*. London: Jacana Media.

Ranganathan, Malini, and Carolina Balazs. 2015. "Water Marginalization at the Urban Fringe: Environmental Justice and Urban Political Ecology across the North-South Divide." *Urban Geography* 36(3): 403–423.

Robinson, Jennifer. 2014. "New Geographies of Theorizing the Urban: Putting Comparison to Work for Global Urban Studies." In *The Routledge Handbook on Cities of the Global South*, edited by Susan Parnell and Sophie Oldfield, 57–69. London: Routledge.

Robinson, Jennifer, and Ananya Roy. 2015. "Debate on Global Urbanisms and the Nature of Urban Theory." *International Journal of Urban and Regional Research* 40(1): 181–186.

Rose, Gillian. 1997. "Situating Knowledges: Positionality, Reflexivities and Other Tactics." *Progress in Human Geography* 21(3): 305–320.

Rouch, Jean. 2003. *Ciné-Ethnography*. Edited and Translated by Steven Feld. Minneapolis: University of Minnesota Press.

Roy, Ananya. 2014. "Worlding the South: Toward a Postcolonial Urban Theory." In *The Routledge Handbook on Cities of the Global South*, edited by Susan Parnell and Sophie Oldfield, 9–20. London: Routledge.

Roy, Ananya, and Aihwa Ong. 2011. "Introduction: Worlding Cities, or the Art of Being Global." In *Worlding Cities: Asian Experiments and the Art of Being Global*, edited by Ananya Roy and Aihwa Ong, 1–26. Malden, MA: Wiley-Blackwell.

Said, Edward. 1983. *The World, the Text and the Critic*. Cambridge, MA: Harvard University Press.

Silver, Jonathan. 2014. "Incremental Infrastructures: Material Improvisation and Social Collaboration across Post-Colonial Accra." *Urban Geography* 35(6): 788–804.

Simone, AbdouMaliq. 2001. "On the Worlding of African Cities." *African Studies Review* 44(2): 15–41.

Sinclair, Paul J. J., Gullög Nordquist, Frands Herschend, and Christian Isendahl. 2010. *The Urban Mind: Cultural and Environmental Dynamics*. Uppsala: Uppsala University: Department of Archaeology and Ancient History.

Sitte, Camillo. 1889. *Der Städtebau nach seinen künstlerischen Grundsätzen* [City planning according to artistic principles]. Vienna: Verlag von Carl Glaeser.

Smith, Neil. 1984. *Uneven Development: Nature, Capital and the Production of Space*. Oxford: Basil Blackwell.

Sörlin, Sverker. 1998. "Monument and Memory: Landscape Imagery and the Articulation of Territory." *Worldviews: Environment, Culture, Religion* 2: 269–279.

Sörlin, Sverker. 2012. "Environmental Humanities: Why Should Biologists Interested in the Environment Take the Humanities Seriously?" *Bioscience* 62(9): 788–789.

Sörlin, Sverker, and Paul Warde. 2009. "Making the Environment Historical—An Introduction." In *Nature's End: History and the Environment*, edited by Sverker Sörlin and Paul Warde, 1–19. London: Palgrave Macmillan.

Spivak, Gayatri Chakravorty. 1988. "Can the Subaltern Speak?" In *Marxism and the Interpretation of Culture*, edited by Cary Nelson and Lawrence Grossberg, 271–313. London: Macmillan.

Swyngedouw, Erik. 2004. *Social Power and the Urbanization of Water*. Oxford: Oxford University Press.

Truelove, Yaffa. 2011. "(Re-)Conceptualizing Water Inequality in Delhi, India, through a Feminist Political Ecology Framework." *Geoforum* 42(2): 143–152.

Tsing, Anna. 2005. *Friction: An Ethnography of Global Connection*. Princeton, NJ: Princeton University Press.

van Dooren, Thom, and Deborah Bird Rose. 2012. "Storied-Places in a Multispecies City." *Humanimalia* 3: 1–27.

von Heland, Jacob, and Henrik Ernstson. 2018. *One Table Two Elephants*. Documentary film, 84 minutes. World premiere at CPH:DOX Copenhagen International Film Festival, March 20 http://bit.ly/1T2E-film.

von Thünen, Johann Heinrich. 1826. *Der isoli[e]rte Staat in Beziehung auf Landwirtschaft und Nationalökonomie* [The isolated city in relation to agriculture and economics]. Hamburg: Perthes.

Whatmore, Sarah. 2009. "Mapping Knowledge Controversies: Environmental Science, Democracy and the Redistribution of Expertise." *Progress in Human Geography* 33(5): 587–598.

Windelband, Wilhelm. 1901. *A History of Philosophy*. 2nd ed. New York: Macmillan.

Wittgenstein, Ludwig. 2001 [1953]. *Philosophical Investigations*. Oxford: Blackwell.

Contributors

Volume Editors

Henrik Ernstson is Lecturer in Human Geography at The University of Manchester. He is also part-time Research Fellow at KTH Royal Institute of Technology in Stockholm, and in 2018 he was appointed Honorary Associate Professor at the African Centre for Cities at the University of Cape Town. He has held postdoctoral positions at Stanford University, Stockholm University, and the University of Cape Town. He is an interdisciplinary urban environmental scholar who has led research in Cape Town, Kampala, Luanda, New Orleans, and Stockholm and produced analyses of collective action, urban infrastructure, environmental expertise, and postcolonial urbanisms. In 2012 he founded the Situated Ecologies Platform, which draws on art, design, and film to expand critical modes of research, and in 2014 he cofounded the Situated Urban Political Ecologies Collective. His work has been published in *Antipode*, *Progress in Planning*, *Theory, Culture & Society*, and *Urban Studies*, among others, but also in environmental science journals such as *Ecology & Society*, and *Landscape & Urban Planning*. His latest book, coedited with Erik Swyngedouw, is *Urban Political Ecology in the Anthropo-Obscene: Interruptions and Possibilities* (Routledge, 2019). With Jacob von Heland, he is developing a film-based research practice, and in 2018 at the CPH:DOX Copenhagen film festival their cinematic ethnography *One Table Two Elephants* (84 minutes) was premiered, which interrogates how race, nature, and knowledge are intimately intertwined in a postcolonial city.

Sverker Sörlin is Professor of Environmental History in the Division of History of Science Technology and Environment at KTH Royal Institute of Technology, Stockholm, where he was also cofounder of the KTH Environmental Humanities Laboratory in 2011. He has held visiting positions at the University of California, Berkeley, the University of Cambridge, the University of Oslo, the University of Cape Town, the University of British Columbia, and the Institute for Advanced Study in Princeton, NJ. Over a long career he has researched the history of natural resources, nationalism, urban and landscape history, and government policies on research and higher education. In more recent years he has focused on the science, history, and politics of climate change. He is coeditor of *The Future of Nature: Documents of Global Change* (Yale University Press, 2013) and coauthor of *The Environment: A History of the Idea* (Johns Hopkins University Press, 2018), both with Libby Robin, Australian National University, and Paul Warde, University of Cambridge. He also has served as a policy advisor to the Swedish government on environmental policies and urban development and, starting in 2018, became a member of Sweden's Climate Policy Council. In Sweden he is also a public intellectual and a prize-winning author of popular history and narrative nonfiction.

Chapter Authors

Martín Ávila is a designer, researcher, and Professor of Design at Konstfack (School of Arts, Crafts, and Design) in Stockholm. He works through a design-driven research method that addresses forms of interspecies cohabitation. His postdoctoral project, "Symbiotic Tactics" (2013–2016), explored cohabitation with scorpions, cockroaches, and nonhuman animals that we dislike or that pose risks to us, without attempting to elide the tensions of such cohabitation. See also www.martinavila.com.

Amita Baviskar is Professor of Sociology at the Institute of Economic Growth, Delhi. Her research focuses on the cultural politics of environment and development in rural and urban India. Her book *In the Belly of the River: Tribal Conflicts over Development in the Narmada Valley* (Oxford University Press, 1995) and her other writings explore the themes of resource rights, popular resistance, and discourses of environmentalism. She is currently studying food and agrarian environments in western India. Her recent publications include the edited books *Contested Grounds: Essays on Nature, Culture and Power* (Oxford University Press, 2008); *Elite and Everyman: The Cultural Politics of the Indian Middle Classes* (with Raka Ray) (Routledge, 2011); and *First Garden of the Republic: Nature in the President's Estate* (Government of India, 2016). She has taught at the University of Delhi and has been a visiting scholar at Stanford University, Cornell University, Yale University, Sciences Po in Paris, and the University of California at Berkeley. She was awarded the Infosys Prize for Social Sciences in 2010.

Jia-Ching Chen is Assistant Professor of Global Studies at the University of California, Santa Barbara. His research interests lie at the intersections of urban, development, and environmental studies. Currently, his research examines China's role in shaping the global green economy and the spread of Chinese urban planning expertise through its international development activities.

James Evans is a professor in the Department of Geography at the School of Environment, Education and Development, The University of Manchester. His research focuses on how cities learn to become more sustainable in the face of multiple challenges, and he currently leads projects on smart cities, informal mobility, and resilience. He also leads the Smart and Sustainable Cities research theme as part of the Manchester Urban Institute.

Lisa M. Hoffman is Professor of Urban Studies at the University of Washington, Tacoma. She holds a PhD in cultural anthropology and an MA in China Regional Studies. Her research focuses primarily on contemporary governmental and subject formations in China, with attention to questions of urban processes and spatialities. She is the author of *Patriotic Professionalism in Urban China: Fostering Talent* (Temple University Press, 2010) and coeditor (with Heather Merrill) of *Spaces of Danger: Culture and Power in the Everyday* (University of Georgia Press, 2015). She also has worked on US-based projects on topics such as subject formation and homelessness, and she is currently engaged in a project on identity and community at Tacoma's Japanese Language School.

Jens Lachmund is Lecturer in Science and Technology Studies at Maastricht University. His has published widely on themes in the historical sociology of medicine. In his more recent research he has drawn on concepts and methods from the social studies of sciences to explore the relationship between nature, science, and the politics of space. His books include *Greening Berlin: The Co-Production of Science, Politics, and Urban Nature* (MIT Press, 2013). With Raf de Bont he is coeditor of the volume *Spatializing the History of Ecology* (Routledge, 2016).

Joshua Lewis is a geographer and urban ecologist at Tulane University in New Orleans. His research examines the intersection of water infrastructure, ecosystem change, and urban politics.

Lindsay Sawyer is an urbanist who is currently a Leverhulme Early Career Fellow in the Department of Urban Studies and Planning at the University of Sheffield, and she is an Honorary Fellow at the Global Development Institute at The University of Manchester. Since 2011 she has been part of the project "Planetary Urbanization in Comparative Perspective" involving comparisons of Lagos with Kolkata, Shenzhen, Mexico City, and Istanbul. Her research in Lagos has focused on the plot-by-plot development of ordinary neighborhoods and has considered what "informal" means in regard to African cities, the role of customary authorities in the urbanization process, and ways to analyze, represent, and compare grounded urban realities.

Anne Whiston Spirn is the Cecil and Ida Green Professor of Landscape Architecture and Planning at the Massachusetts Institute of Technology. The American Planning Association credits her first book, *The Granite Garden: Urban Nature and Human Design* (Basic Books, 1984), with launching the ecological urbanism movement and named it one of the one hundred most important books of the twentieth century. Her second book, *The Language of Landscape* (Yale University Press, 1998), argues that landscape is a form of language with its own grammar and metaphors, and that failure to learn and use this language endangers humanity. In recent books Spirn has continued to develop the concept of landscape literacy as part of visual thinking.

Since 1987 Spirn has directed the West Philadelphia Landscape Project (WPLP), an action research project whose mission is to restore the natural environment and rebuild community through strategic design, planning, and education programs. In 2001 Spirn received Japan's International Cosmos Prize for "contributions to the harmonious coexistence of nature and mankind." For more, see www.annewhiston spirn.com.

Lance van Sittert is Associate Professor in the Department of Historical Studies at the University of Cape Town. He has written extensively on the environmental histories of the city and its hinterland.

Richard A. Walker is Professor Emeritus of Geography at the University of California, Berkeley, where he taught for forty years. He works in the fields of economic, urban, and environmental geography, chiefly with a focus on California and the continental United States. His books include *The Capitalist Imperative* (with Michael Storper) (Blackwell, 1989), *The New Social Economy* (with Andrew Sayer) (Blackwell, 1992), *The Conquest of Bread* (New Press, 2004), *The Country in the City* (University of Washington Press, 2007), and the *Atlas of California* (with Suresh Lodha) (University of California Press, 2013). His latest book is *Pictures of a Gone City: Tech and the Dark Side of Prosperity in the San Francisco Bay Area* (PM Press, 2018). He is currently director of the Living New Deal project, which documents and maps all public works of the 1930s (https://livingnewdeal.org). Dr. Walker splits his time between Berkeley and Burgundy, France.

Index

Urban and Industrial Environments

Series editor: Robert Gottlieb, Henry R. Luce Professor of Urban and Environmental Policy, Occidental College

Ronald Sandler and Phaedra C. Pezzullo, eds., *Environmental Justice and Environmentalism: The Social Justice Challenge to the Environmental Movement*

Julie Sze, *Noxious New York: The Racial Politics of Urban Health and Environmental Justice*

Robert D. Bullard, ed., *Growing Smarter: Achieving Livable Communities, Environmental Justice, and Regional Equity*

Ann Rappaport and Sarah Hammond Creighton, *Degrees That Matter: Climate Change and the University*

Michael Egan, *Barry Commoner and the Science of Survival: The Remaking of American Environmentalism*

David J. Hess, *Alternative Pathways in Science and Industry: Activism, Innovation, and the Environment in an Era of Globalization*

Peter F. Cannavò, *The Working Landscape: Founding, Preservation, and the Politics of Place*

Paul Stanton Kibel, ed., *Rivertown: Rethinking Urban Rivers*

Kevin P. Gallagher and Lyuba Zarsky, *The Enclave Economy: Foreign Investment and Sustainable Development in Mexico's Silicon Valley*

David N. Pellow, *Resisting Global Toxics: Transnational Movements for Environmental Justice*

Robert Gottlieb, *Reinventing Los Angeles: Nature and Community in the Global City*

David V. Carruthers, ed., *Environmental Justice in Latin America: Problems, Promise, and Practice*

Tom Angotti, *New York for Sale: Community Planning Confronts Global Real Estate*

Paloma Pavel, ed., *Breakthrough Communities: Sustainability and Justice in the Next American Metropolis*

Anastasia Loukaitou-Sideris and Renia Ehrenfeucht, *Sidewalks: Conflict and Negotiation over Public Space*

David J. Hess, *Localist Movements in a Global Economy: Sustainability, Justice, and Urban Development in the United States*

Julian Agyeman and Yelena Ogneva-Himmelberger, eds., *Environmental Justice and Sustainability in the Former Soviet Union*

Jason Corburn, *Toward the Healthy City: People, Places, and the Politics of Urban Planning*

JoAnn Carmin and Julian Agyeman, eds., *Environmental Inequalities Beyond Borders: Local Perspectives on Global Injustices*

Louise Mozingo, *Pastoral Capitalism: A History of Suburban Corporate Landscapes*

Gwen Ottinger and Benjamin Cohen, eds., *Technoscience and Environmental Justice: Expert Cultures in a Grassroots Movement*

Samantha MacBride, *Recycling Reconsidered: The Present Failure and Future Promise of Environmental Action in the United States*

Andrew Karvonen, *Politics of Urban Runoff: Nature, Technology, and the Sustainable City*

Daniel Schneider, *Hybrid Nature: Sewage Treatment and the Contradictions of the Industrial Ecosystem*

Catherine Tumber, *Small, Gritty, and Green: The Promise of America's Smaller Industrial Cities in a Low-Carbon World*

Sam Bass Warner and Andrew H. Whittemore, *American Urban Form: A Representative History*

John Pucher and Ralph Buehler, eds., *City Cycling*

Stephanie Foote and Elizabeth Mazzolini, eds., *Histories of the Dustheap: Waste, Material Cultures, Social Justice*

David J. Hess, *Good Green Jobs in a Global Economy: Making and Keeping New Industries in the United States*

Joseph F. C. DiMento and Clifford Ellis, *Changing Lanes: Visions and Histories of Urban Freeways*

Joanna Robinson, *Contested Water: The Struggle Against Water Privatization in the United States and Canada*

William B. Meyer, *The Environmental Advantages of Cities: Countering Commonsense Antiurbanism*

Rebecca L. Henn and Andrew J. Hoffman, eds., *Constructing Green: The Social Structures of Sustainability*

Peggy F. Barlett and Geoffrey W. Chase, eds., *Sustainability in Higher Education: Stories and Strategies for Transformation*

Isabelle Anguelovski, *Neighborhood as Refuge: Community Reconstruction, Place Remaking, and Environmental Justice in the City*

Kelly Sims Gallagher, *The Globalization of Clean Energy Technology: Lessons from China*

Vinit Mukhija and Anastasia Loukaitou-Sideris, eds., *The Informal American City: Beyond Taco Trucks and Day Labor*

Roxanne Warren, *Rail and the City: Shrinking Our Carbon Footprint While Reimagining Urban Space*

Marianne E. Krasny and Keith G. Tidball, *Civic Ecology: Adaptation and Transformation from the Ground Up*

Erik Swyngedouw, *Liquid Power: Contested Hydro-Modernities in Twentieth-Century Spain*

Ken Geiser, *Chemicals without Harm: Policies for a Sustainable World*

Duncan McLaren and Julian Agyeman, *Sharing Cities: A Case for Truly Smart and Sustainable Cities*

Jessica Smartt Gullion, *Fracking the Neighborhood: Reluctant Activists and Natural Gas Drilling*

Nicholas A. Phelps, *Sequel to Suburbia: Glimpses of America's Post-Suburban Future*

Shannon Elizabeth Bell, *Fighting King Coal: The Challenges to Micromobilization in Central Appalachia*

Theresa Enright, *The Making of Grand Paris: Metropolitan Urbanism in the Twenty-First Century*

Robert Gottlieb and Simon Ng, *Global Cities: Urban Environments in Los Angeles, Hong Kong, and China*

Anna Lora-Wainwright, *Resigned Activism: Living with Pollution in Rural China*

Scott L. Cummings, *Blue and Green: The Drive for Justice at America's Port*

David Bissell, *Transit Life: Cities, Commuting, and the Politics of Everyday Mobilities*

Javiera Barandiarán, *From Empire to Umpire: Science and Environmental Conflict in Neoliberal Chile*

Benjamin Pauli, *Flint Fights Back: Environmental Justice and Democracy in the Flint Water Crisis*

Karen Chapple and Anastasia Loukaitou-Sideris, *Transit-Oriented Displacement or Community Dividends? Understanding the Effects of Smarter Growth on Communities*

Henrik Ernstson and Sverker Sörlin, eds., *Grounding Urban Natures: Histories and Futures of Urban Ecologies*